The Irish in Ontario
A Study in Rural History

When this book first appeared it was the only major study of the Irish in central Canada for over a century; and also the first scholarly examination of the Irish in central Ontario as an ethnic group. A new introduction brings the work up-to-date.

For most of the nineteenth century the Irish were the largest non-French ethnic group in Canada and they were particularly significant in Ontario. They are popularly thought of as urban in their settlement patterns, but Professor Akenson shows that those who took up residence in Ontario were primarily rural and small-town dwellers. Historians have also argued that the Irish experience in the homeland rendered them incapable of settling successfully in North American frontier environments, but in fact the Irish migrants to Ontario largely settled in the hinterlands and did so with marked financial and social success.

The author focuses on two main aspects of the subject. He presents against a background of early settlement characteristics in Ontario a general discussion of Irish behaviour in the province, but he also carries out a close analysis of the process of Irish settlement and adaptation in one particular locale, the township of Leeds and Lansdowne in eastern Ontario. The findings in the case of Ontario call seriously into question established beliefs on the cultural limitations of the Irish, not only in Canada but in the United States. The use of nineteenth-century Ontario as an historical laboratory makes it possible to define more accurately the nature of the Irish migrants and their fortunes in the New World.

DONALD HARMAN AKENSON is professor of history at Queen's University, Kingston, Ontario, and Beamish Research Professor of Migration Studies at the Institute of Irish Studies, University of Liverpool.

The Irish in Ontario

A Study in Rural History

DONALD HARMAN AKENSON

Second Edition

McGill-Queen's University Press
Montreal & Kingston • London • Ithaca

© McGill-Queen's University Press 1984
Introduction to the Second Edition
© McGill-Queen's University Press 1999
ISBN 0-7735-2029-5

Legal deposit 2d quarter 1984
Bibliothèque nationale du Québec

Printed in Canada
Reprinted 1985
First paperback edition 1985
Second edition 1999

Canadian Cataloguing in Publication Data

Akenson, Donald Harman
  The Irish in Ontario
  Includes index
  ISBN 0-7735-2029-5
  1. Irish – Ontario – Leeds and Lansdowne – History –
  19th century. I. Title
  FC3095.L43Z7 1984971.3'730049162   C84-098156-2
  F1059.L43A 1984

To J.H.

Contents

Illustrations

FIGURES

MAPS

Tables

Acknowledgments

Grateful acknowledgment for financial aid in completing this study is made to the Social Sciences and Humanities Research Council of Canada for a three-year Released Time Fellowship, to the Directorate of Multiculturalism of the federal Department of the Secretary of State for a research grant, and to the Advisory Research Committee of Queen's University for funding for cartographic work. This book has been published with the help of a grant from the Social Science Federation of Canada, using funds provided by the Social Sciences and Humanities Research Council of Canada. Financial assistance for publication has also been provided by Multiculturalism Canada. The views expressed, however, do not necessarily reflect the position or policy of the Government of Canada.

Several maps are reproduced by the kind permission of the National Map Collection of the Public Archives of Canada and photographs by the kind permission of the Archives of Ontario. Quotations from the reports of the R.G. Dun and Company collection are by gracious permission of the Baker Library, Harvard University. Chapter 1, which appeared in a considerably different form in *Canadian Papers in Rural History*, volume 3, is reprinted by permission of Langdale Press.

Introduction to the Second Edition: Irish "Emigration" Studies at the End of the Century

When this book appeared fifteen years ago, it had a run of good luck. It was awarded the 1985 Chalmers Prize for the best book on Ontario history and the 1987 Landon Prize for regional history. And in 1990 the Social Sciences and Humanities Research Council of Canada named it one of the twenty most important publications in the social sciences in the previous half-century in Canada.

For that I can only be grateful; but I think I should briefly explain why that run of luck occurred. It was because I was able to make in a single text a set of points that historical readers and scholars were ready to embrace: namely, that the history of Ireland and the history of Canada are each too important to be left as merely domestic matters. Like a really good cocktail (say an ice-cold, tongue-numbing classic Martini) each history acquires an electric synergy if properly combined with other compatible elements.

When I began this book, it seemed that a glacial mass blanketed the field that it examines. First, there was no concept of what is today called "the Irish diaspora" but instead a long and doleful historiography on Irish emigration. Collectively, the historical literature was a threnody, with migration from Ireland being defined as a tragedy. Secondly, the individual migrants were almost universally treated as passive flotsam on history's woeful tide. Thirdly, the history of Irish out-migration was dominated almost entirely by the story of the Irish who went to the United States of America. (A few historians elsewhere – such as Patrick O'Farrell in Australia – fought this American imperialism, but they were lonely heroes.) And, fourthly, the Canadian historiography was totally subservient to the "American Model." The leading authorities, Kenneth Duncan and H. Clare Pentland, bought the American concept that the Irish were almost entirely Catholic in religion, urban in residence,

unskilled in occupation – a lumpenproletariat who were unequipped to deal with a modernizing economy, especially one whose driving engine was the in-filling and exploitation of a vast, seemingly empty frontier.

Fortunately, beneath this historiographical ice-sheet, tectonic changes were occurring. To mention only the most obvious: David Fitzpatrick began a critical re-examination of what the data on Irish-outmigration really meant. Patrick O'Farrell continued his work on the Antipodes and with his leadership a strong contingent of scholars of Irish-Australia emerged, confidently resistant to American hegemony. Donal McCracken founded a small but vigorous association devoted to the Irish diaspora in Southern Africa. And breakthrough work was begun on the sector of Irish migration that dominates the twentieth century: that to Great Britain, especially England. Roger Swift and Sheridan Gilley were the pioneers in their generation. All this work was in train, although little of it was published when *The Irish in Ontario* came out. So the international context in which a study of the Irish in Canada would be read was changing quickly. And within the Canadian historical community, which has always had a love-hate relationship with u.s. scholarship, historians of ethnicity were becoming less willing to import formulae from the United States. Thus, both internationally and domestically, this book had the good fortune to appear just when the old doctrinal glacier was ready to fracture and, as later events have shown, to crumble.

The Irish in Ontario assayed two tasks. The first was to accurately define the basic characteristics of the Irish in central Canada. I am proud of how this was done, because I did not have a cent in computer research money or any research assistants. However, by using techniques from accounting (that being one of the few useful subjects I learned in university) and employing the entire population base of Ontario, I arrived at two conclusions that were directly counter to the accepted wisdom of the time: (1) most Irish migrants to Ontario and most persons of Irish ethnicity were Protestants and (2) both Catholics and Protestants were mostly a rural people. Those points are easily stated, but they turned the literature upside down. Here I must emphasize that the data base on which these conclusions were founded was not a sample but the entire population of Ontario, as defined in various governmental enumerations. This is necessary because some quantitatively untrained historians have somehow managed to infer that these conclusions were based on a sample, and a very small and non-random one at that. No: the entire population. Later, very sophisticated studies of the census

data conducted by Gordon Darroch and Michael Ornstein confimed my basic conclusions, while producing much subtler shadings of the basic picture.

The second task was to examine how Irish migrants and their descendants might function within the context of a local social system, defined as broadly as possible. I chose Leeds and Lansdowne Township because that is where I live and I was fairly curious about my neighbours: especially the fact that the most successful farmers were of Irish-Catholic background. I wondered how long that pattern had existed. It should be absolutely clear to any reader of this book that this tiny social system is studied in the same way a physiologist studies a cell: not as typical, not as randomly selected and therefore representative of *structures* of some larger entity, but as indicative of *processes* that are interesting in themselves. These processes being shown to occur in one locale should therefore be on the list of things-to-watch-for when other scholars examine other places. That's all – Leeds and Lansdowne is not presented as the centre of the world.

Undeniably, however, *The Irish in Ontario* has become part of a globe-circling, long-term research agenda that has a clear import: to reduce the sectarian stain that besmirches so much of the historiography on the Irish diaspora and to accomplish this without denying the uniqueness and importance of each of the religious and cultural traditions that derive from the Irish homeland. Simply put, the Irish Protestants have to be built into the story; and, simultaneously, the virtually racist depiction of the Irish Catholics that stems from the u.s. literature – the Irish Catholic immigrants as feckless, pre-modern, culturally handicapped, passive exiles – has to be erased. Such stereotyping, even though conducted by the great-grandchildren of those same migrants, does not honour them, least of all because the stereotype is demonstrably inaccurate.

Perhaps this is the appropriate point to evaluate the present state of Irish "emigration" studies, considered worldwide. Actually, I am convinced that emigration as a concept in the analysis of Irish history is virtually mined-out. Let me be clear here: I do not mean that the term "emigration" as a *descriptive* reference to out-migration from Ireland has lost its validity. To the extent that we can ever hold in common the meaning of words, "emigration" is one that we can share to describe a real historical process, a common life-tactic employed by many members of Irish society. However, in the historical literature (and, indeed, in present-day policy

statements), "emigration" as a higher-level concept has become almost useless because it is used both to denominate a set of events (a set of effects, in other words) and the cause of those events. It has become an omnibus construct because many observers use "emigration" both to mean the leaving of Ireland and the effects upon Irish society of those departures. And "emigration" has become a term so emotion-laden as to preclude clear historical and political thought, for it wraps the behaviour of individual human beings in a smothering blanket of implied judgement. Och, emigration, the forever tragedy.[1]

Too often, the application of "emigration" as a concept involves a tiny, constant bullying, and at the heart of that bullying is the tyranny of the Irish homeland. (I'm speaking here, obviously, of the home country as a cultural icon, not as a physical force.) You see, in its present usage, "emigration" is usually understood as a vector that starts in a primary place and slides towards a second one. Emigration is always *from* Ireland. Well and good: that's a matter of linguistic definition. But, if we are trying to understand the larger world, this privileging of the Irish homeland may have less value than if we were to reverse the valence, for explanatory purposes. That is, instead of thinking of movement being from Ireland, let's conceive of it as being *towards* someplace else. The gradations on the metre stick by which one assesses the activities of the migrants (and of their children and their grandchildren) alter radically and thereupon the meaning of the act of migration is transformed.

The iconic tyranny of the homeland also must be excised in a second way. It is generally, albeit unconsciously, assumed that whatever social, cultural, and intellectual practices occur "abroad" (that is, outside of Ireland) most approximate those that occur in Ireland, are most "Irish." That is a standard which often results in a lead sector – an area of very rapid social adaptation by migrants – being assayed in some way as pernicious or iniquitous. And cities, provinces, neighbourhoods wherein people of Irish background adapt new economic and social mores are seen as less historically important than those that resemble the old home country.

Instead of seeing the homeland as the equivalent of ancient Rome – the capital by which all other locales are judged – it might be more productive if we conceive (if only for brief moments) of the sum total of Irish migration patterns – the entire Irish diaspora – as being a phenomenon that has no single metropole. Instead of seeing it as a flat-earth exercise, judged from "Rome," we might well conceive of the Irish diaspora as a massive reticulation of

invisible webbing, stencilling itself all over the face of the globe. That webbing has no centre, but instead, if one stands at any point, it possesses lines that stretch out infinitely and in all directions. Viewing this diaspora from Wellington, Sydney, Cape Town, Boston, Toronto, Liverpool is just as revealing and just as legitimate an exercise as is the adoption of the Customs House, Dublin, as our vantage point.

Obviously, I am implying that Irish migration forms a text that is polysemous and that it should be multiply conceptualized. I am particularly evangelical on this matter, because one of my missions over the years has been to convince historians of countries that previously avoided doing so to build Irish migrants into their own national histories as fully articulated entities.[2] But the Irish will be given their appropriate place in the various national histories as real, complex peoples – not as ethnic stereotypes and not as filiopietistic burlesques of reality – only if the data on Irish migrants can be appropriated by each national history.[3] This requires that the vantage point not be limited to Dublin, nor the meaning of migration determined solely by Old World criteria.

Both as part of my small crusade to convince historians of other nations that the Irish migrants really are much more important than those national historians realized, and as a general improvement of Irish historiography as well, I hope to coax as many scholars as possible to consider the validity of a doctrine that runs through Irish historiography. This is the "Doctrine of Irish Exceptionalism," and the belief – more an unconscious attitude than a specific articulation – that Irish history has worked by different rules than those which apply to the rest of the western world.[4] Of course Ireland has been unique – *every* culture is – but much of what we view as Irish history is a local subset of a much larger, general pattern, and this is as true in migration history as in any other area. In particular, Irish migration patterns from roughly 1600 onwards were part of the larger phenomenon which, for want of a better term, is often called "the expansion of Europe." The promise of the next generation is that it will meld the Irish research base with the data-bases of other European countries. There is especial promise in working with scholars of migration from other, relatively small nations on the periphery of Europe. The Scandinavian material, for example, is particularly rich. But non-European comparisons are also possible. For example, some of the post-Famine labour flows seem to bear comparison to data being produced by the Southern African Migration Project at Queen's University, Ontario. And there are other examples.[5]

Now, in melding the research base of Irish migration studies with those of other countries, the work will in the first instance be historical and social scientific. One recognises that within the community of Irish scholars social scientists have not had the influence that they deserve to have had. (Still, one has to stretch far to find in Ireland the dour sense of vengeance-served found in a Toronto *Globe and Mail* backpage headline [25 July 1997] "Social Scientist elected president in Albania.") To my mind, the great virtue of social scientists as they approach the global matter of the Irish diaspora is that they are not afraid to draw generalisations: tight, rigorous, limited in scope: testable generalisations. This is in contrast to the practice in my own line, history, in which the cheap-trick that we teach all honours students and post-graduates is that everything is unique, and thus out-liers in any data set are taken to mean that central propensities and common properties can be ignored. And the social scientists, in framing their generalisations, operate in contrast to most of those scholars operating in what is vaguely called "cultural studies," wherein no generalisation is uttered unless it is incapable of being either proved or disproved, but merely illustrated. Or so it seems.

Actually, if there is a danger in social scientists having a major, perhaps dominant, position in Irish diaspora studies, it is only the general one that affects that broad band of disciplines worldwide: a curious propensity for reversing cause and effect. In that regard I instance only an American example, from the *Journal of Fallacious Research*, where it was reported that a physical geographer who had collected hundreds of video tapes of violent meteorological phenomena had demonstrated, at a high level of statistical significance, that mobile trailer parks cause tornados.

One of the sets of inhibitions that we are in the process of slipping off could be called "the spancel of the migrant generation." Because of the way that information on Irish migration was collected (and this holds virtually worldwide), we tend to know quite a lot about the migrating generation in each historical moment and relatively little about the people who are the majority of the Irish diaspora: a group that then-President Mary Robinson estimated in 1990 as being over 70 million persons worldwide.[6] In most cultures, the sense of Irishness (however defined) both changed and diminished over generations, but I would argue that for at least two or three generations it was a significant determinant of the behaviour of most people of Irish descent. Further, I think that even after that, it remained (and indeed remains) as a perduring stream, subterranean, but still partially determining personal behaviour, and

this long after the individuals in question have ceased to think of themselves as Irish. Any concept of Irish migration, then, must not be merely physical and must not deal only with the first generation, but must be cultural and institutional and must deal with the entire multi-generational ethnic group. Operating with such a rich concept of migration is much more challenging than working with simple "emigrant" history, but it has the potential to be infinitely more productive.

I emphasize the potential here, because I think that the Irish diaspora is being sold short by its historians (I include myself here). For, even when building the Irish into our own separate national histories, we have been excessively modest in the following respect: put bluntly, we have not emphasized sufficiently strongly that the Irish diaspora is a very big deal in world history. It deserves presentation as part of as a multi-generational cultural and institutional web that interacts with other diaspora. The ones that are especially important are (1) the Spanish diaspora. One of the great virtues of present-day scholarship is that attention finally is being paid to the Irish and the Hispanic world, for the Hispanic diaspora has interacted with the Irish one from the earliest days of European expansion; (2) second, the African diaspora, the intersections with the Irish diaspora being frequently tragic; and (3) that of the English (more of that later).[7]

Notice that I included "cultural and institutional web" in the preceding paragraph. From that you can infer that I believe it is self-defeating to limit migration studies simply to the geographic transfer of human beings from one spot to another. The really interesting part is the migration of cultural patterns – physical culture, technology, institutions, and "soft" culture – into and out of Ireland as part of a great globe-circling matrix. Let me mention only three examples as instances of the sort of phenomenon that deserves further investigation.

The first is in the field of Irish commercial relationships with other countries. A case that obviously comes to mind is that of Beamish and Crawford. Founded in 1792, the firm had assimilated a technological history that ran back to the outbreak of the Irish civil war of 1641, being built on one of the oldest brewing sites in Ireland. How does an enterprise that has a mercantile genealogy that goes back before Cromwell come to be part of one of the massive commercial empires of our own day (the Scottish-Courage Group which now has one-quarter of the beer market in Ireland and England)? And what does it say about the iconographic enthusiasms of the Irish as an ethnic group that Beamish remains a cult

drink among Hibernophiles from Mombasa to Montreal?[8] (Here, I shudder to think that I may set a phalanx of graduate students off to deconstructing the meaning of a pint. Still, in academics one never knows where one will make one's fortune: I stand in awe of the recent acquisition by the French film director Luc Besson of the film rights to a book about the making of the *Oxford English Dictionary*. He paid £750,000 for a story that concerns Dr. W.C. Miner, a wealthy U.S. Civil War surgeon who contributed to the OED while imprisoned in Broadmoor as criminally insane.)

Secondly, I think a really important book lies in tracing the globe-circling impact of the Irish national schools and, simultaneously, of the Irish Catholic church's attitudes towards primary education. Whomever takes on this task will discover that in several important places in the English-speaking world the "official culture" of the masses – that is, the state-approved and government-funded culture taught to children – had as its direct genealogical antecedent the national system of education in Ireland. The school systems of Ontario, British Columbia, and parts of the Canadian prairies were modelled directly on those of Ireland, and in their early days professors of education were imported directly to the Canadas to show the locals how things should be done.[9] Related to this is the seemingly globe-circling fact that the Roman Catholic church fought, first, to bend the Irish-national system of education into a form that it could approve, and then held this up as a model to be emulated. It achieved these ends – involving a segregation of Catholic from Protestant children and a clerical control over state-provided tax monies – in most of Canada, in New Zealand, and (partially) in some Australian states. And, mostly, these patterns of "official culture" were won by Irish-educated priests and bishops, or by clergy trained in Irish-founded seminaries in their respective countries.[10] Irish ideas migrated; Ireland ruled.

This brings me to the third example of cultural migration. Curiously, the migration of Christianity to Ireland and its migration from Ireland is relatively little studied. More than any other ideational matrix, Christianity influenced (some would say determined) the pivotal aspects of Irish cultural and social life. And, more importantly to historians of other nations, nineteenth- and early twentieth-century Ireland was the source of the numerically greatest diaspora in the history of the Christian religion. For the better part of a century, the heart of the Catholic church in the United States of America, in English Canada, in Australia, and in New Zealand was Irish. Only within living memory has this changed. So, Christianity and its flow in and out of Ireland should

be one of the central themes of Irish historical writing. Yet, when one looks at the literature, one encounters very little that embodies the appropriate sense of wonder, or attempts to see the wholeness of the process. Instead, one has (with one or two notable exceptions) narrow institutional studies and isolated chapters plucked from the M.Litt. theses of antiquarian parish priests.[11] Christianity deserves better. I suggest this with both disappointment and strong conviction, because I have spent a portion of my own research time over the last two decades writing a book which has just appeared. Entitled *Surpassing Wonder. The Invention of the Bible and the Talmuds*, it has as its dominant tone my own awe at just how magnificent an achievement the invention of our Judaeo-Christian heritage actually was; and how fundamentally determinative of most of our later social and intellectual concepts were the texts, the poetry, the hymns, the historical narratives of the Ancient Near East.[12] Something akin to that same awe should seize Irish historians as they see those same concepts interact with a proud and unbroken Celtic world and thereby produce a culture that, in its religious components, was perduring, adaptable, and thus, ultimately, transportable the world around.

I am optimistic that the parochial concept of Irish emigration is being replaced by the more robust, more international, more ecumenical one of "migration." And the accompanying concept of Irish exile, gvetching and vaguely paranoid as it is, is being replaced by the idea of Irish diaspora, so that scholars of Irish migration are empowered to approach with confidence topics of genuine international significance, and to discuss matters within their ken from which the historians of other countries can learn a good deal.[13] But perhaps I am being blithe and Pollyannaish. So, let me conclude my conspectus of Irish migration studies by citing some of the subfields in which scholars have turned the corner and are producing a good deal of work distinguished simultaneously by imagination and integrity. (I do not detail specific scholars here, because it is the contours of the field as a collective enterprise that are here important).

The most significant of these developments, in my view, is the creation virtually *ex nihilo* of a substantial literature on female migration. Such a literature would be necessary in virtually any culture, but for the Irish it is particularly salient, for Ireland was unusual among European countries in having nearly as many women who chose to out-migrate as men. There are still scores of

unsettled basic questions concerning women in the Irish diaspora – the most difficult to ponder being whether or not migration out of Ireland was an emancipating experience – but the grounds of debate are now becoming clearly established.[14]

Indeed, the work on women's migration has had an impact on Irish diaspora studies in general: it has helped to spur a recognition of Irish migrants as active participants in their own life stories, not mere flotsam on the running tide of social history. Just as a recognition of the personal independence and personal agency of females has been a central item in the field of women's history in general, so the demonstration that Irish women were capable of a remarkable degree of self-direction in the migration process has led to a recognition that the entire group of migrants – men included – had a greater degree of agency than previously was granted. The notion of the Irish emigrant as passive victim served for several generations as an analgesic within the Irish homeland, and to a lesser degree throughout the diaspora, but it was patronizing to the emigrants and culturally debilitating to those who promulgated it. If one reads the classic documents on Irish emigration – for example, the Commission on Emigration and Other Problems of 1948–54 – one finds a pervasive sense of the failed male.[15] The tone is the same as that of the first generation of men in our own time whose wives went to work. They had a sense of failure, that they were not real men because they could not "keep" their wives. The same sense of failed maleness holds for most Irish discussion of out-migration conducted before, roughly, the early 1980s: we have failed because we cannot keep our young people. No, it's all right if your wife works in Dunne's stores, and it's o.k. if your kids work in California. That's just the way the world is: no fault implied.

Now, further, I am optimistic because we have learned within the last decade or so to live with the fact that ethnicity – which is a construct central to understanding the behaviour of the Irish diaspora – is a hollow concept: hollow not in the sense of being meretricious, but as being susceptible to situational modification. The best work that I read now assumes that ethnic identity is both a matter of self-identification and of taxonomies developed by the host society, and thus the nature of Irish ethnic identity evolves both over time and according to locale.[16] So, really good ethnic history is simultaneously a rigorous documentation of the behaviour of a specific group of individuals and equally a chronicle of their evolving consciousness. Thus, what begins as emigration history becomes part of what is sometimes called "the history of consciousness."

Moreover, I am delighted to encounter, year-by-year, an ever-diminishing amount of "ball-gown and tiara history." That is a term from the museum trade. It refers to a phenomenon universal in both material and cultural history: the most ubiquitous and widespread items disappear and the unusual ones – the tiaras and ball gowns of a previous culture – are those that are most often preserved. So it is relatively easy, but very misleading, to set up a museum exhibit which gives pride of place to the unusual and the atypical, while ignoring what was general, perhaps universal. Similarly, in the New Worlds to which the Irish migrants went, it is important to document and honour the cultural treasures that were brought from the homeland and were preserved – the Irish language in some places, ascetic Presbyterian psalmody in others – but only if they are placed in societal context. To judge the historical importance of any given practice according to the degree to which it either preserved or replicated usages from the Old Country is to confuse migrants with curators. Fortunately, most historians of the Irish diaspora now do not privilege, say, early twentieth-century male migrants who played Gaelic games, but, rather, follow the bulk of the migrants to the places they really played: baseball parks, rugby fields, and football pitches, depending where in the wide world they turned up. That is a metonym of a larger and promising historiographic development, attending to the migrants on their own historical terms, not ours.

Further, I am heartened that, finally, historians of Irish migration and historians of the Irish diaspora have begun to face directly what has until recently been the single most-avoided matter in the field, namely the relationship of the Irish and empires. (Note the plural: empires); and particularly that we are beginning to analyse the way the successive ranks of Irish migrants to New Worlds were, however unconsciously in most instances, the foot soldiers of empire.[17] This requires a breaking of the perceptual set, the idea that Irish migrants were not like other Europeans (the Doctrine of Irish Exceptionalism again), that because they had been imperialised, and at home had frequently fought against imperialism, they could not be imperialist. To break this misleading perceptual set, several focal recalibrations are in train. First, focus is being shifted from formal activities that relate to empire to informal ones. Crucially, the actions of individual migrants (whether in rural or urban areas) made them participants in imperial systems, and this despite most of them having no involvement with any official imperial apparatus.[18] Second, a confusion of cause and effect is being erased. It is true that the motives of most Irish migrants leaving their homeland had nothing

to do with enthusiasm for imperialism – many were virtually forced to migrate – but the effects upon native cultures in the various New Worlds occurred nonetheless. Behaviours, not motive, is becoming our chief focus. And, empires being very complex social systems, whether an Irish migrant joined a regiment in the Maori Wars or was a tally man in the Winchester arms factory in Connecticut made little difference: participation in the system inevitably implied an effect. Crucially, the American Empire is becoming recognized as the place where the Irish migrants and their descendants made their most underestimated contribution to imperialism, not least in the displacement and destruction of indigenous cultures.[19] The post-1850 expansion of the United States to embrace most of the habitable portions of North America was nothing less than the creation of a kingdom; and, in our own century, the American Republic has become, first, the world's leading imperial power and, in our own time, the only one of any consequence. And, at last, scholars are facing the possibility that the educational and religious institutions that issued forth from Ireland – both Catholic and Protestant – were more effective in breaking down indigenous cultures than were entire regiments of the armies of the British Empire or of the various American governments.[20] Tough issues, certainly, but the discipline is sufficiently mature to engage them.

Finally, I am most optimistic about the direction and energy of Irish migration studies because I see each year just a little less of the unconscious, but pervasive, sectarianism that has bespeckled so much of the historiography of Irish migration. Sectarianism is a very easy disease to catch, not least because one of the chief causal determinants of Irish history has been (and still is) the existence of hostile, mutually hate-ridden sects. The chief way that the historiography of the global Irish diaspora exhibited the effects of this toxin was either to segregate the history of the Protestant migrants or, more commonly, to ignore that history completely.[21] Those practices are fading, but building the Protestants (I am here using the term in its modern sense, to include all the Protestant denominations, not just the Church of Ireland) into the worldwide story is notoriously difficult: they left fewer markers than did their Catholic counterparts and they held more complex and protean, multiple identities, so they disappeared more quickly into host populations than did the Catholics.

If I think that we can look forward to a very productive, paradigm-shifting decade or two in Irish migration studies, I am also aware

that this work eventually will be found factually insufficient and its conceptual base inadequate by some subsequent generation. Good: that is one version of how the Great Chain of Being operates and it should not bother us a bit. However, we should be mildly concerned with a side-effect of the way that we use, wear out, and discard concepts. Though that is the way professional scholars do their work, it can be very unsettling to the general public, who confuse the verities with the unvarying. And, often, the general public wants historians not to uncover the facts, but to obscure them.

I recently received a letter from my old Harvard mentor John Kelleher, the founding-figure of Irish Studies in North America. He was talking about a set of pictures in the *New York Times* which showed various sets of para-militaries posing without their balaclavas on. "Makes one sense the real reason for the ski-masks," he noted.

Within Ireland at the present time, a strong minority within the scholarly community and (probably) a minority of the general public are in search of heritage rather than history, belief rather than evidence, sectarian and political exclusivity rather than cultural diversity. They want the old songs, the old methods, the old hatreds. They want the ski-masks back on.

It is much too early to guess how the *Methodonenstreit* within the scholarly profession in Ireland will be resolved. I am confident, however, that the scholars who study the Irish migrants worldwide, their culture, their institutions, their ethnic consciousness, will not do an abrupt about-face and march back to the false security of the tiny walled towns constructed by the frightened and the resentful. We have already come too far for that.

Donald Harman Akenson
April 1999

NOTES

1 Examples include John A. O'Brien, *The Vanishing Irish: The Enigma of the Modern World* (London: W.H. Allen, 1954); Carl Wittke, *The Irish in America* (New York: Russell and Russell, 1956); George Potter, *To the Golden Door. The Story of the Irish in Ireland and America* (Boston: Little, Brown and Co., 1960); William V. Shannon, *The American Irish* (New York: MacMillan, 1963); Laurence J. McCaffrey, *The Irish Diaspora in America* (Bloomington: Indiana University Press, 1976). Some scholars in the field of Irish migration history continue to support this view. Kerby Miller's *Emigrants and Exiles*, which appeared in 1985, is the *ne plus ultra* of books in the victim-tradition of Irish-America historiography. An extended study of immigrant letters led him to the conclusion that emigration posed "severe social, cultural, and even psychological problems" for Irish Catholics. According to Miller, the "fatalism," "dependence," and "passivity" which characterized traditional Irish Catholic culture forced upon immigrants a view of emigration as exile, and conditioned their response to life in North America. Miller's views on the culture of exile have been endorsed recently in Matthew Frye Jacobson, *Special Sorrows: The Diasporic Imagination of Irish, Polish, and Jewish Immigrants in the United States* (Cambridge: Harvard University Press, 1995). For a critique of Miller's approach, see D.H. Akenson, *Being Had: Historians, Evidence, and the Irish in North America* (Toronto: P.D. Meany, 1985). In his essay "Revising the Diaspora," Alan O'Day observes that other historians, including Patrick O'Farrell, Cecil Houston and William Smyth, have made extensive use of immigrants' letters without reaching Miller's conclusions. See Alan O'Day, "Revising the Diaspora," in D. George Boyce and Alan O'Day (eds.), *The Making of Modern Irish History: Revisionism and the Revisionist Controversy* (London: Routledge, 1996), Chapter 10. O'Day's reference is to Cecil J. Houston and William J. Smyth, *Irish Emigration and Canadian Settlement: Patterns, Links and Letters* (Toronto: University of Toronto Press, 1990), 20–31. Roy Foster's remarks on this subject in "Marginal Men and Micks on the Make" in *Paddy and Mr. Punch. Connections in Irish and English History* are also worth consulting. (London: Penguin Books, 1993), 288–89.

2 I consider the importance of such an international perspective in the following works, which deal with Irish communities in different parts of the diaspora. *Being Had: Historians, Evidence and the Irish in North America* (Toronto: P.D. Meany, 1985); *Small Differences: Irish Catholics and Irish Protestants, 1815–1922. An International Perspective* (Montreal and Kingston: McGill-Queen's University Press and Dublin: Gill and MacMillan, 1988); *Half the World from Home. Perspectives on the Irish in New Zealand, 1860–1950* (Wellington: Victoria University Press, 1990); *Occasional Papers on the Irish in South Africa* (Grahamstown: Institute of Social and Economic Research, Rhodes University, 1991); "The Historiography of English-Speaking Canada and the Concept of Diaspora: A Skeptical Appreciation," *Canadian Historical Review* 76 (1995): 377–409; *The Irish Diaspora. A Primer* (see note 1); *If the Irish Ran the World: Montserrat, 1630–1730* (Montreal and Kingston: McGill-Queen's University Press, and Jamaica: University of West Indies Press, 1997).

3 Statistics on Irish out-migration are incomplete, but see the available data in the standard sources, N.H. Carrier and J.R. Jeffrey, *External Migration: A Study of the Available Statistics, 1815–1950, being No. 6 In the General*

Register Office's "Studies on Medical Population Subjects" (London: HMSO, 1953); and *Commission of Emigration and other Population Problems, 1948–1954* (Dublin: Stationery Office, 1954). Where possible, original emigration statistics should be consulted in the relevant House of Commons Parliamentary Papers.

Census data on the ethnicity and religious affiliation of populations varies in quantity and quality among the various English-speaking countries of the Irish diaspora. For Australia, the *Census for the Commonwealth of Australia, 1911* was the first full census for the population and included cross-tabulations on place of birth and religious affiliation. These data are broken down in my *Small Differences*, chapter 3. For the earliest detailed breakdown of population according to religious affiliation in New Zealand see *Results of a Census on the Dominion of New Zealand, 1921*. The available data are summarized and explained in Akenson, *Half the World From Home*, chapter 3. Data on immigrants to South Africa are unfortunately meagre. In 1891 and 1926 the authorities attempted to collect information on the ethnicity of the population, but the effort was unsuccessful. Still, an estimate of ethnicity can be calculated based on the existing data. See *the Results of the Census of the Colony of the Cape of Good Hope ... 1891; Results of the Census ... 1926*, and my commentary in *Occasional Papers on the Irish in South Africa*, chapter 3. Statistics for the later period are more complete; see F.G. Brownell, *British Immigration to South Africa, 1946–1970* (Pretoria: Government Printer, 1985).

The study of the Irish in the United States remains seriously impaired by the fact that the 1969–70 census was the first to ask questions concerning the ethnicity of respondents. Even then, the collection of the data was bungled and no firm conclusions could be reached; further attempts in 1980 and 1990 were mishandled and the ethnicity question remained unproductive due to the authorities permitting individuals to list several ethnicities. More extraordinary, the United States census authorities have *never* collected information on the religious affiliation of specific individuals, and the historical relationship between religion and Irish ethnicity in America cannot be determined using official census data. Instead, studies of the Irish in America must refer to data collected as part of a random survey carried out by the Graduate Center of the City University of New York in 1989–90. The study enquired into the religion, ethnicity, and race of the members of 113 000 American households, a very large sample indeed. See Barry Kosmin et al., *Research Report: the National Survey of Religious Identification, 1989–90* (New York: CUNY Graduate Center, 1991). For comparable data collected in smaller surveys, see Andrew M. Greeley, "The Success and Assimilation of Irish Protestants and Irish Catholics in the United States," *S.S.R.* 72, no. 4 (1988): 229–236; George Gallup, Jr. and Jim Castelli, *The People's Religion: American Faith in the '90s* (New York: Macmillan, 1989). Also, consult the recent article by Michael Hout and Joshua R. Goldstein, "How 4.5 Million Irish Immigrants Became 40 Million Irish Americans: Demographic and Subjective Aspects of the Ethnic Composition of White Americans," *American Sociological Review* 59 (1994): 64–82.

Finally, for the most substantial data on the ethnicity and religious affiliation of a nineteenth-century population, see the results of the 1870–71 Dominion of Canada Census reproduced in aggregate form in *Census of Canada, 1931*. The data for the 1861 and 1871 censuses has been retabulated from the original census manuscripts by Gordon Darroch and Michael Ornstein of York University, Ontario. Together they have constructed a data base that, on matters of

ethnicity, religion, occupation, and social class, is the most sophisticated research design in North American ethnic historical studies, and should serve as a model for the construction of ethnic profiles in other countries. See A.G. Darroch and M.D. Ornstein, "Ethnicity and Occupational Structure in Canada in 1871: the Vertical Mosaic in Historical Perspective," *Canadian Historical Review* 61 (1980): 305–333; A.G. Darroch and M.D. Ornstein, "Ethnicity and Class, Transitions over a Decade: Ontario, 1861–1971," *Historical Papers* (Canadian Historical Association, 1984), 111–37; A.G. Darroch, "Half-Empty or Half-Full" Images and Interpretations in the Historical Analysis of the Catholic Irish in Nineteenth-Century Canada," *Canadian Ethnic Studies* 25, no.1 (1993).

4 There are encouraging signs that this idea is being replaced in scholarship by a more ecumenical approach to Irish history and migration. For example, see L.M. Cullen and Francois Furet (eds.), *Ireland and France: Towards a Comparative Rural History* (Paris: Editions de l'Ecole des Hautes Etudes en Sciences Sociales, 1981). In a study of Irish migrant labour, Jim McLaughlin favours such a comparative approach which avoids the pitfalls of "national exceptionalism." Jim MacLaughlin, "Ireland: An 'emigrant nursery' in the world economy," *International Migration* 31, no. 1 (1993): 149–170. Timothy Guinnane challenges explicitly the notion of Irish exceptionalism in *The Vanishing Irish: Households, Migration, and the Rural Economy in Ireland, 1850–1914* (Princeton: Princeton University Press, 1997), Chapter 1. See also, Ullrich Kockel, "Irish Migration to Mainland Germany," in Russell King (ed.), *Ireland, Europe and the Single Market* (Dublin: Geographical Society of Ireland, 1993), 128–136.

5 Collections include Dirk Hoerder (ed.), *American Labor and Immigration History, 1877–1920s: Recent European Research* (Urbana: University of Illinois Press, 1983); George E. Pozzetta, *American Immigration and Ethnicity, Volume 2: Emigration and Immigration. The Old World Confronts the New* (New York: Garland Publishing, 1991); Rudolph J. Vecoli and Suzanne M. Sinke (eds.), *A Century of European Migration, 1830–1930* (Urbana: University of Illinois Press, 1991); Dirk Hoerder and Horst Rossler (eds.), *Distant Magnets: Expectations and Realities in the Immigrant Experience, 1840–1930* (New York: Holmes and Meier, 1993). For the earlier period, see the recent collection of essays edited by Nicholas Canny, *Europeans on the Move. Studies on European Migration, 1500–1800* (Oxford: Clarendon Press, 1994). The chapters on English, Scottish, Irish, Dutch, German, and French migrations are accompanied by more specialized bibliographies.

   H. Arnold Barton examines the history of Scandinavian-American migration studies and the current state of scholarship in "Where Have the Scandinavian-Americanists Been?," *Journal of American Ethnic History* 15, no.1 (1995): 46–55. Also see Odd S. Lovoll (ed.), *Scandinavians and Other Immigrants in Urban America: The Proceedings of a Research Conference, October 26–27, 1984* (Northfield, 1985); Harald Runblom and Dag Blanck (ed.), *Scandinavia Overseas: Patterns of Cultural Transformation in North America and Australia* (Uppsala: Uppsala University Press, 1986); Hans Norman and Harald Runblom, *Transatlantic Connections: Nordic Migration to the New World after 1800* (Oslo: Norwegian University Press, 1988); Robert C. Ostergren, *A Community Transplanted: The Trans-Atlantic Experience of a Swedish Immigrant Settlement in the Upper Middle West* (Madison: University of Wisconsin Press, 1988); Odd S. Lovoll (ed.), *Nordics in America: The Future of their Past* (Northfield, 1993); Janet E. Rasmussen, *New Land New*

Lives: Scandinavian Immigrants to the Pacific Northwest (Northfield: North American Historical Association, 1993). There is an extensive literature on Italian migration, including some valuable local and regional studies. For example, see the excellent article by Russell King and Brian Reynolds, "Casalattico, Dublin and the fish and chip connection: a classic example of chain migration," *Studi Emigrazione* 31, no. 115 (1994): 398–426. Also see Donna R. Gabaccia, *Militants and Migrants: Rural Sicilians become American Workers* (New Brunswick: Rutgers University Press, 1988); Franc Sturino, *Forging the Chain: a Case Study of Italian Migration to North America, 1880–1930* (Toronto: Multicultural History Society of Ontario, 1990); S. Baily, "The village outward approach to the study of social networks: a case study of the Agnonesi diaspora abroad, 1885–1989," *Studi Emigrazione* 29, no. 105 (1992): 43–67. For trends in migration scholarship, see J. Salt, "Contemporary trends in international migration study," *International Migration* 15 (1987): 241–251; Silvia Pedraza-Bailey, "Immigration Reseach: A Conceptual Map," *Social Science History* 14, no.1 (1990): 43–67; Ewa Morawska, "The Sociology and Historiography of Immigration," in Virginia Yans-McLaughlin (ed.), *Immigration Reconsidered: History, Sociology, Politics* (New York: Oxford University Press, 1991).

6 President Robinson provided this estimate in her inaugural address on 3 December 1990. *Canadian Journal of Irish Studies* 17 (July 1991): 109.

7 For the history of the Irish in southern Africa, see the pioneering work of Donal P. McCracken, "The Irish in Colonial South Africa: An Overview," *Southern African-Irish Studies* vol.1 (Durban-Westville: Department of History, University of Durban Westville, 1991), and the essays edited by McCracken as part of the Southern-Africa Irish Studies series, *Southern African-Irish Studies* 1 (1991); *The Irish in Southern Africa, 1795–1910* vol.2 (1992); *Ireland and South Africa in Modern Times* vol.3 (1996). The remaining historical literature is rather thin, but see R.H. Henderson, *An Ulsterman in Africa* (Cape Town: Uni-Volkspers, 1944); Kathleen M. Cox, *Immigration into South Africa, 1940–67: A Bibliography* (Cape Town: University of Cape Town Libraries, 1970); E. Morse Jones, *Roll of the British Settlers in South Africa, Part I: Up to 1826* (Cape Town: A.A. Balkema, second ed., 1971); Graham B. Dickason, *Irish Settlers to the Cape: A History of the Clanwilliam 1820 Settlers from Cork* (Cape Town: A.A. Balkema, 1973); Pamela M. Barnes, "Irish Immigration to South Africa: A Historical Introduction," *The Irish at Home and Abroad* 4, no.4 (1997): 165–67.

The literature on the Irish elsewhere in Africa, and throughout the West Indies and the Spanish Empire is scarce. The following works indicate the opportunity for research on this aspect of the Irish diaspora: Robert MacAdam, "Is the Irish Language Spoken in Africa?," *Ulster Journal of Archaeology* 7 (1859): 195–200; Joseph J. Williams, *Whence the "Black Irish" of Jamaica* (New York: Dial Press, 1932); John C. Messenger, "The Influence of the Irish in Montserrat," *Caribbean Quarterly* 13 (June 1967): 3–26; Stephen Clissold, *Bernardo O'Higgins and the Independence of Chile* (London: Rupert Hart-Davis, 1968); Hilary Beckles, *White Servitude and Black Slavery in Barbados, 1627–1715* (Knoxville: University of Tennessee Press, 1989); J. Lorimer, *English and Irish Settlement on the River Amazon, 1550–1646* (London: Haklyut Society, 2nd ser., 171, 1989); Hilary Beckles, "A 'Riotous and unruly lot': Irish Indentured Servants and Freemen in the English West Indies, 1644–1713," *William and Mary Quarterly* 47 (October 1990): 503–522; Robert

Burrett, "The Eyre Brothers: Arthur and Herbert," *Heritage of Zimbabwe* 9 (1990): 37–46; Grainne Henry, *The Irish Military Community in Spanish Flanders, 1586–1621* (Dublin: Irish Academic Press, 1992); D.H. Akenson, *If the Irish Ran the World. Montserrat, 1630–1730* (Montreal and Kingston: McGill-Queen's University Press, 1997); Jose C. Moya, *Cousins and Strangers: Spanish Immigrants in Buenos Aires, 1850–1930* (Berkeley: University of California Press, 1998).

The intersection of the African and Irish diasporas in North America produced the infamous New York City draft riots in 1863. See Adrian Cook, *The Armies of the Streets: The New York City Draft Riots of 1863* (Lexington: University Press of Kentucky, 1974); Iver Bernstein, *The New York City Draft Riots* (New York: Oxford University Press, 1990). For relations between the Irish and African-Americans in Philadelphia, see Dennis Clark, *The Irish Relations: Trials of an Immigrant Tradition* (Rutherford: Fairleigh Dickinson University Press, 1982).

8 An indication of the rich possibilities of commercial histories if well-done, is Patrick Lynch and John Vaizey, *Guinness's Brewery in the Irish Economy, 1759–1876* (Cambridge: Cambridge University Press, 1960), 89–90, 132. See also, T.R. Gourvish and R.G. Wilson, *The British Brewing Industry, 1830–1930* (New York: Cambridge University Press, 1994), and Andy Bielenberg, *Cork's Industrial Revolution, 1780–1880* (Cork: Cork University Press, 1991), 50–60.

9 Franklin A. Walker, *Catholic Education and Politics in Upper Canada* (Toronto: J.M. Dent, 1955); J. Donald Wilson, "The Ryerson Years in Upper Canada," in J. Donald Wilson, Robert M. Stamp, and Louis-Philippe (eds.), *Canadian Education: A History* (Scarborough: Prentice Hall, 1970); D.H. Akenson, *The Irish Education Experiment: The National System of Education in the Nineteenth Century* (London: Routledge and Kegan Paul, 1973); R.D. Gidney, "Making Nineteenth-Century School Systems: The Upper Canadian Experience and its Relevance to English Historiography," *History of Education* 9, no. 2 (1980): 101–116.

10 The influence of the (Irish) Catholic Church on systems of education throughout the empire has been studied only incidentally, as part of national or local histories, or as part of studies in education, but see the following: my *Half the World from Home*, chapter 6; Geoffrey Sherington, "Australian Immigration, Ethnicity and Education," *History of Education Review* [Australia] 20, no. 1 (1991): 61–72; Margaret Pawsey, "The introduction of payment by results into Victoria's schools," *History of Education Review* [Australia] 23, no.2 (1994): 1–17; David L. Salvaterra, *American Catholicism and the Intellectual Life, 1880–1950* (New York: Garland Publishing Inc.,1988); Janet A. Nolan, "Irish-American Teachers and the Struggle over American Urban Public Education, 1890–1920: A Preliminary Look," *Records of the American Catholic Historical Society of Philadelphia* 103, nos. 3–4 (1992) 13–22.

11 An important exception is the pioneering work of the late Kathleen Hughes, *The Church in Early Irish Society* (London: Methuen, 1966). See also a collection of her essays in Hughes, *Church and Society in Ireland, A.D. 400–1200* (London: Variorum Reprints, 1987). For an entry into the Patrician literature, see T.F. O'Rahilly, *Early Irish History and Mythology* (Dublin: Dublin Institute for Advanced Studies, 1964). An older but classic work is James Heron, *The Celtic Church in Ireland: the Story of Ireland and Irish Christianity from Before the Time of St. Patrick to the Reformation* (London: Service and Paton, 1898).

12 D.H. Akenson, *Surpassing Wonder. The Invention of the Bible and the Tal-muds* (New York and London: Harcourt Brace; Montreal: McGill-Queen's University Press, 1998).

13 For example, James S. Donnelly, Jr., "The Construction of the Memory of the Famine in Ireland and the Irish Diaspora, 1850–1900," *Eire-Ireland* 31, nos. 1–2 (1996): 26–61; Allen Feldman, "'Gaelic Gotham': Decontextualizing the Diaspora," *Eire-Ireland* 31, nos. 1–2 (1996): 189–201. The Irish diaspora has also become the focus of general surveys; see the entry on Ireland in Gerard Chaliand, *The Penguin Atlas of the Diasporas* (New York: Viking, 1995). More importantly, the *New History of Ireland* devotes substantial sections to the history of the Irish abroad. For the nineteenth and twentieth centuries, see the entries by David Fitzpatrick, David Noel Doyle, and Patrick O'Farrell in W.E. Vaughan (ed.), *The New History of Ireland: Volume V, Ireland Under the Union, 1801–1870* and *Volume VI, Ireland Under the Union, 1870–1921* (Oxford: Clarendon Press for the Royal Irish Academy, 1989 ff). A comprehensive bibliography is included in Volume VI, "Bibliography: History of the Irish Abroad," 845–851. The multi-volume collection of essays on aspects of the Irish diaspora in *The Irish World Wide* series, edited by Patrick O'Sullivan, confirms the increasing depth and breadth of Irish migration research. In addition, L.M. Cullen addresses an earlier and often neglected period of Irish migration in his chapter, "The Irish Diaspora of the Seventeenth and Eighteenth-Centuries," in Nicholas Canny (ed.), *Europeans on the Move. Studies on European Migration, 1500–1800* (Oxford: Clarendon Press, 1994). For a survey of the current state of scholarship on the Irish diaspora, see the essay by Alan O'Day, "Revising the Diaspora," in D. George Boyce and Alan O'Day (eds.), *The Making of Modern Irish History. Revisionism and the Revisionist Controversy* (London and New York: Routledge, 1996), 188–215. Two of the more important works of larger imagination deal with the Antipodes: James Belich, *Making Peoples. A History of the New Zealanders from Polynesian Settlement to the End of the Nineteenth-Century* (London: Penguin, 1996), and David Fitzpatrick, *Oceans of Consolation. Personal Accounts of Irish Migration to Australia* (Ithaca and London: Cornell University Press, 1994).

14 A valuable collection of essays appears in Volume 4 of *The Irish World Wide* series edited by Patrick O'Sullivan, *Irish Women and Irish Migration*, op cit. For additional reading on the history of women and Irish migration, see the following: Robert E. Kennedy Jr., *The Irish: Emigration, Marriage and Fertility* (Berkeley: University of California Press, 1973); C. Groneman, "Working-Class Immigrant Women in Mid-Nineteenth Century New York: the Irish Women's Experience," *Journal of Urban History* 4, no. 3 (1978): 255–274; Hasia Diner, *Erin's Daughters in America: Irish Immigrant Women in the Nineteenth-Century* (Baltimore: Johns Hopkins University Press, 1983); Pauline Jackson, "Women in 19th Century Irish emigration," *International Migration Review* 18 (1984): 1004–1020; David Fitzpatrick, "'A share of the honeycomb': Education, Emigration and Irishwomen," *Continuity and Change* 1, no. 2 (1986): 217–234; Janet Nolan, *Ourselves Alone: Women's Emigration from Ireland 1885–1920* (Lexington: University Press of Kentucky, 1989); Ide O'Carroll, *Models for Movers. Irish Women's Emigration to America* (Dublin: Attic Press, 1990); Malcolm Campbell, "Irish Women in Nineteenth-Century Australia: A More Hidden Ireland'," in Phillip Bull, Chris McConville, and Noel McLachlan (eds.), *Irish Australian Studies* (Melbourne: La Troube University, 1991); Donna Gabbaccia, "Immigrant Women. Nowhere at Home?,"

Journal of American Ethnic History 10, no. 4 (1991): 61–87; Ann Rossiter, "Bringing the Margins into the Centre: a Review of Aspects of Irish Women's Emigration," in Sean Hutton and Paul Stewart (eds.), *Ireland's Histories* (London: Routledge, 1991); Sheelagh Conway, *The Faraway Hills are Green: Voices of Irish Women in Canada* (Toronto: Women's Press, 1992); Lara Marks, "'The Luckless Waifs and Strays of Humanity': Irish and Jewish Immigrant Unwed Mothers in London, 1870–1939," *Twentieth Century British History* 3, no. 2 (1992): 113–137; Grace Neville, "She never then after that forgot him: Irishwomen and Emigration to the United States in Irish Folklore," *Mid-America* 74, no. 3 (1992): 271–289; Sydney Stahl Weinberg, "The Treatment of Women in Immigration History: A Call for Change," *Journal of American Ethnic History* 11, no. 4 (1992): 25–46; Laurie K. Mercier, "'We Are Women Irish': Gender, Class, Religion and Ethnic Identity in Anaconda, Montana," *Montana* 44, no. 1 (1994): 28–41; Suellen Hoy, "The Journey Out: the Recruitment and Emigration of Irish Religious Women to the United States, 1812–1914," *Journal of Women's History* 6, no.4 and 7, no. 1 (Winter/Spring 1995): 64–98; Joan Grant (ed.), *Women, Migration and Empire* (1996). Literature on contemporary women migrants from Ireland includes Jenny Beale, *Women in Ireland. Voices of Change* (London: Macmillan, 1986); Mary Lennon, Masie McAdam, and Joanne O'Brien, *Across the Water: Irish Women's Lives in Britain* (London: Virago, 1988); Joy Rudd, "Invisible Exports: The Emigration of Irish Women This Century," *Women's Studies International Forum* 11, no. 4 (1988): 307–311; Kate Kelly and Triona Nic Giolla Choille, *Emigration Matters for Women* (Dublin: Attic Press, 1990); Breda Gray, "Irish Women in London: National or Hybrid Diasporic Identities?," *NWSA Journal* 8 (Spring 1996): 85–109.

15 *Commission of Emigration and other Population Problems, 1948–1954* (Dublin: Stationery Office, 1954).

16 Charles Price, who virtually established serious ethnic history in Australia, points out that there are two sorts of ethnic identification: subjective and objective. The objective aspects include place of birth, religious affiliation, and first language. The subjective aspects are more intriguing, and include how people feel about their cultural heritage and how they identify themselves. Charles Price, "Ethnic Composition of the Australian Population," in Price (ed.) *Australian Immigration. A Bibliography and Digest* No. 4 (Canberra: Australian National University, 1981). Also see Christopher McAll, *Class, Ethnicity, and Social Inequality* (Montreal and Kingston: McGill-Queen's University Press, 1990); A.P. Cohen, "Culture as Identity: An Anthropologist's View," *New Literary History* 24, no. 1 (1993): 195–209. For discussions of ethnicity in the United States, see K.N. Conzen et al., "The Invention of Ethnicity: A Perspective from the U.S.A.," *Journal of American Ethnic History* 12, no. 1 (1992): 3–41; Rudolph Vecoli, "An Inter-Ethnic Perspective on American Immigration History," *Mid-America* 75, no.2 (1993); Elliott R. Barkan, "Race, Religion, and Nationality in American Society: A Model of Ethnicity – From Contact to Assimilation," *Journal of American Ethnic History* 14, no. 2 (1995): 38–101.

17 See Ronald Robinson, "Non-European Foundation of European Imperialism: Sketch for a Theory of Collaboration," in Roger Owen and Bob Sutcliffe (eds.), *Studies in the Theory of Imperialism* (London: Longman, 1972): 117–42. The relationship of the Irish to empires is beginning to be explored by historians. See Scott B. Cook, "The Irish Raj: Social Origins and Careers of Irishmen in

the Indian Civil Service, 1855–1914," *Journal of Social History* 20, no. 3 (1987): 506–29; Hiram Morgan, "An Unwelcome Heritage: Ireland's Role in British Empire-Building," *History of European Ideas* 19, nos. 4–6 (1994): 619–25; Ann Daniel, "Undermining British Australia: Irish Lawyers and the Transformation of English law in Australia," *Studies* 84, no.333 (1995): 61–70; Keith Jeffery (ed.), *"An Irish Empire?" Aspects of Ireland and the British Empire* (Manchester: Manchester University Press, 1996). The role of Irish soldiers in the British army is explored throughout the collection by Thomas Bartlett and Keith Jeffery (eds.), *A Military History of Ireland* (Cambridge University Press, 1996). Also see H.J. Hanham, "Religion and Nationality in the Mid-Victorian Army," in M.R.D. Foot (ed.), *War and Society: Historical Essays in Honour and Memory of J.R. Western, 1928–1971* (London: Paul Elek, 1973); Peter Karsten, "Irish Soldiers in the British Army, 1792–1922: Suborned or Subordinate?," *Journal of Social History* 17 (1983): 31–64; A.J. Cook, "Irish in the British Army in South Africa, 1795–1910," in Donal P. McCracken (ed.), *The Irish in Southern Africa, 1795–1910* (Southern African-Irish Studies Volume 2, 1992); Terence Denman, *Ireland's Unknown Soldiers: The 16th (Irish) Division in the Great War, 1914–1918* (Dublin: Irish Academic Press, 1992). Irish soldiers have also filled the ranks of foreign armies. For example, see Alfred Hasbrouck, *Foreign Legionaries in the Liberation of Spanish South America* (New York: Octagon Books, 1969); James Belich, *The New Zealand Wars and the Victorian Interpretation of Racial Conflict* (Auckland: Auckland University Press, 1986); Donal McCracken, *The Irish Pro-Boers, 1877–1902* (Johannesburg: Perskor, 1989); Grainne Henry, *The Irish Military Community in Spanish Flanders, 1586–1621* (Dublin: Irish Academic Press, 1992); Myles Dungan, *Distant Drums: Irish Soldiers in Foreign Armies* (Belfast: Appletree Press, 1993); John Gallaher, *Napoleon's Irish Legion* (Carbondale: Southern Illinois University Press, 1993). Ireland's military history journal, *The Irish Sword*, is a treasury of information on Irish involvement in both the British army and many foreign armies. For a discussion of the origin of policing systems throughout the empire, and the adoption of the Royal Irish Constabulary as a model for colonial police forces, see David M. Anderson and David Killingray (eds.) *Policing the Empire: Government, Authority and Control, 1830–1940* (Manchester: Manchester University Press, 1991). Richard Hawkins is skeptical about the adoption of an Irish model to colonial police systems; see chapter 2 in Anderson and Killingray: "The 'Irish Model' and the Empire: a Case for Reassessment." However, other contributors to the volume confirm links between the Royal Irish Constabulary and policing in the colonies.

18 In an important article, Brian Stoddart argues that the consolidation of the British empire was achieved in large part through the import of "cultural power," the set of ideas, beliefs and conventions concerning social behaviour that was carried throughout the empire by civil servants, military officers, traders, settlers, and educators. He points to the English language as a primary example. Also crucial was the introduction of British sports and games into the colonies, and his article sets a framework for an analysis of the elaboration of cultural power through sport. Brian Stoddart, "Sport, Cultural Imperialism, and Colonial Response in the British Empire," *Comparative Studies in Society and History* 30, no. 4 (1988): 649–73.

19 For an entry into the literature on the Irish in North America, see Seamus Metress, *The Irish American Experience: A Guide to the Literature* (Washington, D.C.: University Press of America Inc., 1981 and subsequent editions);

R.A. Burchell, "The Historiography of the American Irish," *Immigrants and Minorities* 1 (November 1982): 281–305; David Noel Doyle, "The Regional Bibliography of Irish America, 1800–1930: A Review and Addendum," *Irish Historical Studies* 23 (May 1983): 24–283; D.H. Akenson, "An Agnostic View of the Historiography of the Irish-Americans," *Labour/Le Travail* 14 (1984): 123–59; Michael F. Funchion, "Irish-America: An Essay on the Literature Since 1978," *The Immigration History Newsletter* 17 (November 1985): 1–8; Kenneth W. Keller, "The Origins of Ulster Scots Emigration to America: A Survey of Recent Research," *American Presbyterians* 70, no. 2 (1992): 71–80; David Noel Doyle, "Small Differences" The Study of the Irish in the United States and Britain," *Irish Historical Studies* 29, no. 113 (1994): 114–19; Graham Davis, "Models of Migration: The Historiography of the Irish Pioneers in South Texas," *Southwestern Historical Quarterly* 99, no. 3 (1996): 327–45.

20 The history of the Irish in America has been well-served by regional and community studies: Dennis Clark, *The Irish in Philadelphia: Ten Generations of Urban Experience* (Philadelphia: Temple University Press, 1973) and *Erin's Heirs: Irish Bonds of Community* (Lexington: University Press of Kentucky, 1991); Patrick J. Blessing, *West among Strangers: Irish Migration to California, 1850–1880* (Los Angeles: University of California Press, 1977); R.A. Burchell, *The San Francisco Irish 1848–1880* (Manchester: Manchester University Press, 1979); Timothy Meagher, *From Paddy to Studs: Irish-American Communities in the Turn of the Century Era, 1880–1920* (Westport: Greenwood Press, 1986); L.J. McCaffrey et al., *The Irish in Chicago* (Urbana: University of Illinois Press, 1987); B.C. Mitchell, *The Paddy Camps: The Irish of Lowell 1821–1861* (Urbana: The University of Illinois Press, 1988); Grady McWhinney, *Cracker Culture: Celtic Ways in the Old South* (Tuscaloosa, 1988); P.J. Drudy (ed.), *Irish Studies 4: The Irish in America: Emigration, Assimilation and Impact* op. cit.; Patrick J. Blessing, "Paddy: The Image and Reality of Irish Immigrants in the American Community: a Review Essay," *Journal of American Ethnic History* 9 (Fall 1989): 112–19; David M. Emmons, *The Butte Irish: Class and Ethnicity in an American Mining Town, 1875–1925* (Urbana: University of Illinois Press, 1989); Rory Fitzpatrick, *God's Frontiersmen: The Scots-Irish Epic* (London: Weidenfeld and Nicolson, 1989); David Noel Doyle, "The Irish as Urban Pioneers in the United States," *Journal of American Ethnic History* 10 (Fall 1990/Winter 1991): 36–59; Michael A. Gordon, *The Orange Riots: Irish Political Violence in New York City, 1870 and 1871* (New York: Cornell University Press, 1993); Malcolm Campbell, "The Other Immigrants: Comparing the Irish in Australia and the United States," *Journal of American Ethnic History* 14 (1995): 3–22; Thomas H. O'Connor, *The Boston Irish: A Political History* (Boston: Northeastern University Press, 1995); Ronald H. Bayor and Timothy J. Meagher, *The New York Irish* (Baltimore: Johns Hopkins University Press, 1996); H. Tyler Blethen and Curtis W. Wood, Jr. (eds.), *Ulster and North America: Transatlantic Perspectives on the Scotch-Irish* (Tuscaloosa and London: University of Alabama Press, 1997).

The history of the Irish in America is actually the history of the Irish in North America, and the high quality of literature on the Irish migrant group in Canada is frequently overlooked by historians of the Irish in the United States. As a corrective, see the following: Bruce S. Elliott, *Irish Migrants in the Canadas: A New Approach* (Montreal and Kingston: McGill-Queen's University Press; Belfast: Institute of Irish Studies, 1988); Robert O'Driscoll and

Lorna Reynolds (eds.), *The Untold Story: The Irish in Canada*, 2 vols. (Toronto: Celtic Arts, 1988); Thomas Power (ed.), *The Irish in Atlantic Canada. 1780–1900* (Fredericton: New Ireland Press, 1988); David Wilson, *The Irish in Canada* (Ottawa: Canadian Historical Association, 1989); Margaret E. Fitzgerald and Joseph A. King, *The Uncounted Irish in Canada and the United States* (Toronto: P.D. Meany, 1990); Cecil J. Houston and William J. Smyth, *Irish Emigration and Canadian Settlement: Patterns, Links, and Letters* (Toronto: University of Toronto Press, 1990); Gerald L. Pocius, *A Place to Belong: Community Order and Everyday Space in Calvert, Newfoundland* (Montreal and Kingston: McGill-Queen's University Press, 1991); Catherine Anne Wilson, *A New Lease on Life: Landlords, Tenants, and Immigrants in Ireland and Canada* (Montreal and Kingston: McGill-Queen's University Press, 1994).

There is a rich literature in fiction on the Irish experience in America. See Finley Peter Dunne, *Mr. Dooley in the Hearts of His Countrymen* (Boston: Small, Maynard and Co., 1899); Finley Peter Dunne, *Mr. Dooley's Philosophy* (New York: R.H. Russell, 1900); James T. Farrell, *Studs Lonigan: A Trilogy* (*Young Lonigan, The Young Manhood of Studs Lonigan, Judgement Day*) (New York: Vanguard Press, 1978); Edwin O'Connor, *The Last Hurrah* (Boston: Little, Brown and Co., 1956). The literature is reviewed with commentary and a comprehensive bibliography in Charles Fanning, *The Irish Voice in America: Irish-American Fiction from the 1760s to the 1980s* (Lexington: University Press of Kentucky, 1990). Literature on the Irish experience in Canada is not nearly as extensive, but see Brian Moore, *The Luck of Ginger Coffey* (Boston: Little, Brown and Co., 1960), and Jane Urquhart, *Away* (Toronto: McClelland and Stewart, 1993). For a unique perspective on the Irish in New Zealand, Dan Davin's works of historical fiction are required reading. See Dan Davin, *Selected Stories* (Wellington: New Zealand University Press, and London: Robert Hale Ltd., 1981).

21 For the most part, the influence of the Irish Catholic and Protestant churches on the British empire has been explored only incidentally, through studies of specific congregations, missions and key figures in ecclesiastical history. Most, but not all, of the literature focuses on the Roman Catholic church. The following literature confirms the significance of Irish religious influence in every corner of the diaspora and invites research in this understudied area of scholarship. Rev. John Colgan, "Irish Missionaries in South Africa," *Studies* (December 1931): 611–26; Aubrey Gwynn, "The First Irish Priests in the New World," *Studies* 21 (June 1932): 213–28; Henry Koren, *The Spiritans: A History of the Congregation of the Holy Ghost* (Pittsburgh: Duquesne University, 1958); W.E. Brown, *The Catholic Church in South Africa* (London: Burnes and Oates, 1960); W.J. Lowe, "The Lancashire Irish and the Catholic Church, 1846–71: The Social Dimension," *Irish Historical Studies* 20, no.78 (1976): 129–55; Antoine Demets, *The Catholic Church in Montserrat, West Indies, 1756–1980* (Plymouth, Montserrat: privately published, 1980); Cecil J. Houston and William J. Smyth, *The Sash Canada Wore: A Historical Geography of the Orange Order in Canada* (Toronto: University of Toronto Press, 1980); Patrick Carey, *An Immigrant Bishop: John England's Adaptation of Irish Catholicism to American Republicanism* (Yonkers: U.S. Catholic Historical Society, 1982); Edmund Hogan, "African Conversion to Roman Catholicism," *African Ecclesiastical Review* 24, no. 2 (1982): 71–80; Sheridan Gilley, "The Roman Catholic Church and the Nineteenth-Century Irish Diaspora," *Journal of Ecclesiastical History* 35, no. 2 (1984): 188–207; Norman W. Taggart, *The Irish in World*

Methodism, 1760–1900 (London: Epworth Press, 1986); Paul O'Leary, "Irish immigration and the Catholic Welsh district, 1840–50," in G.H. Jenkins and J.B. Smith (eds.) *Politics and Society in Wales, 1840–1922: Essays in Honour of Ieuan Gwynedd Jones* (Cardiff: University of Wales Press, 1988); Hugh McLeod, "Popular Catholicism in Irish New York, c.1900," in W.J. Shiels and Diana Woods (eds.), *The Churches, Ireland and the Irish* (London: Basil Blackwell, 1989); Edmund M. Hogan, *The Irish Missionary Movement: A Historical Survey, 1830–1980* (Dublin: Gill and Macmillan, and Washington D.C.: Catholic University of America Press, 1990); Elaine McFarland, *Protestants First: Orangeism in Nineteenth Century Scotland* (Edinburgh: Edinburgh University Press, 1990); Louis McRedmond, *To the Greater Glory: A History of the Irish Jesuits* (Dublin: Gill and Macmillan, 1991); William Sloan, "Religious Affiliation and the Immigrant Experience: Catholic Irish and Protestant Highlanders in Glasgow, 1830–1850," in T.M. Devine (ed.) *Irish Immigrants and Scottish Society in the Nineteenth and Twentieth Centuries* (Edinburgh 1991); J.B. Brain, "The Irish Influence on the Roman Catholic Church in South Africa," in Donal P. McCracken (ed.) *The Irish in Southern Africa, 1795–1910* (Southern African-Irish Studies Volume 2, 1992); M.M. Goedhals, "The Road to Disestablishment: Irish Anglicans in Nineteenth-Century South Africa," in Donal P. McCracken (ed.) *The Irish in Southern Africa, 1795–1910* op. cit.; Leo J. Hynes, *The Catholic Irish in New Brunswick 1783–1900: A History of Their Prominent Role in the Shaping of the Province and the Structuring of the Roman Catholic Church* (Moncton: Leo J, Hynes, 1992); Brian P. Clarke, *Piety and Nationalism: Lay Voluntary Associations and the Creation of an Irish-Catholic Community in Toronto, 1850–1895* (Montreal and Kingston: McGill-Queen's University Press, 1993); Terrence Murphy and Gerald Stortz (eds.), *Creed and Culture. The Place of English Speaking Catholics in Canadian Society, 1750–1930* (Montreal and Kingston: McGill-Queen's University Press, 1993); Patricia T. Rooke, "Papists and Proselytizers: Non-denominational Education in the British Caribbean after Emancipation," *History of Education* 23 (1994): 257–73; Joseph Akinyele Omoyajowo (ed.), *Makers of the Church in Nigeria* (Lagos: CSS Bookshops, 1995); James White McAuley, "Under an Orange Banner: Reflections on the Northern Protestant Experiences of Emigration," in Patrick O'Sullivan (ed.) *The Irish World Wide* Volume 5, *Religion and Identity* op cit.; Michael J. McNally, "Diocesan Clerical Life in Florida," *Records of the American Catholic Historical Society of Philadelphia* 106, nos.3–4 (1995): 50–62.

Although the influence of the Irish Catholic Church worldwide has been underestimated, the emerging history of Irish Catholicism in Australia provides a growing exception to this rule, much of the work being a continuing footnote to the pioneering work of Patrick O'Farrell. See the following: Michael Gilchrist, *Daniel Mannix, Priest and Patriot* (Victoria, 1982), and a critique of the Mannix literature in R.M. Sweetman, "Daniel Mannix and his Biographers," *Australian Studies* 1 (June 1988): 61–71; Helen Holzer, "The Sisters of Mercy in Auckland of the 1850s and 1860s," *Auckland Waikato Historical Journal* 44 (1984): 30–35 and 45 (1984): 22–28; Patrick O'Farrell, *The Catholic Church and Community in Australia: A History* (Kensington: New South Wales University Press, new ed. 1985); A.E. Cahill, "Cardinal Moran's Politics," *Journal of Religious History* [Australia] 15, no.4 (1989): 525–31; Marie Therese Foale, *The Josephite Story* (Sydney: St Joseph's Generalate, 1989); M.S. McGrath, *These Women! Women Religious in the History of*

xxxix Introduction to the Second Edition

Australia: Sisters of Mercy, Parramatta 1888–1988 (Sydney, 1989); Ruth Schumann, "The Catholic Priesthood of South Australia, 1844–1915," *Journal of Religious History* [Australia] 16, no. 1 (1990): 51–73; Jane Tolerton, *Convent Girls* (Auckland: Penguin, 1994); Lyndon Fraser, "'The Ties that Bind': Irish Catholic Testamentary Evidence from Christchurch, 1876–1915," *New Zealand Journal of History* 29, no. 1 (1995): 67–82; Janice Tranter, "The Irish Dimension of an Australian Religious Sisterhood: The Sisters of St. Joseph," in Patrick O'Sullivan (ed.), *The Irish World Wide* Volume 5, *Religion and Identity*, op cit.; Patrick O'Farrell, "The Irish in Australia and New Zealand, 1870–1990," in W.E. Vaughan (ed.) *A New History of Ireland Volume VI: Ireland Under the Union, 1870–1921* (Oxford: Clarendon Press, 1996); Rory Sweetman, *Bishop in the Dock: The Sedition Trial of James Liston* (Auckland: Auckland University Press, 1997). For a contrast, a throwback to the old idea (albeit wrapped in post-modernspeak) that the Protestants were not really Irish, see Mary J. Hickman, *Religion, Class and Identity. The State, the Catholic Church and the Education of the Irish in Britain* (Aldershot: Avebury, 1995).

22 Two classic books which served as a model for this virtually racialist distinction between the Ulster Scots and the Irish Catholics in North America are Charles A. Hanna, *The Scotch-Irish, or, The Scot in North Britain, North Ireland, and North America* (New York: Knickerbocker Press, 1902) and Henry Ford Jones, *The Scotch-Irish in America* (Princeton: Princeton University Press, 1915). For a revival of this opinion, see R. Hanna, *Land of the Free: Ulster and the American Revolution* (Lurgan: Ulster Society, 1992). The related assumption that Irish migrant communities are culturally homogenous continues to distort current scholarship. See James White McAuley's critique in "Under an Orange banner," op. cit. 43–44 and *passim*. Also see the thoughtful essay by Kenneth W. Keller, "What is Distinctive about the Scotch-Irish?," in Robert D. Mitchell (ed.), *Appalachian Frontiers* (Lexington: University Press of Kentucky, 1991).

The Irish in Ontario

CHAPTER ONE

Ontario: Whatever Happened to the Irish?

Part I

I

"Emigrant behaviour, in addition to its intrinsic interest, can tell us much about the society from which the emigrants have emigrated."[1] So writes M.A.G. O'Tuathaigh as part of an authoritative survey of recent Irish historiography produced by the Irish Committee of Historical Sciences. His observation suggests one of the three facets of meaning inherent in any useful study of Irish emigrants and their dependants: it will cast light, most probably indirectly and reflexively, upon the history of the home land. What the emigrants were able to achieve in the New World suggests something about the nature of the cultural assets and liabilities they brought with them from the Old. In the study which follows, this point is not reiterated at any length because to do so would be otiose. That the history of the Irish abroad is in some sense a part of the historiography of the Irish at home is taken as a fundamental principle, as integral to the progress of this study as an endoskeleton is to vertebrate locomotion, and it is assumed that the reader is familiar with the recent literature on nineteenth-century Irish social history.

A second facet of any valid emigration study is that it inevitably is comparative in that it must be both written and read within the context of the large international literature on the "Irish diaspora." The adaptation of the Irish in general to conditions in nineteenth-century Ontario, and their specific reactions to the local environment of Leeds and Landsdowne township, which is the case

1 M.A.G. O'Tuathaigh, "Ireland, 1800–1921," in *Irish historiography 1970–79*, ed. Joseph Lee (Cork: Cork University Press 1981), 106. O'Tuathaigh makes special reference to Patrick O'Farrell, "Emigrant Attitudes and Behaviour as a Source for Irish History," in *Historical Studies X*, ed. G.A. Hayes-McCoy (Connemara: 1976), 109–31.

analysed here, illustrates one sort of adaptation (out of several sorts) that the Irish made in their diaspora. Of course, in comparative terms, the Irish experience in the United States is the most relevant to that of the Irish in central Canada, but this study's concluding chapter suggests that the Ontario data can help to correct some failings in the American literature.

A third, equally important, aspect of an emigrant study is the light it casts upon the history of the host country. The story of the Irish in Ontario comprises the bulk, though certainly not the entirety, of the history of the Irish in nineteenth-century Canada: in 1871, for example, 66.1 percent of persons of Irish ethnicity in the dominion of Canada lived in Ontario.[2] Any generalizations about the Irish in Canada must therefore begin with the Irish in Ontario as their base line.

Because rural microstudies (or, if one does not like that term, analytic local histories) are done relatively rarely in Canada by professional historians, they are particularly vulnerable to misreading. The key point is not that the specific community being studied is of great importance in itself but that a thorough case-study permits examination of a fundamental historical process (in this case, ethnic adaptation and acculturation) with the detail provided by an electron microscope for living organisms. This, or course, is not the only perspective historians can or should use in studying a given historical process (history needs its general ecologists as well as its microbiologists), but the study of historical process at a specific microlevel certainly can make a valid contribution to our overall understanding.

Thus the question of the "typicality" of a given locale for microstudy is misplaced. No area is typical. What one needs to know instead is, first, whether the area for the microstudy had specific environmental or social characteristics that influenced the data, and, second, where the community fit in the spectrum of local variance in the entire province of Ontario. The effect of these issues on the microstudy of Leeds and Landsdowne township is addressed in chapters 2 and 7.

Within the Canadian context, this book is intended primarily as a contribution to ethnic studies. Yet the reader will notice that the Canadian literature on ethnicity is rarely referred to, although the author is well aware of it and is respectful of the wide-ranging work being done in the field. A knowledgeable observer, the former editor of *Canadian Ethnic Studies*, has noted that the "traditional con-

2 See *Census of Canada, 1931*, 1: 710–23.

cept" of ethnic history in Canada has focused "on groups other than the original British and French colonizers or the various native peoples."[3] There is indeed a massive amount of work being done on the more than sixty non-charter Canadian ethnic groups, most notably the twenty-five or more major ethnic histories being funded by the federal Department of the Secretary of State. Unfortunately, the ethnic literature as it deals with Ontario focuses almost entirely on groups that (1) were separated by language from the bulk of the receiving population, (2) had not had experience in their homeland with political and administrative systems of the sort operative in Canada, (3) experienced a considerable degree of racial discrimination (sometimes very gross discrimination indeed), and (4) largely settled in urban concentrations which in many instances constituted ghettos.

There is a real problem in trying to assimilate into the ethnic historical literature the experience of groups that (1) spoke English with facility even before they migrated to Ontario, (2) were familiar with how a British-derived system of representative government worked and knew how to find the hidden levers of power, (3) experienced relatively minimal discrimination (usually based on their state as bedraggled immigrants rather than on perduring ethnic characteristics), and (4) largely settled in the countryside, most commonly in the nineteenth century as farmers.[4]

This problem would exist even if there were no temporal gap between the history of the charter groups and that of the modern ethnic groups. The crucial periods, however, in the history of the Irish, Scots, English, and American immigrants all occur before the twentieth century, while virtually all the ethnic data that relate to Ontario have been generated in the twentieth century, mostly from World War II onwards. Thus, to attempt to apply theoretical models based upon the mid-twentieth-century experience of ethnic minorities to the experience of nineteenth-century immigrants who

3 Howard Palmer, "Recent Studies in Canadian Immigration and Ethnic History," *The History and Social Science Teacher* 17 (Winter 1982): 97. Palmer believes, however, that the British, French, and native peoples should fall within the boundaries of ethnic history.

4 That the Irish in Ontario (both Catholics and Protestants) most commonly became farmers is a point that will be discussed in detail in the pages which follow. For a useful review, which indicates that not only the Irish but the Scots and English as well were most commonly farmers, see the study of the 1871 census conducted by A. Gordon Darroch and Michael D. Ornstein, "Ethnicity and Occupational Structure in Canada in 1871: The Vertical Mosaic in Historical Perspective," *Canadian Historical Review* 61 (September 1980): especially table 7, 326–7.

virtually comprised majority groups requires an excessive leap of faith. Instead, one should try, however haltingly, to deal with ethnicity in late eighteenth- and nineteenth-century Canada on its own terms, avoiding anachronistic approaches and scratching hard for evidence. For the moment that undoubtedly is the slowest method of progress, but ultimately it probably will be the surest.

As a first step to dealing with ethnicity in nineteenth-century Ontario, we would do well to develop an unambiguous terminology. There exists a vexing semantic tangle concerning the groups from the British Isles, and until this is straightened out to the general satisfaction of ethnic historians each study will have to be read with an eye to the author's own peculiar set of definitions. (This is to put aside the whole question of whether there ever has been a satisfactory definition of ethnicity itself.)[5] The problem is that certain words used both by contemporaries and by modern historians have meanings that not only are ambiguous but are in themselves constituents of "semantic nests."[6] For example, the word "English" as used in mid-nineteenth-century Canada could have been taken as referring to someone from England, someone from Wales (the United Kingdom census categories group the English and the Welsh), or an English Canadian (that is, a Canadian of English or Welsh origin). Further, it was used to refer to such concepts as the English parliamentary tradition (although there had been no such thing as an English parliament since the union with Scotland in 1707) and such institutions as the Church of England (which since 1801 actually had been part of the United Church of England and Ireland).

The word "British" is even worse. Ethnically, it referred to a semantic nest comprising the inhabitants of Great Britain (English, Scots, and Welsh) and their descendants in Canada. Often, however, it also was (and is) used to include Irish Protestants and sometimes Irish Catholics, that is, all groups from the British Isles and their descendants in Canada. This latter encompassing usage is common among historians of the several twentieth-century ethnic groups to describe a particular group's history against the undifferentiated backdrop of "British" groups in Canada.

5 See Wsevolod W. Isajiw, "Definitions of Ethnicity," in *Ethnicity and Ethnic Relations in Canada: A Book of Readings*, ed. Jay E. Goldstein and Rita M. Bienvenue (Toronto: Butterworths 1980), 14–25.

6 The discussion here was stimulated by the schematic presented by David H. Stymeist, "Non-Native Ethnicity in Crow Lake," in Goldstein and Bienvenue, 35.

As for the term "Irish," in both the contemporary literature and later scholarly studies the fallacy of floating terminology is endemic.[7] "Irish" is sometimes used to refer to all migrants from Ireland, regardless of their religious faith. At other times, "Irish" means "Irish Catholic," and at still other times it means a poverty-stricken Irish Catholic from one of the poorest areas of Ireland. Often "Irish peasant" is used to mean "Irish Catholic." This is invalid, for pauperized peasants of the Protestant faith emigrated from Ireland, while conversely many of the Catholic small tenant farmers who emigrated were well above the poverty line. The remedy for this ambiguity is simple enough: one should always make clear that Irish Catholics and Irish Protestants were part of a larger general body – the Irish – and, when the Irish are not being discussed collectively, one should specify clearly whether the subject is Irish Catholics or Irish Protestants. Sometimes, it is convenient to refer to the Irish and their descendants in the New World either as a single ethnic cohort, "the Irish," or as "Irish Catholics" or "Irish Protestants." In such cases the context should make clear that one is referring to the multi-generational ethnic cohort and not simply to the first generation of migrants from the Old World.

Such considerations make it obvious that, until we, as historians of ethnic groups in nineteenth-century Ontario, learn to describe our subjects with precision, we would do well not to immerse ourselves too deeply in the complex theoretical literature which has been developed concerning twentieth-century ethnic groups. Ultimately, however, one hopes that an integration of nineteenth- and twentieth-century ethnic studies as they appertain to Ontario will be possible. Integration is a two-way word. It implies, certainly, that at some stage the students of the nineteenth-century charter groups will be able to assimilate the appropriate aspects of twentieth-century studies on non-charter minorities. But it also implies that those doing modern ethnic studies will realize that ethnic history is like a pyramid and that each course of stones must be solid and true if the next is to hold. It is not only reverse racism but self-defeating to build a history of any recent ethnic group upon a foundation which designates the earlier arrivals as some kind of undifferentiated "Anglo" or "British" lump. Only if there is a sympathetic understanding of the complexities of the history of the early groups will it

7 For specific examples of the misuse of the terminology concerning "the Irish," taken from the modern Canadian historical literature, see Donald H. Akenson, "Ontario: Whatever Happened to the Irish?" *Canadian Papers in Rural History* 3 (1982): 222–5.

be possible to construct sensible, accurate, and lasting histories of the groups which arrived later.[8]

2

To anyone interested in the history of the Irish and of their diaspora in the nineteenth and twentieth centuries their settlement in Ontario is doubly fascinating. In the first instance their settlement and assimilation indicate that the generally accepted American pattern of urban concentration cannot be taken as the universal norm: the "American pattern" (if indeed it actually existed) almost certainly was a result of factors peculiar to that country rather than of cultural determinants set down in the Old World. Second, the paucity of historical literature on the subject is noteworthy and, indeed, strange. Once one has referred to Nicholas Flood Davin's *The Irishman in Canada* (1878) and to John J. Mannion's *Irish Settlements in Eastern Canada: A Study of Cultural Transfer and Adaptation* (1974), one has mentioned all the books and monographs that deal directly with the Irish in Ontario as an ethnic group. Fortunately, there are several monographs available that deal with the Irish as a political group and others that deal with institutional matters, but these skirt the central issue of ethnicity. The dearth of studies on Irish ethnicity in the region that is now Ontario is underscored when one makes the natural comparison to the Irish Americans. In the nineteenth century, they wrote massive volumes memorializing the Irish contribution to the rise of urban America and to their part in the creation of American democracy and they sometimes put forth a modest claim for the Hibernian basis of all western civilization. In recent times there has developed a corpus of scholarship tracing in depth and detail the history of the Irish as an ethnic group in the United States, but there are no cognate bodies of literature for the Upper Canadian Irish.[9]

8 For pioneering work on the English as an ethnic group in Manitoba in the twentieth century, see Ross McCormack, "Cloth Caps and Jobs: The Ethnicity of English Immigrants in Canada 1900–1914," in *Ethnicity, Power, and Politics in Canada*, ed. Jorgen Dahlie and Tissa Fernando (Toronto: Methuen 1981), 38–54; and also his "Networks among British Immigrants and Accommodation to Canadian Society, 1900–1914" (paper presented to the University of Kent Conference on the Diaspora of the British, June 1981).

9 Unhappily, demographers have largely evaded the question of ethnicity in nineteenth-century Ontario. This is especially disappointing as the numerical contours of an ethnic population must be determined before one can speak of their secondary cultural characteristics with much certainty. One can look forward, however, to the work of the sociologists A. Gordon Darroch and Michael D. Ornstein. Some of their early material is found in "Ethnicity and Oc-

These lacunae become all the more striking when one realizes that the Irish in Upper Canada (later called Canada West and later still Ontario) were much more important to Canadian society than the American Irish were to that of the United States. For most of the nineteenth century the Irish were the single largest European group in Upper Canada. This point with regard to Upper Canada will be developed in the text which follows. Here, one should note as demographic context for that later discussion that the Irish were the largest ethnic group throughout British North America in the nineteenth century. From the end of the Napoleonic Wars until the mid-1860s, emigrants from Ireland to all parts of British North America exceeded those from England and Wales and from Scotland in almost every single year and, indeed, until the mid-1850s usually exceeded the *combined* total from the rest of the British Isles. Not surprisingly, when the censuses of 1841–2, 1851, 1861, 1871, and 1881 tallied the birthplaces of all persons in British North America, Ireland was the most common homeland of those born outside the country. Not until 1891 were there more English-born than Irish-born in British North America.[10]

One wonders what, in fact, happened to the Canadian Irish and to their history. Especially, one would like to know why so little is known about them in Upper Canada, where they settled in the largest numbers.[11] Part – but only part – of the explanation for the

cupational Structure in Canada in 1871," 61: 305–33. This article stands in impressive contrast to the slighting treatment of ethnicity in, for example, Warren E. Kalbach and Wayne W. McVey, *The Demographic Bases of Canadian Society,* 2d. ed. (Toronto: McGraw-Hill Ryerson 1979).

    For reasons of space, I am not able to discuss in detail the various books about the political or institutional life of the Ontario Irish. See particularly the books and article cited below, n 46.

10 See *Census of Canada, 1870–71* 4; *Census of Canada, 1665 to 1871* passim; M.C. Urquhart and K.A.H. Buckley, *Historical Statisics of Canada* (Toronto: Macmillan 1965), 20.

11 There is, of course, a mass of material in the parliamentary papers of the United Kingdom which relates to Irish emigration to British North America. For the pre-Famine period, the most useful of these are as follows (in chronological order as they appear in the papers):
Report from the Select Committee on Emigration from the United Kingdom, HC 1826 (404), iv.
Estimate of the sum required for facilitating emigration from the South of Ireland to the Canadas and the Cape of Good Hope, HC 1823 (491), xiii; HC 1825 (131), xviii; HC 1826–7 (160), xv.
Report from the Committee appointed to inquire into the expediency of encouraging emigration from the United Kingdom, HC 1826–7 (88), v; HC 1826–7 (237), v; HC 1826–7 (550), v.
Report from the select Committee appointed to take account of the state of the

lack of documentation is that our information on the movement of the Irish to Upper Canada is fragmentary, at least before the mid-nineteenth century. (For convenience, "Upper Canada" will be used in Part I of this chapter to denominate the area first called Upper Canada and later Canada West.) As a start, then, it is appropriate to sort out what we know and what we do not know about this great Irish migration.

Initially, one should note that the post-1815 migrations from the British Isles (see table 1) were the by-product of a series of population explosions that remain to this day among the most perplexing phenomena in modern history. Firm population figures are not available for Great Britain before 1801, or for Ireland before 1821, but it is clear that during the eighteenth century and the first half of the nineteenth century population in the British Isles grew at a rate as fast as that which presently holds for many "third world" countries and which we now view as a portent of inevitable disaster for the nations involved. The causes of the population explosions were not everywhere the same throughout the British Isles and must have varied from region to region within each country. Nor were the results everywhere the same; in Ireland, for example, the population boom in the region of industrializing Belfast produced radically different social configurations from those in deepest Connaught. As

---

poorer classes in Ireland and the best means of improving their condition, HC 1830 (667), vii.

Reports from the commissioners for emigration to the colonial secretary, HC 1831–2 (724), xxxii.

Emigration, North America and Australia, HC 1833 (141), xxvi.

Emigration. Return ... 1833, HC 1833 (696), xxvi.

Emigration. Return ... 1835, HC 1835 (87), xxxix.

Report from the agent-general for emigration from the United Kingdom, HC 1837–8 (388), xl.

Number of persons who have emigrated from the United Kingdom ... between 1832 and 1836, HC 1837–8 (137), xlvii.

Emigration. Return ... , HC 1839 (536-1), xxxix.

Correspondence relative to emigration to Canada, HC 1841 (298), xi.

Emigration. Return ... , HC 1841 (61), iii, sess. 2.

Emigration and Crown Lands, HC 1842 (231), xxxi.

Despatch from the governor-general of British North America to a transmitting of the annual reports of the agents for emigration in Canada [373], HC 1842, xxxi; HC 1843 (109), xxxiv; HC 1844 (181), xxxv.

Reports by the emigration agents of Canada, etc., HC 1843 (109), xxxiv.

General report of the colonial land and emigration commissioners, HC 1842 (567), xxv; HC 1843 (621), xxix; HC 1844 (178), xxxi; HC 1845 (617), xxvii.

TABLE 1

Emigration from the British Isles to Major Extra-
European Countries (unrevised data), 1815–45

Year	British North America	United States	Australasia
1815	680	1,209	N/A
1816	3,370	9,022	N/A
1817	9,797	10,280	N/A
1818	15,136	12,429	N/A
1819	23,534	10,674	N/A
1820	17,921	6,745	N/A
1821	12,955	4,958	320
1822	16,013	4,137	875
1823	11,355	5,032	543
1824	8,774	5,152	780
1825	8,741	5,551	485
1826	12,818	7,063	903
1827	12,648	14,526	715
1828	12,084	12,817	1,056
1829	13,307	15,678	2,016
1830	30,574	24,887	1,242
1831	58,067	23,418	1,561
1832	66,339	32,782	3,733
1833	28,808	29,109	4,093
1834	40,060	33,074	2,800
1835	15,573	26,720	1,860
1836	34,226	37,774	3,124
1837	29,884	36,770	5,054
1838	4,577	14,332	14,021
1839	12,658	33,536	15,786
1840	32,293	40,642	15,850
1841	38,164	45,017	32,625
1842	54,123	63,852	8,534
1843	23,518	28,335	3,478
1844	22,924	43,660	2,229
1845	31,803	58,538	830

Source: Carrier and Jeffery, External Migration, 95

a whole, however, the Irish population was growing faster than the
nation's economic production.[12]

On the key question of the Irish and their move to North America,
table 2 indicates the number of individuals migrating from Irish

12 The basic English census data from 1801 onwards are most conveniently available in B.R. Mitchell and Phyllis Deane, Abstract of British Historical Statistics

TABLE 2

Migration from Irish ports to North America (unrevised data), 1825–45

| Year | To British North America | | To the United States | |
	From Irish ports	As percent of UK total to BNA	From Irish ports	As percent of UK total to U.S.
		(percent)		(percent)
1825	6,841	78.3	4,387	79.0
1826	10,484	81.8	4,383	62.1
1827	9,134	72.2	4,014	27.6
1828	6,695	55.4	2,877	22.4
1829	7,710	57.9	4,133	26.4
1830	19,340	63.3	2,981	12.0
1831	40,977	70.6	3,583	15.3
1832	37,068	55.9	4,172	12.7
1833	17,431	60.5	4,764	16.4
1834	28,586	71.4	4,213	12.7
1835	9,458	60.7	2,684	10.0
1836	19,388	56.6	3,654	9.7
1837	22,463	75.2	3,871	10.5
1838	2,284	49.9	1,169	8.2
1839	8,989	71.0	2,843	8.5
1840	23,935	74.1	4,087	10.1
1841	24,089	63.1	3,893	8.6
1842	33,410	61.7	6,199	9.7
1843	10,898	46.3	1,617	5.7
1844	12,396	54.1	2,993	6.9
1845	19,947	62.7	3,708	6.3

Source: Carrier and Jeffery, *External Migration*, 95

(Cambridge: Cambridge University Press 1962). The pre-1801 estimates of population which were cited so confidently as recently as fifteen years ago have been shown to be untrustworthy and of necessity have been abandoned. With them have gone the several complex explanations of the eighteenth-century demographic explosion. What remains is the certain knowledge that there was an extraordinary boom in England and Wales in the eighteenth century, but its exact magnitude is now highly problematical. See M.W. Flinn, *British Population Growth 1700–1850* (London: Macmillan 1970) for a compact summary of the problems with the data.

For the Scottish situation see Michael Flinn, ed., *Scottish Population History from the 17th Century to the 1930s* (Cambridge: Cambridge University Press 1977).

The standard study of eighteenth- and early nineteenth-century Irish popula-

ports, beginning in 1825, the first date for which we have even a rough approximation.

Sailing from an Irish port however, did not mean that the individual migrant actually was an Irishman, any more than sailing from a British port made him a Scotsman or an Englishman. Actually, the number of Irish migrants was even greater than the tally of the numbers leaving Irish ports would indicate, because

---

tion growth remains K.H. Connell, *The Population of Ireland, 1750–1845* (Oxford: Clarendon Press 1950). See also Connell, "The Population of Ireland in the Eighteenth Century," *Economic History Review* 16 (1946): 111–24, and Michael Drake, "Marriage and Population Growth in Ireland, 1750–1845," *Economic History Review*, 2d ser., 16 (December 1963): 301–13.

The most complete compendium of the data on emigration from the British Isles, which includes both the actual data and a discussion of the limits on its reliability, was compiled for the General Register Office of the United Kingdom, as N.H. Carrier and J.R. Jeffery, *Studies on Medical and Population Subjects, No. 6: External Migration, a Study of the Available Statistics, 1815–1950* (London: HMSO 1953).

Two older works are still highly serviceable: Stanley C. Johnson, *A History of Emigration from the United Kingdom to North America, 1763–1912* (London: Routledge and Kegan Paul 1913; reprint, London: Frank Cass and Co. 1966), and William Forbes Adams, *Ireland and Irish Emigration to the New World from 1815 to the Famine* (New Haven: Yale University Press 1932). A considerably less sophisticated volume from the same era is Helen I. Cowan, *British Emigration to British North America, 1783–1837* (Toronto: University of Toronto Library 1928). This was later revised (1961), but not greatly improved. A précis of this work is Helen I. Cowan, *British Immigration before Confederation* (Ottawa: Canadian Historical Association Booklets 1968). Norman MacDonald, *Canada, 1763–1841, Immigration and Settlement: The Administration of the Imperial Regulations* (London: Longmans, Green and Co. 1939), is chiefly descriptive and is imprecise on numerical matters.

H.J.M. Johnston, *British Emigration Policy, 1815–1830* (Oxford: Clarendon Press 1972), deals chiefly with pauper emigration but includes some shrewd redactions of emigration statistics. Lynn Hollen Lees, *Exiles of Erin. Irish Migrants in Victorian London* (Ithaca: Cornell University Press 1979) deals primarily with intra-British migration but it assesses data that are relevant to external migration as well.

A convenient compendium of Irish data is W.E. Vaughan and A.J. Fitzpatrick, eds., *Irish Historical Statistics. Population, 1821–1971* (Dublin: Royal Irish Academy 1978).

The data on Scottish migration are discussed in Flinn, *Scottish Population History from the 17th Century to the 1930s*, 91ff. See also the précis of James M. Cameron's PHD thesis (University of Glasgow 1970), "Scottish Emigration to Upper Canada, 1815–55: A Study of Process," in *International Geography 1972*, ed. W. Peter Adams and Frederick Helleiner (Toronto: University of Toronto Press 1972), 1, 404–6. See also Cameron, "The Role of Shipping from Scottish Ports in Emigration to the Canadas, 1815–55," in *Canadian Papers in Rural History*, ed. Donald H. Akenson, 2 (1980): 135–54.

On the migration by lowland Scots before the time of their move to Upper

many Irishmen sailed from ports in Great Britain while relatively few Britishers sailed from Irish ports. In particular, two British ports were attractive and accessible to the Irish, Liverpool, which in the 1830s was the third leading English port of emigration, and Greenock, which in the same period was the leading Scottish emigration port.[13] The number of actual Irish migrants was underestimated for two additional reasons: because there was a substantial illegal migrant trade and because children were counted (or discounted) in an eccentric fashion. The matter of the children is especially confusing since from 1817 to 1833 inclusive children coming to British North America were counted as one-half, one-third, or not at all, according to their age. Thereafter, they appear to have been counted as adults.[14]

The most successful attempt at resolving all these difficulties is William Forbes Adams's classic study (1932). Given below are Adams's final figures, indicating his upward revision of Irish estimates of the Irish migration to North America.[15]

Adams's revised estimate of Irish emigration to British North America from all United Kingdom ports

Year	Figures
1825	8,893
1826	13,629
1827	11,969
1828	8,824
1829	10,148
1830	25,679
1831	54,514
1832	50,305

Canada see M. Perceval-Maxwell, *The Scottish Migration to Ulster in the Reign of James I* (London: Routledge and Kegan Paul 1973), and R.J. Dickson, *Ulster Emigration to Colonial America, 1718–1755* (London: Routledge and Kegan Paul 1966). Dickson's "Critical Note on Authorities" deals succinctly with the available data and published work for the American colonial period.

13 For statistics for all United Kingdom emigration ports, 1831–4, see *Report on Canadian Archives, 1900,* "Emigration," 58–9. The statistical series is continuous through 1860, in C.M. Godfrey, *The Cholera Epidemics in Upper Canada, 1832–1866* (Toronto: Secombe House 1968), 70–2.

14 Adams, 411–13.

15 Ibid., 413–14. Although the best available revision, Adams's materials is not above reproach. In particular, he seems somewhat cavalier in his treatment of migration from Greenock. I have interpolated the estimate for 1836 myself, from data found in Carrier and Jeffery, 95. It should be added that Adams believed the original data for 1827 to have been seriously below the true situation.

1833	23,139
1834	32,315
1835	10,764
1836	22,528
1837	26,102
1838	2,908
1839	10,943
1840	28,756
1841	30,923
1842	42,884
1843	14,668
1844	17,725
1845	26,708

When combined with the raw data in tables 1 and 2, the conclusion is inescapable: well before the Great Famine, the Irish were the single most important group of migrants to British North America.[16]

When one turns directly to Upper Canada, one finds that the various censuses were not nearly as accurate or as probing as one would wish, but the 1842 enumeration did inquire into place of birth of the province's residents. In that year, Upper Canada had 78,255 Irish-born inhabitants, making the Irish by far the largest non-indigenous group.[17]

In interpreting table 3, the crucial point to note is that, large though the immigrant numbers were, the enumeration procedures radically underrepresented the extent of new additions to Upper Canadian society. This occurred because the census authorities recorded only the birthplace, not the ethnic background, of each individual. Thus, although the mother and father in a family of recent arrival were enumerated as being of European birth, their children, so long as they were born in Canada, were recorded as

16 The reader may notice that for 1825 and 1826 Adams's revised estimates of Irish migrants to British North America exceeds the unrevised official emigration figures for all of the British Isles. It would be natural – but quite wrong – to see this as indicative of a flaw in Adams's procedures. Actually, Adams made allowances for children and for illegal migrants, which the official version of the figures did not do. A "true" version of the official figures would have to include the same compensation to figures for all of the British Isles which Adams made only for the Irish.

Strictly speaking, then, the data in table 1 and those in Adams's work are incompatible, but as confirmation of the point made in the text about the prepotence of Irish migration, they are more than adequate.

17 The 1842 census is found in Appendix (FF) to the Journals of the Legislative Assembly, 1843. It is reprinted in altered form in Census of Canada, 1870–71 4, Censuses of Canada, 1665 to 1871, 134–40. The reprint is preferable, as arithmetical errors in the original are corrected in the reprint. The differences, however, are relatively small.

TABLE 3
Birthplaces of Upper Canadian Population, 1842

Country of birth	Numbers	Proportion of UC population (percent)
CANADIAN-BORN		
English Canadian	247,665	50.8
French Canadian	13,969	2.9
Subtotal Canadian-born	261,634	53.7
FOREIGN-BORN		
British Isles:		
Ireland	78,255	16.1
England and Wales	40,684	8.4
Scotland	39,781	8.1
Subtotal British Isles	158,720	32.6
United States	32,809	6.7
Continental Europe	6,581	1.4
Subtotal Foreign-born	198,110	40.7
Not known	27,309	5.6
TOTAL POPULATION	487,053	100.0

Source: Derived from 1842 census, as found in Census of Canada, 1871 4: 136

native Canadians, with no distinctions in the records between them and the children of, say, third-generation loyalists. At minimum, one should define as members of an identifiable ethnic group not only those born abroad but at least the first generation born in Canada; indeed, in many groups the sense of identifiably ethnic identity has run considerably longer. The magnitude of the native-born Canadian population was a statistical chimera not reflective of the actual ethnicity of the people.

Ideally, the 1842 census should be reprocessed in its entirety. Failing that, there are three methods of redacting the 1842 data, each helpful in part but none totally satisfactory. First – Revision A – one can begin with the base population of Upper Canada before heavy emigration started and define this group, plus the numbers accruing to it by natural increase, as the "native Canadian" population. This figure will be less than the native-born category as defined in the 1842 census. The difference between the two numbers presumably will consist of the first generation of offspring of foreign-born parents, and their grown children, in cases of early migrants. Then one adds this ethnic figure to foreign-born populations as shown in the 1842 census to obtain an aggregate total of the foreign-born and their offspring. Next one adds a portion of this

corrected ethnic figure to each ethnic group in proportion to its existence in the population in 1842 and, in theory, obtains a more accurate indication of the relative numerical importance of each group than is provided in the original census data. Specifically, if one takes the base population of Upper Canada to have been 100,000 in 1812[18] and the rate of natural increase to have been 30 percent per decade,[19] then the "true" native indigenous population in Upper Canada in 1842 would have been approximately 219,700. One could then estimate the ethnic derivation as follows:

Revision A

	(percent)
Indigenous Canadian	45
Irish	18
English and Welsh	10
Scottish	10
United States	8
Continental Europe	2
Unknown	7

For many reasons, in particular, the shakiness of the estimate of the base population (in 1812 it may well have been closer to 70,000 than to 100,000) and the arbitrary nature of the percentage of rate of natural increase, these estimates are highly questionable.

Thus, we must abandon Revision A and attempt Revision B. Fundamentally, this is an attempt to estimate the first-generation ethnic population, add this number to the figures for the foreign-born, and thus provide an indication of ethnicity over two generations. Here we (1) "correct" the raw population data for 1842 by distributing the "unknown" category among the various ethnic categories in proportion to the relative size of each group. This is not unreasonable – they were born somewhere, and a proportional distribution makes more sense than any alternative allocation.[20] (2) We now determine the hypothetical number of families in Upper Canada (an actual number was not enumerated). We do this by

18 The two relevant estimates – of 95,000 and 135,000 – can be taken as co-eval, as they both deal with the situation before heavy transatlantic immigration began. (Michael Smith, *A Geographical View of the Province of Canada*, 1813, and Joseph Bouchette, *Topographical Description*, 1815.) Most observers have taken the lower estimate as most likely to be closer to the truth.

19 I am here following the procedure and, in the absence of Upper Canadian figures, the usage of a rate of natural increase taken from the United States, as found in Johnston, 111.

20 Because of the arithmetical corrections necessary in the 1842 census, one cannot accept their proportional distribution of the "unknown" category but must do it oneself.

dividing the number of married people – 155,304 – by two and then multiplying by 1.028 to take into account single-parent families (this multiple is derived from the 1848 census, as comparable information was not available for 1842).[21] This yields an estimate of 79,826 family units in Upper Canada in 1842. (3) We assume that both the propensity to marry and family size do not vary by ethnic group. Actually, this assumption is conservative, because in most societies immigrant groups have larger families than do long-established residents. The conservative procedure guarantees that our revision will, if anything, err on the side of caution. (4) To obtain the average number of children in each family, we divide the number of children fourteen years of age and under – 224,023 – by the estimated number of families and obtain 2.8 children per family. The reader will recognize that this too is a highly conservative procedure as far as estimating ethnicity is concerned, both because many children stayed *en famille* beyond the age of fourteen, and because the *completed* family size (the total number of children born in the lifetime of a marriage) is greater than the actual number in the family at any given time. (5) Finally, we subtract the imputed number of the first generation born in Canada from the "Canadian" total and add it to the appropriate ethnic total. These procedures yield the following estimate of the ethnicity of Upper Canada's population in 1842.

Revision B

Ethnicity	Estimate	Percentage
Born in Ireland or born in Canada of Irish-born parentage	120,949	24.9
Born in England or Wales or born in Canada of English- or Welsh-born parentage	62,884	12.9
Born in Scotland or born in Canada of Scottish-born parentage	61,480	12.6
Subtotal for British Isles	245,313	50.4

21 Census of 1848, in *Census of Canada, 1870–71* 4, *Censuses of Canada, 1665–1871*, 164. The multiplier obviously is low, but I suspect that any error is self-correcting. Many widows and widowers probably were tallied (incorrectly) as being married, even though they had no spouses. Thus, the married figure probably is artificially high and the multiplier artificially low. The final result of the estimates of total families, however, should be reasonably accurate.

Born in the United States or born in Canada of American-born parentage	50,720	10.4
Born in Continental Europe or born in Canada of European-born parentage	10,169	2.1
Canadian – defined as all second and succeeding generations born in British North America	180,851	37.1
Grand total	487,053	100.0

The revisions suggested above are conservative in part because they were based on an assumption of average family size – 2.8 children per family – that is very small indeed. This figure comes from a statistical definition of family size as including only children of fourteen years of age or younger.

Revision c follows the same procedures and makes the same assumptions as Revision B, with one exception: instead of taking 2.8 as the average number of children in each family, we will take 5.76 as the average family size (including parents). This figure comes from the census of 1851, which enumerates as family members all those living in the family unit, regardless of their age. (The 1851 census was the first to collect data permitting this kind of calculation.) [22]

Revision c

Ethnicity	Estimate	Percentage
Born in Ireland or born in Canada of Irish-born parentage	134,363	27.6
Born in England or Wales or born in Canada of English- or Welsh-born parentage	69,859	14.3
Born in Scotland or born in Canada of Scottish-born parentage	68,298	14.0
Subtotal for British Isles	272,520	55.9

22 *Census of Canada, 1851–52* 1: 308 shows 152,336 families, comprising 863,971 members actually resident and an additional 13,651 family members temporarily absent, for a total of 877,622 family members.

Born in the United States or born in Canada of American-born parentage	56,348	11.6
Born in Continental Europe or born in Canada of European-born parentage	11,296	2.3
Canadian – defined as all second and succeeding generations born in British North America	146,889	30.2
Grand total	487,053	100.0

Whereas Revision B was a conservative recension of the ethnicity data, Revision C probably goes too far: when transposed to the 1842 data, the average family size calculable from the 1851 census leaves too few single people in the society. Revision B and Revision C together, however, produce a set of bracketing figures which can be considered the boundaries of probability. Somewhere between them will be found the truth of the matter.

The long paperchase through the extant statistical sources leads to two sets of conclusions. The first indicates that even if ethnic identity is defined very narrowly (as lasting through the first generation born in Canada and no longer) only a moiety, or less, of the Upper Canada population in the early 1840s can be considered native Canadian. The ethnic groups from the British Isles constituted, at minimum, half of the population, and among all ethnic groups the largest was the Irish, a quarter of the population at least and probably more, even *before* the massive Irish migrations of the Famine years. Second, the necessity of making long calculations and employing unverifiable (albeit reasonable) assumptions on a number of points, and the complete lack of data on other matters (such as place of birth before the year 1842) help to explain why the history of the Irish in Upper Canada has been largely avoided by all but a few Canadian social historians, by historians of the Irish in America, and by historians of the Irish nation and its diaspora.

3

Here it would be comforting to introduce a simplification and claim that the main reason for the thinness of the historical literature on the Irish in Upper Canada is that the Irish who migrated there were predominantly of the "wrong sort," in the sense that they were not from the Catholic majority of the Irish population. From that Catholic majority arose Irish nationalism

which not only triumphed in the home country but was celebrated by the predominantly Catholic Irish who settled in America. Historians love winners, but the Protestant Irish who predominated in Upper Canada were not part of the romantic, victorious, and memorable tradition of Irish nationalism and are hence easily (although wrongly) consigned the role of reactionary, uninteresting, and (in the context of Irish historiography) forgettable losers.

This explanation actually is more plausible than stating it in so bald a fashion may imply, as it is based on some sensible observations about the general nature of large migrations. That the major causes of human migrations are economic was the observation that underlay Ravenstein's classic Laws of Migration formulated in the 1870s and 1880s.[23] This is not merely a truism but an important operational point in analysing Irish migration, for economically induced or motivated migration – as distinct from compelled migrations such as the expulsion of almost the entire Acadian population – is selective.[24] This selectivity, taking all migrants together, almost always tends to be bimodal. In most societies from which migrants issue there is a sharp distinction between those who leave because of "plus factors" (such as, say, a young shopkeeper who leaves to seek better commercial opportunities in another city) and those who respond chiefly to negative factors (as, say, the herdsmen of Eritrea, forced to move by dearth of vegetation). The one group is positively selected, the other negatively, and if one plots the characteristics of migrants by almost any index, whether of education, class, or financial position, one can expect to get a J-shaped or U-shaped curve.[25]

This bimodality would be interesting in any population, but for the Irish it is absolutely crucial, for Irish society in the first half of the nineteenth century was itself rent by a series of social dichotomies. The Catholics and Protestants were virtually endogamous tribal groups, the economic distinction between the agricultural subsistence sector and the rest of the economy was severe, and the northeastern quarter of the country (roughly equivalent to present-day Northern Ireland) was geographically, socially, and economically distinct from the rest. These various Irish dualities were not coterminous but they did overlap. As they are related to Irish

23 For a useful formulation of Ravenstein's laws in modern terms, see D.B. Grigg, "E.G. Ravenstein and 'the Laws of Migration'," *Journal of Historical Geography* 3 (1979): 41–54.
24 On the various forms of migration, see William Petersen, "A General Typology of Migration," *American Sociological Review* 23 (June 1958): 256–66.
25 Everett S. Lee, "A Theory of Migration," *Demography* 3 (1966): 56.

migration to Upper Canada, the Irish dichotomies might be taken to imply not merely that there was a radical change in the character of Irish migration consequent upon the Famine, but that the pre-Famine migration to Canada was overwhelmingly Protestant and that which occurred thereafter mostly Catholic.

But reality intervenes. Neither pre- nor post-Famine emigration fits neatly into this pattern. Granted, it is well known that the Irish port from which, in most pre-Famine years, the largest number emigrated to British North America was Belfast;[26] and it is undeniable that Protestants were predominant in Ulster. It is a long way, however, from these two points to concluding solidly that the bulk of pre-Famine emigrants were Protestants or indeed that most migrants actually hailed from Ulster – as distinct from embarking there – whatever their religion.

S.H. Cousens has made a remarkable series of studies of the pre-Famine Irish demographic data, the most important for our purposes being a discussion of regional variations in emigration from 1821–41. In the absence of trustworthy direct emigration figures he has calculated reliable indirect indicators of emigration before the Famine, region by region, through analysis of population change in each census district. His research reveals that migration came mostly from the northern half of Ireland (from Ulster and the neighbouring parts of Leinster and Connaught) and least from the south. Counties Longford, Westmeath, Londonderry, and Donegal had the highest pre-Famine rates of outward migration. Emigration was especially strong in areas in which there was a domestic textile industry, since it was severely hurt by the post-Napoleonic slump combined with the spread of textile mechanization. That the fringe areas of the domestic textile industry were hurt more than the central Lagan valley industry is a reasonable assumption; the rise of mechanical production in Belfast and environs absorbed thousands of otherwise displaced textile workers. In the southern half of Ireland emigration was especially strong from small pockets (in particular, parts of counties Limerick, King's, Queen's, Wicklow, and Cork) of Protestant minorities engaged in weaving. In contrast, the subsistence agricultural areas of Connaught and Munster produced relatively few emigrants. (Counties Clare, Kerry, and Gal-

26 Adams constructs a set of interesting tables on emigration ports in the years immediately after the Napoleonic Wars (420–5). On later emigration to Upper Canada from specific Irish ports, see *Report on Canadian Archives, 1900* ("Emigration," 58–9); *Second Report from the Select Committee on Emigration from the United Kingdom*, HC 1826–7 (237), v, 70; *Emigration. Return ...* , *1833*, HC, 1833 (696), xxvi, 3; *Emigration. Return ...* , HC, 1839 (536-I), xxxix, 34.

way had the lowest emigration rates from 1821 to 1841.) It is fair to assess the pre-Famine emigration as composed largely of migrants who were in reduced circumstances but were well above the poverty line.[27]

Thus from Irish data we know that in most pre-Famine years Belfast was the most common port of out-migration, that most migrants came from the northern half of Ireland, that most came from the relatively prosperous areas of the country, not from the subsistence regions, and that Protestants had a higher propensity to emigrate than did Catholics.

Yet, in the absence of direct data on out-migration, we can *not* conclude that most migrants came from Ulster. The northern half of Ireland and the province of Ulster are not at all the same thing, and it was the Leinster and Connaught counties which border on Ulster that had the highest out-migration rates while parts of Ulster (in particular, County Antrim) had very low emigration rates. Nor can we conclude that the bulk of pre-Famine migrants necessarily were Protestants. Although Protestants certainly had a higher propensity to emigrate than did Catholics, there were fewer Protestants in the general population. As far as Irish sources are concerned, we can go no further.

In trying to escape from this trap, one might be tempted to posit that, as far as Upper Canada was concerned, a socio-religious filter operated through which Irish Catholics tended to go to the United States and Irish Protestants to Upper Canada. This would fit well with the traditional notion that Protestants, being loyal to the Crown, wished to continue to live under the Union Jack and that Catholics, being instinctively nationalist and therefore republican, chose to live in the republic to the south. For such a comforting simplicity, I can find no convincing evidence, at least for the pre-Famine migration. Probably most people who migrated before the Famine – mostly individuals with some financial resources, information on alternate economic opportunities, and the will to act decisively to better their chances in life – found the constitutional niceties and geopolitical boundaries to be a virtual irrelevance.

27 S.H. Cousens, "The Regional Variation in Emigration from Ireland between 1821 and 1841," *Institute of British Geographer, Transactions* 37 (December 1965): 15–30.

There are several studies of the Irish textile industry, of which the most important segment in relation to emigration in this period is the linen industry. An admirably succinct summary is W.H. Crawford, *Domestic Industry in Ireland: The Experience of the Linen Industry* (Dublin: Gill and Macmillan 1972).

Upper Canadian data bearing directly on the issue of ethnicity and religious affiliation are lacking; the 1842 census tallied both country of birth and religious affiliation but did not cross-tabulate these categories. What then can one do? The answer is, quite a bit, provided one proceeds with a large degree of humility and sedulously avoids the "fallacy of false precision." Ideally, one would like to see a complete retabulation of the 1842 census for the entire province, but that would be too expensive a proceeding. Failing that, a random sampling of several thousand cases would be desirable, and perhaps some day that will be done. For the present, however, one must be satisfied with accounting procedures which permit a reformulation of the aggregate data. The reformulation detailed below, which gives an estimate of the Protestant-Catholic breakdown among the Irish, should be read as being the most likely division within a possible range of two to three percentage points either way. Given the assumptions which one must make in the reformulation process and given the shaky nature of the 1842 census, to claim any greater degree of precision would be to invite hubris.

The Right Reverend Alexander Macdonnell, the Catholic bishop of Kingston and one of the best-informed observers of the Upper Canadian religious situation, stated in 1838 that "the Catholics, who compose a great proportion of the population of Upper Canada, are either Irish emigrants, Scots highlanders, or French Canadians."[28] This categorization can be employed as the basis for a formula for estimating the religious composition of the Irish, as follows. Begin with the Catholic population as reported in 1842: 65,203. From this, subtract the total of French Canadians.[29] Doubtless there were some French-Canadian Protestants, but assume that their numbers equal those of Catholics born in Continental Europe, England, Wales, and the United States, or those of the first generation of such parentage. Assume that 3 percent of the Scots-born and of the first generation born in Canada of Scots parentage and 3 percent of the second generation Canadian-born

28 Alexander Macdonnell to Lord Durham, 22 June 1838, reproduced in Lord Durham's *Report on the Affairs of British North America*, 3, *Appendixes*, ed. C.P. Lucas (Oxford: Clarendon Press 1912), 20.

29 Two points: (1) one employs the number of native-born French Canadians as given in 1842 census, without any redaction for first-generation immigration (this is not a methodology incompatible with Revisions B and C, as it is assumed that the first-generation ethnic populations all were tallied in the census as part of the non-French, native-Canadian category); (2) the French-Canadian native-born numbers must be slightly augmented, however, to distribute the "unknown" category, as was done in estimating the total ethnic population.

inhabitants of non-French origin were Catholics, and subtract these figures from the preceding subtotal. (Actually, this may underestimate somewhat the Catholic proportion of the Scots-born and first generation Scots populations and overstate that of the non-French second generation Canadian-born group.)[30] The remaining number of Catholics can be taken to equal the number of Irish inhabitants (either Irish-born or first generation) who were Catholics. This

30 Here let me re-emphasize the need for humility in interpreting the data and also the necessity of keeping in mind the arithmetic of the formula employed. As discussed below, the Scots Catholic percentages employed are highly problematical, but they deal with a very small percentage of subcategories of the total population so that the effect of any error in the data would be very small on the final result. That said, one is dealing in each instance with speculation, albeit of an informed sort. Intentionally, I have probably somewhat overestimated the Catholic percentage of the non-French second-generation Canadian-born population. That a number as high as 3 percent is even within the bounds of possibility rests on the fact that among the earliest settlers (whose descendants by 1842 often were second-generation born in Canada) were the considerable numbers of Glengarry Fencibles. The probable overestimation should compensate for any underestimation of the Catholic proportion of the Scots-born and first-generation Scots, for I have opted for the low end of the possibility range in dealing with the Scots Catholics. Unfortunately, the only data on Scots which I can find indicate that in 1871 (a very late date for my purposes) 10 percent of the Scots throughout Canada were Roman Catholics (Darroch and Ornstein, 312). This figure can be taken as the top edge of the possibility range for Upper Canada in 1842. But I am loath to project a national figure for the 1870s onto this province for the 1840s, especially in view of the relatively large communities of Scottish-derived Catholics in various parts of the Maritimes.
    What do the contemporary data for Upper Canada suggest? Unfortunately, one cannot deal with data on Scottish religious persuasion by reference to the Upper Canada census data of 1842. It would be temptingly simple to determine the actual number of Scots Catholics by subtracting the number of adherents of the Church of Scotland from the Scots ethnic total (taken to be the average of that given in Revisions B and C in the text). However, because of adhesions from other ethnic groups in Canada, the membership of the Church of Scotland in 1842 *exceeded* the Scots ethnic population! Thus, we must turn to religious data from the home country. This is such a vexed matter that even Flinn's massive work on Scottish demography virtually avoids the entire religious question. The earliest information we have comes from the religious census of 1851, with its well-known shortcomings and double-counting.
    Our problem is even worse, as we know that the Scots who emigrated did not form a representative profile of the entire population; in particular, one needs to know more about the position of highlanders' emigration (for, as Bishop Macdonnell suggested, highland Catholics were an important element of his flock). "Which part of Scotland supplied the most immigrants?" Scotland's most distinguished demographer recently has asked. His reply: "On this point the available records are at their most intransigent." (Flinn, *Scottish Population History*, 453.) The most careful and useful studies are by James Cameron (see above, n 12). If one takes Cameron's data on emigration from Scottish ports

number is slightly under 44,000. Finally, by comparing this figure to the inferred total for Irish ethnicity,[31] one has a figure for the Catholics among the Irish-born and first generation of Irish-born in Upper Canada in 1842 of 34.5 percent.

Forget now all the procedures and the individual numbers. Instead, focus on the two key points that have emerged, that before the Famine the Irish population in Upper Canada was mostly Protestant, but that the Irish-Catholic minority was formidable – indeed, much larger than was supposed by contemporaries and by later historians. The Protestant-Catholic split is best described as roughly 2:1. One can accept this with considerable confidence. Changes in detail of our calculations would budge the results a percentage point or, at most, two or three either way, but the historian who is content to deal in words can be confident in accepting that there were about twice as many Protestants as Catholics among the Irish in Upper Canada.

---

to the St Lawrence for 1831–7 inclusive and also takes into account the proportion of highlanders sailing from the Clyde, then it appears that roughly (very roughly) 44 percent of those emigrating in that period were highlanders. (Derived from Cameron, in *Canadian Papers in Rural History*, figures 2 and 3.) For an array of non-statistical data, see *First Report from the Select Committee on Emigration. Scotland*, HC (82), 1841, vi and *Second Report from the Select Committee on Emigration, Scotland*, HC 1841 (333), vi. Also helpful is Ronald Sunter, "The Scottish Background to the Immigration of Bishop Alexander Macdonnell and the Glengarry Highlanders," *Study Sessions 1973, The Canadian Catholic Historical Association*, 11–20.

Now, if one tallies the number of attendants at public worship on Sunday, 31 March 1851, and assumes that because the Protestant practice in many parishes of holding two services a day led to a one-third over counting of Protestants, one finds that the proportion of Catholics in the highlands was approximately 5.5 percent (calculated from *Census of Great Britain, 1851. Religious Worship and Education. Scotland* [1764], HC 1854, lix, 6–20). Juxtaposing this with Cameron's data, and assuming that all the Catholic Scots came from the highlands, then a reasonable estimate is that 2.4 percent of all Scots emigrants were Catholic. Unfortunately, for our purposes, the Catholics were not distributed evenly over the population but were found in pockets. Moreover, Scottish emigration was noted for being highly localized, large numbers of whole parishes emigrating together or within a year or two of each other. Upper Canada was especially attractive to some of these groups. Thus, in employing 3 percent, I am trying to minimize any underestimating of the numbers of Scots Catholics. Further, in cognizance of Darroch and Ornstein's work, I have built in further compensation for possible underestimation of the Scots Catholics when dealing with the second-generation non-French cohort born in Canada (see above).

31 In all the calculations above, the ethnic estimates used are the mean of those shown in Revisions B and C in the text.

4

This was the proportion *before* the Famine. Note how complicated the picture has now become. Instead of a simple dichotomy between early arriving Protestants and later Famine-starving Catholics, one must instead deal among the Irish with two groups of early emigrants, Protestant and Catholic, each of whom had emigrated with resources in hand and aspirations intact, and each of whom would have relationships with the later arrivals. (Implicit in this observation is the point that most pre-Famine Catholics were not pauper peasants, although there were pauper emigrants among both Catholics and Protestants.) The problems of the early arrived and relatively prosperous Catholics in dealing with their post-Famine coreligionists were infinitely more difficult than those posed for the early arrived Protestants, who treated the Famine Catholics as members of a lower and alien order.

Indirectly, by establishing that the Catholics comprised such a large proportion of the pre-Famine population, one opens the door to another level of understanding – and of complication. If one compares the probable religious persuasion of those of Irish derivation in 1871 with that calculated for 1842, one discovers that the Catholic proportion of the Irish in Upper Canada has stayed virtually constant, not risen as one might expect following the Famine: it was approximately 34.5 percent in 1842 and 33.8 percent in 1871.[32] Either there was a high degree of apostasy among Irish

32 The 1871 religious estimate is based on data in the *Census of Canada, 1870–71*, 1: 142–4, 280–1; 364–5. Of necessity, the religious-ethnic proportions are derived differently than those for 1842, but the data and procedures are sufficiently comparable to support strongly the conclusion argued in the text. The 1871 census was the first to provide data not only on place of birth but on the ethnic origin of all respondents. This was basically a self-definition item, and, as such, it defined ethnicity in a manner that varied according to each individual's perception; thus, for example, a third-generation Scot might define himself as Scots, while a first-generation individual of another ethnic group might refuse any ethnic label at all. This apparent messiness was actually the strong point of the ethnicity census, for it employed self-definition rather than arbitrary and imposed external criteria. See *Manual containing "The Census Act" and the Instructions to Officers employed in the taking of the First Census of Canada (1871)* (Ottawa: Queen's Printer 1871), 22–3.
    As for the calculation, it was derived by (1) taking the total Roman Catholic population as a starting figure; (2) subtracting the number of French-derived ethnicity, under the presupposition that the French Canadians were overwhelmingly Catholic; and (3) assuming that whatever number of French Canadians had turned Protestant was equalled by Catholics in the English, American, and Continental European-derived population; then (4), as was done in the

Catholics (a suggestion that cannot be considered even remotely possible) or, despite the Famine in Ireland generally having affected the Irish Catholics more severely, the stream of migrants was still a dual stream and the bulk of emigrants to Upper Canada continued to be Protestant.

Thus the complexity of relationships within the Irish ethnic community increases almost exponentially. A history of the Irish in Upper Canada must then not only take into account the relationship to each other of the relatively well-off Protestants and Catholics who migrated before the Famine and indicate how each group dealt with the post-Famine Catholics, but the social history of the Irish must show how the later post-Famine Protestants related to both sets of earlier pre-Famine settlers, and how the Protestant and Catholic Irish of the Famine and post-Famine years related to each other in the New World. All this must be taken into account in addition to defining the relationships of these several sectors to the outside society.

Part II

I

The Great Famine of 1846–9 is the one event in modern Irish history that is familiar to the educated layman throughout the English-speaking world.[33] Within Irish society, the Famine effected a social, cultural, and economic upheaval more thoroughgoing than could conceivably be produced by a merely political revolution. In its

---

calculation for 1842, assuming that 3 percent of the Scots in Canada were Catholic and subtracting from the previous total. This leaves 188,912 catholics among a total Irish ethnic population of 559,442. My figure of 33.8 percent is close to that of William J. Smyth, who calculated that, in 1871, "thirty-six percent represents the absolute maximum proportion of Irish who could have been Catholic." (William J. Smyth, "The Irish in Mid-Nineteenth Century Ontario," *Ulster Folk Life*, 23 [1977]: 100.) In an excellent recent book, Cecil Houston and William J. Smyth, *The Sash Canada Wore: A Historical Geography of the Orange Order in Canada* (Toronto: University of Toronto Press 1980), the authors estimate that there were in 1871 182,000 persons in Ontario of Irish Catholic background (186 n27). This estimate, which equals 32.5 percent of the Irish ethnic population, well may be more accurate than mine as my formula may have underestimated the number of Scots Catholics and, unlike the case of 1842, there is no item in the 1871 formula to compensate for such overestimation. This said, my point in the text is buttressed, not weakened, by Houston and Smyth's work, as, if they are accurate, it would mean that there were slightly fewer Catholics than I posit. If true, my point that the post-Famine migration to central Canada was not composed wholly, or even chiefly, of Catholics, is strengthened.

33 From an historiographical viewpoint, the most striking thing about the Famine is that there has been so very little scholarly work done on it. One can cite

course, the bulk of the Irish population at home completely redefined its marriage and inheritance patterns and its agricultural practices. Abroad, the English-speaking colonies and the United States received the Irish outpouring, which at times was more of a flood than a diaspora. The Irish outflow did not end with the passing of the Famine. The new Irish social and economic arrangements that came in the train of the Famine (in particular, the replacing of partible with impartible inheritance of land and the increase of pastoral farming at the expense of intensive tillage) meant that for a full century after the Famine Ireland extruded sons and daughters for whom there was no place at home. At least three million persons left Ireland between 1845 and 1870, and another 1.1 million emigrated between 1871 and 1891. In 1891, 39 percent of all Irish-born individuals in the world were living outside Ireland.[34]

Until 1853 the figures for Irish migration to British North America are less than completely reliable. (Table 4 gives the total British Isles emigration figures as a context for viewing the Irish pattern; the table is a continuation of table 1.)[35]

The unrevised figures for migrants from Irish ports to North America between 1846 and 1852 inclusive are as follows:[36]

Year	To British North America	To the United States
1846	31,738	7,070
1847	71,253	24,502

only three major volumes: R. Dudley Edwards and T. Desmond Williams, eds., *The Great Famine: Studies in Irish History, 1845–52* (Dublin: published for the Irish Committee of Historical Sciences by Browne and Nolan, 1956) and Cecil Woodham-Smith, *The Great Hunger: Ireland, 1845–9* (London: Hamish Hamilton 1962). Joel Mokyr, *Why Ireland Starved: A Quantitative and Analytical History of the Irish Economy, 1800–1850* (London: George Allen and Unwin 1983).

34 Robert E. Kennedy, Jr, *The Irish: Emigration, Marriage and Fertility* (Berkeley: University of California Press 1973), 27.

35 From 1846 onwards, the material in the United Kingdom parliamentary papers concerning emigration is copious and does not bear direct listing here. The following items, however, are especially useful: The annual *General Report* of the Colonial Land and Emigration Commissioners; *First Report from the Lords Select Committee on Colonization from Ireland*, HC 1847–8 (415), xvii; *Second Report*, HC 1847–8 (593), xvii; *Third Report*, HC 1849 (86), xi; *Papers relative to Emigration to the British Provinces in North America* [777] and [824], HC 1847, xxix; [932], [964], [971], and [985], HC 1847–8, xlvii; HC 1847–8 (50), xlvii; [1025], HC 1849, xxxviii; HC 1851 (384), xl; [1474], HC 1852, xxxiii; *Despatch transmitting report ... showing the facilities afforded to Emigrants from Europe for reaching the interior by the completion of the St. Lawrence Canals*, HC 1850 (173), xl; *Report from the Select Committee on the Passenger Acts*, HC 1851 (632), xix.

36 Carrier and Jeffery, 95.

1848	20,852	38,843
1849	26,568	43,673
1850	19,784	31,297
1851	23,930	38,418
1852	17,693	23,371

These figures, however, do not include any indication of the large numbers of Irish who embarked from British ports, especially Liverpool, and they make no provision for illegal passengers. For the sake of comparability to pre-1846 data, I am employing William Forbes Adams's formula to revise the data as follows:[37]

Year	To British North America	To the United States
1846	40,667	68,730
1847	104,518	119,314
1848	24,809	157,473
1849	33,392	181,011
1850	26,444	183,672
1851	31,709	219,453
1852	23,389	194,874

37 Adams never stated his formula except in roundabout literary terms, but it can be expressed as follows:

Migration to either BNA or USA	= official migration figure to BNA or to USA	+ 10 percent of official figure to account for illegals	+ 90 percent of Liverpool embarkations to BNA or USA

See Adams, 412–13. Adams suggested that the 90 percent Liverpool figure probably was too high, but that it was compensated for by the numbers which sailed to North America from other British ports, especially Greenock and Glasgow.

I employ Adams's formula with some hesitation since it seems to be more accurate for the 1840s than for the early 1850s. In particular, I suspect that its use overestimates, by a tenth to a fifth, the Irish figures for the early 1850s.

The Liverpool data which are necessary for employing Adams's formula are found in: *Appendix to the Seventh General Report of the Colonial land and Emigration Commissioners*, 36 [809], HC 1847, xxxii; *Eighth General Report of the Colonial Land and Emigration Commissioners*, 36 [961], HC 1847–8, xxvi; *Ninth General Report of the Colonial Land and Emigrating Commissioners*, 32 [1082], HC 1849, xxii; *Tenth General Report of the Colonial Land and Emigration Commissioners*, 36 [1204], HC 1850, xxiii; *Eleventh General Report of the Colonial Land and Emigration Commissioners*, 32 [1383], HC 1851, xxii; *Appendix to the Twelfth General Report of the Colonial Land and Emigration Commissioners*, 74 [1499], HC 1852, xvii; *Appendix to the Thirteenth General Report of the Colonial Land and Emigration Commissioners*, 66 [1647], HC 1852–3, xl.

TABLE 4

Total Migration from the British Isles to Major
Extra-European Countries (unrevised data),
1846–71

Year	British North America	United States	Australasia
1846	43,439	82,239	2,277
1847	109,680	142,154	4,949
1848	31,065	188,233	23,904
1849	41,367	219,450	32,191
1850	32,961	223,078	16,037
1851	42,605	267,357	21,532
1852	32,873	244,261	87,881
1853	31,779	190,952	54,818
1854	35,679	153,627	77,526
1855	16,110	86,239	47,284
1856	11,299	94,931	41,329
1857	16,803	105,516	57,858
1858	6,504	49,356	36,454
1859	2,469	57,096	28,604
1860	2,765	67,879	21,434
1861	3,953	38,160	20,597
1862	8,328	48,726	38,828
1863	9,665	130,528	50,157
1864	11,371	130,165	40,073
1865	14,424	118,463	36,683
1866	9,988	131,840	23,682
1867	12,160	126,051	14,023
1868	12,332	108,490	12,332
1869	20,921	146,737	14,457
1870	27,168	153,466	16,526
1871	24,954	150,788	11,695

Source: Carrier and Jeffery, External Migration, 95

With this revision, one can present a numerical outline of Irish
migration to British North America and the United States from the
beginning of the Famine through 1871. (See table 5.)

For the sake of convenience, from now on I shall refer to the
territory involved as "Ontario." Although the official name for
Upper Canada became "Canada West" at the union of the Canadas
and stayed so until Confederation, the name was not fully adopted
by contemporaries and, since most of the important data concerning
the Irish were collected soon after Confederation, "Ontario" is quite
appropriate. So cataclysmic was the Irish Famine and so forceful the

TABLE 5

Irish Migration to North America from all Ports in
the United Kingdom, 1846–71 (including revised
data: 1846–52)

Year	Total to North America	To the United States	To British North America
1846	109,397	68,730	40,667
1847	223,832	119,314	104,518
1848	182,282	157,473	24,809
1849	214,403	181,011	33,392
1850	210,116	183,672	26,444
1851	251,162	219,453	31,709
1852	218,263	194,874	23,389
1853	179,361	156,970	22,391
1854	134,004	111,095	22,900
1855	63,270	57,164	6,106
1856	63,131	58,777	4,354
1857	70,516	66,060	4,456
1858	33,656	31,498	2,158
1859	42,271	41,180	1,091
1860	53,318	52,103	1,215
1861	30,054	28,209	1,845
1862	36,628	33,521	3,107
1863	98,424	94,477	3,947
1864	99,978	94,368	5,610
1865	89,274	82,085	7,189
1866	90,515	86,594	3,921
1867	84,153	79,571	4,582
1868	61,354	57,662	3,692
1869	69,776	66,467	3,309
1870	70,768	67,891	2,877
1871	68,652	65,591	3,061

Source: Carrier and Jeffery, External Migration, 95, and revised
estimate for 1846–52, given above in text

resultant tidal wave of migration that it is easy to misinterpret the
pattern of Irish migration in so far as Ontario is concerned. It is
tempting but wrong to infer either that the Famine-induced
migration changed completely the character of the human flow
between Ireland and Ontario or that the Famine sent to Ontario a
group of humans so pulverized by poverty as to be socially
indistinguishable as storm-tossed stones upon a shingle beach. Such
a lack of discrimination is easy enough to fall into because both
contemporary observers and later historians often did so fall. For

example, writing in the autumn of 1847, the chief emigration agent for Canada West noted that three-quarters of the immigrants in that year were Irish, "diseased in body and belonging generally to the lowest class of unskilled labourers."[38] And in 1931 Gilbert Tucker employed an oft-quoted phrase in the pages of the *American Historical Review*: "during that baleful year, 1847, there poured into Canada the most polluted as well as relatively the most swollen stream of immigration in the history of that country."[39]

Whatever the Irish multitudes may have seemed to contemporary observers (and one can readily understand their being overwhelmed by the unprecedented influx), there is no excuse for present-day historians treating the Irish immigrants as a faceless lumpen-proletariat. As the work of S.H. Cousens clearly has demonstrated, the Irish who emigrated during the Famine were not by and large the decimated paupers of the poorest regions of Ireland: the inhabitants of the most cruelly affected regions of the country, the west and southwest, if they escaped starvation and epidemic were far too poor to migrate. Of course, few migrants were people of significant means: emigration was lowest in the areas of Ulster where the Famine had the least effect. The Irish migrants came chiefly from the same areas and the same economic strata that had been the source of migration before the Famine, the areas of Leinster, southern Ulster, and northern Connaught that can be denominated "north-central Ireland." These were areas in which the increase in poor rates (caused by local destitution consequent upon the potato failure) was most pronounced. These rates fell most heavily upon the small tenant farmers, and they led the flight from Ireland, exchanging the proceeds of their last cash crop in Ireland for a ticket to a New World. The emigration rate in the commercial farming areas of north-central Ireland, where most families operated small tenant farms, was two to three times as high as in the counties such as Cork, Kilkenny, Waterford, and Tipperary, which had the highest proportion of landless labourers. Landless labourers who could afford to migrate went largely to England. North America was for the relatively well-off.[40]

38 A.B. Hawke to the Civil Secretary, 20 September 1847, quoted in Gilbert Tucker, "The Famine Immigration to Canada, 1847," *American Historical Review* 36 (April 1931): 537.

39 Ibid.

40 S.H. Cousens, "The Regional Pattern of Emigration during the Great Irish Fam-ine, 1846–51," *Institute of British Geographers Publications* 29 (1968): 119–34, is a brilliantly succinct clarification of the entire issue of Irish migration. Also relevant (if less successful) are his "Regional Death Rates in Ireland during the Great Famine, from 1846 to 1851," *Population Studies* 14 (1960–1): 55–73, and

The Irish migrant to Ontario arrived in terrible physical condition, but his bodily emaciation should not be equated with cultural impoverishment or with technological ignorance. Typically, he had not been a landless labourer and he did not now become a lumpenprol. Instead, he had been the manager of a small-scale commercial farming enterprise, which had been scuttled not by his own ineptitude but by a natural disaster of overwhelming magnitude. As will be shown, in Ontario he passed through the cities on the way to settling successfully in the commercial farm economy of small towns and isolated farmsteads.

The pattern of geographic provenance within Ireland and the economic background of the overseas emigrants from Ireland were remarkably similar before and during the Great Famine and a parallel continuity can be discerned in the religious composition of the group which migrated to Ontario. Here, recall the calculations from Part I which indicated that the religious divide in the Irish ethnic population was close to the same in 1871 as it had been in 1842: Catholics composed approximately 34.5 percent of the Irish ethnic population in 1842 and 33.8 percent in 1871. The continuity in patterns of origin, both geographic and economic, among Irish migrants and the remarkably stable pattern of religious distribution should give some pause to anyone who wishes to view the Irish (in Ontario) as some great force by which at mid-century the world began to be turned upside down.

2

The question in dealing with the Irish who came during and after the Famine is, where did they settle, in cities, towns, and villages, or on farms? This question is applicable to all Irish migrants but is especially pertinent to the Catholics. The dominant view of what happened to the Famine and post-Famine Irish migrants is expressed most clearly by Kenneth Duncan in the single most influential article on the Irish in Ontario: "To sum up, disease, ignorance, and poverty made the entry into agriculture exceedingly difficult for the famine migrants and they became, it would appear, urban by

"The Regional Variation in Mortality during the Great Irish Famine," *Proceedings of the Royal Irish Academy* 63, sec. C: 127–49. See also *Report of the Commission on Emigration and Other Population Problems* (Dublin: Stationery Office 1955) and Lees, *Exiles of Erin*, 39–41; Oliver MacDonagh, "The Irish Famine Emigration to the United States," *Perspectives in American History* 10 (1976): 409, 414, 418–26.

compulsion. Later, however, when circumstances altered, the Irish remained urban."[41] Urban? Let us see.

The censuses of 1851 and 1861 tallied the birthplaces of all inhabitants of Ontario and also indicated whether the populace lived in cities, towns and villages, or in the countryside. These enumerations had their flaws but they are quite serviceable for defining the fundamental characteristics of the population. Irritatingly, however, the census authorities did not cross-tabulate place of birth and place of residence, so one must do this task oneself. The job is clerical and tiresome but not methodologically controversial. The results show that in 1851 14.0 percent of the inhabitants of Ontario who had been born in Ireland lived in cities the average size of which was 14,253 inhabitants; in 1861, 13.6 percent of the Irish-born lived in cities the average size of which had risen to 20,777.[42] A group urban by compulsion? Hardly.

But let us be generous and include as urbanites all those who lived in incorporated towns and villages, irrespective of how small those settlements were. We find then that an additional 7.1 percent of the Irish-born are included as of the 1851 census, living in towns and villages the average size of which was 2,111. In 1861, 12.0 percent of the Irish-born in Ontario resided in towns and villages whose average size was 1,957.[43] It is hard to see how living in a town of

41 Kenneth Duncan, "Irish Famine Immigration and the Social Structure of Canada West," Canadian Review of Sociology and Anthropology (1965): 19–40, reprinted in Studies in Canadian Social History, ed. Michiel Horn and Ronald Sabourin (Toronto: McClelland and Stewart 1974), 140–63. The quotation is from this reprint, 146. The article is also reprinted in Canada: A Sociological Profile, ed. W.E. Mann (Toronto: Copp Clarke 1968), 1–16.

42 Computed from Census of the Canadas, 1851–52 1: 4–37, and from Census of the Canadas, 1860–61 1: 48–80; and cf. 128–60.

43 Ibid. The concept of an urban-rural breakdown of population data is a relatively new one and was not used by the census authorities for the three censuses (1851, 1861, and 1871) with which I deal in Part II. In employing incorporated cities, towns and villages as the unit whereby to compute "urban" populations, I am following the examples of the historical analysis done in the 1920s and published in Seventh Census of Canada, 1931. (See 1: 81 and 154, for a justification of this procedure.) This procedure will underestimate all urban percentages to the extent that (a) urban areas were unincorporated or (b) two separately incorporated areas merge physically into each other but remain distinct municipal entities. Point (b) is a serious problem in evaluating twentieth-century census data but had little import in the nineteenth. Although there were unincorporated towns of two to three thousand, the inclusion of villages as small as four to five hundred as urban more than offsets the potential underestimation on this account.

I should warn any reader who wishes to do a similar calculation for another

2,000, in the typical case, can be viewed as an urban experience, but, if one wishes to accept it as such and add these town and village residents to the inhabitants of the cities, one still finds that in 1851 only 21.1 percent of the Irish-born in Ontario lived in cities, towns, and villages, averaging 4,030 residents in size, and in 1861 the proportion was 25.6 percent, living in towns, villages, and cities whose average size was 3,077.

The unavoidable fact is that, even employing the broadest possible definition of "urban," one has to conclude that the overwhelming majority of Irish migrants to Ontario settled in the countryside. In 1851, 78.9 percent of the Irish-born lived in rural areas, and in 1861 the percentage was 74.4, and that by the most narrow of definitions of rural.

Those figures deal with the Irish-born. Perhaps their children drifted to the cities and perhaps the real urban predisposition of the Irish came out only in the first and second generations born in North America. The 1871 census provided a self-definition question in which each individual's national descent was to be recorded "as given by the person questioned."[44] In modern terms, this is a subjective ethnicity item, dependent wholly upon the self-perception of the individual tallied. Of the individuals in Ontario who reckoned themselves of Irish descent (whether Irish-born, or sub-

---

ethnic group of a vexing problem: one cannot relate one's totals for the cities, towns, and villages as shown in the 1851 and 1861 enumerations to the overall figures of urban life as given in the historical sections of the 1931 census. The reason is that the census authorities, in doing their historical work, "corrected" the 1851 and 1861 returns but did not indicate where, why, or how they did this. As a result, the urban total given in the historical section of the 1931 census (see 1: 366) is higher than that reported district by district in 1851 but lower than 1861. Fortunately, in many cases for 1851, and in most for 1861, one can infer what the 1931 investigators did and proceed according to their pattern. Even so, the figure one derives for 1851 is 3.5 percent less than that in the historical section of the 1931 census, and that for 1861 is one-tenth of 1 percent higher. Because returns for cities seem to have been unambiguous and thus not needing "corrections" by the historical census workers for the 1931 volume, it is clear that most of the changes were made in the figures for the towns and villages. For the purpose of the argument put forward in the text, the possible underenumeration of "urban" Irishmen is not serious: it amounts only to a possible 3.5 percent in 1851 and this consists almost entirely of individuals who lived in small towns and villages, whose claim to be urban would be dubious at best. For those working on other ethnic groups, however, it means that they must (as I have done in this study) calculate not only the city, town, and village components of their respective population but most also calculate by exactly the same criteria the total urban segments of the entire population of the province so that valid comparisons can be made to the general population. If the 1931 data are used as a shortcut, the comparisons will be invalid.

44 *Manual containing "The Census Act" and instructions to officers,* 23.

sequent generations born in Canada), their place of residence was as follows:[45]

Cities (average size: 26,517)	9.5 percent
Towns and villages (average size: 2,148)	13.0 percent
Total urban (including all cities, towns, and villages (average size: 3,266)	22.5 percent
Total rural	77.5 percent

Clearly, actually to describe the experience of the Irish migrants and their descendants in Ontario as having been an urban one requires an act of faith sufficient to move mountains.[46]

45 *Census of Canada, 1870–71* 1: 86–145; cf. 252–81.
46 In attacking the dominant view in Canadian historical writing that the Irish were an urban group, I do not wish to tar all commentators with the same brush. There have been several scholars who have got the basic facts straight; no small achievement. Of the older generation, see Frances Morehouse, "Canadian Migration in the Forties," *Canadian Historical Review* 9 (1928): 309–29. During the 1950s and 1960s, Professor John Irwin Cooper of McGill University supervised a number of graduate theses that were sensible. Mostly, these dealt with Quebec, but not entirely. Cooper's own view was that "the bulk of the Irish who remained in Canada chose a predominantly rural world. Those who emigrated to the United States, if they joined their brethren, entered the area of greatest urban concentration." (John Irwin Cooper, "Irish Immigration and the Canadian Church before the Middle of the 19th Century," *Journal of the Canadian Church Historical Society* 2 [May 1955]: 5.) More recently, three articles of diverse topic and approach have each dealt with the Irish as a rural people: William J. Smyth, "The Irish in Mid-Nineteenth Century Ontario," *Ulster Folk Life* 23 (1977): 97–105; R. Cole Harris, Pauline Roulston, and Chris de Freitas, "The Settlement of Mono Township," *The Canadian Geographer* 19 (1975): 1–17; and G.J. Parr, "The Welcome and the Wake: Attitudes in Canada West toward the Irish Famine Migration," *Ontario History* 66 (1974): 101–13.
   There is also a good deal of valuable work about the Protestant Irish, particularly as related to the Orange Order in both its rural and urban manifestations. See especially Gregory S. Kealey, "The Orange Order in Toronto: Religious Riot and the Working Class," in *Essays in Canadian Working Class History*, ed. Gregory S. Kealey and Peter Warrian (Toronto: McClelland and Stewart 1976), 13–35, and 195–9. Kealey's argument is reproduced, substantially unchanged, in chapter 7 of his *Toronto Workers Respond to Industrial Capitalism, 1867–1892* (Toronto: University of Toronto Press 1980.) Especially useful is Cecil Houston and William J. Smyth, "The Orange Order and the Expansion of the Frontier in Ontario, 1830–1900," *Journal of Historical Geography* 4 (1978): 251–64. In *The Sash Canada Wore*, Houston and Smyth provide a great deal of data relevant to Ontario. Their material on the distribution of the lodges is especially valuable.
   Earlier work concerning the Order in Ontario was done by Hereward Senior, *Orangeism in Ireland and Britain, 1795–1836* (London: Routledge and Kegan Paul, 1966); "The Character of Canadian Orangeism," in *Thought from the Learned Societies of Canada, 1961* (Toronto: W.J. Gage 1961), 177–89; *Orange-*

3

There may be a plausible explanation. Possibly, the Roman Catholics among the Irish-born or Irish-descended lived in urban areas and thus underwent the Handlinesque trauma of being a religious minority and an impoverished immigrant group in an urban society.

Here, the available data present us with a double difficulty: not only was there no cross-tabulation relating to the urban-rural breakdown of ethnicity in the 1871 census, but no attempt was made to cross-tabulate religious persuasion and ethnic origin. (And, of course, before 1871, ethnicity was not dealt with at all.) However, a reasonably simple two-stage redaction of the 1871 data permits us to view the Irish-descended Catholics as a distinct group. A simple bit of bookkeeping tallies the residence pattern of each of the major ethnic groups; one then employs the equation developed in Part I to distinguish the imputed number of Roman Catholics among the Irish in each major type of residential area.[47] The results for 1871 are as follows:

Catholics of Irish descent, living in cities (average size: 26,517)	14.7 percent
Catholics of Irish descent, living in towns and villages (average size: 2,148)	19.0 percent
Total urban Catholics of Irish descent including all cities, towns, and villages (average size: 3,266)	33.7 percent
Total Catholics of Irish descent living in rural areas	66.3 percent

---

ism: The Canadian Phase (Toronto: McGraw-Hill Ryerson 1972); "The Genesis of Canadian Orangeism," Ontario History 60 (1968): 13–29; "Orangeism in Ontario Politics, 1872–1896," in Oliver Mowat's Ontario, ed. Donald Swainson (Toronto: Macmillan 1972), 136–53; "Ogle Gowan, Orangeism, and the Immigrant Question, 1830–1833," Ontario History 66 (1974): 193–206; "Ogle Robert Gowan," DCB, 10.

47 The source of the raw data is the Census of Canada, 1870–71 1: 86–145.

Because the basic argument of this section is that most Irish Catholics did not live in cities and were not socially acclimatized in Ontario in the generally accepted American pattern, the formula used to estimate the number of Irish Catholics in cities, towns, and villages is biased so as to err, if at all, in the direction of overestimating their urban numbers: in particular, it may do so by under-estimation of the number of Scots Catholics. In other words, the case against the Irish Catholics being an urban people could easily have been made even stronger. The formula is as follows: Irish-born urban Catholics = total of urban Catholics − 100 percent of urban French Canadians − 3 percent of urban Scots. This is the same formula used for the general population. See note 32 above. Note that this formula should be used only with large populations and not to calculate the Irish Catholics in any specific municipality.

Given that only one in three Irish Catholics in Ontario settled in areas that can even remotely be considered urban, and given the fact that only one in seven settled in cities, it is impossible to apply the "American model" to the Canadian situation, as it involves either Catholics or Protestants.[48] We must deal with the Canadian Irish on their own, not borrowed, terms.

This is inconvenient. First, it means we must now discard all the analogies so easily drawn from the American literature and the Canadian studies which were based, either directly or indirectly, on it. Second, it is clear that we desperately need studies of the Ontario Irish, both Protestant and Catholic, in typical places where they settled, not in cities, or even towns and villages, but in rural areas. We need to reconstruct several representative rural townships, farm by farm, family by family, correlating data of ethnicity and religion with records of landholding and with economic data from the assessment rolls. This is a difficult and time-consuming task, and the cumulative results will emerge only after many scholars have put in years of work. But to proceed in any other way would be to cheat and to risk a return to the misinformation and misinterpretation that have characterized most modern studies of the Irish in Canada.

Third, we must face the inconvenience of jettisoning most of our preconceptions about the Irish process of settlement in Ontario. No more can we accept the easy, lazy phrases, such as H.C. Pentland's that the Irish "[were] left as sediment on the seaboard."[49] Of course the newly arrived Irish were debouched in the major cities and towns – communication links end in cities and towns, after all, not in the middle of the countryside – but eventually most of them settled in rural areas. Thus, in all probability, a multi-stage (and in some instances multi-generational) migration occurred from the

48 For purposes of comparison, the reader may wish to note the residential pattern of the Protestants of Irish descent for 1871:

Protestants of Irish descent living in cities
(average size: 26,517)   6.9 percent

Protestants of Irish descent living in towns and villages
(average size: 2,148)   9.9 percent

Total urban Protestants of Irish descent
(including all cities, towns, and villages,
average size: 3,266)   16.8 percent

Total Protestants of Irish descent living in rural areas   82.2 percent

49 H.C. Pentland, "The Lachine Strike of 1843," *Canadian Historical Review* 29 (September 1948): 257. Incidentally, as a footnote to the same page, Pentland states: "Oscar Handlin's *Boston Immigrants, 1790–1815* (Cambridge, Mass. 1941), provides an excellent discussion of the character of Irish immigration into America. Most of the findings for Boston apply equally to Irish immigration into Canada."

points of disembarkation to the farmsteads. The technical problems in tracing this multi-step Irish migration to the backwoods are immense, but, like the microstudies of individual townships, the work must be done.[50]

Although the aggregate census data indisputably establish that the vast majority of both Catholic and Protestant Irish settled in rural areas, they do not establish that the great bulk were farmers: only township-by-township studies or a large-sample survey will settle that point for certain. For the moment, we can posit that it is very highly probable that farming was the most common occupation among Irishmen and that an additional segment became farm labourers.[51] It is quite clear that the Irish migrants of both religious persuasions possessed the necessary technical adaptability to cope with everyday agriculture practices in Ontario. S.H. Cousens established that the bulk of the Famine migrants came, not from the totally pauperized or the landless labourers, but from among the small tenant farmers, individuals whose holdings, though small, were part of the cash economy and who already possessed at least minimal commercial skills. These people when they emigrated were broke, not culturally broken.

They could adapt, and in rural Canada they did: the Irish became farmers, and reasonably successful ones. Precisely how successful awaits intensive local study. The only microstudy of this question of which I am aware, Guy Ferguson's study of the Peter Robinson settlers in Emily township, reveals both a high degree of continuity on their original farmsteads and a standard of agricultural achievement comparable to that of neighbours from other ethnic backgrounds. Ferguson's work on a group of pauper Catholic settlers from the Blackwater River Valley in County Cork (a group probably less

---

50 I am heartened to read the research reports of Darrell A. Norris for the projected Historical Atlas of Canada. Norris is doing remarkable work on what he calls the "stepwise" migration pattern into Euphrasia Township, Ontario. Many of the settlers in that township were Irish. The reader may be familiar with the multi-stage migration of Wilson Benson, an Ulster Protestant whose peregrinations were the heart of the chapter on "Transiency and Social Mobility," in Michael B. Katz, *The People of Hamilton, Canada West: Family and Class in a Mid-Nineteenth-Century City* (Cambridge: Harvard University Press 1975), 94 ff. Since Katz was interested only in a single urban area, he rather obscured the central fact that despite sixteen moves in residence and approximately two-and-a-half dozen changes of occupation and location, Benson spent most of his mature years as a farmer, and most of that working the same farmstead.

51 Certainly the early work of Darroch and Ornstein confirms this speculation as of 1871: studies of earlier years still are required, however. (See especially 326.)

technically advanced than the dispossessed tenant farmers of the
Famine era) shows that about 45 percent of the farms settled in the
mid-1820s were still held in 1861 by the original owners or their
descendants, a strikingly high degree of continuity compared to the
mobility which held for pioneer settlements in general. Despite
initial disadvantages, by 1861 the Irish Catholics had the same
levels of capital accumulation and were as firmly committed to
mixed commercial agriculture as their non-Catholic and non-Irish
neighbours.[52]

Obviously, one cannot generalize from a single study (especially
because the Robinson settlement was unusual in its origin), but,
from aggregate census data, one can infer that the Irish, both
Catholic and Protestant, were successful farmers, in the sense of
their surviving and making a livelihood in the activity, and from the
fact that they did not pour back into the cities, towns, or villages. In
1871, when 78.0 percent of the population of Ontario was rural, 77.5
percent of those of Irish descent lived in rural areas. In 1901, when
57.1 percent of Ontario's inhabitants were rural, 58.4 percent of
those of Irish descent lived in the countryside.[53] If anything, it may
be argued that the Irish were slower to drift to the cities, towns, and
villages than was the general population.

To return to the larger question of what happened to the Irish
Catholics in Ontario, it is clear why they became, if not historically
invisible, at least thoroughly camouflaged. Unlike the American
Irish Catholics, those in central Canada dispersed among the larger
rural population, and in all probability their economic activities
were fundamentally no different from those of their neighbours. Of
course, they were distinguished by their religion and consequent
upon their faith followed certain political controversies (especially
concerning education); to this day, party political lines in rural
Ontario follow religious lines.[54] Yet these divisions were formed by
the practical politics of a group which was not prepared to be shoved
about in their new homeland, not by the embittered "buy-the-
dynamite," "God-free-Ireland" nationalism with which so many
Irish Americans reacted to the harsh experience of the American
urban ghetto. As far as Irish nationalism was concerned, few Irish
Canadian Catholics could be bothered. And thus, few historians of

---

52 Guy R. Ferguson, "The Peter Robinson Settlers in Emily Township, 1825 to 1861"
(MA diss., Queen's University, Kingston 1979), passim.
53 Computed from *Seventh Census of Canada, 1931* 1: 716.
54 See John Meisel, *Working Papers on Canadian Politics*, 2d enlarged ed. (Montreal: McGill-Queen's University Press 1975), passim.

Ireland have bothered about them.[55] The historian of the nineteenth century can well argue that the near-invisibility of the Irish Catholics is itself a prime indication of their success in adapting to life in this part of the New World.

4

A final, seemingly incongruous, note is in order concerning the Irish (especially the Irish Catholics) and the cities. Although it is clear that the first step in dealing with the historical experience of the Irish in nineteenth-century Ontario is to deal with them in their predominantly agrarian setting, the Irish in cities will demand special study. (By cities, I refer to Hamilton, Kingston, London, Ottawa, and Toronto, jurisdictions which had an average size in 1851, 1861, and 1871 respectively of 14,253, 20,777, and 26,517.)

In 1851, the Irish were overrepresented in the cities,[56] but by 1871 the Irish as a group semed to have settled in. The great Famine-induced flood was over, subsequent migration had gradually been reduced, and the Irish migrants and their offspring had completed their trek to the Canadian farmsteads: in 1871, 9.5 percent of persons of Irish descent were living in the five major cities. The comparable statistics for the entire population were strikingly similar, 8.2 percent. Thus, the Irish generally were not a new and deviant immigrant group but a part of the majority pattern. The consistency of the Irish pattern in the overall one is noteworthy; in 1871, 13.0 percent of those of Irish descent lived in small towns and villages, and 77.5 percent were rural residents. The figures for the overall population were respectively 13.8 percent and 78.0 percent, a virtually identical profile.[57]

This profile, however, masks an internal distinction among the Irish. Although both Catholics and Protestants became predominantly rural, the Catholics were more apt to linger behind in the cities. This point can be illustrated by data for 1871, the first year when one can distinguish between Protestants and Catholics of Irish descent:

55 For a preliminary survey, useful not only on Fenianism, but on the general character of Canadian-Irish nationalism, see Hereward Senior, *The Fenians and Canada* (Toronto: Macmillan 1978). Also interesting is D.C. Lyne and Peter M. Toner, "Fenianism in Canada 1874–84," *Studia Hibernica* 12 (1972): 27–76.

56 In 1851, 14.0 percent of the Irish-born lived in cities as compared to 7.5 percent of the overall population. The parallel figures for 1861 were 13.6 percent and 7.4 percent. Compiled and computed from *Census of the Canadas, 1851–52* 1: 4–37 and *Census of the Canadas, 1860–61* 1: 48–80; and cf. 128–60.

57 Compiled and computed from *Census of Canada, 1870–71* 1: 86–145 and 252–81.

I   A. Proportion of all Irish-descended Catholics
        who lived in the five major cites   14.5 percent
        Proportion of all Irish-descended Protestants
        who lived in the five major cities   6.9 percent

     B. Proportion of all Irish-descended Catholics
        who lived in rural areas   66.3 percent
        Proportion of Irish-descended Protestants
        who lived in rural areas   83.2 percent

II   A. Irish-descended Protestants as proportion
        of total population of Ontario   22.9 percent
        Irish-descended Protestants as proportion
        of total population of the five major cities   19.3 percent

     B. Irish-descended Catholics as proportion
        of total population of Ontario   11.6 percent

        Irish-descended Catholics as proportion
        of total population of the five major cities   20.7 percent[58]

In attempting to explain this difference between Protestants and Catholics, it is tempting to grab on to the simplistic notion that Catholics in Ireland lived in densely populated agricultural areas and were therefore predisposed to live in cities, while Protestants, on the other hand, came from isolated farmsteads and were predisposed to become agricultural isolates in the New World. There is as yet no evidence to back up these ideas, and one must be highly skeptical. In particular, one must be cautious because the areas of the classic isolated Protestant farmstead, Antrim and Down, were the very regions where the rate of emigration was lowest. It is likely that most Protestant emigration came from the north-central region and was especially high in the "border" counties of Monaghan and Cavan. Probably landholding in these areas was not signally different from Catholic landholding in the same region and in the contiguous midland areas. In other words, there is at present no compelling evidence that Catholics and Protestants who migrated to the New World came from residential backgrounds in Ireland sufficiently distinct to explain their residential patterns in Ontario.

Instead of casting about in the Old World for some vague cultural factor that would explain the differing Protestant and Catholic settlement patterns, it would be more sensible to look to more mundane reasons. Two possible explanations occur on examination. First, in terms of skills and experience as farmers, the Famine migrants by and large were considerably better off than those who followed in the decade after the Famine. They left, but the really

58 Ibid.

poor, the landless labourer, and the Gaeltacht peasant could not. After the Famine, when poor rates dropped and the economic position of the small farmer improved, he was less apt to leave Ireland. Simultaneously, the position of the landless labourer improved enough for him to scrape together sufficient money to leave. These processes especially affected the character of Catholic migration. The post-Famine emigration contained a higher proportion of people from the south and west than previously, a small proportion of individuals who had operated their own farms, and a large proportion of single men (the Famine migration had largely been a family affair). All of these characteristics were of the sort that would naturally bear the new arrivals towards life in cities.[59]

A second explanation is closer at hand. It is helpful to ask who, in Ontario, were the greater deviants from a "normal" pattern, the Catholics who were proportionately overrepresented in the cities or the Protestants who were underrrepresented? The answer is the Protestants, because it is natural to expect that any group of relatively recent immigrants would be overrepresented in the cities, where they disembarked, and even in a predominantly rural society such as Ontario the move to the countryside often took years. Thus, in the decade 1871–81, when the English overtook the Irish as the largest incoming group in Ontario, they showed the same basic pattern of overrepresentation in the cities that had prevailed among the Irish Catholics in 1871.

1881

A. English-born as proportion
of total population of Ontario .... 7.2 percent

English-descended as proportion
of total population of the five major cities .... 14.1 percent

B. English-descended as proportion
of total population of Ontario .... 27.8 percent

English-descended as proportion
of total population of the five major cities .... 35.8 percent[60]

Hence, any explanation of the difference between Catholics and Protestants must take into account not only matters that influenced

59 See S.H. Cousens, "Emigration and Demographic Change in Ireland, 1851 to 1861," *Economic History Review*, 2d ser. 14 (August 1961): 275–88, and David Fitzpatrick, "The Disappearance of the Irish Agricultural Labourer, 1841–1912," *Irish Economic and Social History* 7 (1980): 66–92.

60 Compiled and computed from *Census of Canada, 1880–81* 1: 58–93, 262–95, 360–94.

the Catholics' overrepresentation in the cities (such as the changing character of migration from Catholic areas of Ireland after the
Famine was over but also those that influenced the Protestants'
underrepresentation.

My own guess (and at this stage of our knowledge it can scarcely
be more than that) is that institutions and practices peculiar to
Ontario rather than factors relating to the Irish homeland influenced the Protestants. One can account for their underrepresentation in the cities in 1871 only by making two assumptions. (1) In
general, the Protestants arrived earlier than did the Catholics.
There is as yet no demographic evidence to suggest that this was
indeed the case, and the constancy of the religious proportions of the
Irish ethnic population between 1842 and 1871 implies that Protestants and Catholics actually came in relatively constant dual
streams. (2) More likely, the Protestants possessed organizational
mechanisms for speeding their migration to rural areas. The Orange
Order comes immediately to mind. The question is an open one,
however, especially because it is not yet clear whether the Protestants moved out of the cities and into the countryside proportionately more often than did the Catholics, or whether they simply did
so more quickly.

Just as one cannot convincingly argue, on the basis of present
evidence, that the Irish Catholics were culturally predisposed to
live in cities, one cannot argue that those who did live in cities (only
one-seventh of the Irish Catholic ethnic group in 1871) were
alienated from the general population and ghettoized in the same
way as the Irish Catholics in the eastern seaboard cities of the
United States. There is a vast gap in the historical literature on this
point and, until a direct study of the Irish in the various major
cities of Canada is undertaken, the case will remain open. In a
report on his research in progress on the adjustment of the Irish
immigrants in Toronto between 1840 and 1860, the Reverend D.S.
Shea states that the "Boston model" did not fit Toronto. The Irish
were not perceived as an economic threat: although they tended to
concentrate in specific neighbourhoods, the availability and accessibility of building land and rental accommodation prevented the
Toronto Irish from becoming enclosed in a ghetto. Single-family
residences, rather than multiple-family tenements, prevailed. The
newcomer faced some discrimination, but it was relatively mild
when compared to the American situation, and upward occupational mobility was commonplace. Shea concludes that there was
enough evidence to "suggest that the Irish never remained a massive

lump in the Toronto community, undigested and indigestible."[61]
Studies of Montreal and Halifax dictate much the same conclusion,
that the Irish Catholics faced hardship but found many avenues to
upward mobility and did not undergo an embittering ghetto
experience.[62]

This returns us to our final incongruity. The Irish (Protestant and

---

61 D.S. Shea, "The Irish Immigrant Adjustment to Toronto: 1840–1860," *Study
Session, 1972 ... The Canadian Catholic Historical Society*, 55.

Susan E. Houston, in "The Impetus to Reform: Urban Crime, Poverty, and
Ignorance in Ontario, 1850–1875" (PHD diss., University of Toronto 1974),
includes an interesting case study (186–226) of the Famine Irish and their
impact upon welfare resources in Toronto. She correctly emphasizes that stren-
uous efforts were made to move the Irish out of the main port towns of Toronto,
Hamilton, and Kingston. In the summer of 1848, for example, only about 200
of the 4,219 Irish who arrived in Toronto stayed on (196). As for the larger issue
of whether the Catholic Irish became ghettoized and alienated from the
general population, the impressionistic nature of the demographic data in Houston's study makes them too limited to permit any conclusion being drawn about
social mobility in Toronto. Much the same evaluation holds for Murray W.
Nicholson's bizarre doctoral thesis, "The Catholic Church and the Irish in
Victorian Toronto" (PHD diss., University of Guelph 1980). On the other
hand, Darroch and Ornstein's study of a 10,000 person case study for 1871
for all of Canada (including a large sample from Ontario) is unambiguous.
It argues strongly against the historian's usual notion that occupational
status and ethnicity were closely related. In particular, they found a striking
range of occupations and of occupational status among Irish Catholics.
Because of the nature of their sample, however, it remains to be seen
whether or not, within a pattern of general occupational mobility, there were
pockets of intransigence and insuperable discrimination in specific cities.
Paul C. Appleton, "The Sunshine and the Shade: Labour Activism in Central
Canada, 1850–60" (MA diss., University of Calgary 1974), indicates that the
urban Irish were successful in penetrating the "middle rank trades" and were
very active in the unions of their day. He argues against a simple two-tier
model of the urban labour pool, with the Irish on the bottom.

62 See especially Dorothy S. Cross, "The Irish in Montreal, 1867–1896" (MA
diss., McGill University 1969), and George R.C. Keep, "The Irish Migration to
Montreal, 1847–1867" (MA diss., McGill University 1948). Also relevant is
Daniel C. Lyne, "The Irish in the Province of Canada in the Decade Leading to
Confederation" (MA diss., McGill University 1960). On Halifax, see Terence
Punch, "The Irish in Halifax, 1836–71: A Study in Ethnic Assimilation" (MA
diss., Dalhousie University 1976).

There is a good deal of valuable material about the Irish in Michael Katz's *The
People of Hamilton, Canada West*, but it is hard to know what to make of it,
as the study's numbers are presented in a virtual historical vacuum. The Irish
Catholics, it is clear, had a harder time of it than did most ethnic groups and had
a more difficult time rising from the lower rungs of the social ladder. On the
other hand, Katz denies that there were ghettos in Hamilton and argues that
the anti-immigrant Know-Nothingism of American politics did not have a coun-
terpart in Hamilton.

Catholic taken together) formed the largest ethnic group in the cities of Ontario: the Irish-born comprised 34.7 percent of the populace of the five major cities in 1851 and 25.1 percent in 1861; 40.0 percent of the residents of the five major cites in 1871 were of Irish descent. Yet for both Protestants and Catholics the city life was a relatively minor part of their collective experience: only 14.5 percent of Catholics of Irish descent lived in cities in 1871, and an even smaller proportion of Protestants of Irish descent – 6.9 percent – lived in the cities. Thus, one might well reverse the usual arguments which present urban societies as forces that acted upon the Irish and instead concentrate upon the Irish as major causal factors in determining the shape of the Canadian cities. To put it another way, the Irish were more important to the cities than the cities were to the Irish. This is because, by and large, the Irish immigrants and their children in nineteenth-century Ontario were farmers, agricultural labourers, rural craftsmen and tradesmen, merchants, and workers in small towns and hamlets. The Irish were not a city people.

CHAPTER TWO

Leeds and Lansdowne Township in the Loyalist Era, 1787–1816

I

According to J.J. Lee, Professor of Modern History at University College, Cork, "the development of emigrant communities in new environments is the closest one can come to constructing a national laboratory," to help historians distinguish the perduring aspects of Irish culture from those based on immediate environmental circumstances and thus relatively ephemeral.[1] Of course, many questions of method arise from a complex set of cultural observations, and these matters will be addressed in the text and notes which follow. The most difficult matter, however, is not any specific methodological point but the necessity of keeping in mind the phrase "as if": one is treating a portion of North America as if it were an ethnic laboratory and one must remember that this is merely a useful fiction. Unlike a laboratory in the sciences, the specific environment employed was not designed with the purpose of yielding undistorted data. The social systems under examination had a life of their own whose independence and integrity must be recognized before inferences can be drawn about ethnic elements that eventually were introduced into them.

That granted, in a sense all of nineteenth-century Ontario can be treated as if it were a laboratory which permits us to observe the propensities and abilities of Irish immigrants and their descendants in a primarily rural environment. A specific township, Leeds and Lansdowne township in eastern Ontario, can be employed as if it were one particular room or compartment in the overall laboratory, and in the conclusion of this study the effect of the Irish immigrants

[1] Taken from a Thomas Davis Lecture of J.J. Lee, broadcast late in 1972, quoted by Patrick O'Farrell, "Emigrant Attitudes and Behaviour as a Source for Irish History," in *Historical Studies X*, ed. G.A. Hayes-McCoy (Connemara: The Irish Committee of Historical Sciences 1976), 120.

and their children on certain key variables in this specific township will be compared to the province-wide pattern. Because the heavy influx of persons from Ireland into Upper Canada did not begin until after the conclusion of the Napoleonic Wars, it is important to describe the nature of the social and economic system that was established before they arrived. Only if one knows what existing arrangements the Irish encountered can one accurately describe and judge their adaptation. As will eventually be seen, the local social system as it evolved before 1815 was particularly vulnerable to attack by later immigrants who played by rules from a different social universe.

Leeds and Lansdowne township[2] is a particularly useful setting for a microstudy, for it permits us to view the actions of the settlers of the loyalist era undistorted by the flux and stress of the initial migration. Although surveyed in 1788,[3] the township did not receive any considerable number of settlers until the 1790s. This at first glance seems strange as it is situated midway between two major areas of early loyalist settlement, roughly indicated by the areas around present-day Kingston and in Elizabethtown township, whose present centre is Brockville. In fact, the first surveyors had stopped at the western boundary of Elizabethtown and had begun again upriver, skipping Yonge, Leeds and Lansdowne, and Pittsburgh.[4] An abstract of the loyalist population of July 1784 shows that in the five easterly settled townships (Charlottenburgh to

2 As this study progresses the reader will notice that the terminology for Leeds and Lansdowne township changes somewhat. The townships were surveyed separately but formed a single municipal entity until 1850 and even after the rearrangement of that year they still comprised a single social community. Hence, most often the phrase "Leeds and Lansdowne township" is employed. However, in later chapters, specificity in referring to subunits of this overall social system sometimes will require other usages: e.g., at times the census authorities reported separately on Leeds township and on Lansdowne township, and the data, when aggregated, become those on "Leeds and Lansdowne townships."

3 Ruth McKenzie, "Historical Sketch of Leeds and Grenville," in *Illustrated Historical Atlas of the Counties of Leeds and Grenville, Canada West* (Kingston: Putnam and Walling 1861–2; reprint, Belleville: Mika Publishing 1973), 8.
Robert Gourlay's respondents for Lansdowne (four members of the Landon family and six other settlers) stated that it was in June 1788 that Leeds and Lansdowne was surveyed. Robert Gourlay, *Statistical Account of Upper Canada, Compiled with a View to a Grand System of Emigration* (London: Simpkin and Marshall 1822), 1: 503.

4 On map 3 the reader will notice that the eastern neighbour of Leeds and Lansdowne is Escott. Escott was not recognized as a separate entity until 1794, being part of Yonge. Even then, the 'recognition was terminological, not political, as it was not until 1844 that Escott became a separately governed township. (McKenzie, "Historical Sketch," 9.)

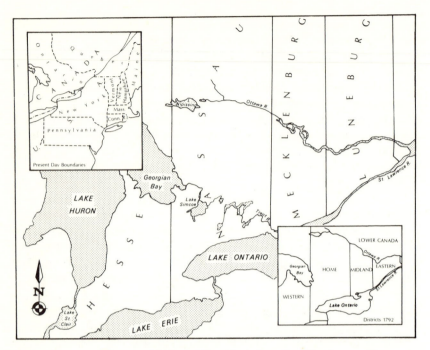

Map 1   The administrative districts, 1788

Matilda inclusive) there were 1,462 settlers, from Edwardsburgh to Elizabethtown inclusive, 495, and from Cataraqui (Kingston) to the Bay of Quinte, 1,819 (including forty-four German soldiers and twenty-eight loyalist Mohawk Indians).[5] In terms of population Leeds and Lansdowne was a void.

The township was perceived as being largely uninhabitable, which, considering the character of much of the land on which the earliest settlements were made, is a harsh judgment indeed. After travelling down the Gananoque River from the Rideau, Lieutenant Gershom French reported in October 1783 that there were "a few

5 "Abstract of men, women and children settled on the new townships on the River St. Lawrence," Haldimand Collection, BM, add MS 21,828, reproduced in *Report on Canadian Archives, 1888*, 753. In comparing the designation of the settled townships with the townships indicated on map 3, one will note that the township of Lancaster, the most easterly in Upper Canada, is left out of the population abstract. One rarely finds it referred to in early records, and in the days before the townships were named (being merely numbered), township no. 1 was Charlottenburgh. This was because Lancaster was thought to be valueless by reason of its topography, being denominated colloquially the "Sunken Township." Thaddeus W.H. Leavitt, *History of Leeds and Grenville* (Brockville: The Recorder Press 1879), 17.

small tracts of good Land near the River but scarcely sufficient in a place for a farm." He concluded that "from our entrance in the River Gananoncoui to its fall into St. Lawrence I did not discover as much good land conveniently situated as would serve one farmer."[6] Similarly a surveyor general's report at the end of the 1784 season noted that after the eighth township (Elizabethtown) the lands were "unfit to lay in townships or seigniories." He noted, however, that "many places in the necks and coves can be found advantageous for several families to settle."[7] Yet another 1784 report indicated that on the St Lawrence River, beginning five miles below Cataraqui, "the land was exceedingly bad, being a constant succession of stoney ledges and sunken swamps altogether unfit for cultivation."[8]

These reports did not accurately reflect the physical character of Leeds and Lansdowne township: later settlers found prime agricultural lands in spots not on the original exploration routes. But contemporary perceptions of the land resulted in the area being left virtually untouched by the first hurried, almost forced, settlement of the loyalists from the south.[9]

Consequently, the township became a sizeable bank of over 104,000 acres[10] of what contemporaries viewed as second quality land[11] and what for historians is a natural laboratory. When in the

6 Journal of Gershom French, 29 October 1783, in Haldimand Papers, B 31, 31–41, published in *The Settlement of the United Empire Loyalists on the Upper St. Lawrence and Bay of Quinte in 1784. A Documentary Record*, ed. E.A. Cruikshank (Toronto: Ontario Historical Society 1934), 17 and 18.

7 The report was dated 26 October 1784. Quoted by Leah Beehler, "Haldimand and the Loyalists" (MA diss., Queen's University, Kingston 1927), 39.

8 Captain Justus Sherwood was the chief of the party which made this report. Quoted in McKenzie, "Historical Sketch," 7.

9 The negative reports about the region continued well into the nineteenth century. John Galt reported in 1832 of Leeds: "soil indifferent; advantage of a stream of water," and of Lansdowne: "Soil indifferent; indifferently situated." John Galt, *The Canadas as they at present commend themselves to the enterprise of Emigrants, Colonists and Capitalists* (London: Effingham Wilson 1832), 144. In 1839 Hugh Murray reported that in Lansdowne "the ground bordering on the river is stony and ill cultivated; but the rear ... shows a very considerable improvement and contains some excellent farms ... Leeds is still less favoured by nature, being throughout rugged and rocky, though including scattered patches of good land, and in the rear some fine farms." Hugh Murray, *An Historical and Descriptive Account of British America, etc.* (Edinburgh: Oliver and Boyd 1839), 1: 296–7.

10 Jesse E. Middleton and Fred Landon, *The Province of Ontario – A History, 1615–1927* (Toronto: Dominion Publishing Co. 1927), 2: 1155.

11 An amusing indirect indication of the second-line character of the area in the contemporary official view is found in the township's name. Unlike the original

1790s a trickle of settlers began, it was composed of individuals who came by choice, not compulsion, and whose behaviour was volitional, not merely expedient. The actions of most of the early loyalist settlers in the original townships inevitably had been forced behaviour in that circumstances pressed upon them decisions about fundamental economical matters (especially land allocations) in conditions of considerable haste and in a time of frightening confusion. In contrast, the individuals who settled in Leeds and Lansdowne in the 1790s were no longer refugees but persons who now had a realistic picture of their new home province and sufficient economic substance to wish to acquire further pieces of real property. The former Americans who came from the south in the 1790s as "late loyalists" or simply as settlers did not come to Upper Canada under the same kind of political and military pressure experienced by the first loyalists. They moved on the basis of their own personal advantage.

The Upper Canadian government provided mechanisms sufficiently flexible to allow individuals in places such as Leeds and Lansdowne township to operate freely in acquiring their share of the society's basic resource, land. The settler could obtain land from the government or from a private individual who had himself previously acquired it from the government. Free government grants were made to loyalists and their descendants as part of a series of implied and explicit contracts compensating them for their losses in the American Revolution and rewarding them for their loyalty. Later settlers were either encouraged or permitted to settle in Upper Canada (the warmth of welcome varied according to the colonial administrator of the time). They were charged fees and required to

------

line of loyalist townships, whose names were associated with British royalty, Leeds and Lansdowne township derived its name from two contemporary politicians of noble birth, Francis Godolphin Osborne, fifth Duke of Leeds and foreign secretary under Pitt from 1783–91, and William Petty-Fitzmaurice, first Marquis of Lansdowne. The latter was a longtime opposition politician with a predilection for a soft line on the American question. He briefly headed his own administration which conceded independence to the Americans and made peace with France and Spain. He was generally recognized as one of the most unpopular politicians of his era and was credited with insincerity and commonly known as "Malagrida." This occasioned Goldsmith's biting remark, "I never could conceive the reason why they call you Malagrida, for Malagrida was a very good sort of man." On toponymics of the region see G.H. Armstrong, *The Origin and Meaning of Place Names in Canada* (Toronto: Macmillan 1930; republished 1972). For biographical details of the various British individuals memorialized in Canadian local names, see the *Dictionary of National Biography*.

do settlement duties, the nature of which changed almost annually in the first quarter century after the province was formed. If a settler dealt with a private individual for property instead of seeking a government grant it usually was in a "bargain and sale," the contemporary legal term for an outright purchase. This was the most common private transaction, although land could pass from one individual to another through free gift or by inheritance.[12]

The original system for recording land transactions was notable for its confusion. Settlers rested proof of their land titles upon scraps of paper – location tickets, copies of orders in council, self-drawn deeds of transfer, and holographic wills – and the central system of records was so diffuse as to be chaotic. Fortunately, in the mid-1790s (by 35 Geo. III, c.5) a uniform scheme for patenting land titles was introduced and eventually all land titles in Upper Canada were examined by governmental officials, certified as correct or disallowed as the case might be, and recorded. Subsequent transactions

12 Of course here one is necessarily oversimplifying a highly complex set of practices and regulations, the details of which are not germane to this study. There is an extensive literature on the early land granting and transfer practices. Impressive and still valuable pioneering work was done by G.C. Patterson, and published as "Land Settlement in Upper Canada," in *Sixteenth Report of the Department of Archives for the Province of Ontario, 1920*. It should be juxtaposed with Lillian F. Gates's monumental *Land Policies in Upper Canada* (Toronto: University of Toronto Press 1968). Useful supplementary pieces are Theodore D. Regehr, "Land Ownership in Upper Canada, 1783– 1796: A Background to the First Table of Fees," *Ontario History* 55 (1963): 35–48, and J. Howard Richards, "Land and Policies: Attitudes and Controls in the Alienation of Lands in Ontario during the First Century of Settlement," *Ontario History* 50 (1958): 193–203. An admirably succinct summary of procedures and of the documentary evidence such procedures generated is the (unpublished) Finding Aid for the RG 1 series in the Archives of Ontario, 36ff. (Hereafter AO) The annual reports of both the provincial and the national archives have several times transcribed primary material dealing with land granting. Particularly useful are the *Second Report of the Bureau of Archives for the Province of Ontario, 1904*, 11–25, and *Fourth Report of the Bureau of Archives for the Province of Ontario, 1906*, passim.

Aside from questions of administrative policy, there is the technical matter of surveying systems employed in dividing Upper Canadian townships into habitable lots. Leeds and Lansdowne was surveyed according to a single front system of two hundred acre lots whose character is easily discernible in the maps of land distribution which follow in the text. For background information see R. Louis Gentilcore, "Lines on the Land: Crown Surveys and Settlement in Upper Canada," *Ontario History* 61 (1969): 57–73; J.E. Hietala, "The Land Survey System," in *Second Annual Agricultural History of Ontario Seminar: Proceedings*, ed. T.A. Crowley (Guelph: University of Guelph 1978), 5–25; W.F. Weaver, "Ontario Surveys and the Land Surveyor," *Canadian Geographical Journal* 32 (1946): 181–91.

– sales, mortgages, gifts, inheritances, and all land later granted by the government and subsequently patented – were recorded, usually in a district registry. Admittedly, the early data in the patent records are less than perfect in that initial patenting was left to the individual, who in some instances did not bother to patent his land until long after he located on it. Nevertheless, the data are much better than for any other aspect of Upper Canadian life in the loyalist era. Within scribal limits the patent records are comprehensive, since they deal with all land, not merely with an arbitrary and unrepresentative sample, and they are standardized in that they provide the same pieces of information, in the same way, for each piece of property.[13]

13 Like any set of documents the patent records have their flaws. For example, in Leeds and Lansdowne, one discovers cases of an individual patenting his land and then three years later patenting it a second time, a procedure which, at minimum, makes difficult whatever numerical analysis one is attempting. There are also problems of identity in the case of loyalist women who received land grants upon marriage, patented the land in their maiden names, but subsequently sold it in their married names. The greatest problem with the land patents is their apparent lateness in some individual instances. For example, one finds many cases of individuals buying land (the "bargain and sale" of the time) and not bothering to have the transaction registered until three, five, or sometimes fifteen years later. The evidentiary difficulties in such instances, however, are more apparent than real: the patent records give both the date of the original transaction (say, 1799) and the date of registry (perhaps as late as 1815). Actually the most delicate problem in using the records occurs in interpreting the date of first patenting. Here the key is to avoid overreading the data. Inevitably, a time lag was built into the patenting system. After obtaining a location ticket, an individual had to find his property, perform whatever settlement duties were required at the time, and then go through the administrative procedures of having his application for a land patent approved. Some eccentric individuals waited years before ever starting the patenting procedure. Thus, one cannot use the patent dates to determine when a specific piece of land was first settled or the actual date when a specific family settled. However, if one is considering a community as a whole (as distinct from individual genealogies), then one is on surer ground. Over a large body of data the distortions caused by individual eccentricities are reduced, although not entirely eliminated. Indeed, one can plausibly (if not entirely convincingly) argue that in the study of entire communities the time lag in the patenting procedure is an inherent corrective to an opposite distortion, the cases in which individuals fraudulently convinced the authorities that they had performed their settlement duties and thereby obtained a patent, thus, as far as the records go, introducing the opposite of a time lag and a spurious acceleration in the record dating. In sum, none of the problems mentioned here is insuperable, and the patents of land remain by far the most consistent and thorough set of early Upper Canadian records.
Because the patenting system was not established until 1795 (see Patterson,

The laboratory of Leeds and Lansdowne township thus has six primary characteristics. It was *empty* at the beginning of the relevant period of social observation. It was *open*, not only to any original loyalists who wished to move from their first residence or to pursue an economic speculation but also to late loyalists, the children of loyalist settlers, and to former Americans who came north not out of any political predilection but simply to improve their economic position. The behaviour of those who either settled or speculated in the township's lands was *untainted* in the sense that the individuals entered the local economic system of their own volition, not as part of a refugee stream. There were *mechanisms* whereby individuals could acquire land, the primary resource, and thereby conduct economic activities. A comprehensive and standardized *system* was maintained to record these, the society's most

---

52), an historian studying one of the earliest loyalist communities obviously will not be able to use patent records as his chief entry point into its social history. Even in Leeds and Lansdowne there are minor problems, such as Oliver Landon in Lansdowne in 1787 or 1789 and Joel Stone in Leeds in 1792, and some locations were given to other settlers in 1793–5 (see AO, "Locations in Eastern District, 1793," RG 1-ser. C-1-4, and AO, "Locations in Eastern District, 1795," RG 1-ser. C-1-4-vol. 2). Nevertheless, in a community such as Leeds and Lansdowne the number of pre-1795 settlers was very small.

In later communities, such as Leeds and Lansdowne, the heir and devisee data are useful supplements to land patents. One should understand, however, that as compared to the land patents they lack comprehensiveness (they are available only for a skewed sample of the lots in any given community) and comparability (in that nearly every case was unique with its own idiosyncratic documentation). On the first Heir and Devisee Commission, see Lillian F. Gates, "The Heir and Devisee Commission of Upper Canada, 1797–1805," *Canadian Historical Review* 38 (1957): 21–36. On its successor see H. Pearson Gundy, "The Family Compact at Work: The Second Heir and Devisee Commission of Upper Canada, 1805–1841," *Ontario History* 66 (1974): 129–46.

There are not many items referring to Leeds and Lansdowne township because the small number of settlements made before the patenting system came in obviated the need to go to the Heir and Devisee Commission. What little there is is found in the Public Archives of Canada (hereafter "PAC"), RG 1, L5 Heir and Devisee Reports 12, dealing with the Johnstown district, 13 giving notices of claims, and 17–23 inclusive, providing documentation for each specific claim. The relevant Heir and Devisee material in AO is indexed on MS 174, and the reports and decisions in RG 1-ser. A-II-5, 1–17. Actually, much more productive are the "Township Papers – Lansdowne," and "Township Papers – Leeds," in AO, RG 1-C-IV. For interesting details of what could happen to a location ticket in the Eastern district in the early days, see the reminiscences of Mrs Burritt, "The Settlement of the County of Grenville," *Ontario Historical Society: Papers and Records* 3 (1901): 104–5.

fundamental economic transactions.[14] Finally, as will be discussed later, a local system of government emerged which enforced many property rights and limited social friction; in so doing, it indirectly produced documentation concerning the form of *social contract* dominant in the locality. The township, then, provides a clear window on the activities of settlers who were recreating from scratch an economic and social order in the wilderness.

2

Upper Canada in its early years resembled a massive Monopoly board, divided into rectangles and virtually empty.[15] Upper Canada's internal boundaries, however, unlike those of a game board, were

14 Legislation of 1865 required each county registry to compile an abstract of the patent data in their keeping and this, in the form of the Abstract Index to Deeds, is available in each county registry and on microfilm in AO. For an explanation of the meaning of the legal terms used in the abstract records and examples of the type of analysis of early settlement papers which the records permit, see John Clarke, "Land and Law in Essex County: Malden Township and the Abstract Index to Deeds," *Histoire Sociale/Social History* 11 (1978): 475–93, and R.W. Widdis, "Tracing Property Ownerships in Nineteenth Century Ontario: A Guide to the Archival Sources," in *Canadian Papers in Rural History*, ed. Donald H. Akenson (Gananoque, Ontario: Langdale Press 1980) 2: 83–102. The most analytically sophisticated use of the land patent data which I have seen is R.W. Widdis, "A Perspective on Land Tenure in Upper Canada: A Study of Elizabethtown Township, 1790–1840," (MA diss., McMaster University 1977).

15 Two points are in order about geopolitical units and boundaries as employed in this study. (1) As a matter of expository convenience I have employed the term "Upper Canada" to refer to the relevant area before 1791, although strictly speaking, Upper Canada was not formed until the proclamation of the order-in-council of 24 August 1791. (2) Although the basic shiring of the province was accomplished by royal proclamation of 16 July 1792, as represented on map 2, one should be aware that from 1792 to 1800 the county, district, and township boundaries were not everywhere coterminous. In the case of the eastern boundary of Leeds and Lansdowne township, the township boundary was set at the western boundary of Pittsburgh township. This coincided with the county boundary between Leeds and Frontenac counties. But the dividing line between the Midland and the old Eastern district was the Gananoque River. This arrangement left a slice of Leeds and Lansdowne township (and a small portion of Leeds county) in the Midland district and the bulk in the old Eastern district. Legislation of 1798, effective in 1800, removed this anomaly and map 3 indicates the situation prevailing from 1800 onwards, when the township, county, and district lines in question were identical. Most of the information upon which maps 1, 2, and 3 are based is provided by James L. Morris's valuable series of maps, "Ontario and its Subdivisions, 1763–1867" (PAC A/400, c. 1942). These are more accurate than those of George W. Spragge, "The Districts of Upper Canada, 1788–1849," *Ontario History* 39 (1947): 91–100. For the full text of the royal message of 25 February 1791 and the subsequent order-in-council

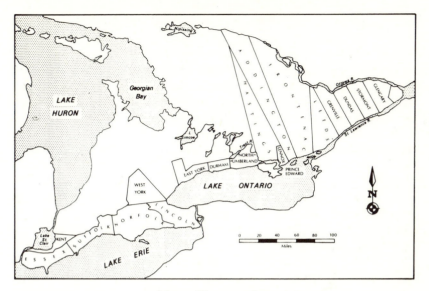

Map 2 The counties, 1792

not static: the great spaces were frequently divided and subdivided
as the population increased. From a practical viewpoint the area of
the province was almost incomprehensibly large, 413,000 square
miles, three and a half times the size of the British Isles, and for
effective governance and settlement the territory had to be cut into
manageable portions. The process of subdivision proceeded logi-
cally almost to a fault: geographic portions were often cut with
purely geometric logic to form straight lines on paper instead of

---

of 24 August 1791 which divided the previous Province of Quebec into Upper and
Lower Canada, see *Fourth Report of the Bureau of Archives for the Province
of Ontario ... 1906*, 158ff. For the full text of the royal proclamation of 16 July
1792 creating the nineteen counties, see ibid., 177ff. The legislation renaming
the four districts (15 October 1792) is 32 Geo. III c. 8.
   Other relevant information is found in J.F. Pringle, *Lunenburgh or the Old
Eastern District: Its Settlement and Early Progress* (Cornwall: Standard Printing
House 1890), 42–3 and 49, and in J.D.W. Darling and W.H. Wallace, *Sketch
of the Early History of the Front Concessions of Lansdowne and Thousand
Islands Group* (Gananoque: privately published 1925), 6–7. See also the his-
torical introduction by William F.E. Morley to the reprint edition of the *Illus-
trated Historical Atlas of Frontenac, Lennox, and Addington Counties, Ontario*
(Toronto: J.H. Meacham and Co. 1878; reprint, Belleville: Mika Publishing Co.
1977); and see the "Historical Sketch of the County of Lanark," reprinted
(with source unspecified) in the *Illustrated Atlas of Lanark County 1880 ...
Renfrew County 1881 ...* (Toronto: H. Beldon and Co. 1881; reprint, Owen
Sound: Richardson, Bond and Wright Ltd. 1972).

following the natural meanderings of rivers and irregularities of terrain.

The division of Upper Canada into administrative districts in 1788 and 1792 is indicated in map 1. As population increased, the number of such districts frequently was also increased until the middle of the nineteenth century when counties replaced districts as units of local government. For the purposes of this study the relevant districts are the "old" Eastern district as it existed until 1800 and the Johnstown district which was carved out of it in 1800 (a "new" Eastern district continued in existence but is not germane here).

Working as they did from British models, the administrators of Upper Canada divided the inhabited parts of the province into counties, as indicated on map 2.[16] Within the counties were townships. These were cognates of the English parish, upon which they were loosely modelled, but lacked its ecclesiastical basis and most of its political and administrative functions. Significantly, along the St Lawrence River the exigencies of loyalist settlement resulted in several townships being established in the 1780s, before the administrative superstructure of districts was constructed. Map 3 indicates the township boundaries in eastern Ontario and shows

16 A chronology of the boundary decisions relevant to the township of Leeds and Lansdowne is as follows:
1788 Four districts were proclaimed covering what later became Upper Canada. Most of Leeds and Lansdowne lay in the Luneburg district, a small portion in Mecklenburg district.
1791 Upper Canada established.
1792 The four districts in Upper Canada renamed. Most of Leeds and Lansdowne was in the old *Eastern* district, a small portion being in the *Midland* district.
1792 Much of Upper Canada shired. Leeds and Lansdowne township lay entirely in *Leeds* county which at this time stretched from the St Lawrence to the Ottawa River.
1798 A general revision was made, becoming effective in 1800. Leeds county and Leeds and Lansdowne townships now were entirely within the *Johnstown* district. This district was taken mostly from the former Eastern district (a new, reduced, Eastern district, somewhat confusingly for historians, continued to exist) and in small part from the Midland district. The Johnstown district now comprised the counties of *Leeds and Grenville*, and newly established *Carleton*. This new county was formed chiefly from the northern halves of land previously assigned to Leeds and to Grenville counties. At this stage, the district, not the county, was the basic governmental unit. A valuable source of information on these and related matters of civil administration is Frederick A. Armstrong, *Handbook of Upper Canadian Chronology and Territorial Legislation* (London, Ontario: Lawson Memorial Library 1967).

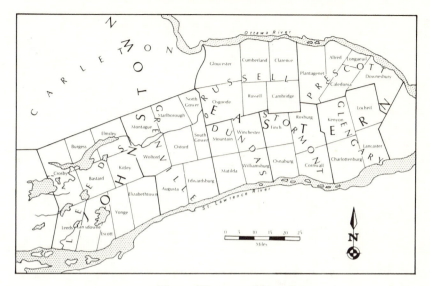

Map 3 The townships, 1800

the county boundaries as revised in 1800 (note especially that of
Leeds county). The regular, rectilinear, and arbitrary character of
the boundaries is obvious.

From the viewpoint of the individual citizen, neither the county
nor the township boundaries were very important in themselves.
The lines which counted most were those which marked individual
tracts of land. Except on the St Lawrence River front, these parcels
were sharply defined rectangles, each containing, in the usual case
in the Johnstown district, two hundred acres. It was at this
fundamental level of local ownership that a township most resembled a precisely ruled game board on which the new settlers
played out their lives. The acquisition of real property (or the
attempt to do so) was the one behaviour that was almost a cultural
universal. Virtually every family was involved.

How many people were in the township in the loyalist era?
Unfortunately, census data for Leeds and Lansdowne township (as
for the entire Johnstown district) are extremely spotty until the
1820s. The only reasonably trustworthy information for the entire
township indicates that there were 361 persons (men, women, and
children) settled in 1805 and 359 in 1806. The next trustworthy
information is for 1815, when there were 505 inhabitants. In 1820,
the next year for which there are data, there were 814 inhabitants.[17]

17 See Appendix A, table 1.

Maps 4–7 Land patents by five-year intervals, 1796–1815

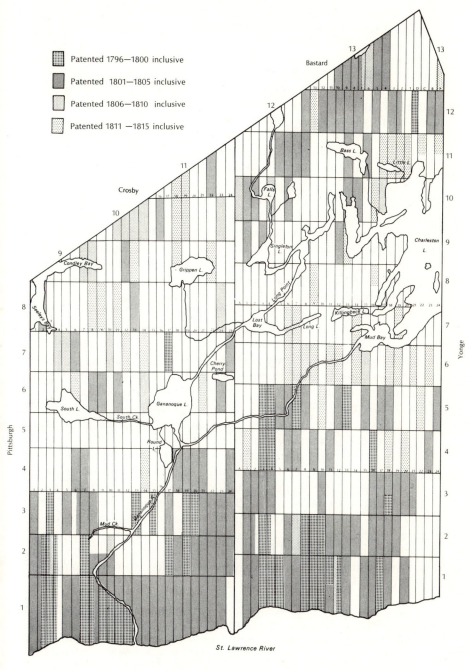

Map 8 Lands patented, cumulative pattern,
1796–1815 inclusive

The signal point about the distribution of population in the township is that it violated the invisible rule of settlement in Upper Canada, namely, that settlement was thickest along the St Lawrence River front. Maps 4 and 5 indicate that the first land patents were concentrated on the river front, but by 1805 most of the population resided in the rear (236 of 361 persons, 65 percent of the inhabitants).[18] A further underscoring of this peculiarity is the fact that although considerably more land was patented in the front of Leeds and Lansdowne (as maps 4–7 indicate) throughout the period 1795–1815, the predominance of the rear concessions in terms of population continued until at least 1815.[19]

Behind this apparent paradox is a pattern. As elsewhere in Upper Canada the St Lawrence River front was settled first, because of its ease of accessibility. However, because of the geological structure of the area many of the river front lots and the lots in the second and third concession were rocky and infertile, so that settlers interested in prime agricultural land moved inland with more alacrity than usual. Individuals with an eye to non-agricultural ways of making a living or of turning a profit looked to the rivers and especially to the Gananoque River which runs north through Leeds township. This created a vertical fissure in the customary horizontal pattern of tiers of settlement running east and west parallel to the St Lawrence. The Gananoque River not only gave access to inland farming areas but its shores were forested in prime woods that were valuable for spars and masts and that could easily be moved by being floated down to the St Lawrence. What held for the Gananoque River itself held for the lakes to which it gave access. Moreover, because the tributary system of the Gananoque was articulated almost like the veins on a human hand, there were several potential sites for mills, all well inland. Finally, in the ninth, tenth, and eleventh concessions of Lansdowne, settlers congregated near the town now known as Lyndhurst, then called by the descriptive name of "Furnace Falls," bog iron being found in the area and processed at the falls. Thus the unusual predominance of the rear of the township in terms of population is accounted for in part by the Gananoque River which opened a pathway inland and in part by the nature of the two inland industries, lumbering and iron mining, both of which were rela-

18 These maps are based on the relevant individual entries in the Abstract Index of Deeds for Leeds and Lansdowne Township in the AO.
19 The front of Leeds is defined as the first six concessions of Lansdowne and the first five concessions of Leeds. These eventually become a separate municipality of the front of Leeds and Lansdowne in 1850. The division before then was practical, not official.

tively labour intensive and thus supported a larger population than a similar area of unimproved agricultural land.[20]

3

This description of settlement patterns is clearly justified by the evidence, but it is too impersonal to be entirely satisfying. History, after all, eventually comes down to individual human beings and their specific decisions. Limits of space preclude discussing in detail most of the colourful, sometimes bizarre, personalities among local loyalists; three cases will suffice. The first of these, Oliver Landon, is indicative of the activities of an only moderately successful loyalist. The second, that of Sir John Johnson, is of an entirely contrasting sort: a participant in the local economic system who was so successful that he did not settle in the area himself and thus had little to do with the social system. The third case, that of Joel Stone,

20 In presenting an empirically based description of the settlement pattern in Leeds and Lansdowne, one is not depreciating the theoretical work of geographers in the field of location study. Their theories are helpful. For an excellent summary of geographical location theory in non-technical language, see Michael Chisholm, *Rural Settlement and Land Use* (London: Hutchinson University Library 1962). Also of relevance is Donald Denman and S. Prodana, *Land Use: An Introduction to Proprietary Land Use Analysis* (London: George Allen and Unwin 1972). Considerably more technical is Peter Haggett, *Locational Analysis in Human Geography* (Toronto: Macmillan 1965). Of greater direct relevance than these, however, is David Wood, ed., *Perspectives on Landscape and Settlement in Nineteenth Century Ontario* (Toronto: McClelland and Stewart 1975).

An interesting comparison and contrast to the case of Leeds and Lansdowne is R.L. Gentilcore's study of a 10 percent sample of Upper Canadian townships. Gentilcore found that settlement in the early years had little to do with the physical condition of the land but was dictated chiefly by accessibility and the action of the military authorities. Gentilcore's conclusions are in part borne out by the Leeds and Lansdowne case, for certainly accessibility was important. However, (1) the military authorities played no part in directing the settlement pattern; (2) economic desirability, not merely accessibility, influenced the configuration, as the Furnace Falls settlement indicates, and (3), no matter how accessible, certain areas were not settled, and this certainly was because of the physical condition of the land. In particular, concession 5 in Leeds was virtually empty and unclaimed despite being easily accessible by water. In fact, the land was desperately inhospitable, veering between marsh on the one hand and barren rock face on the other. Thus, from the very first days, physical quality of land *did* enter the picture. See R. Louis Gentilcore, "Change in Settlement in Ontario (Canada), 1800–50: A Correlation Analysis of Historical Source Materials," in *International Geography, 1972*, ed. W. Peter Adams and Frederick M. Helleiner (Toronto: University of Toronto Press 1972), 1: 418–19.

reveals in detail the attitudes and activities of a successful individual in the loyalist era.[21]

Oliver Landon (1755–1820) came from Litchfield, Connecticut, the family originally having emigrated to the American colonies from England in the seventeenth century. He was part of a large and tangled family network and he had no less than twenty male first cousins living on the eve of the American Revolution. Many of his cousins and uncles obtained lands in the vicinity of what is now the New York–Vermont state border. Eventually several of these relatives came to Upper Canada as loyalists, settling chiefly in Augusta township, but they had already made marriage alliances with several families that were to be important in the eastern section of the new province, notably the Sherwoods, Colvins, Reads, and Everts.

Unlike many of his relatives, Oliver Landon seems not to have taken lands in the speculative areas of New York and Vermont but to have come directly to Upper Canada from Connecticut. Either in 1787 or 1789 (accounts vary) he arrived in Lansdowne from Connecticut. He was the first recorded settler in the township and obviously he was a man of some determination for at least one hundred miles of his journey to the township was through uncut woods. As was common among the first generation of settlers, Landon wore out his first wife, who died in 1800, and took a second in 1801. He had nine sons by the first and at least one daughter (some sources say three) by the second. Had Landon's business ability matched his physical vigour he probably would have owned the entire township before his life was over. As it was, he merely did well. Originally granted eight hundred acres, he managed to patent only three hundred acres of the free grant land on his own behalf, plus a partnership share in another two hundred acres. He did, however, acquire a further one hundred acres by private treaty. In economic dealings with his children, Landon followed the unromantic practice prevalent in the early loyalist days: he did not give them land or will it to them; he sold it to them at the going market price.[22]

21 In this section and hereafter, when reference is made to patented land transactions, the documentation is the Abstract Index of Deeds in AO. For resolving ambiguous items it is useful to consult the copybooks of land registrations which are found for Leeds and Grenville counties for the years 1797–1847 in Queen's University Archives, Kingston. The reader should be aware that, despite the regular geometric nature of most land grants, the early acreage figures for irregular plots and for parts of lots are to be treated as approximate only.

22 Material on Oliver Landon and his family is found in the Landon papers in Queen's University Archives, Kingston. Within that collection there is a confus-

Sir John Johnson (var.: Johnston) was the most socially distinguished and most aloof of the township's landowners. Sir John was an absentee and played little direct role in local affairs, although in the early 1790s he had grist and saw mills constructed at Gananoque. Because of his political influence, however, he had a potential veto over almost any local decision, should he have decided to take an interest. He was the son of Sir William Johnson, an Irish-born soldier who served with General Amherst and was knighted for his services. During the American Revolution the younger Johnson followed his father's example and served the Crown with distinction. He not only formed and commanded his own unit (the Royal Greens) but in 1783 was appointed superintendent general of Indian affairs, a not entirely inappropriate appointment as his father, Sir William, had been superintendent of northern Indians and had taken an Indian for his second wife after his common-law wife died.

In 1784 the younger Johnson was placed in charge of the initial loyalist settlement operation, a position which obviously gave him immense power and prestige. The prestige is clear from the prevalence of his name in the old Eastern district: what is now Cornwall was named New Johnstown for a time and the area around it referred to as New Johnstown township. Further upriver there was a village of Johnstown in Edwardsburgh township and in 1800 the administrative district of Johnstown (which included Leeds and Lansdowne township) was carved out of the old Eastern district.

Despite his position in the area, Sir John had no intention of settling in the new loyalist townships but stayed in Lower Canada

---

ing but useful paper by Fred C. Landon, written in June 1940, entitled "Three Hundred Years of Landons." A genealogical article by Aline G. Hornaday, "The Landons in Ontario: A Loyalist Family," *Canadian Genealogist* 1, no. 1 (1979): 4–23, focuses on Asa Landon but sheds light on the entire family history. See also Leavitt, 139, and Howard W. Warner, "South Augusta and Its Environs" (Grenville County Historical Society 1964), 29–30. Both Hornaday (15) and Landon (unpaginated) state that Oliver Landon arrived in Lansdowne in November 1787. In this they are using Leavitt (139), who states that his source is "an account book which has been preserved," this book making it "clear that Mr. Landon had settled in the township as early as 1787." He quotes a note in the book as saying "arrived at Lansdowne November 5th," presumably in 1787. McKenzie dates Oliver Landon's arrival in Lansdowne as 1789, "or thereabouts," but this is done without reference. Ruth McKenzie, *Leeds and Grenville: Their First Two Hundred Years* (Toronto: McClelland and Stewart 1967), 27. In McKenzie's favour is a note made by Joel Stone early in 1789 saying that Mr Oliver Landon was going to move to the area, clearly implying that Landon had not settled as of early 1789 (PAC, MG 23 H II 1, McDonald-Stone papers, no. 370, draft, Joel Stone to unnamed, 29 January 1789).

where he was the seigneur of Argenteuil. He did want lands in Upper Canada, however, and these he easily obtained. In July 1789 he was granted 1,000 acres on the east side of the Gananoque River, and an attorney general's fiat of 1800 redefined this grant as 1,534 acres. It included not only valuable lands along the river but two modest-sized islands lying in the St Lawrence at the mouth of the Gananoque River and two major islands further up the St Lawrence system, Howe Island and Amherst Island. He patented his Leeds and Lansdowne township holdings in 1802 but did not superintend them himself, putting one of his discharged soldiers in residence as an agent cum watchman. Aside from milling ventures, Sir John did not improve the property. In 1824 he made it over to his sister, a widow, and she sold it the next year to John McDonald, a Gananoque merchant and miller. In a sense it was unfortunate that Sir John never resided, for he was a man of energy and ability. It is reported of him that at the age of ninety he vaulted a six-foot fence in much the same style as a gymnast over a pommel horse and, having dropped to his knees upon landing, exclaimed in surprise, "By God! I believe I am getting old." Whatever his failings, Sir John was a natural aristocrat and not one of the jumped-up sham squires of the Upper Canadian wilderness.[23]

Joel Stone (1749–1833) demands particular attention. He was not the largest landowner in Leeds and Lansdowne, but he was the most important and he actually resided there. Using property at the mouth of the Gananoque River as his lever, he raised himself and the

23 Freeman Britton, *Souvenir of Gananoque and Thousand Island, with short sketch of first owners, early settlement and other historical notes of the town* (Gananoque: Gananoque Reporter 1901), 9–10, 12; Frank Eames, *Gananoque Blackhouse, 1813–1859: Appendices to Gananoque Blackhouse – 1813–1859* (Gananoque: privately printed 1951; portions originally published in *Ontario History and Records* 32 [1937]: 85ff), 9; Herbert S. McDonald, "Memoir of Colonel Joel Stone, a United Empire Loyalist and Founder of Gananoque," *Ontario Historical Society: Papers and Records* 18 (1920): 73–4. Agnes M. Machar, "The Story of a Canadian Loyalist: Col. Joel Stone, Founder of Gananoque," *The United Empire Loyalists Association of Ontario: Annual Transactions* (1899): 64–5; AO, Crown Land Papers, RG 1-C-IV, Township Papers, Leeds, "Extract from the Land Book 14 July 1789;" AO, Crown Land Papers, RG 7-C-IV, Township Papers, Leeds, fiat to Sir John Johnson, 15 September 1800; McKenzie, *Leeds and Grenville*, 5, 7, 9–10, 12–13.

Incidentally, the 1789 land board minute refers to the River Gananoque, "now called Thames," and reflects a short-lived attempt to change the aboriginal name of the river. The 1788 proclamation creating the four administrative districts had also referred to the Thames. By the mid-1790s, it was once again universally referred to as the Gananoque River, albeit with variant spelling. For an unusual and not entirely convincing antiquarian investigation see Frank Eames, *Gananoque: The Name and Its Origin*, 2nd ed. (Gananoque: privately printed 1942).

entire river valley from obscurity to economic respectability. He was a source of energy for the economy and the civic order. In his behaviour he was the embodiment of the local economic and social morality, and his progress shows what was and was not permissible under the local rules. Thus, chronicling and analysing Stone's behaviour is not indulging in what has been derided as "élite" history but rather using him as a convenient source of data that will help infer the rules of the local game. An analogy will make this clear: if a total foreigner to modern North American society attempted to infer the rules of baseball from watching the game and looking at baseball records, he conceivably could learn as much from studying the on-field behaviour of a mediocre utility infielder who batted .187 and had a poor arm as he could from charting Gary Carter. Both players conform to certain rules which can be inferred from watching either of them. But Carter will have performed more and left more records and therefore study of his career will yield more detailed and accurate information about the nature of the game in which both men were engaged.

The best way to summarize Stone's career is to say that he was a prospector, in the sense of a searcher for economic opportunity or an edge in competition in business deals. Not that he was vicious – he was notably loyal in personal matters, protective of the weak, and in later life tiresomely religious – but he was a classic eighteenth-century merchant, the kind of person who never needed to read Adam Smith's *Wealth of Nations* (1776), for he lived it.[24]

Stone came from a family that had long been established in New England. His first direct ancestor in the region settled in the Quinnipiac area of Connecticut (near New Haven) in 1639. Joel was born in Litchfield where his father farmed. Then, as now, the life of a farmer's son was difficult and upon reaching his majority in 1771 Stone became a Yankee pedlar, buying small goods, travelling about the countryside selling at a profit, and returning home to buy more goods. This he did for three years with considerable success and in

24 There is no full biography of Joel Stone in print, although there are several articles which are referred to below. One should pay more than passing respects, however, to the unpublished work of H. William Hawke. His studies of Joel Stone exist in various unpublished forms, the most satisfactory being "Joel Stone of Gananoque, 1749–1833: His Life and Letters," which he completed in 1966 and a copy of which is in Queen's University Archives. Elizabeth M. Morgan's "Joel Stone: Connecticut Loyalist (1749–1833)" (MA diss., Queen's University 1980) adds very little to Hawke's work. Stone's papers are divided largely between PAC (the McDonald-Stone papers), AO, Queen's University Archives, and a smaller number of items in the Toronto Public Library. Most of the outgoing correspondence is in the form of drafts of letters, not verbatim copies.

1774 he was able to enter a mercantile partnership with a Jabez Bacon of Woodbury, Connecticut, his intentions being no longer peripatetic but long-term and substantial. The partnership was for six years and each partner put up £350 in goods. At the age of twenty-five, Joel Stone was on his way to being an established merchant.[25]

Then occurred the least adequately explained event in his life: Joel Stone found himself on the losing side of the American Revolution. Stone was not an introspective or reflective man and even in his petition of 1784 to the British government for redress for his losses as a loyalist his statements of loyalty were brief and stereotyped. He had no articulate ideology and the best that one can do is chart his behaviour. We know that, when in 1775 he was called upon by a patriot committee to declare his position, he managed to avoid making a commitment while the rebels directed their rage at his father, whose loyalism was more overt. When a year later he did finally commit himself it was not a spontaneous affirmation of loyalty but a forced response occasioned by the demand of a local patriot committee that he either take up arms against the established government or provide a substitute. Only then did Joel Stone declare himself a loyalist and leave Connecticut for New York. Still, however disoriented he may temporarily have been, he continued as an instinctive, almost perpetual prospector for advantage.[26] Between his affirmation as a loyalist and his arrival in Canada in October 1786, Stone prospected continually: he acted as a recruiting agent for Wentworth's army, tried his hand at privateering, married a woman of substantial family, looked after the probating in London of a will that benefited his new wife's family, and successfully pursued a pension from the British government for his loyalist service, which he eventually received in the amount of forty pounds annually. While in London Stone became acquainted with Sir Guy

25 Hawke, 2–4; Herbert S. McDonald, *Memoir of Colonel Joel Stone, a United Empire Loyalist and Founder of Gananoque* (np., privately printed c. 1920), 3–5; this is a reprint of the article of the same title, cited in n 23, with the pagination changed. A copy of the partnership agreement is found in AO, Stone papers, 5 February 1774. At age 81 Stone left a two-page summary of his life (PAC, McDonald-Stone papers, no. 1638) which is full of error and should not be used for factual reference.

26 PAC, McDonald-Stone papers, nos. 1770ff, "Narrative and Will" of Joel Stone (of nearly thirty pages) is a copy of the narrative he provided to the British government in 1784 in support of his petition for compensation for losses. "The Narrative of Joel Stone" is conveniently available in James J. Talman, ed., *Loyalist Narratives from Upper Canada* (Toronto: The Champlain Society 1946), 323–36.

Carleton and other influential figures, and this apparently determined his settling in Canada.

A fundamental rule for prospectors of every sort is to arrive first, and here Stone was at a disadvantage. He initially chose to settle in New Johnstown (Cornwall) which was already populated with early loyalists. Stone arrived there in the spring of 1787 and was pleased by what he saw. "Verily," he wrote to his London agent, "I find it as good land in general as ever I set my foot on," an observation that indicates a buoyant optimism if not a great sense of geology.[27] Stone pressed the government hard for lands, on the basis of his losses and his various services, especially his militia captaincy, and he came to understand that he would draw perhaps as much as one thousand acres of free government land. But he soon discovered that the desirable lands around New Johnstown were already allocated. Therefore, he bought a small house and a small holding of fourteen acres and began to brew beer and distil spirits. This activity had been part of his plans since soon after his arrival in British North America and he had sent three stills ahead of him in February 1787. Soon he built a brew house and was in business.[28]

Things did not go well, however. Stone was financially overextended and chronically short of cash. Moreover, he and his wife were fighting and eventually he had to agree to legal separation and an expensive maintenance agreement. To escape from his financial impasse Stone became what one observer presciently has termed a "prospector of water-privileges,"[29] and, after a vexed period of fighting off rival claimants and dealing with bungling government officials, he eventually received a large grant of land on the west bank of the Gananoque River in Leeds and Lansdowne township. Previously Stone had been promised seven hundred acres as a reward for his loyalism but somehow the actual grant became eleven hundred acres.[30] Stone now felt confident in engaging two millwrights and a blacksmith in the spring of 1789 as preparation for setting up business on the Gananoque River. His land certificate was

27 (Copy) Joel Stone to Charles Cooke, 9 May 1787 (Toronto Public Library, Stone papers).

28 (Draft) Joel Stone to Thomas Swan, 8 February 1787 (Queen's University Archives, Stone papers); (draft) Joel Stone to General Hope, 5 February 1787 (PAC, McDonald-Stone papers, no. 287).

29 Machar, 61.

30 How Stone's grant grew from seven hundred to eleven hundred acres is highly problematical. The official entries in the Upper Canada Land Books (see below) referred to his grant as being seven hundred acres, these entries being made in 1796 and 1799. However, a survey done for Stone by Reuben Sherwood in 1799 showed him to have just under eleven hundred acres in his

signed by John Hollins, the deputy surveyor general, on 2 August 1789 and sometime in 1790–1 Stone had a house built on his new property and a tenant placed in occupancy. Early in 1792 he came to reside in person, his long period of insecurity almost over. The fulfilment came with the creation of the land patenting system in the mid-1790s. His 1796 application for deed led to his lands being patented (after the usual administrative fumbling) in part in 1798 and the rest by the close of 1801.[31]

The key to the remainder of Stone's career is that he was not an absentee speculator but built directly upon the natural advantages of his property, adding new improvements year by year. (Not that he was interested in capital improvements to the exclusion of all other forms of acquisition; in October 1792 he had the impudence to petition the government for an entire township and in 1799 he sought more free grants as "family lands"; both these efforts failed,[32]

---

primary parcel (PAC, McDonald-Stone papers, no. 516). A somewhat different version of the survey, yielding the same conclusion, is in Toronto Public Library, Stone papers. This conclusion, that he actually received eleven hundred acres, tallies well with the Abstract Index of Deeds indicating the lands Stone eventually patented. It appears that he later acquired half of one large lot – the east of lot 8, concession 1 – before patenting, but otherwise the holding stayed the same (see AO, Abstract Index of Deeds). It has been suggested that Stone received an additional grant of two hundred acres for each of his children, thus bringing the total up to eleven hundred acres (Donald McMurrich, "Joel Stone and the Founding of Gananoque," *Historic Kingston* 15 [1967]: 32). This explanation has an appealing arithmetical precision, but I am skeptical of its validity for two reasons. First, Stone was denied family lands in 1799, as "the application for family lands is too late" (PAC, "Upper Canada Land Book D," 13 February 1799, 271–2). Second, the land was patented by Stone, not by his children. In the case of land grants to loyalist children the patents almost always were taken out in their own names when they came of age or, in the case of young women, when they married. My own guess is that we have here an example of a more general situation in Upper Canada, an extraordinarily high degree of slippage in the administrative machinery, combined with aggressive and aggrandizing actions on the part of those who wanted particularly valuable lands. In his 1789 petition (Stone to Peter Russell and council, 11 February 1789, quoted in Hawke, 46), Stone had described the parcel as constituting seven hundred acres. The verbal description he gave tallies with the parcel which was surveyed in 1799 and found to be eleven hundred acres. Given that by his residence and improvements Stone effectively occupied the land, the land patenting system later brought the acreage on the land record to correspond with the reality in the field.

31 Hawke, 46–7; PAC, RG I LI "Upper Canada Land Book B," 12 December 1796, 186, and "Upper Canada Land Book D," 13 February 1799, 271–2. See also Abstract Index of Deeds, AO.

32 PAC, "Upper Canada Land Book A," 17 October 1792, 29; "Upper Canada Land Book D," 13 February 1799, 271–2.

but he did acquire land on the open market after the turn of the century.)

Stone had competition, for by 1792 Sir John Johnson had completed a saw- and grist-mill on his side of the Gananoque River, with provision for batteaux or small vessels to go right up to the mill door.[33] However, by 1795 Stone had his own sawmill operating. This was a sizeable piece of machinery, with fifteen saw blades, most of which were adjustable to size and thickness of cut. The water coming over the falls not only powered the blades but was also harnessed to lift logs on to the sawing plane, a fairly sophisticated technological achievement.[34] In these early years Stone cut canals on the west river bank and he and the agent for Sir John cooperated in erecting two dams designed to control the water for the two milling operations.[35]

For Stone, the Ganonoque River was a source of great economic opportunity, but for many others it was a problem: getting across it was awkward. Stone saw a chance for a profitable investment, and in 1801 he set up a ferry service, operated it,and then sold it a year later.[36] That was profitable, but he really wanted a good bridge and in May 1806 Stone (now a justice of the peace) and another JP convened a meeting of the freeholders and inhabitants of the township to petition the authorities for a bridge across the Gananoque River joining Sir John Johnson's property and his own. Undeniably the Stone-Johnson millpond was the easiest place to build a bridge, but equally undeniably the benefits to Stone were greater than to anybody else, for now the traffic on the King's Highway between Montreal and Kingston had to pass through his land. Stone did not have to pay any more than his rate-payer's share of the seventy-five pounds the structure cost, but as a supervisor of highways and as the nearest resident justice of the peace he was given responsibility for letting the contract and supervising the job. In short, a significant capital investment project, paid for by public funds, was controlled as tightly by Stone as if he had been spending his own money.[37]

On his site on the west bank of the Gananoque River, Stone set up a general trading operation that grew from a slovenly inn and

33 Deposition by Alexander Atkins, deputy provincial surveyor, 6 November 1792, cited in Hawke, 28.
34 "La Rochefoucault-Liancourt's Travels in Canada, 1795," ed. William R. Riddell, in *Thirteenth Report of the Bureau of Archives for the Province of Ontario, 1916*, 521 (original pagination).
35 Hawke, 60.
36 Ibid., 55.
37 (Copy) Joel Stone to Lemuel Mallory, 12 June 1806 (AO, Stone papers); Hawke, 55–6; Leavitt, 59.

general store into a prosperous business. To facilitate his trading ventures he had built in 1793–4 a seventeen-ton schooner, the *Leeds Trader*.[38] Seemingly he would buy, stock, and sell almost anything that might turn a profit: an account of 1810 includes an impressive range of items, from one gallon of madeira to six silk handkerchiefs, a barrel of pork, a frying pan, five gallons of spirits, and some soap.[39]

Together Stone's activities represent a substantial capital investment in machinery, buildings, and inventory. He operated before the era of audited annual balance sheets (indeed, before the time of double-entry bookkeeping) and there is no way precisely to determine increases in his net worth over time. One can indirectly chart his increasing prosperity, however, as he moved from his original log house to the "Red House" of framed timber and later to a larger, almost stately "Yellow House." By 1816 he was a substantial merchant dealing with Montreal merchants in bills of exchange drawn for one thousand pounds in Halifax currency.[40]

How did Stone finance his capital improvements? He cannot have done it directly on his loyalist compensation, for his forty pounds a year military pension, while adequate for living modestly in the English countryside (recall Goldsmith's country preacher, "passing rich with forty pounds a year"), was hardly enough money to finance a complex set of investments in the New World. Nor can one infer that the legacy he obtained on behalf of his wife was any underpinning for his fortune, as Stone himself felt that his wife was a heavy financial burden, both before and after their separation. He does not seem to have gained much in direct financial resources from his second marriage in 1799 to the widow of a Quaker small farmer living in the township of Burford, near Brantford. The widow had a small amount of landed property but this was rented out and its management seems to have cost Stone more trouble than it was worth. In his new wife, Abigail, Stone found a shrewd helpmeet for his various business enterprises but not a source of risk capital.[41] Stone entered into three business partnerships, traditionally a form

38 "Agreement between Joel Stone and William Eadus," 5 April 1798 (PAC, McDonald-Stone papers, no. 506); Hawke, 49; Machar, 66; McDonald, 24.
39 Account with Peter Smith, Kingston, 1810 (Stone papers, Queen's University Archives).
40 Britton, [11]; Hawke, 48–9; bill of exchange of 27 July 1816 (PAC, McDonald-Stone papers, no. 2045).
41 The date of the marriage is unknown, as is even the month in 1793 when Stone's first wife died. Probably he was remarried in the summer of 1799 (Hawke, 53). Machar (67) has a long, ghoulish, and unintentionally funny anecdote about the widow-to-be who, upon noting that her first husband was beginning to pine away, at once sent twenty-five miles for a set of seasoned cherry boards. Her husband noticed and was not cheered by her foresight. On Mrs Stone's

of pooling capital and thus of facilitating major investments, but none of these can have been the source of any money. The first of these was an unsuccessful speculative agreement with Daniel Jones whereby Stone and Jones were to spy out and obtain the land at the mouth of the Gananoque River. This agreement dissolved, probably because the administrative authorities objected to giving lands to Jones, who had already received his grant. A second partnership, with a scruffy Frenchman named Carey, was only a temporary alliance of convenience. When Stone moved permanently to Gananoque in 1792 he found Carey on a nearby island and the two men moved to the mainland and together set up a public house and store. They kept two cows, the milk of which they bartered with the Indians for fish and game, and sold stale biscuits and provided dirty accommodation to travellers. When Governor Simcoe's party visited the place in 1792 it was so filthy that they decided to pitch a tent for the night although it was raining heavily. This partnership broke up when the house burned, the arrangement having provided Stone with temporary shelter but little else.[42] The third partnership was entered into after he was securely established. In 1810 he made some form of association (the details are not clear) with Charles McDonald, an American merchant from Troy, New York. Probably this association was dictated by domestic considerations, rather than economic ones. In 1809 Stone's only son had died, depriving him of his chief deputy, and Charles McDonald filled the void. In 1811, McDonald married Stone's only surviving child, Mary, and soon began providing grandchildren (the first of whom was named William after Stone's dead son). In any case, by 1810 Stone no longer was capital starved; indeed, one soon finds him giving valuable parcels of land to the young couple. This third partnership, then, was a means of obtaining managerial help and perpetuating his family line, not a source of funds.[43]

Burford township property, see letters of Reverend Thomas Whitehead to Joel Stone, 12 January 1816, 31 July 1816, and 21 April 1823, and (copies) Joel Stone to Reverend Thomas Whitehead, 1 March 1823, 27 August 1825, 5 July 1828, 23 September 1828, and 27 December 1828 (all in Stone papers, Queen's University Archives). Concerning Stone's domestic arrangements, it could be added that in the 1790s he lived with a housekeeper and by Jinny Hagerman in 1796 had an illegitimate child. This Jinny was married in the same year to a Lewis Bissonnett (Hawke, 50–1).

42 McDonald, 24; *The Diary of Mrs John Graves Simcoe*, ed. J. Ross Robertson (Toronto: Ontario Publishing Co. 1934), 106; Frank Eames, "Briefs of Local Lore: Gananoque and Lady Simcoe's Four Rests" (Gananoque: privately printed by author 1951), 4.

43 See H. William Hawke, "The McDonald Family of Gananoque" (unpublished paper, McDonald family papers, Queen's University Archives, 2–3); Abstract

No portion of his capital came from sales of his land, for Stone engaged in speculation for development, not for resale. Far from selling any of his considerable land holdings, Stone added to them by purchase. He sold none of his original eleven hundred acre tract and in subsequent years his acquisitions exceeded his sales both in value and extent. His biggest reduction in land holdings was in the form of a gift in 1811 of over five hundred acres of valuable St Lawrence River frontage, downriver from his own primary holding, to his son-in-law and daughter.[44] Stone did make some money from land rents as a town grew up at the mouth of the Gananoque River, but these opportunities did nor arise in any number until the second decade of the nineteenth century, long after he was fully established.[45] Occasionally he made money from land by acting as a sales agent for absentees, but such instances were late and infrequent.[46]

Stone apparently acquired most of his investment capital in resource stripping and in daily, continual hard dealing and profit taking in each of his mercantile ventures. He had become involved in the lumbering trade almost as soon as he arrived, but it was not until his sawmills were fully functional in 1794–5 that he entered the business in a big way. The most spectacular aspect of this trade was the rafting of large quantities of sawed timber down the river to Montreal, which he began to do as early as 1795.[47] More prosaic but also highly profitable was the local sale of sawed timber. Stone not only sold in Leeds and Landsdowne but competed energetically for the Kingston custom: in 1795 the Kingston price of an hundred feet of inch board (of unspecified width) was five shillings; Stone's price for boards of the same dimensions was three shillings.[48] His eye for the market is well indicated in a letter that he wrote to his second

Index of Deeds, AO (references to Hawke which follow are to his Stone biography, not the McDonald essay, unless specifically noted otherwise).

44 See Abstract Index of Deeds (AO), indenture, Cynthia Caroll to Joel Stone (PAC, McDonald-Stone, no. 671); grant, to Joel Stone, 10 September 1811 (PAC, McDonald-Stone, no. 554); indenture, Hugh McIlmoyle to Joel Stone, 5 May 1797 (PAC, McDonald-Stone, no. 500). For information on Stone's wild lands in Montague township, see Glenn J. Lockwood, *Montague: A Social History of an Irish Ontario Township, 1783–1980* (Smiths Falls: Township of Montague 1980), 54–5.

45 Indenture, Joel Stone to John Brounson (PAC, McDonald-Stone, no. 950). This provides a sale with provision for fiteen years' ground rents to Stone. See also indenture, Joel Stone to Charles and John McDonald, 3 February 1824, and *Kingston Gazette*, 13 January 1818.

46 For an instance see *Kingston Gazette*, 13 January 1818.

47 Britton, [11]; Hawke, "The McDonald Family of Gananoque," 3.

48 "La Rochefoucault-Liancourt's Travels in Canada, 1795," 521–2 (original pagination).

wife while he was away on a business trip. They should, he said, "get all the boards and planks they possibly can." Although it presently was a time of low prices, "remember that after a storm comes a calm. Let us not fail to be prepared with dishes when it may rain!"[49]

Stone's most ambitious attempt at resource exploitation fell through, but it nevertheless indicates his instinct. In 1810 he came to an agreement for the development of possible iron deposits on his Gananoque River property with an American entrepreneur, Jonas Broughton, who was ceded the right to discover, mine, and manufacture any ore on Stone's land. This agreement was what one would today call an option. It was conditional, the relevant phrase being "provided the quality of oar proves good." In that case Stone would sell two hundred acres of river front to Broughton, including control of the rapids, and give him mining rights on the rest of the property. In return, Stone would receive one thousand guineas, no small sum. In the event, the option, which ran for a year, was never acted upon: there was no iron on the land Stone owned.[50]

If in his willingness to strip primary resources from the land Joel Stone resembled a twentieth-century Canadian, in his mercantile behaviour he was a creature of the eighteenth-century British counting house. Everything, small, large, whatever the transaction, was turned to a profit. Like the archetypal merchant adventurers of his time, he did not specialize. Any product and almost any service was his business, provided there was a profit in it. Sometimes the profit was considerable. For example, if, instead of buying sawn timber cut from Stone's own forest rights, a settler wished to have his own timber sawn, the fee was half of the sawn boards.[51] These Stone could then sell to other customers at the retail price. The ferry that Stone established across the Gananoque River in 1801 was not a big money maker (the tariff was 3d. for a single man, 1s. for a man and horse, and 1s.6d. for a boat load) but in the succeeding year Stone sold to one Silas Pearson the entire operation as a going concern.[52] Mostly, Stone simply bought goods as cheaply as possible and sold them as expensively as he could, a prescription dear to classical economists. Most of the goods were brought upriver from Montreal, but he was not above bartering or selling local produce: at one point he instructed his wife to provide as many as ten barrels of

49 Quoted in Machar (no date given), 70.
50 Hawke, 58–9, gives the text of the agreement between Stone and Broughton, 8 September 1810.
51 "La Rochefoucault-Liancourt's Travels in Canada, 1795," 521 (original pagination).
52 Hawke, 55.

wheat to a settler in Lansdowne who had hired four labourers from Scotland and was possibly short of bread. In return, he expected to get some farm work from the labourers himself.[53]

The most expensive goods that Stone retailed (manufactured products, wines, fine goods) came from Montreal and this aspect of his operation was admirably efficient. His downstream rafting operations gave either Stone or his son the opportunity to conduct two transactions at once, closing of the timber deal and then arranging for retail goods to be sent upstream to Gananoque. In other words, his exploitation of resources and his mercantile ventures were complementary, arranged so that the travel overheads for two separate operations were integrated into a single cost. The seventeen-ton schooner that he had had constructed in 1793–4 gave him an inexpensive method of transporting goods between the La Chine Rapids and Gananoque, or Kingston, or the Bay of Quinte. Even so, he apparently could not keep the vessel busy all the time and in 1798 he leased it to a mariner for four years for thirty pounds a year so that it was working for him even when it was not under his own cargo.[54] He always had a percentage or a profit, and these small slices added up to one big portion.

It seems then that in Joel Stone we have a case of self-generated economic development, the kind of personal financial levitation so beloved of nineteenth-century moralists and twentieth-century developmental economists. Two questions remain, one a matter of substantive economics, the other of pertinent curiosity. First, one would like to know to what extent credit arrangements made possible Stone's heavy capital development program. Vexingly, there is no adequate answer. Land records show that Stone did not take out a mortgage on his properties; on the other hand, it is clear that he was short of cash until almost 1810, as the forced sale of his property in Cornwall in the 1790s clearly indicates (see above, p. 69). A demand note signed by Stone in 1804 for a loan of slightly over £186 was not redeemed for over five years.[55] In all probability, however, most of the credit he received was invisible, in the sense that wholesale merchants at the time gave retailers up to a year's credit on goods they purchased but did not openly charge interest. They simply added the credit cost to their overheads and thus the price of any item purchased (except for cash purchases) included

53 Joel Stone to Abigail Stone, 25 June 1801 (Stone papers, Queen's University Archives).

54 Agreement between Joel Stone and William Eadus, 5 April 1798 (PAC, McDonald-Stone papers, no. 506).

55 Demand note of 8 September 1804 (PAC, McDonald-Stone papers, no. 594).

the cost of the implicit loan. These arrangements were virtually unrecorded. In his turn, Stone provided credit to his customers as an unrecorded portion of the price of the article that he finally sold. Credit from the Quebec wholesalers doubtless was crucial in allowing Stone to set up and continue his mercantile operation, but it cannot have financed his major capital investments, which demanded not credit but cash. A reasonable (though emphatically tentative) conclusion is that Stone's day-to-day trading operations were based on wholesalers' credit but that his major capital developments were paid for by the profits on these trading operations and by his sales of timber.

Second, one is curious as to whether fraud, deceit, or unnecessarily hard dealings were part of Stone's personal economic miracle. My own judgment is that he was a hard man but straight. The only instance of possible chicanery on his part that I have found (though inevitably this is a highly subjective area) is his representation of his original claim to the administrative authorities as seven hundred acres and his later accurate patenting of it as eleven hundred. It is unclear whether this was due to an error in surveying or intentional on his part. There was also an instance in 1813 when Stone bought a pair of oxen, a yoke, and an ox bell from a woman while her husband was away from home; the husband returned to protest vigorously. The situation, one feels, reflects nothing more than a certain degree of domestic breakdown between the couple and a shrewd eye on the part of Stone.[56] A fortune could be made in Upper Canada by a hard, honest man and probably Stone was such a man.[57]

56 Receipt from Margaret Sheriff, 13 August 1813 (PAC, McDonald-Stone, no. 872) and Allan MacLean on behalf of William Sheriff to Joel Stone, 18 August 1813 (PAC, McDonald-Stone, no. 876).

57 Left aside as totally profitless is the question of whether Stone used his position as an important local civic figure to feather unethically his nest as an economic baron. He held almost every possible local position of power and in our own time one would have a *prima facie* case of conflict of interest: he was perpetually a justice of the peace and as such often served as chairman of the court of general sessions (the "quarter sessions") that administered most laws below the felony level in the Johnstown district. At various times he was coroner for the district, deputy customs collector, postmaster, overseer of the roads and highways, colonel and commander of the second regiment of the Leeds militia (whence he generally became known locally as "Colonel Stone"), returning officer for the election to assembly of Upper Canada, a commissioner to administer the oath of allegiance to suspicious people (during the war of 1812), commissioner under the alien act of 1814, commissioner to administer oaths to those claiming military pensions, and, in 1819, member of the newly created land board for the Johnstown district. However, the conflict of interest question is

In March 1833, well into his eighty-fourth year, Joel Stone made a list of rateable property in Leeds and Lansdowne township. It included one large frame house, 1,220 acres in the first concession of Leeds, 200 acres of wild land in Lansdowne, fifty acres of wild land to the interior of Leeds, three horses, two oxen, fourteen milk cows, and seven head of beef cattle.[58] Actually, this understates his true wealth. In a will made in August of the same year he stated that he had fifteen hundred acres of land in the first concession of Leeds. This included roughly half the mercantile and industrial land in the village of Gananoque. In addition he held fifty acres of land in Leeds, 200 acres in Lansdowne, as well as the 200 acres his wife had inherited in Burford township and 2,200 acres of wild land in various parts of Upper Canada.[59] All this was in addition to his personal property and cash, the details of which were not specified in the will. In November 1833, six weeks after thus listing his earthly winnings, Joel Stone died, old, respected, and rich.

---

useless, because it is anachronistic. In business ethics Stone and the people of his time recognized a line between fraudulent and ethical, albeit hard, practices, but no such line was drawn between economic power and civic power. The concept of conflict of interest is a very recent idea, not only alien to eighteenth-century civic morality but actually diametrically opposed to it. It was believed that economic power and civic power, far from being distinct, should reinforce each other. The British aristocrat or country squire was the model. Economic privilege was supposed to be balanced by civic responsibility, and the large landowner who did not accept unpaid civic appointments was looked upon as abnegating his duties.

On Stone's various appointments see warrant, Isaac Brock to Joel Stone, 27 February 1812 (PAC, no: 795–6); John B. Robinson to Joel Stone and Charles Jones, 20 January 1820 (AO, Stone papers); Livius P. Sherwood to Joel Stone, 16 June 1802 (Queen's University Archives, Stone papers); indenture of June 1812, installing Stone as returning officer (Queen's University Archives, Stone papers); *Kingston Gazette*, 26 April 1814, 4 May 1814, and 6 July 1816; Britton, [8]; *Fourteenth Report of the Bureau of Archives for the Province of Ontario, 1917*, 455; McDonald, 33–4.

58 Copy of list by Joel Stone, 11 March 1833 (Toronto Public Library, Stone Papers).
59 The 6 August 1833 will is given in full in Hawke, 103–5. The will was complexly entailed, in part because his daughter Mary McDonald (the widow of Charles McDonald who died in 1862) had for a long time been of unsound mind and required special provision. Thus, the final probate, breaking entail, was not done until 6 May 1848, although some portions were distributed in the early 1840s (PAC, MG 23 HII-I, 4, oversized item in vertical file, 2020–2). That Stone did not list large business interests in this will is less surprising than it might at first appear. After being joined by Charles McDonald in 1810, he appears to have gradually turned over his mercantile affairs to McDonald (who formed a partnership with his brother under the firm name of C. and J. McDonald in 1818). This was not unnatural, as in 1818 Stone already was sixty-nine years old and, additionally, Charles McDonald was carrying the heavy domes-

4

As in any competitive individualistic game, the relationships between the people who settled in Leeds and Lansdowne township were ambivalent, vacillating between alliance and aggression. When Joel Stone set a certain price for a barrel of flour as delivered to Oliver Landon, his margin of profit took from Landon money that Landon could have used for something else; and, when in his turn Landon did not pay the account for fourteen months, he was reclaiming some of that money by using it interest-free for a troublesomely long period of time. Each was trying to take something from the other. Yet when they struck a bargain these same two men were also entering into an alliance of sorts, for by placing a limited trust in each other they were able to complete a transaction that left both of them slightly better off. Unhappily, we cannot document these day-to-day instances of aggression and alliance in any detail, for they are part of the historian's Law of Disappearing Evidence: the more common and pervasive a human activity or artifact, the more likely it is to disappear without trace. Things that were taken for granted, such as customary social and economic usages, were so ingrained as to be automatic and were rarely directly recorded. Thus, in the case of Leeds and Lansdowne township we are forced to examine events that are rather more important than we would like, that is, at instances of aggression and alliance that were unusual enough to be recorded. With caution, these events can be used as examples of the ways in which the social and economic fabric was both stretched and stitched, and as analogues for the tens of thousands of unrecorded everyday behaviours.

One example is the fundamental matter of economic alliances. It appears that the settlers could cooperate to the extent of buying and selling to each other and would involve themselves in short-term collective matters (such as construction projects) but that even simple economic partnerships were unusual. Most heads of house-

---

tic burden of his wife: Stone's daughter had begun to be unstable mentally after her marriage to McDonald in 1811. In a sense, in stepping aside in the day-to-day mercantile trade in favour of the McDonalds Stone was implicitly contributing to the support of this daughter (see Hawke, 80). A reasonable supposition is that after moving into the background on the local mercantile scene, Stone began his acquisition of wild lands. Whether he received any significant cash settlement (other than rents) from the McDonalds is unclear. However, even if he received nothing from them, reducing or liquidating his mercantile stock would have given him the funds with which to speculate in the wild lands.

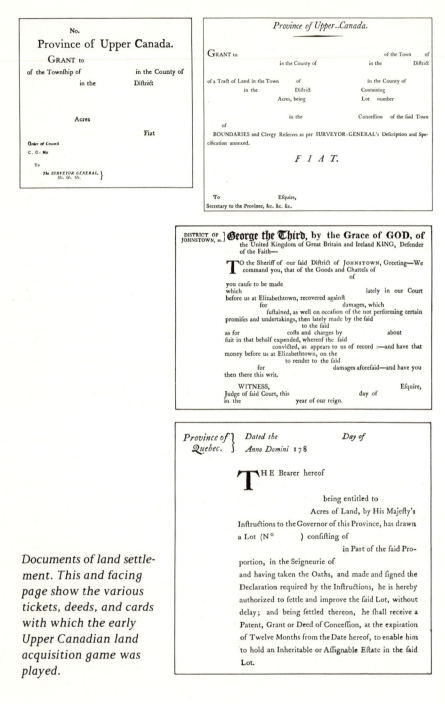

Documents of land settlement. This and facing page show the various tickets, deeds, and cards with which the early Upper Canadian land acquisition game was played.

81 Leeds and Lansdowne Township

N°. CERTIFICATE of the Board appointed by His Excellency the Governor for the Diftrict of in the Province of Quebec, under the Rules and Regulations for the Conduct of the Land Office Department, dated Council-Chamber, Quebec, 17th. February, 1789.

THE Bearer having on the day of preferred to this Board a Petition addreffed to His Excellency the Governor in Council for a grant of Acres of land in the Townfhip of in the Diftrict of We have examined into his loyalty and character and find him duly qualified to receive a SINGLE LOT of about two hundred Acres, the oath of fidelity and allegiance directed by law having this day been adminiftered to him by the board, in conformity to the fourth article of the Rules and Regulations aforementioned.

Given at the Board at this day of one thoufand feven hundred and

To

Acting Surveyor for the Diftrict of

N°. Certificate of the Acting Surveyor.

I Affign to the Bearer the Lot N° in the Townfhip of in the Diftrict of containing Acres, Chains

which lands he is hereby authorized to occupy and improve. And having improved the fame, he fhall receive a grant thereof to him and his heirs or devifees in due form, on fuch terms and conditions as it fhall pleafe his Majefty to ordain. And all perfons are defired to take notice, that this affignement, and all others of a fimilar nature, are NOT TRANSFERABLE by purchafe, donation, or otherwife, on any pretence whatever, except by an act under the fignature of the Board for the Diftrict in which the lands are fituated, which is to be endorfed upon this certificate.

Given at this day of one thoufand feven hundred and

Acting Surveyor for the Diftrict of

TOWNSHIP of

Lot Number Conceffion

Commencing at a Poft in front of Conceffion, marked

Then North Chains 27 Links ;

Then Weft, 9 Chains Links ;

Then South Chains Links ;

Then Eaft, Chains Links ;

To the place of beginning :

Containing Acres, more or lefs,

for which acres fevenths are referved as per margin.

LOT No.

CONCESSION.

Acting Surveyor-General.

With

Certificate

Number

This Indenture, made the Day of in the year of the Reign of his Majefty Lord by the Grace of God of the United Kingdom of Great Britain and Ireland, King, Defender of the Faith, &c. and in the year of our Lord One Thoufand Eight Hundred and between of the Townfhip of in the Diftrict in the Province of Upper Canada of the one part ; and of the other part, WITNESSETH, That for and in confideration of the fum of good and lawful money of the faid Province, to the faid in hand well and truly paid by the faid at or before the fealing and delivery of thefe prefents, the receipt whereof is hereby acknowledged, and thereof, and therefrom, and of and from the fame, and every part thereof, the faid Do by thefe Prefents acquit, releafe, and forever difcharge, the faid Heirs, Executors, Adminiftrators and Affigns, and every of them forever : the faid Ha Granted, Bargained, Sold, Aliened, Releafed, Conveyed and Confirmed ; and by thefe Prefents Do Grant, Bargain, Sell, Alien, Releafe, Convey, and Confirm, unto the faid Heirs and Affigns, all That Piece, Parcel, or Tract of Land, fituate, lying, and being, in the Townfhip of in the County of in the Diftrict in the Province of Upper Canada aforefaid, with all and every of the appurtenances, containing by admeafurement be the fame more or lefs, being compofed of Conceffion ; together with all the Buildings, Improvements, Woods and Waters thereon erected, made, lying and being, under the Refervations, Limitations, & Conditions, expreffed in the Original Grant from the Crown Which faid of Land, are butted and bounded, or may be otherwife known as follows, that is to fay, Commencing of the faid Conceffion, of the faid Lot ; Thence Degrees Chains more or lefs, to the of the faid Conceffion ; Thence Degrees Chains more or lefs, to the ; Thence Degrees Chains more or lefs, to the of the faid Conceffion ; Thence Degrees Chains more or lefs to the place of beginning : And the reverfion and reverfions, remainder and remainders, yearly and other rents, iffues, and profits thereof, and alfo all the Eftate, right, title, inheritance, ufe, truft, poffeffion, property, claim and demand whatfoever, both at Law, and in Equity, of --the faid of, in, to, or out of the faid Premifes, or any part thereof ; TO HAVE AND TO HOLD the faid Piece, Parcel, or Tract of Land, and all other the Premifes mentioned to be hereby Granted and Releafed as aforefaid, with their, and every of their appurtenances, and every part and Parcel thereof, unto the faid Heirs and Affigns ; to the only proper ufe, benefit, and behoof, of the faid Heirs and Affigns forever. And the faid for Heirs, Executors, and Adminiftrators, and for every of them, Do Covenant, Grant, Promife, and agree, to and with, the faid Heirs and Affigns in manner following : that is to fay, that the faid now the true, lawful, and rightful owner of all and fingular the Land and Premifes abovementioned, with the appurtenances, and of every part, and parcel thereof, and now lawfully, and rightfully, feized in own right, of a good, fure, perfect, abfolute and indefeafible Eftate of inheritance, in Fee-Simple, of and in the Premifes hereby Granted, Bargained and Sold, or intended to be Granted, Bargained, and Sold, without any Condition, Limitation of ufe or ufes, or any other matter or thing, to alter, charge, change, incumber, or defeat the fame—And alfo, that the faid and Heirs fhall and will *Warrant*, and forever *Defend* the faid Heirs and Affigns, and every of them forever, in the peaceable and unmolefted poffeffion of the faid Land and Premifes, and every part and parcel thereof, againft all and every other perfon, or perfons, having or lawfully claiming, or who fhall, or may have or lawfully claim, any Eftate, Right, Title, Truft, or Intereft, at Law or in Equity, of, in, to, or out of the faid Piece, Parcel, or Tract, of Land and Premifes, or any of them, or any part thereof, by or under, or in truft for or by or under anceftors, or any of them : And FURTHER, that the faid and Heirs, and all other perfons, having or lawfully claiming, or who fhall, or may have, or lawfully claim, any Eftate, Right, Title, Truft, or Intereft, at Law, or in Equity, of, in, to, or out of, the faid Piece, Parcel, or Tract of Land and Premifes, or any of them, or any part thereof, by or under, or in truft for or by or under anceftors, or any of them fhall, and will, from time to time, and at all times hereafter, upon every reafonable requeft of the faid Heirs, or affigns, or any of them, make, do, acknowledge, levy, fuffer, and execute, or caufe, or procure to be made, done, acknowledged, levied, fuffered, and executed, all, and every fuch further, and other, lawful and reafonable act and acts, thing and things, deed and deeds, devices, conveyances, and affurances in the law whatfoever, for the further, better, more perfect, and abfolute, Granting, Conveying, and Affuring the faid Piece, Parcel, or Tract of Land and all other the Premifes hereby bargained, and fold or intended fo to be, and every part and parcel thereof, with their, and every of their appurtenances, unto and to the ufe of the faid Heirs and Affigns forever, be the fame by fine, or fines, Deed, or Deeds, enrolled, or not enrolled, the enrollment of thefe prefents, or any other matter of Record, or not of Record, or otherwife howfoever, as by the faid Heirs or Affigns, any, or either of them, their, or any of their Counfel, learned in the Law, fhall be lawfully, and reafonably devifed, or advifed and required ; IN WITNESS WHEREOF, the Part firft above named, have to thefe prefents, fet, and put, hand and feal the day and year firft above written.

Signed Sealed and Delivered
In the Prefence of US,

holds operated as individual economic units. Joel Stone entered into three partnerships, but even these were either very short-lived or (as in the case of his association with his son-in-law) dictated by non-economic considerations. In the fundamental matter of land ownership, Stone was not interested in partnerships and in his attitude he was typical of his fellow citizens. Of the 396 land transactions recorded in the township of Leeds and Lansdowne from the beginning of the patenting system through 31 December 1815, only seven (1.8 percent) involved partnerships.[60] As far as the community's basic economic resource, land, was concerned, it was an atomistic universe.

5

The chief and natural exception to this atomism was the development of the iron ore manufactory at Furnace Falls, and even this involved as much backstabbing and financial intrigue as it did cooperative behaviour. In October 1784, Edward Jessup, one of two loyalist officers sent ahead to make preliminary settlement arrangements, reported to the authorities in Quebec that he had been told that a good place to build an iron works would be between the settlements of "Oswatia" and "Catraque," as he had learned of an "iron oar bed" in that region.[61] Under the provisions of the land regulations of June 1787, reported in February 1789 (see the illustration on p. 83), mineral rights were reserved to the Crown and arrangements for their use had to be made through the governor-in-council.[62] Hence, anyone wishing to develop the ore sites had to spend as much time dealing with the central authorities as he did

60 Computed from Abstract Index of Deeds, AO.
61 Edward Jessup to Major Matthews, 5 October 1784, reproduced in Cruik-shank, *The Settlement of the United Empire Loyalists*, 170. Jessup did not specify where the bed was, either for reasons of security or because he really did not know exactly. Cruikshank (170 n1) identified the iron bed as being in the township of Lansdowne, but even that is not certain. The ironic point about the early iron working in Lansdowne township is that we know a good deal about the furnace and associated works but cannot be sure where most of the ore (often described as "bog-iron") actually was found. One should not assume that the large acreage appropriated to the iron makers around the Lyndhurst site actually included the iron bog as well, for an iron mill needed large amounts of timber, etc., to keep going and the grant therefore may well have been for purposes of aiding processing. McKenzie (*Leeds and Grenville*, 32) says that "it is believed that the ore was located nearby, on the tenth concession of Bastard township" but gives no evidence for this speculation or any indication of her source. See note 68 below.
62 Patterson, 26.

EXTRACT from the Rules and Regulations for the Conduct of the Land Office Department, dated Council-Chamber, 17th. February, 1789.

IV. THE safety and propriety of admitting the Petitioner to become an inhabitant of this Province being well ascertained to the satisfaction of the Board, they shall administer to every such person the oaths of fidelity and allegiance directed by law. After which the Board shall give every such Petitioner a certificate to the Surveyor general, or any person authorized to act as an Agent or Deputy Surveyor for the District within the trust of that Board, expressing the ground of the Petitioner's admission. And such Agent or Deputy Surveyor shall within two days, after the presentment of the certificate, assign the Petitioner a single lot of about two hundred acres, describing the same with due certainty and accuracy under his signature. But the said certificate shall nevertheless have no effect, if the Petitioner shall not enter upon the location and begin the improvement and cultivation thereof within one year from the date of such assignment, or if the Petitioner shall have had lands assigned to him before that time, in any other part of the Province.

VII. The respective Boards shall, on petitions from Loyalists already settled in the upper Districts for further allotments of land under the instructions to the Deputy Surveyor-general, of the 2d of June, 1787, or under prior or other orders for assigning portions to their families, examine into the grounds of such requests and claims, and being well satisfied of the justice thereof, they shall grant certificates for such further quantities of land, as the said instructions and orders may warrant, to the acting Surveyors of their districts respectively, to be by them made effectual in the manner beforementioned ; but to be void nevertheless, if, prior to the passing the grant in form, it shall appear to the Government that such additional locations have been obtained by fraud.— And that of these, the Boards transmit to the Office of the Governor's Secretary, and to each other, like reports and lists as herein before, as to other locations, directed.

VIII. And to prevent individuals from monopolizing such spots as contain mines, minerals, fossils, and conveniences for mills and other singular advantages of a common and public nature, to the prejudice of the general interest of the settlers, the Surveyor-general and his Agents or Deputy Surveyors in the different Districts, shall confine themselves in the locations to be made by them upon certificates of the respective Boards, to such lands only as are fit for the common purposes of husbandry, and they shall reserve all other spots aforementioned, together with all such as may be fit and useful for ports and harbours, or works of defence, or such as contain valuable timber for shipbuilding or other purposes, conveniently situated for water-carriage, in the hands of the Crown.

And they shall without delay give full and particular information to the Governor or Commander in Chief for the time being, of all such spots as are herein before directed to be reserved to the Crown, that order may be taken respecting the same.

And the more effectually to prevent abuses, and to put individuals on their guard in this respect, any certificate of location given contrary to the true intent and meaning of this regulation is hereby declared to be null and void, and a special order of the Governor and Council made necessary to pledge the faith of Government for granting of any such spots as are directed to be reserved.

Land Regulations, February 1789

overcoming the practical difficulties on the actual site. The need for water power in any processing arrangement made the only realistic site in the rear of Leeds and Lansdowne at a waterfall known to some as "the Great Gananoque Falls" (a contemporary usage soon to disappear) or more commonly as the "Furnace Falls."[63] On a modern map the falls are found at "Lyndhurst" (concession ten, lots 2 and 3 in Lansdowne township), a town so named in 1846 in defiance of the

63 On Furnace Falls and the Great Gananoque Falls being the same, see Eames, "Gananoque Blockhouse," 3–4.

prevailing Upper Canadian tradition of naming places after Englishmen of unexceptionable mediocrity.[64]

Abel Stevens, Baptist leader, imaginative speculator, energetic settlement provost, and late arrival (he came to Upper Canada in May 1793), was the first individual to push seriously for permission to develop the iron bed. In the fall of 1794 he petitioned the council, claiming to have discovered a vein of iron ore and asking for permission to open the vein, manufacture from it, and, to this end, received one thousand acres at the falls. This petition for water privileges was contested by Justus and Thomas Sherwood, personages of high importance in the early community, but they soon tired. Stevens persevered, repeatedly petitioning the council and buttressing his claims by pointing to large numbers of American settlers that he had brought to the empty reaches of Bastard and Kitley townships. In the autumn of 1798–9 he went so far as to organize the building of a road from Kingston Mills to the falls where he wished to set up the iron manufactory, a distance of thirty-one miles. For this road construction Stevens and his sixteen associates were recompensed with four hundred acres of land each; but, more important, Stevens obtained leverage on the government, and, in February 1799, the committee of the executive council concerned with Crown land, chaired by Chief Justice Elmsley, finally gave Stevens permission to erect his iron works. However, there was a time limit: he had six months to provide a detailed plan, including evidence of adequate credit. Stevens searched for funds, first finding a Montreal financier as backer. When this man withdrew, Stevens tried to form a company in the United States, but all this took longer than six months and when Stevens still did not have a practical plan a year later, the council declared his licence void.[65]

Stevens himself was largely responsible for the cancellation of his

64 McKenzie, "Historical Sketch of Leeds and Grenville," 10. John Singleton Copley, Baron Lyndhurst (1827), was the son of the great American portrait painter of the same name. Copley was a lawyer of unusual independence, making his reputation in popular cases, such as his 1812 defence of a Luddite rioter; in a widely unpopular case, he conducted the prosecution of Queen Caroline in 1820. He served three times as lord chancellor (see DNB). Lyndhurst was also known as an exceptional womanizer. Disraeli records Lyndhurst's reply to the question of whether or not he believed in having a platonic friendship with a woman: "After, but not before" was the answer (Robert Blake, *Disraeli* [Garden City: Anchor Books 1968], 110).

65 The details of Stevens's activities are documented in an admirably full article by E.A. Cruikshank, "The Activity of Abel Stevens as Pioneer," *Ontario History* 31 (1936). See 57–72 on matters up to the cancellation of Stevens's licence.

licence as he had engaged in some very tricky financing. He had sold his own interest in the site to Matthew Wing of Augusta township but had continued to raise money and hire workmen in the United States as if nothing at all had taken place. Only when Wing brought up the subject in February 1800 did the executive council cast an eye over the matter (they had let the original six months' deadline to Stevens slip by unnoticed) and then it recognized Wing's claim and gave *him* six months to submit a suitable working plan. Now, despite Stevens's attempt to defraud Wing, the two men worked out an alliance. Wing was under pressure of time and Stevens had brought back from the United States several workmen and a master manufacturer, Wallis Sunderlin, to direct them. Under their agreement, the workmen began constructing the iron works. This turned out to be Wing's undoing, for when in July 1800 he applied to the executive council for an extension of his six months' planning period, he was turned down on the grounds that he had presumed actually to erect iron works on the land in question before he had permission to occupy it.[66] Soon thereafter Stevens was dismissed, for when in August 1800 the government received yet another petition from him it was curtly endorsed, "Mr. Stevens already having received a final answer from the Executive council, he is referred to it."[67]

The only man left was the Vermont iron maker Wallis Sunderlin, who in September 1800 quickly stepped forward to petition to be allowed to set up an iron works in his own right. Sunderlin, in partnership with three other Americans from Connecticut, was granted permission and by November 1801 he was producing iron bars in small quantities. By early 1802 he had completed a furnace, forge, bellows, sawmill, and bridge near the falls and was operating to the government's satisfaction. It therefore granted him twelve hundred acres as a premium for setting up the works, reserved for it the rights to ten thousand acres of swamp land further north for the supply of bog iron, and hinted that he would receive additional land grants in the future.[68] As was often the case with such grants, Sunderlin was able to expand his lands so that, although originally granted twelve hundred acres, he managed to patent closer to

66 Ibid., 72–4.
67 Ibid., 74.
68 Ibid., 76–7. That bog land was reserved upstream of Furnace Falls implies that McKenzie may well be correct in believing that the ore bed lay in the township of Bastard. After setting up his iron manufactory, Sunderlin found iron ore in lots 11, 12, and 13 in the fifteenth concession of Lansdowne (Cruikshank, 79).

eighteen hundred. Successful as Sunderlin's achievement was as a method of land acquisition, the iron works was not terribly efficient, producing only about a ton of cast iron a day,[69] almost certainly at a financial loss.

That matters were not going well is indicated in the reaction of the executive council in April 1804 to Sunderlin's application for a second grant of twelve hundred acres of Crown lands. This was rejected because "it is believed that Mr. Sunderlin is not the real petitioner on this occasion."[70] Almost certainly this indicates financial troubles and points to the *sub rosa* role of Ephraim Jones, sometime commissary for the loyalist settlers and now the most successful gombeen man in the Johnstown district. Whether because the enterprise was undercapitalized to begin with or because Sunderlin was a bad production manager, he looked to Jones for financial succour, but Jones soon displaced everyone save himself. In 1804 Sunderlin sold approximately seven hundred acres to Jones for five hundred pounds and he also sold about three hundred acres to two other purchasers. In 1805 Jones advanced Sunderlin more than one thousand pounds (the records are contradictory as to the precise amount) on the remaining parcels, acquiring not only mortgages on the land but also a mortgage on shares in the furnace and associated works. Sunderlin never managed to discharge these mortgages but in 1809 sold out his interests to Jones for one-quarter less than their amount. Commissary Jones had done very well indeed, for he had acquired nearly twelve hundred acres of the Sunderlin grant, half of the water rights at the Furnace Falls, a one-quarter share in the furnace and forge, and a one-half share in the local sawmill. Sunderlin and his partners were left with half of the water rights, a three-quarters share in the furnace and forge, and a one-half interest in the sawmill, and against these assets they still had liabilities to other creditors.[71] Sometime after the sale to Jones, Wallis Sunderlin and Ellis Barlow, one of the partners, died. In 1811 the factory was destroyed by fire, and in January 1812 Ephraim Jones died.[72]

This unedifying and at times Byzantine narrative suggests a

69 Ibid., 80.
70 Ibid., 78. Although a Crown grant was refused, some kind of reserve (probably of mineral rights only) of twelve hundred acres was made for the iron works to take up in future if necessary. This reserve was still intact as late as April 1831, despite several offers by entrepreneurs to purchase it (AO, RG I ser. C-I-2, Box 8).
71 These conclusions are drawn from the Abstract Index of Deeds, AO. See also Cruikshank, 80.
72 Ibid., 79.

signal characteristic of economic life in Leeds and Lansdowne township and perhaps in much of Upper Canada at the time, that the society was not yet capable of cooperative economic ventures on any significant scale. It was possible for Abel Stevens to gather sixteen men and build a road from the Furnace Falls to Kingston Mills, but this was a simple and atomistic venture: road building is easily gauged and each man received an equal amount of land as his reward. In other words, they were working directly and simply for themselves. In contrast, the more complex cooperative matter of raising risk capital and putting together a manufacturing operation could not be achieved by Stevens using the resources at his call in Upper or Lower Canada. He had to go to the United States for both money and expertise, while his American successor, Wallis Sunderlin, and his associates were unable to run a profitable enterprise and eventually fell into the grasp of Commissary Jones. Having no way of eliciting venture capital from benign sources (such as occurs in our own time when a firm offers common stock on the market), they were forced to deal with one of the most aggressive financial operators in the entire province.

This lack of a mechanism of economic cooperation is not surprising. Even in England, the most economically advanced nation of the time, it was very difficult until 1825 to form a company of any sort (as distinct from a simple partnership) and it was not until enactments of 1855–6 that a limited liability company could be formed without requiring a Crown charter or an act of Parliament. Thus the dominant economic customs of the time – embodied in the extreme individualism of single-proprietor or simple-partnership mercantilism – were reinforced by the realities of an underpopulated landscape and by an economy characterized by rudimentary agriculture and resource stripping and were limited by legal impediments to cooperative economic ventures. It was, indeed, every man for himself.

6

Of course individuals cooperated in economic ventures that were short-lived and required no complex legal arrangements and in which the rewards were obvious (such as the Abel Stevens road-building scheme), but this does not undercut the basic point and neither do the instances of short-term social cooperation. Some of the most interesting of these involved the collective manipulation by the more eminent local citizens of the mechanism of government in order to gain direct private and personal benefits for themselves.

The classic local case involved the land board created in the autumn of 1792 for Leeds and Grenville counties (this should not be confused with the board which operated from 1788–92 along district lines or the Johnstown district land board constituted in 1819).[73] The board was entrusted with the primary decisions in the allocation of land in the two counties. The board members paid particular attention to the political loyalty of the applicants and in the case of single lots (two hundred acres) they seem to have had complete discretionary powers in certifying eligibility for grants. In the case of larger parcels (roughly all those five hundred acres and above) they made recommendations to the governor-in-council on both the suitability of the applicant and the appropriate amount of land. The five members of the Leeds and Grenville board were Johnstown district worthies: Justus Sherwood, Ephraim Jones, William Fraser, Thomas Fraser, and Peter Drummond. The secretary was Dr Solomon Jones. This group considered many requests for small parcels and acted upon them with an administrative regularity that probably indicates probity. Large parcels, however, were another matter. On 12 March 1798 the board dealt with their own claims. William Fraser was granted five hundred acres, in addition to five hundred he already held. In a later meeting he was recommended for another two thousand acres and for fifteen hundred acres adjoining his extant holdings on behalf of his late father. Ephraim Jones sat on the committee that considered his petition for one thousand acres in addition to the thousand he had already acquired and had it approved. The same day the petition of Dr Solomon Jones, who was present in his capacity as secretary, was considered. It was recommended that he receive eleven hundred acres in addition to the nine hundred that he had already drawn, and on behalf of his late brother David he was recommended for fifteen hundred acres, on top of the five hundred that had already been drawn on the late brother's behalf. The petition of Daniel Jones, the brother of Dr Solomon, was read the same day and the board recommended that he be granted sixteen hundred acres in addition to the four hundred he had received already.[74] All in all, a remarkable day's work by unpaid public-spirited citizens.

One would not suggest however, that any fraud or deceit was here

73 Patterson, 24 and 39–40.
74 "Land Board: Leeds and Grenville, Minutes and Records, 1792–1794," (AO, RG 1, L4, 14). The minute book contains 152 pages, mostly of routine small claims. See, however, 22ff.

involved.[75] Each of the individuals mentioned above was entitled to land grants in return for his loyalist services. We do have, though, a clear case of temporary and essentially simple cooperation, where the men involved acted together, using a civic agency to guarantee property benefits to themselves as individuals. The differences between the actions of the local élite using political agencies in this way and those of the new Baptist settlers under Abel Stevens putting together a road are more apparent than real. Each example essentially involved a set of temporary and simple alliances which bore direct and obvious material rewards for each individual participating. No abstract entity (such as the "public good" or the modern "corporate welfare") was being served; they were serving themselves. At the bottom of society and at the top the pattern was the same.[76]

7

Here we must turn a corner and view the one aspect of early life in eastern Ontario in which it might appear that there was a cooperative instinct that went beyond mere immediate self-interest, local government. Historical writing has its pendulum

75 There probably were fraudulent claims, although specific cases are not available. In October 1793 Simcoe and council considered the problem of individuals who obtained United Empire Loyalist grants under false pretences. Upon advice of the colonial secretary it was decided that those who already had successfully defrauded the government should be left undisturbed, provided they had improved their lands and behaved properly. Care was to be taken, though, not to repeat the mistakes (Patterson, 48). In the event, even after the abolition of the land boards in 1794 successful frauds were perpetuated to an extent disturbing to the government. The frauds were not perpetuated solely by Americans coming north and posing as loyalists but also by the loyalists themselves. In 1799 the government issued a broadside saying that there was reason to believe that "very frequent frauds have been committed by persons who are entitled to land free of expense having asked for and received the same two and three times over" (Marie Tremaine, A Bibliography of Canadian Imprints [Toronto: University of Toronto Press 1952], 564).

76 The land boards were abolished by Simcoe in November 1794. Their power of recommending grants of single lots was vested in the individual local magistrates, larger grants coming under direct central control (Gates, Land Policies in Upper Canada, 29–30). Large grants continued to be made, more in Grenville than Leeds, however (See "Docket Book of Grants of Land, Home, Eastern, Western and Midland districts, 1793–98," AO, RG 1, ser. C-I-8, 1). With the slacking of the land thirst of the original loyalist settlers, the size of grants diminished sharply. Thus, the average-sized grant made in Grenville county in 1808 was 205 acres, and in Leeds 195 (Report on Canadian Archives, 1893, 9).

swings and the willingness of an earlier generation to credit involvement in local civic activities to a form of selfless public service is being replaced with a cynicism that depicts most agencies of local government as "agencies of social control," a phrase which is often code for upper-class tyranny. This latter interpretation is especially fashionable in British historical writing about eighteenth- and nineteenth-century government and is increasingly producing its Canadian derivatives. There is some use in both the old and the new views, but as far as the society here being studied is concerned, each of these views is a mere caricature. The operation of the local government system is best understood in terms neither of moral approbation nor of ideologically based condemnation but only on local terms which are described below.

The local civic arrangements were certainly agencies of social control and few citizens would have disagreed with the belief that a system of limiting violence, protecting property, punishing fraud, and providing for such basic amenities as roads was necessary. No one had to impose a system of local government on the loyalists; they demanded it. As early as April 1785 the leading settlers in what is now eastern Ontario (then Quebec), headed by Sir John Johnson, petitioned the Crown for the substitution of English for French law and for the creation of a county or district system of local government.[77] This petition was repeated, with tertiary additions, in April 1787.[78] The settlers received most of what they wanted in a series of enactments of 1788–91 inclusive. In asking for reasonably sized local governmental districts and in petitioning for the English system of law, the loyalists were implicitly asking for the introduction of the English system of local government by justices of the peace. Indeed, it is clear that they appointed "magistrates" – a contemporary synonym for JPs – as early as 1786 in some locales, even though there was at that time no provision in statute law for such an office.[79] The English system as adopted in Upper Canada is

77 Printed in whole in A.C. Casselman, "Pioneer Settlements," in *Canada and its Provinces*, ed. Adam Shortt and Arthur G. Doughty (Toronto: Publishers' Association of Canada 1913–17), 17 (1914): 30–5.

78 This petition was also signed by five leading loyalists from west of Cataraqui. It is reproduced in whole in Casselman, 35–9. This second petition was itself partly based on the original of 1785 (which was duplicated and sent again to the Crown authorities) and partly on a letter sent to Sir John Johnson from the "magistrates" assembled at New Oswegatchie, 18 December 1786. For the letter see Adam Shortt and Arthur G. Doughty, *Documents Relating to the Constitutional History of Canada, 1759–1791* (Ottawa: King's Printer 1918), part II, 945–6.

79 See the magistrates' letter, cited above, note 78. The eighteenth-century

too well known to require much description.[80] Justices of the peace were appointed by the central authorities. They were convened at varying intervals (originally four times a year, whence the common misnomer "quarter session" for a meeting of the JPS) and in their collective capacity simultaneously controlled most matters of local government and administered justice in minor criminal cases. The remarkable thing about this system of local government is that it was based upon a model which had evolved over the centuries in the manicured and ordered English countryside, yet it was transported to the Upper Canadian wilderness with only minor modification. Surprisingly, it worked, chiefly because the English system of local government was a system of *mixed* social control providing exactly what was required in the new regions, a combination of local civic management and the control of anti-social behaviour. Conditioned as we are to believe that specialization is the key to efficiency, it is easy to miss the fundamental and admirable efficiency of a system of local government in which a group of substantial and perhaps sapient citizens could meet at, say, six-weekly intervals and in a single meeting set a rate for the local highway, let a bridge contract, try several cases of assault and battery, and grant a licence to a tavern keeper.[81]

English use of the word "magistrate" to mean justice of the peace should not be confused with the nineteenth-century Irish usage, in which a magistracy was a paid office in contradistinction to the unpaid justice of the peace; The English usage was a synonym for justice of the peace: the Irish was virtually an antonym.

80 The standard treatise is J.H. Aitchison, "The Development of Local Government in Upper Canada, 1783–1850" (PH D diss., University of Toronto 1953). More conveniently available is Aitchison's "The Municipal Corporations Act of 1849, Ontario," which, despite its title, has a good deal of material on early local government (*Canadian Historical Review* 30 [1949]: 107–22). See also Adam Shortt, "Municipal History, 1791–1867," in Shortt and Doughty, 18: 403–52 and G.P. de T. Glazebrook, "The Origins of Local Government," in *Aspects of Nineteenth-Century Ontario: Essays Presented to James J. Talman*, ed. F.H. Armstrong, H.A. Stevenson, and J.D. Wilson (Toronto: University of Toronto Press 1974), 36–47. The following early statutes (UC) are especially important: 32 Geo. III c.4, 32 Geo. III c.6, 32 Geo. III c.8, 33 Geo. III c.8, 33 Geo. III c.2, 33 Geo. III c.3, 33 Geo. III c.4, 33 Geo. III c.6.

81 The criminal and various higher courts are not being discussed here. These courts dealt with serious forms of social deviance and matters of "high law". Unlike the quarter sessions, they were not part of any discrete local social system. Their judges were governmental functionaries, not locals acting in their roles as citizens, as were the JPS. An admirable series of articles on the various early courts was written by William R. Riddell. See especially "Criminal Courts and Law in Early (Upper) Canada," *Ontario Historical Society: Papers and Records* 22 (1925): 210–21; "The 'Ordinary' Court of Chancery in Upper

The men appointed as justices of the peace were the economically dominant figures in the area. In the case of the Johnstown district, the men who, by virtue of their appointment by the lieutenant governor, attended the first general sessions for the district included Solomon Jones, Ephraim Jones, Joel Stone, and William Fraser, each of whom has been encountered earlier. James Breakenridge, lieutenant of Leeds county, joined them before the session was over. All were names of weight in the local area prior to their appointment as JPS.[82]

A false syllogism can easily be constructed from the preceding two points, namely, that one is viewing a system of social control forced upon the middle and lower orders by and to the advantage of the local élite. Such a conclusion is based upon two unspoken minor premises in the syllogism, neither of which can actually be accepted, (A) that the JPS were imposed, not merely appointed, from above, and (B) that the JPS, the system they embodied, and the actions they carried out were not desired by the bulk of the population. Premise A is not acceptable because it is based upon the notion that someone who is not directly chosen by ballot is therefore not representative of this community. In fact, eighteenth-century British politics were based on the idea of virtual representation and contemporaries would have found incomprehensible the idea that direct election was a proper way to choose a true representative of the people, since in their view, the mob would elect the person who most pandered to their base prejudices. To impose twentieth-century conceptions of direct democracy upon a system established in the late eighteenth century is anachronistic in the extreme. Locally a person such as Joel Stone was a perpetual JP and in practice became the representative of Leeds and Lansdowne at the quarter sessions, all without elections. He was permanently

---

Canada," *Ontario Historical Society: Papers and Records* 22 (1925): 222–38; "The Prerogative Court in Upper Canada," *Ontario Historical Society: Papers and Records* 23 (1926): 397–412. See also the papers by Riddell republished from the *Canadian Law Times* as *Upper Canada Sketches: Incidents in the Early Times of the Province* (Toronto: Carswell Co. 1922).

82 "Johnstown District, General Quarter Sessions Minutes, 1800–1818," AO, RG 22, ser 7, entries for 22 and 24 April 1800. This was the first session of the Johnstown district. Earlier there had been a court of quarter sessions for the district of Lunenburgh (var: Luneburgh) whose first recorded meeting was 15 June 1789. The Lunenburgh district became the Eastern district in 1792 and the Johnstown district was carved out of it in 1800. On the pre-1800 arrangement see Marjorie E. Lyons, "Elizabethtown: A Typical St. Lawrence River Township, some phases of its settlement and development to 1850" (MA diss., Queen's University, Kingston 1935), 53–4.

resident in the township and had spent more of his own money and energy on improving his property than had any other individual. As long as the governing officials of Upper Canada did not impose JPS upon the local communities but instead chose them from among the existing local leaders (as certainly was the case in the Johnstown district between 1800 and 1816), the JP system of government was not dissonant with the local social structure but was a logical outgrowth of it.

Premise B is unacceptable because there is no convincing evidence that the locals abstained from the system of civic administration. Case after case shows the opposite situation that the JPS provided social services that the individual inhabitants desired, sometimes desperately. Certainly desperation was the feeling of those who had to deal with Lewis Nadeaux in 1797. Nadeaux assaulted and beat Samuel Osborn, a master mariner on the St Lawrence, and when Joel Stone, as JP, had him confined for the night he escaped and went to the Osborn home. Finding only the wife and small children at home, he demanded and received a gill of rum from the terrified woman, and then left, or seemed to have done so. But after he had disappeared the children discovered that the house was alight. It burned. Nadeaux was gaoled but was so violent that when he came to trial in September Joel Stone himself appeared before another JP and James Breakenridge, the deputy lieutenant of the county, stated that he was personally in great fear because of the violent threat made against himself and his property by Nadeaux, and pleaded for Nadeaux to be kept confined.[83] Less dramatic, but clearly of great concern to the individuals involved, were the scores of cases of assault, or assault and trespass, that fill the quarter sessions minutes. In responding to these claims for protection and redress, and to parallel cases involving everything from petty larceny to embezzlement or libel, the quarter sessions were providing a much demanded service.[84] A simple indication that the system

---

83 (Draft) minute by Joel Stone, 17 April 1797; (copy) Joel Stone to John White, 12 September 1797, and affidavit of Joel Stone, 20 September 1797 (AO, Stone papers).

84 This brief list is taken from the several hundred cases recorded in "Johnstown District General Quarter Sessions Minutes, 1800–1818." These minutes are spare and are not transcripts but merely records of charge and outcome. They leave no doubt, however, of the demand for a service to redress grievances. In theory, the quarter sessions had unlimited criminal jurisdiction, but in practice all capital felonies and most felonies of a serious nature such as sodomy, rape, murder, and grand larceny were passed on to the higher professional courts. See Riddell, "A Criminal Circuit in Upper Canada a Century Ago," in *Upper Canada Sketches*, 34 n1 and 107–8.

was not imposed upon an unwilling people is the construction of the district gaol, not primarily by a compulsory levy on the rate payers, but by voluntary subscriptions.[85] As for other services, the most important, bridge building and road provision, involved the imposition of a local rate which grumblingly the populace paid; there are few cases of tax sales for non-payment of rates.[86] The system provided many other services, including the performance of marriages in isolated areas[87] and the administration of oaths, and under the aegis of the court of general sessions a "court of requests" was established in each locality for the recovery of small debts.[88]

85 AO, RG 22, ser. 7, "Court of General Session – Johnstown District, Sundry Municipal Papers," Box D, "List of Subscribers for the Building of the Court House and Gaol at Elizabethtown, 1805–1818."

86 It should be noted, though, that temporary non-payment was not uncommon. However, the rates were low, being limited to a penny in the pound rateable value and confined to roads, highways, and some civic expenses such as a contribution to the salary of the local member of the legislative assembly. In the Abstract Index of Deeds, there are only two occurrences up to 31 December 1815 that conceivably could be interpreted as tax seizure of properties.

87 The general sessions also were in charge of licensing non-Anglican and non-Kirk ministers to perform marriages. On the legal background see the following articles by William Riddell, "The Criminal Law in Reference to Marriage in Upper Canada," *Ontario Historical Society: Papers and Records* 21 (1924): 233–5; "The Law of Marriage in Upper Canada," *Canadian Historical Review* 2 (1921): 226–48; "Quaker Marriages in Upper Canada," *Ontario Historical Society: Papers and Records* 24 (1927): 507–11; "Criminal Courts and Law in Early (Upper) Canada," *Ontario Historical Society: Papers and Records* 22 (1925): 215.

88 The court of requests for the recovery of small debts is an excellent example of the responsiveness of the civic system to local needs. One of the most pressing and vexing problems facing individual settlers was how to collect small sums without personally having to resort to force. The courts of request, created in 1792 (32 Geo. III, c.6) provided that in each district a number of "divisions" be created, where two justices of the peace could judge claims for debts. At first, jurisdiction was limited to debts of not more than forty shillings, although this was raised to five pounds in 1816 (34 Geo. III, c.2). The important characteristics of these courts were, first, that they met regularly, usually on two Saturdays each month; second, that they were inexpensive; costs for a summons being sixpence and the cost of judgment one shilling; third, the divisions of the court were plastic and were increased and rearranged as population grew. Thus, when in July 1801 the court of requests was established for the newly formed Johnstown district, it had five divisions. This was increased to eight in 1807, and several times after 1815 new court divisions were added. Leeds and Lansdowne township was split. The front of Leeds and Lansdowne was grouped with Elizabethtown and Yonge, the rear of Leeds and Lansdowne with Bastard, Kitley, and the largely uninhabited areas north of the Rideau. See "Johnstown District General Quarter Sessions Minutes, 1800–1818," especially sessions of 14 July 1801 and 19 May 1807; J.H. Aitchison, "The Court of Requests in Upper Canada," *Ontario History* 41 (1949): 125–32; Pringle, 300–5.

There is a possibility, therefore, that the JP system of government provided a system of limited, voluntary, and consensual compacts among the local inhabitants and that virtual representation served their needs as well as, or better than direct electoral democracy.

Against this suggestion it may be objected that the English quarter session system of local government had been introduced coercively, to the exclusion of the New England system of democratic township meetings. In a limited sense, this is true. The act of 1793 that delineated the function of township meetings made the calling of a meeting contingent upon the agreement of two JPs, and originally the township meeting was envisaged as only an annual affair summoned to fill minor township offices: a clerk, two assessors, and one rates collector were to be appointed, two to six overseers of highways and roads and one pound keeper selected, and in areas with an Anglican church two churchwardens installed. Except for fixing the minimum height of roadside fence, the town meeting had no legislative power.[89] This toothlessness of township government stemmed from the great, indeed excessive, fear which the central government authorities had of anything which smacked of republicanism.

However, it does not follow from these facts that the local community actually wanted direct electoral control of local government.[90] If they had, it is reasonable to expect that they would have used the existing system as their forum, and that the "democratic" forces would have taken charge of the township system and then expanded their influence from there. In fact, the populace of the Johnstown district, far from wanting more involvement in electoral government, wanted less. The township meetings were unpopular, in part because travel to and from the meeting in an era of primitive transport was time-consuming and, more importantly, because the local offices were onerous and unpleasant. The 1793 act which set up the township meeting included a provision for fining anyone who was elected to an office and refused to serve. In May 1805, Joel Stone, acting as a JP, summoned three men, two of whom had been elected assessors and one a collector of rates for Elizabethtown, to appear and either take their oaths of office or be fined. The three appeared but would not take the oaths. They were fined and new assessors and a collector were appointed.[91]

89 33 Geo. III, c.2 (UC); Landon, "The Evolution of Local Government in Ontario," 2–3.
90 Glazebrook develops this point at greater length. "The Origins of Local Government," 38–42.
91 There is a nice sting to the story. The three men who were fined for refusing to do the jobs for which they were chosen by vote of the township meeting were

Actually, one can plausibly argue that, far from being shut out of their own governance, the citizens of Leeds and Lansdowne township suffered from an excess of opportunities for participation. The number of available civic offices was very high in relation to the actual population. Under the legislation creating the quarter sessions and the subordinate township government, there was a possibility of thirteen township offices; in practice, there were also at least two JPS from the township, in addition to one or more constables appointed by sessions and a varying number of overseers of roads and highways. To this one should add the frequently convened twelve man petit jury and the larger grand jury which drew men from every township in the district.[92] All these offices existed in relation to a population of 103 male property owners in 1805.[93] In addition, the incumbents of most township offices were changed annually and the various juries empanelled and discharged several times a year. Most male residents must thus have had experience of participating in local government arrangements several times in a lifetime spent in the area. When this is compared to the modern situation, in which only a minuscule portion of any population in Canada actually holds municipal office or sits in courts of justice, it is obvious why there was no need for direct electoral democracy. In an area such as the township of Leeds and Lansdowne there was virtually no distance between the governed and the governing. As with face-to-face business deals, a limited social contract was possible whereby the citizens of the township

---

themselves justices of the peace: Samuel Wright, Truman Hicock, and James Breakenridge. They did not at all object to being removed from the unpleasant civic offices, but they fought the fines on the technical grounds that the constables did not make a proper return of the meeting, Hicock on the additional grounds that he was not a freeholder in the township of Elizabethtown and Breakenridge on the grounds that he, as a JP and the deputy lieutenant of the country, was not liable for such service. Stone, heading the court, thereupon fined them each two pounds and the matter was referred to higher courts on appeal. See letters of Joel Stone to James Breakenridge, 23 May 1805, and to Samuel Wright and to Truman Hicock; (copy) minute by Joel Stone of a special session of 24 May 1805; and "A True Copy of my Records as Given to the Solicitor General August 1805" (PAC, McDonald-Stone papers, nos. 612–620).

92 This necessarily imprecise listing (necessarily, because the practice changes year by year, township by township) is derived from 33 Geo. III, c.2 and from the "Johnstown District General Quarter Sessions Minute, 1800–1818," passim. If anything, in comparison to other townships, the estimate of the number of functioning local civic offices is low: in Augusta township in 1813, for example, the number of participants in the civic process was greatly increased by the appointment of fourteen fence viewers. (Ibid., entry for 18 May 1813.)

93 Computed from Abstract Index of Deeds.

paid taxes and served in tiresome civic offices in return for that most basic of governmental "products," civil order. Local government, like economic life, was formed of clear, simple, volitional, and limited bargains.

8

It is arguable that the settlers possessed an "ideology" which made them act as they did. Properly used, ideology refers to an articulate political viewpoint that both interprets the past and gives prescriptions for the future. In this sense the average settler in the township had no ideology at all. Ideology is also sometimes improperly used to refer to fragmented and only partially articulated political and social attitudes which can be stitched together by an historian into an ideology which the contemporary individual did not know he had. Evidence for a loyalist ideology in this meaning of the word is sometimes constructed from snippets in the contemporary press, including the Tory press in the American colonies before the Revolution. This process is objectionable, in part because the attempt to discern an ideological pattern that was invisible to people who lived at the time too easily degenerates into an exercise in the imposition of the historian himself upon the past, and in part because the evidence employed is wildly unrepresentative. The written word, whether in newspaper editorial, printed broadside, or pamphlet, cannot be taken as indicative of the viewpoint of any given population: the one thing we know for certain about people who publish their views is that they are atypical. Even if one could find enough material to posit an ideology for the people of the Johnstown district in general and of Leeds and Lansdowne in particular, it would be only of antiquarian interest, because it would not be the most economical explanation of the population's behaviour consonant with the data. Ockham's razor cuts through history as it does through all social science. The simplest explanation is the best, and thus reference to ideologies is unnecessary. In the local area under study the people were not called upon to give allegiance to any system of local government as an abstract entity. Rather, they made a deal, a concrete arrangement undertaken in the same way as a trade in economic life. It was a very limited and practical form of cooperation.

The fact that the early inhabitants of Leeds and Lansdowne township behaved in civic arrangements as they did in economic matters implicitly makes a statement about their collective culture that could be misconstrued as derogatory. In treating civic and

economic relations as a system of short-term contracts between each individual and his neighbours, the citizens showed a preference for the concrete and the immediate rather than for the abstract and the long-term. To note this is not to criticize an intellectual failing but merely to describe a cultural fact. It is only in the present century that the majority of people in the industrialized world have come to perceive their economic and civic systems in terms of abstract entities and long spans of time. In this context, the development of the large impersonal corporations, which is an abstract entity, has a juridical personality of its own, and is vested with rights and liabilities that transcend the contracts or actions of any specific individual, has forced a quantum leap in the popular culture. By its very existence, the corporation teaches its employees, shareholders, customers, and suppliers that an abstract economic entity can exist and have longevity. This is in sharp contrast to the partnership of the eighteenth and nineteenth centuries which typically was small in number of associates and in any case was destroyed the moment any one of the principals deceased or decided to withdraw from the original contract.

Similarly, it is clear that in the eighteenth and nineteenth centuries the majority of people did not, and probably could not, conceive of government in abstract terms (whether the majority can do so today is a moot point). Walter Bagehot's classic *The English Constitution* (1867) brings this point home. The value of the monarchy, Bagehot convincingly argued, was that it allowed the vast majority of people, those incapable of understanding any theory of government, to feel allegiance to the Queen, a concrete embodiment of the abstract concept of sovereignty.

In Leeds and Lansdowne township it would be an indecency to patronize the isolated inhabitants of a seemingly vast and often frightening wilderness for not thinking abstractly, as it would be an offensive condescension to ascribe to them an ideology which they never held. One should not devalue the early loyalist community on the grounds that they did not think as we do, any more than one would condemn the early Desert Fathers for not being Thomists. The loyalists had minds of their own, tough, concrete, self-protecting.

9

Inevitably, contracts came apart, partnerships dissolved, and people sometimes came to hate each other. Some of the breakdowns in the system of limited social and economic alliances are of interest in themselves, and all are culturally diagnostic. Just as the aetiology of

a disease tells us how a healthy body should operate, so inter-personal conflicts reveal both the stress points and the strengths of the local social system.

For example, although continual competition among individuals was the impelling norm of the social machinery, it had to be limited, for competitive behaviour could tear apart the mechanism. The case of Sir John Johnson and Joel Stone struggling, but not fighting, over valuable lands at the mouth of the Gananoque River is instructive in this regard. Stone (and his fair-weather partner, Daniel Jones) had priority on his side in claiming the river mouth, for he had had a preliminary survey done in the winter of 1786–7 and had received a government grant of several hundred acres in the Gananoque area dated 14 July 1787.[94] The private surveying of the lands before the government survey was later held to be improper, although it seems that Stone made an honest mistake in his interpretation of the land regulations. Thus, although Stone's claim was superior in terms of priority, it was inferior in terms of procedure. Sir John Johnson became aware somewhat later of the desirability of the Gananoque River falls and estuary and he prepared an application for the land in late 1788. In early January 1789 Stone's agent in Quebec, Isaac Ogden, sent him the disquieting word that Sir John was petitioning for the land. Sir John had promised to build mills, so Ogden made the same promise without even waiting for authorization. He presently recognized the real situation, that Stone might have priority of discovery but Sir John had political power, and strongly suggested to Stone that he compromise with Sir John rather than fight, for "remember, if the matter is left to the council that he has many friends of great interest there."[95]

In response to the urging of Ogden, Stone left Cornwall for Quebec on 1 February 1789 and directly presented his own case to the authorities.[96] As one would expect, he was initially outraged that Sir John would try to appropriate the land that he had had surveyed and at first he intended to take the case to courts in England if necessary.[97] For a time he was convinced (as he himself

---

94 Nineteenth Report of the Department of Public Records, Archives of Ontario, 80.

95 Isac Ogden to Joel Stone, 5 January 1789 (PAC, McDonald-Stone papers, no. 363).

96 McDonald, 23.

97 Joel Stone to Daniel Jones, 31 January 1789, cited by McDonald, 23. It is at this point that Daniel Jones slides from the scene. Stone, in the letter of 31 January 1789, asks Jones to put up half the cash for expenses in pursuing the claim, otherwise Stone will proceed for himself only. Apparently Jones then withdrew.

later admitted to Sir John) that Johnson was basing his claim-jumping upon the surveys and plans that Stone had made at his own expense.[98] He felt double-crossed, for he maintained that not long before Sir John filed his petition he had come to recognize Stone's claim and had taken special pains to send an intermediary "to make myself easy for it should be the last thing he would do to disturb me in my right."[99]

Stone, though, was a realist. He recognized Sir John's great political power and when Sir John's counsel put forward to the authorities the argument that Stone had acted improperly in spying out the land before the official government survey was made[100] Stone realized that he was on shaky ground. A prudent retreat was necessary,[101] and Sir John let him retreat with dignity. He did not try to banish him from the field, but instead, during the spring of 1789, the two men worked out a compromise that the council ratified on 14 July 1789. Sir John received the east bank of the Gananoque River mouth, generally conceded to be the most desirable, and Stone the west, and the property division ran to the very centre of the river, so that both had water rights.[102] Later, Sir John tried to trade Stone one thousand acres on Amherst Island for Stone's west bank property, but the offer was declined.[103] Conceivably, Sir John could have used his superior political strength and the technical impropriety of Stone's early survey to dispossess him of his entire claim. Equally, Stone could have tied up Sir John's claim by going to the English courts and thereby initiating a legal snarl that probably would have consumed a decade or longer. By compromising, each man avoided his respective difficulties. More importantly for our purposes, they both indicated a recognition that there were implicit

98 Joel Stone to Sir John Johnson, 13 November 1790 (PAC, McDonald-Stone, no 436).

99 (Draft) Joel Stone to ———— , 29 January 1789 (PAC, McDonald-Stone, no. 372).

100 (Copy) Council's Brief on behalf of Sir John Johnson, 10 February 1789 (PAC, McDonald-Stone, no. 376).

101 In a face-saving letter to his agent, Stone said that it would be easier to fight Sir John, "did I not revere him as a character of universal honor and integrity," a statement that can only be understod in the context of Stone's having come to believe that his agent was less than entirely confidential. (Copy) Joel Stone to Isaac Ogden, 1 March 1789 (PAC, McDonald-Stone papers, no. 385). In letters written by Stone to Sir John after this date Stone is deferential to the point of obsequiousness.

102 Joel Stone to ———— , 19 September 1791 (PAC, McDonald-Stone, no. 42); Sir John Johnson to Joel Stone, 30 October 1790 (PAC, McDonald-Stone, no. 433).

103 Sir John Johnson to Joel Stone, 30 October 1790; Joel Stone to Sir John Johnson, 13 November 1790 (PAC, McDonald-Stone, no. 436).

constraints on economic aggression to avoid rending the very thin social fabric of the new townships.

At times, however, hyper-aggressive individuals stretched the fabric almost to the breaking point. One such case involved Charles Jones, eldest son of Ephraim Jones, and Joel Stone in 1819, although it had its roots as far back as 1804, when Peter Rosback of the township died and left a widow, Margaret. She applied to Stone to become her bondsman in order to allow her to administer her deceased husband's property and Stone agreed. This duty was unpleasant for him as he did not receive any recompense for his expenses, although there were frequent legal transactions, "owing," as he noted, "to the said Margaret's frequent marriages."[104] Nevertheless, Stone maintained his guardianship for well over a decade. In 1816, in front of witnesses, he personally took possession of cattle and other livestock that had been the property of the deceased Peter Rosback (or were the descendants of the livestock Rosback had owned). He did this on Margaret's application on behalf of her sixteen-year-old son, who was the direct heir to the estate, and was to keep them in trust until the boy came of legal age.

In 1819, however, Stone's trusteeship was aborted through the actions of Charles Jones, the markedly avaricious son of Commissary Jones. Stone loathed the younger Jones: in 1816 he had written to a military official that "there has been many things said of Charles Jones, Esq., for many years past respecting his oppressing the poor, taking away their lands, making himself opulent on their ruin etc. during the war that he raised a company of provincial Dragoons, went away to Halifax and left them and the province when the greatest danger appeared."[105] About Christmas 1819 Jones, who was owed money by one of Widow Rosback's husbands (probably her fourth and latest), a man named Conrad Peterson, obtained a court order to seize the cattle and tangible assets and dispose of them at a sheriff's auction. Stone at once tried to interpose, arguing that the livestock were not Peterson's but were held in trust for the son of the late Peter Rosback. Stone threatened the deputy sheriff in charge of proceedings with gross trespass and put him off for a day. Next day, 30 December, the deputy sheriff came back, stole the unguarded cattle away early in the morning and then opened the

104 Memorandum in Stone's hand, 1820 (PAC, McDonald-Stone, item 1232). Reproduced in Hawke, 76. Unless otherwise noted, the factual information on this affray and details in this and subsequent paragraphs are found in Stone's memoranda (1819–20) (PAC, McDonald-Stone, nos. 1232–1234).

105 (Copy) Joel Stone to Nathaniel Coffin, 21 November 1816 (Queen's University Archives, Stone papers).

auction. This time Charles Jones was present, and in what Stone called "very rude and abusive language toward myself" and "very absolute language to the sheriff" ordered him to proceed, "saying in an exulting manner that he took the whole responsibility on himself." The deputy sheriff did proceed, and, although several people were present, not one of them bid on any of the property. Article after article was knocked down to Charles Jones, who took each for whatever trivial price he fancied, a young mare for forty shillings, two cows for forty shillings each, and so on. At day's end an old mare was left behind in a stable and the household furniture that had been seized but not fancied by Jones was left in an open field. Jones took everything else.

The end of this nasty business is not dramatically or morally satisfying. Understandably furious with Charles Jones's apparent violation of the legal trusteeship of the Rosback inheritance, Stone urged young Rosback to prosecute, lent him his attorney's fees and doubtless was pleased when the young man was awarded damages. However, as a by-product of the legal process it was discovered that the ever popular Margaret Rosback had given letters of administration on the Rosback estate to one of the children of her third husband (a man named Henry Miller). This man now sued Nicholas Rosback and Joel Stone jointly and won fifty pounds. Such episodes, initiated by greed and compounded by opportunism and incompetence, were highly destructive of the trust necessary to make the local economic and social system work.

Equally, anything which brought into question the integrity of the local civic-juridical system, the immediate protector of property rights and of personal liberties, necessarily reduced the public trust. One extraordinary barrage of charges and countercharges in court deserves mention. On 21 May 1811, Billa Flint, a prominent innkeeper in Elizabethtown who in the previous session had been selected as foreman of the grand jury, was served with a bench warrant for blasphemy. James Breakenridge, the deputy lieutenant for the county and a JP, was charged with extortion. Levi Soper, a leading settler to the north of Leeds and Lansdowne, was charged with assault and battery and with an additional account (with four other individuals) of riotous assault. Joel Stone was charged with compounding larceny. What the occasion can have been that produced such a panoply of charges against the most substantial of local citizens exceeds the historical record and taxes the imagination, but the striking fact is that both Breakenridge and Stone sat on the bench the next day as justices of the peace. In later outcome Billa Flint in August 1811 was judged not guilty, and in the August assize Levi Soper was found not guilty of assault and battery, but

guilty of riotous assault and was fined £5 15s. But the cases of Stone and Breakenridge, who were charged with serious felonies, were dropped from the record entirely, the charges laid against them were not tried, and no further notice was taken of them. Perhaps justice thereby was done, but certainly it was not seen to have been done. [106]

The least successful activities of the local government system seem to have been in controlling the abuse of liquor, although the records do not permit us to gauge directly the degree of alcohol abuse in the local community. A great deal of effort was expended in trying to control the spirit trade, far in excess of what would have been necessary solely to raise revenue. Annual licences were granted by the quarter sessions to tavern keepers and to owners of shops that sold spirits (usually in connection with a general store). Sureties for good behaviour had to be lodged by innkeepers, ten pounds by owners and five pounds by each of two additional bondsmen. A tally of the licences in the Johnstown district for 1817 shows sixty-two tavern licences, twenty-nine shop permits, and four licences for stills, a large number for the limited population. In Leeds and Lansdowne township in 1819 there were seven licensed innkeepers and an unspecified number of spirit shops. [107] In order to control the spirits trade, the quarter sessions appointed an inspector of shops, taverns, and stills. In 1814, a typical year in the district, he charged six illegal sellers of spirits, three of whom were residents of Leeds and Lansdowne township. [108]

The seriousness of alcohol as a social problem was also shown by the number of assault cases in the quarter session minutes, often page after page. Unfortunately, the JPs did not deal with drunkenness as an offence in itself and the records do not specify those instances in which drink contributed towards social violence. In a frontier society there was always plenty to fight about – straying animals, uncertain property lines, allegedly stolen timber, and so on – but it is not unreasonable to suggest that drink, drinking, and drunkenness were at the heart of many of the brawls and that most men with black eyes and swollen jaws also had hangovers. [109]

106 "Johnstown District General Quarter Sessions Minutes, 1800–1818," entries for 21 May 1811, 22 May 1811, 13 August 1811, and 14 August 1811.

107 "Returns of Tavern Licenses, 1817–29," (AO, RG 22, ser. 7), Court of Johnstown District, Sundry Municipal Papers, Box C, entries for 1817; "Registers of Innkeepers, 1818–43," (AO, RG 22, ser. 7), vol. A, entries for 1818–19.

108 Reports by Oliver Everts, inspector of shop, tavern and still licences (AO, Solomon Jones papers).

109 A general article of relevance, albeit somewhat censorious in tone, is M.A. Garland and J.J. Talman, "Drinking Habits and the Rise of the Temperance Agitation in Upper Canada prior to 1840," Ontario Historical Society: Papers and Records 27 (1931): 341–64.

10

Another apparent failing of the system, the inability of the justices of the peace to control smuggling, may be used to prove the rule put forward in section 8, that the local civic government was not an ideologically derived system, but rather a set of short-term and pragmatic contracts entered into voluntarily by individual citizens. The St Lawrence River was an ideal avenue for illegal commerce, since it is easily navigable in summer by small boats and in winter the ice forms a perfect highway. Whatever the alleged differences of Americans and loyalists, they traded quite happily with each other, but the illicit trade back and forth across the St Lawrence cost the Upper Canadian government revenue. In theory customs duties were payable on most goods, but closing down the trade was more expensive than the duties were worth. The trade flowed in well-developed clandestine channels. One road in Elizabethtown township, running north to the Rideau country, was known as "smuggler's highway" and was said to carry more contraband, both north and south, than any similar road in Canada. According to probably accurate local tradition (collected from eyewitnesses) there was a major wholesale trade from the United States to the Rideau district. In return for tobacco, cotton, and other American goods, the Upper Canadians smuggled live horses, lumber, and potash south. From 1816 onwards (when increasingly stringent laws against trade with the Yankees were invoked) until the mid-1820s, the most frequent conviction by the court of sessions, except for common assault, was for smuggling. A local judicial ritual developed whereby the person charged did not even appear. The particulars of his illicit importation were read into the record and the court took title to them and had them sold. Pork, flour, and salt were the items most commonly seized from smugglers but other items were taken: a shearing machine, a pair of cards for yarn-making, dry apples, and, of course, intoxicating spirits. The apprehended citizens more often than not were substantial landowners. Smuggling was a serious and almost respectable business.[110]

110 The records of the "Johnstown District General Quarter Sessions Minutes, 1800–1818," "1820–22," "1823," and "1824–27" have so many smuggling cases that they preclude specific citation. In 1814 Samuel Sherwood, second son of Justus Sherwood, decided to sell across the border an excess of rum that he could not trade locally. (I am grateful to Shirley Spragge of Queen's University for this Archives information.) Smuggling, clearly, was not a lower-class affair. An interesting discussion based on oral tradition is found in Edwin A. McKim, "Land Marks by the Riverside," unpublished typescript, c. 1933, in Library of University of Western Ontario, 7–8.

The reason for the inability of the quarter sessions to control the smuggling industry was the locals' refusal to accept laws against smuggling as part of the social contract that they had with each other. Had they been instinctively deferential to central government statute or committed to an alleged "loyalist ideology" of an ordered society, they probably would have obeyed the smuggling laws, however grumblingly. Actually, no amount of external coercion, save perhaps a heavy military investment of the border, would have stopped the trade; whatever the law said on paper, it was not part of the bargain they made with each other, and in fact it ran counter to the entrpreneurial individualism which was accepted as the basis of the local economic system.

Therefore, this apparent exception does indeed confirm the rule, for it indicates that, although legal statutes might be engrossed by the central governments, they had to be tacitly ratified by the various local populations or they would be ignored. This implies that in viewing the earliest Upper Canadian communities one should not look so much at statute law as at customary law, that is, at the actual practices which prevailed at the local level, whether or not they were previously articulated in statute. Further, one should emphasize not the centre but the locality. And, if we wish to understand the behavioural norms of the society, we should look not at the top of the governmental pyramid but at the bottom, where the common man and his local government interacted. The idea that law preceded society must be disregarded. Effective law evolved only upon the basis of widespread social acceptance. If creation of government is one of the most sophisticated of human cooperative activities, then in early Upper Canada the real making of government occurred not within the colonial administration but in scores of individual communities, which in their governance were virtually autochthonous.

II

It is not heartlessly empirical to emphasize behaviour rather than belief. The mythological, ideological, and religious beliefs of a community are significant, but they are not the proper starting point for a study of a community formed *de novo* in the wilderness. Jesus Christ said that "by their fruits shall ye know them" (Matthew 7:20), by which he meant that one should pay more attention to what people do than to what they say, and as he indicated in the parable of the talents (Matthew 25:14–30) that one learns more about a person's soul by seeing how he uses his resources than by

listening to all his protestations of intentions. We learn more about the early inhabitants of Leeds and Lansdowne township by looking at their cash ledgers and land patents than by reading their prayer books, and, similarly, their actions in forming their local government tell us more about what really counted in their society than would an exegesis of the nature of the English constitution as embodied in Upper Canadian statute law.

Within the accepted rules which protected property rights and limited social aggressiveness, particularly against the person, an individual took care of himself and his family as his primary, almost sole, responsibility. One is not here suggesting that we should resurrect what Vernon Fowke calls "The Myth of the Self-Sufficient Canadian Pioneer,"[111] for the evidence is strong that various forms of cooperation were adopted, some economic and some social. Nevertheless, it must be kept in mind that almost always these instances of cooperation were limited, direct, bargained, and of short duration. The cooperation of the society was the cooperation of individuals with individuals. In underscoring the individualistic nature of the earliest frontier society, one is not denying the fact that later in the nineteenth century "English Canadian" society came to emphasize collective authority over individual rights and to limit individual social mobility.[112] However, in the earliest stages, in an "empty" township, such as Leeds and Lansdowne was until 1815, individual effort was characteristic and so was a high degree of opportunity for individual advancement.

The acquisition of real property, especially land, was the *leitmotif* that ran through the behaviour of the settler population of loyalist times. In Leeds and Lansdowne township, land was not merely acquired by the pioneer settlers; in most cases, they retained it. This stands in contrast to the general conception that in Upper Canada there were thousands of parcels of land held by speculators who made their profit by acquiring the land and selling it as quickly as possible for as high a price as possible. This mode of behaviour may

111 V.C. Fowke, "The Myth of the Self-Sufficient Canadian Pioneer," *Transactions of the Royal Society of Canada*, ser. 3, sec. 2, 56 (1962): 23–37. For an intriguing argument concerning the social and economic integrity and durability of pre-commercial farming societies such as Leeds and Lansdowne, see Michael Merrill, "Cash is Good to Eat: Self-Sufficiency and Exchange in the Rural Economy of the United States," *Radical History Review* 7 (1977): 42–66. I am grateful to Professor Bryan Palmer for calling this item to my attention.

112 See Allan Smith, "The Myth of the Self-Made Man in English Canada, 1850–1914," *Canadian Historical Review* 59 (June 1978): 189–219.

indeed have characterized much of Upper Canada,[113] but it certainly was not universal. In Leeds and Lansdowne township, individuals usually acquired land in this period not for short-term resale but for holding and developing into a valuable piece of improved property. The case of Joel Stone and his water rights is the most obvious instance of this kind of behaviour, but it is only one example of a general pattern.

The evidence of land resales shows that this was a valid general pattern of behaviour. Of the patents granted in this period, 1796–1815 inclusive, 61.6 percent (167 of 271) were still in the hands of the original patentees as of 31 December 1815. This is a notably high persistence rate, but it actually understates the degree of continuity in land holdings: old age and death inevitably necessitated the passing of land from one generation to another or the sale of assets to support the retired individual, and in this context neither can be looked upon as evidence of speculative transfer in the accepted meaning of the word. Hence, an "actual" persistence rate of 70 or even 75 percent would seem probable.

On the opposite side of the coin, only 7.7 percent (21 of 271) of the original patents were multiply transferred, that is, patented, sold, and then resold. Such land can be designated as speculative in the usual sense of indicating that someone was trying to turn a profit by purchase and resale. There was some resale speculation in Leeds and Lansdowne townships in this period, but most speculation was of an entirely different sort, the acquisition of land for its direct resource values, whether as farm land, rental property, iron ore manufactory, or mill site. Individuals developed the sites and did not merely buy and resell.

The high persistence rate and the type of land-holding evidence in Leeds and Lansdowne township may be so unusual as to be unique; or the pattern may be typical of a subset of Upper Canadian townships, not settled by the first wave of loyalist settlers but still not so far away from the St Lawrence or Lake Ontario as to be considered mere "wild lands" (titles to which were often bought and sold several times over, sight unseen, by the purchaser). And it well

113 Widdis' analysis of land change in Elizabethtown, the most sophisticated study yet done, clearly indicates this pattern. See 15. A contemporary observer, D'arcy Boulton, summarized the situation in 1805: "in truth, any person capable of advancing money may purchase very low, and sell at an advance of one, or even two hundred percent profit, payable by installments." D'arcy Boulton, *Sketch of His Majesty's Province of Upper Canada* (London: 1805; reprint, Toronto: Baxter Publishing Co. 1961), 8.

may be that this particularly stable land-holding picture held only for the first two or three decades of the development of such townships, prior to the heavy immigration that came after the Napoleonic Wars and made resale of lands a more profitable form of speculation than it previously had been. For whatever reason, the stability is undeniable.

In one regard the land-holding patterns in Leeds and Lansdowne differed from those in the wild lands away from the St Lawrence: there were no great magnates who held thousands of acres of speculative lands. As map 9 indicates, the largest landowner in Leeds and Lansdowne, Susannah Jessup, had only approximately nineteen hundred acres. Even if one lumps together all the individuals indicated on map 9 (which is to say the dozen largest landowners), one finds that they owned only a small proportion of the township. Inconsistencies in the early surveying techniques make a precise calculation impossible, but at most they held 10 percent of the township's land.[114]

12

If the atomistic model of behaviour set forward in this book is accurate, it must apply to almost all members of the local society (there will in any community be a small number of social deviants, but they do not disprove the norm). At this point a crucial test is possible: to see whether the description applies equally to the loyalist and the nonloyalist landholders of Leeds and Lansdowne. If so, the model is confirmed; if not, then some neglected factor, such as ethnicity or political ideology, can be seen as prepotent over the individualistic economics and atomistic social ethic depicted here, and the model will require serious revision or abandonment.

Surprisingly, to raise the question of the composition of the early population of Upper Canada is to discover a massive lacuna in Canadian historical writing. Simply put, no one really knows how many original loyalists there were in Upper Canada, how many "late"

114 Map 9 is designed to indicate the maximum influence of large landowners during the period 1796–1815 inclusive. Thus, it shows the holdings of those who held large parcels at any time up to 31 December 1815. The only exceptions are the cases of individuals who completely left the area and were replaced in their property holdings by other large landowners: the chief example is Wallis Sunderlin who, as discussed earlier in the text, lost his considerable holdings near Furnace Falls as a consequence of his iron manufactory being unprofitable. These lands devolved mostly into the hands of members of the Ephraim Jones family.

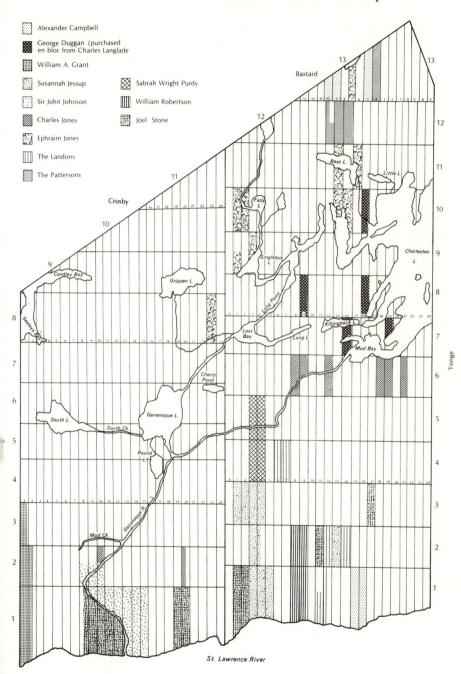

Map 9 Major landholders

loyalists followed, or how many nonloyalist Americans crossed the border from the south. This is a strange black hole in our knowledge, considering the massive literature on the loyalist period and the luminosity of the individuals specializing in the field. Amazingly, the only direct attempts at estimating the total population of Upper Canada were made before 1815 when it was posited that at approximately the time of the war of 1812 there were between 95,000 and 135,000 inhabitants.[115]

Similarly, no one really has anything but the most general view of the ethnic composition of the population, the last plausible (but not very convincing) investigation of this question also having been made before 1815. Because of Governor Simcoe's policy of allowing and tacitly encouraging immigration from the United States from the early 1790s onwards, the loyalist proportion of the population in Upper Canada was probably quite small. If the government's records of 1786 are accurate, there were 5,960 loyalists settled in what became Upper Canada.[116] These were the real hard-shell loyalists. To their number can be added an unknown, but probable, number of later loyalists, who had until mid-1798 to acquire the designation "UE", although one cannot be sure that all of them were loyalists in fact. In any case, the estimates made by Michael Smith in 1812 and after have been taken as acceptable by most Upper Canadian historians, although in my judgment they are so contradictory as to be worthless. Smith, in one of his most quoted estimates, suggested

115 The higher estimate was by Michael Smith in his *A Geographical View of the Province of Canada* (1813), the lower from Joseph Bouchette's *Topographical Description* (1815). A.L. Burt, *The United States and Great Britain and British North America from the Revolution to the Establishment of Peace after the War of 1812* (1940; reprint, New York: Russel and Russel 1961), gives the judgment that Bouchette was the more reliable of the two but was perhaps too conservative in his estimate. This view was adopted by Marcus Lee Hansen, *The Mingling of the Canadian and American People*, vol. 1, *Historical* (New Haven: Yale University Press 1940), who cited Burt as the authoritative source that there were "now about one hundred thousand in 1812" (90). This was not quite what Burt had said. Even if he had read Burt correctly, Hansen still would have been no better off, for Burt had done no research in demography. Yet Hansen's book (which had been prepared for posthumous publication by J.B. Brebner) was cited as an authority ("the most intensive study of population movements between Canada and the United States that has yet appeared"), and Burt's study was cited as an authoritative examination of Upper Canada's population in Fred Landon's *Western Ontario and the American Frontier* (Toronto: The Ryerson Press 1941), 21 n15 and 22 n16. See Note 117 below on the three scholars' use of primary sources.
116 J.J. Talman, "The United Empire Loyalists," in *Profiles of a Province: Studies in the History of Ontario* (Toronto: Ontario Historical Society 1967), 4.

that in 1812 the Upper Canadian population consisted of 20 percent loyalists and their children, 60 percent nonloyalist Americans and their children, and 20 percent immigrants from the British Isles and their children.[117]

117 In one or another of its forms, the three major scholars each endorsed Smith's estimate of the composition of the population (Burt, 181 n25; Landon, 21; Hansen, 90). Their unanimity is suspect. None of the three did any significant demographic research and at best they can claim to have been intuitively perceptive. More impressive than any of these three works was the study of the admirable amateur E.A. Cruikshank, "Immigration from the United States in Upper Canada, 1784–1812 – its Character and Results," *Proceedings of the Thirty-Ninth Annual Convention of the Ontario Educational Association* (1900): 262–83. Cruikshank at least went to the trouble of seeking external verification of Smith's estimate and, through land records, came to his own estimate that there was an immigration from the south of fifty to sixty thousand persons in the first eleven years of the nineteenth century (274).

The trustworthiness of the three men's judgment is seriously undercut when one discovers that they were unaware that their primary source, Michael Smith's book, had gone through several editions, with the result that what he had presented in one edition was contradicted in another. Worse, in the first edition Smith gave two contradictory estimates in the same paragraph, yet none of the three authorities noted this. The six editions of the book are defined in E.A. Cruikshank, "A Study of Disaffection in Upper Canada in 1812–15," *Transactions of the Royal Society of Canada*, sec. 2, 6 (1912): 17–18 n3. Burt (180 n25) used the statement from the April 1813 edition of the Smith book ([Hartford: Hale and Hosmer], 52–3) that one-fifth (20 percent) of the Upper Canadian population were United Kingdom immigrants and their children, one-sixth (16.7 percent) were loyalists and their children, and the rest (61.3 percent) were non-loyalist Americans and their children. Landon (21) and Hansen (90) used a different section of the same paragraph from the same edition, which is contradictory and gives (when the separate fractions are reduced) 20 percent United Kingdom citizens and their children, 20 percent loyalists and their children, and 60 percent non-loyalist Americans and their children.

This contradictory use of the only primary source the three scholars examined might indicate a bit of laziness but no serious flaw, since the two sets of figures are not very far apart. However, fatally for our confidence in the figures, they ignored that in the August 1813 edition ([New York: Pelsue and Gold], 61) Smith, while giving 136,000 for the total population (an upward revision of 1,000), did not give any breakdown of the population. Then, in the 1814 edition ([Baltimore: P. Mauro], 51 n), he gave the following radically new estimates: six parts "natives of the United States and their children born in the British dominions of North America" – that is, 60 percent total for both non-loyalist Americans and their children *and* loyalists and their children – and four parts "Europeans and their children," a doubling, from 20 percent to 40 percent of this figure. This therefore suggests that Smith's contemporary data on ethnicity are not trustworthy and that the material has been improperly used by later historians.

As for Bouchette, the three scholars ignore the fact that, in a later publica-

It seems better to leave the shaky population figures for the whole province and concentrate on a single township for which we have solid data: it is a relatively easy task to relate all the transactions covered on the Abstract Index of Deeds to the standard lists of UE loyalists,[118] and then to see if loyalist and nonloyalists behaved

---

tion, he tacitly abandoned his 1814 estimate of 95,000 (found in the *Topographical Description*, 596). He stated in 1831 that "in 1811 the population calculated from the data given by the assessment returns made to the provincial legislature, amounted to nearly seventy-seven thousand souls" (Joseph Bouchette, *The British Dominions in North America* [London: Longman, Rees, Orme, Brown, and Green 1831] 1: 108). Burt (180 n23) noted this estimate for 1811 but did not take into account what it meant, that Bouchette had tacitly given up his estimate for 1814 as being too high, for Bouchette in his later work cited this as his only authoritative figure for the period 1811–24. The reason for Bouchette's tacit abandonment of his previous estimate for 1814 is that he accepted the 1811 estimate, based on assessment data, as accurate and, given the restriction on in-migration from the United States during the war of 1812 and the difficulty of immigrants from the British Isles coming to Upper Canada during the Napoleonic Wars, it is impossible that the population could have risen to 95,000 by 1814. This entire matter is instructive in that it suggests that perhaps it might be well for historians of loyalist Upper Canada to put aside for a time their more sophisticated studies and answer the humbler questions: how large was the Upper Canadian population, how was it geographically distributed, and what was its composition in terms of ethnicity, national origin, and socio-economic background?

For an heroic, but unsuccessful, attempt at resolving the ethnic issues by using certain military groups as a "sample," see Marla S. Waltman, "From Soldier to Settler: Patterns of Loyalist Settlement in 'Upper Canada', 1783–1785" (MA diss., Queen's University 1981).

118 An order-in-council of 9 November 1789 required that a copy be kept of all United Empire Loyalists who had joined the royal standard before the treaty of 1783. The list, usually called "The Old United Empire Loyalists List," had additions made on it until mid-1798. It was preserved in the Crown Lands Department in Toronto. The list, with various settlements, was published in *The Centennial of the Settlement of Upper Canada by the United Empire Loyalists 1784–1884* (Toronto: Rose Publishing Co. 1885; reprint, Baltimore: Genealogical Publishing Co. 1969). A second standard reference, compiled from individual cases affected by order-in-council was compiled by William Reid, as *The Loyalists in Ontario: The Sons and Daughters of the American Loyalists of Upper Canada* (Lambertville, New Jersey: Hunterdon House 1973). A typescript of this book in Special Collections, Queen's University, includes an original preface which states that United Empire Loyalist statute required the person (1) to have been in the thirteen colonies before 1776, (2) to have joined the royal standard in a loyalist corps (although this was often honoured in the breach), and (3) to have been in Upper Canada before July 1798. Using these lists as standards, one is of course accepting the governmental determination of who was and was not a loyalist and is not worrying about the frequency

differently in acquiring and disposing of landed property.[119] The following table summarizes this information through 31 December 1815.

	Loyalists	Nonloyalists	Total number of cases
Individuals owning patented land as proportion of all inhabitants owning such land[120]	44.3% ± 5%	55% ± 5%	(235)
Patents granted by Crown according to background of first patentee[121]	50.2%	49.8%	(271)
Original patentees who had disposed of their Crown grants by 31 December 1815, by background	49.0%	51.0%	(104)
Instances of land being acquired by means other than Crown grant (bargain and sale, inheritance, etc.), by background	52.0%	48.0%	(125)

The chief point these data suggest is that the loyalists seem to have been slightly overrepresented in the land business in relation

---

of fraud. One hopes that the theory of self-cancelling errors holds and that over the entire group the number of additions by fraud is counteracted by the underreporting which is inherent in any list compiled from scattered sources.

119 The reader will notice that in the data which follow I have used a "sliding census" of loyalist and non-loyalist, derived solely from the records of land patents. (a) By taking all the individuals who acquired land patents in the years 1796–1815 inclusive, it is possible to build up a much larger data base and thus make surer conclusions than if one took a single-day census, such as would be involved in compiling a list of all those who held land on, for example, 31 December 1805, and then following their behaviour. (b) Not only is the data base larger in this way but it is qualitatively better in the sense that it is consonant with the cumulative nature of the records of land transfer to which one is relating loyalist or non-loyalist background.

120 I would suggest that the loyalist/non-loyalist figures be taken as approximations only, with a ± of perhaps as much as five points. (That is a purely arbitrary figure.) The reasons for this degree of tentativeness are that I have less than a full trust in the accuracy of the loyalist lists and, additionally, that there are ambiguities in many of their items. One can say with reasonable confidence that between 40 and 50 percent of the landholders were loyalists, but any claim to precision beyond that would be specious.

121 Town lots are excluded from all the transactions tallied herein.

to their proportion of the population. They were engaged in proportionately more transactions than were the nonloyalists and this makes sense for the most part: they had arrived earlier and had an easier time in acquiring Crown patents. They had also settled longer and were more apt to have the money and knowledge to permit them to acquire land on the open market through bargain and sale procedures. The actual differences, however, are so small as to be remarkable.

And, loyalists and nonloyalists acquired land in similar ways. Of the 201 instances of land acquisition by loyalists, 67.7 percent were by Crown grants and 32.3 percent by bargain and sale or inheritance. Of the 195 instances of land acquisition by nonloyalists, 69.2 percent were by Crown grant and 30.2 percent by bargain and sale or inheritance. These are not significant differences.

Thus, loyalists and nonloyalists behaved similarly after they had acquired a piece of land, either by Crown grant or purchase: 37.5 percent of lots acquired by loyalists were disposed of by them by 31 December 1815. The comparable figure for nonloyalist property was 39.2 percent. These are not real differences.

All the above data lead to a simple, limited conclusion, that in a specific area (in this case Leeds and Lansdowne township) in which loyalists and nonloyalists had roughly equal access to land and its associated resources (unlike the royal range of townships, where the loyalists' early arrival gave them virtual control) and in which the landholding activities of all patentees are studied (not merely of those who left manuscript records or who are recorded because they were politically influential) there was no difference between loyalists and the Americans who arrived later as far as fundamental economic *behaviour* was concerned. Viewing these data one cannot tell that the American Revolution ever happened.

This undramatic conclusion has more significance than its sheer negative formulation might suggest. Almost universally within the British Empire of the time major cultural differences were associated with differences in settlement patterns and in the pattern of land usage. The possession of a distinctive pattern of land usage is often taken as a *sine qua non* of the existence of distinctive cultural systems. A reasonable suggestion would be that here in this fundamental matter loyalist and American settlers did not act differently economically because they were not different culturally.

13

Human systems have a fascination and often a beauty. In its balance of potentially conflicting forces, the Leeds and Lansdowne

community of loyalist times possessed a simple elegance. Joel Stone, Oliver Landon, and their contemporaries would have immediately comprehended our intent if we spoke of their township as being a tiny solar system – the sort modelled so marvellously in those fascinating combinations of carved spheres, propelling chains, and orbiting moons, now found only in museums. Acquisitiveness, aggressiveness, and outright greed acted as centrifugal forces, while the need to form alliances, strike economic pacts, and collectively control violence was centripetal. The forces balanced. Within the system what looked at first like whirl actually was order. Stone and Landon not only would have understood; they would have admired.

CHAPTER THREE

Justification: Neither by Works nor by Faith? 1812–1814

I

Historians have one great disadvantage as compared to natural scientists and to most social scientists: they are not allowed to predict the future. The explanatory networks of the natural scientists and the behavioural models of the social scientists produce hypotheses that actually are predictions of what will happen in the future under certain conditions, for example, how an electron will behave if it is forced to pass through an electromagnetic field of a certain intensity and configuration, or how a human being who has undergone some form of deprivation will respond to an opportunity to alleviate that condition. If a scientist's explanatory network comprehends all the relevant data and his model categorizes and conceptualizes the data accurately, the predictions which he makes (his hypotheses) will be proven valid in sharply scrutinized tests made at some time in the future (that is, in experiments).

Occasionally, however, historians have the good fortune to encounter natural experiments which can be used as equivalents of the laboratory tests of the scientific disciplines. In the present instance, one can use the war of 1812 as an hypothetical experiment to test the behavioural model that was developed in the preceding chapter for the people of Leeds and Lansdowne township. The stress of wartime can be used to measure both the accuracy of the social and economic pattern previously described and the intensity with which the pattern was held. Specifically, the war permits the testing under stress of the following "predictions" (hypotheses) which are derived directly from that model. (1) The locals' response to the war will be predominantly non-ideological; abstract concepts such as the common good or patriotism will not prevail but the war will be judged concretely as a matter of personal advantage or disadvan-

tage. (2) Those individuals who join the war effort will view their involvement in the same light as their other civic involvement, as a set of short-term contracts easily broken, not a series of long-term and abstract commitments. (3) Most individuals will use the war to make a profit, as one would expect in a social system based on individuals' acquisitiveness. (4) To the extent that patriotism is invoked, it will be largely used as a rhetorical gambit to justify wartime profitmaking or to reap postwar rewards. (5) Based on the assertion that locally there were no major differences between the basic behaviour patterns of loyalists and nonloyalists, one would not expect much anti-American feeling. (6) It is implied in each of the predictions made above that the behavioural model described in chapter 2 is etched so deeply upon the population that it will hold even under the stress of wartime. If most of these hypotheses prove to be correct, the model of social and economic behaviour in Leeds and Lansdowne township that was elaborated in the preceding chapter will have received strong confirmation indeed.[1]

Simultaneously, an examination of the response of the local community to that war propels us along an expository path which helps us to understand not only the social and economic system which later immigrants into the area faced after 1815, but also the various barriers which they encountered and eventually overcame. Those who entered early into the economic, civic, and social game as played in Leeds and Landsdowne township had an advantage and understandably they tried to hold their advantage against later immigrants. As justification for their privileged position *vis-à-vis* later arrivals, the early settlers had two alternatives: they could argue that the economic game itself was just and beneficial to all concerned, even the late arrivals, or they could admit that they themselves did indeed hold a privileged position but that it was morally justified because they possessed some inherent virtue or had made some past contribution to the general welfare. The first alternative is intellectually the more satisfactory. There is a wide literature, beginning with Adam Smith and running through the Benthamites and the Philosophic Radicals, which justifies the kind

1 I am not unaware of the considerable volume of work, especially that done by Professor S.F. Wise, which argues for a pervasive ideological influence – essentially British conservative in origin and anti-American in character – upon the behaviour of Upper Canadian loyalists. I am also aware of the work by several younger scholars that questions Wise's work in various ways. Both sides of the argument are irrelevant to the purposes at hand, however, because the argument about the nature of the ideological beliefs of early Upper Canadians does not provide an adequate basis for drawing hypotheses that can be operationally tested.

of atomistic self-interest in economic, social, and political life which characterized the township. According to this line of thought, social competition brought about a spontaneous harmony of egoisms and economic competition yielded the beneficent "invisible hand." This line of thought, however, was virtually unspoken in Upper Canada.

Instead, a "moral" justification for the privileges of the early settlers was to be invoked: their loyalism in leaving the American colonies and, more important, the loyalty shown in the war of 1812 by themselves, their offspring and, crucially, by their later arriving neighbours entitled them to whatever advantages they held in the competition with the post-1815 immigrants.

An examination of the conduct of the people of Leeds and Lansdowne township in the 1812–14 conflict will reveal that their activities in the war permitted the creation afterwards of a patriot mythology which later was used to justify their privileged position in the economic, political, and social game *vis-à-vis* later immigration. Their justification of privilege, however, based as it was on their reputed loyalism, was extremely vulnerable to attack from any group of newcomers whose credentials as loyal citizens of the Empire were strong, and the Irish Protestants who flooded into Upper Canada were not merely loyal but ultra-loyal.

2

Of major wartime matters involving large groups of individuals we have records in detail of only two sets of facts concerning Leeds and Lansdowne township, that there was a militia unit and that Gananoque suffered an American attack.

The militia's organization was not unusual. It followed the Upper Canadian pattern based on the British and Irish yeomanry. A militia had been organized in Upper Canada by Governor Simcoe in 1792 and had hirpled along under the requirement of a single day's training per man per year. In the 1812 war, there were two militia regiments in Leeds county, the second regiment encompassing the men of Leeds and Lansdowne township. The regiment was presided over by a colonel and had one and later two flank companies (consisting of roughly three dozen volunteers who trained six days a month and served as the heart of the regiment), a rifle company, and a fluctuating number of ordinary companies (usually five). The second regiment had 267 men in 1814 and this must have been virtually the entire male population of the area between late

adolescence and late middle age.[2] At the head of this volunteer defensive force was Joel Stone, who was there not by virtue of his limited military experience but almost certainly because he was the most important economic and civic figure in the area. Stone took over the colonelcy by commission of 2 January 1809[3] and wore his rank with the pride of a school prefect. Despite difficulties both considerable and lugubrious, Stone held on to his rank until 1821, when at the age of seventy-two he took offence at an order sent generally to the militia in Upper Canada and resigned.[4]

The militia were not really expected to serve as combat troops and, judging from the experience at Gananoque, that expectation was founded on a realistic assessment of their abilities and enthusiasm. On 21 September 1812 a force under the American Captain Benjamin Forsyth attacked Gananoque and after an easy victory did some damage and left. Forsyth had under his command 100 to 200 men (depending on the sources one reads) to face 40 to 110 defenders, and the Americans either did considerable damage to personnel and the military stores or acted like savages around the women and children but committed more vandalism than strategic damage (again depending on the writer of the account).[5] Four

2 For the military structure of the second regiment of the Leeds militia see L. Homfray Irving, *Canadian Military Institute: Officers of the British Forces in Canada during the War of 1812–15* (Welland: Welland Tribune 1908), 51–2. Stone refers to a second flank company in (draft) Joel Stone to Colonel Vincent, 5 June 1813 (Stone papers, Queen's University Archives). This may have been what Irving calls a rifle company. On manpower in 1814 see the compilation "Returns ... 4 June 1814" in the Stone papers (Queen's University Archives). On the various individual captains' returns see the same papers dated 24 September 1814 (Stone papers, Queen's University Archives). It is not without irony that in peacetime, 1818, the militia regiment grew to nine companies with a total of 553 members ("Annual and Nominal Return ... 4 June 1818, in Stone papers, Queen's University Archives). For useful background see Ruth McKenzie, *Leeds and Grenville: The First Two Hundred Years* (Toronto: McClelland and Stewart 1967), 58–60.

3 Irving (51) gives 1803 as the date of Stone's colonelcy, but this is almost certainly a misprint. A commission of 2 January 1809 is cited by McDonald and this is preferable: see Herbert S. McDonald, "Memoir of Colonel Joel Stone, a United Empire Loyalist," *Ontario Historical Society: Papers and Records* 18 (1920): 85. See also Agnes Maule Machar, "The Story of a Canadian Loyalist: Col. Joel Stone, Founder of Gananoque," *The United Empire Loyalists Association of Ontario: Annual Transactions* (March 1899): 71–2.

4 (Draft) Joel Stone to Nathaniel Coffin, 21 November 1821 (Stone papers, Queen's University Archives).

5 A useful selection of the conflicting accounts is found in H. William Hawke, "Joel Stone of Gananoque, 1749–1833: His Life and Letters" (unpublished mono-

militia men were wounded on the Canadian side, but even so the whole affray had the air of *opera buffa*. No one denies that Colonel Stone was absent (an absence that is not explained adequately), that the crucial flank company was elsewhere (in this case in Kingston under the command of two of Stone's staff), or that the militia were less than fearless in the face of the Americans. In sarcastic tones Colonel R.D. Lethbridge, officer in command, wrote to Stone suggesting "that some omission of necessary vigilance must have occurred," and, he continued ominously, "it is my particular desire that you will distinctly state what number of officers by name, non-commissioned officers and privates were present at this port when the attack on the part of the enemy" took place.[6] The least heroic (but in some ways appropriate) aspect of the American victory was that, failing to find Colonel Stone, the invaders took to firing into his house and hit his wife. Judge McDonald delicately described the wound as being in the thigh; other commentators said the hip,[7] but no historian has yet been so ungallant as to express this occurrence, the chief result of the Forsyth raid, more colloquially.

One would really like to know whether the inhabitants of Leeds and Lansdowne township were loyal. After the war was over, Joel Stone wrote to Gordon Drummond pressing his own claims for compensation for war losses and in the course of the petition complained that "in 1812 ... your memorialist (though surrounded at that time by seditious neighbours)" raised a militia.[8] Nothing happened during the course of the war to change Stone's conviction that large numbers of his neighbours were disloyal. He was especially concerned and informed Richard Cartwright that "a considerable number of persons residing in Yonge and Elizabethtown [nearby townships] were suspected of Treasonable practices." After investigation, he came to the conclusion that "communication

---

graph, 1966, in Queen's University Archives, Kingston), 64–6. See also *Kingston Gazette*, 26 September 1812; Thaddeus W.H. Leavitt, *History of Leeds and Grenville* (Brockville: Recorder Press 1879), 38–9; and Stone to Gordon Drummond, c. 1815 (Stone papers, Queen's University Archives). The Forsyth raid on Gananoque is not mentioned in the latest history of the war, Pierre Berton's *The Invasion of Canada, 1812–13* (Toronto: McClelland and Stewart 1980). This seems to me to be a not unfair assessment of the event's importance.

6 R.D. Lethbridge to Joel Stone, 21 September 1812. Quoted in McDonald, 85, and in Hawke, 65–6. Stone cannot have been far away when the attack occurred, as he was able to get a message to Lethbridge on the same day as the attack.

7 Compare McDonald, 85, Leavitt, 38, and McKenzie, 61.

8 (Draft) Joel Stone to Gordon Drummond, c. 1815 (Stone papers, Queen's University Archives).

with the enemy has been too general – in so much – that provided one half of those accused were to prove guilty – we should be obliged to build new gaols."[9]

This represents an informed opinion, undeniably, but the problem with accepting Stone's evidence at face value is that he had been badly affected personally by an individual case of disloyalty and this may have made him hypersensitive on the topic. The daughter by marriage of Stone's second wife, a girl named Abia, had married Benareh Mallory of a long-standing loyalist family. When the war broke out Mallory, then a member of "parliament" as Stone phrased it, deserted his wife and five children and joined the American army. Abia Mallory at first followed her husband to the United States but after the war she renounced him, returned to Upper Canada, and raised the children on her own. Joel Stone became the family's protector and eventually in the 1820s Mrs Mallory and the two younger daughters came to live in Stone's house. The two younger daughters and an older one married into various connections of the McDonald trading firm in Gananoque, which was an outgrowth of Stone's early trading activities and whose senior partners already were intermarried with Stone's family. So sensitive was Stone to the outrage against loyalty and family committed by Benareh Mallory that the incident formed the major part of one of the last letters he ever wrote.[10] He also became sensitive to disloyalty among prominent UE loyalist families: he listed the son of James Mallory and five other prominent men of distinguished family in a private list of military deserters he made in 1814.[11]

Other observers, however, agreed that something was amiss in the local area. Colonel R.D. Lethbridge, who commanded the region, wrote in August 1812 to Isaac Brock, "There are, I am sorry to say, some exceptions to universal loyalty in the County of Leeds and I wish to be honoured with your instructions in respect of men who have lived as peaceable inhabitants, but who being called on, refuse to take the oath of allegiance."[12]

9 Joel Stone to Richard Cartwright, 17 August 1814, quoted in Hawke, 69.
10 (Copy) Joel Stone to Leman Stone, dated 9 and 15 October 1832 (PAC, McDonald-Stone Papers, no. 1737). The letter is quoted at length in Hawke, 98–9. See also William R. Riddell, "Benijah Mallory, Traitor," *Ontario Historical Society: Papers and Records* 26 (1930): 573–8.
11 List on the back of an envelope, Thomas Smyth to Joel Stone, 29 June 1814 (Stone papers, Queen's University Archives).
12 R.D. Lethbridge to Isaac Brock, 10 August 1812, quoted in E.A. Cruikshank, "A Study of Disaffection in Upper Canada in 1812–15," *Transactions of the Royal Society of Canada*, sec. 2, 6 (1912): 25.

In 1814, Lieutenant-Colonel Pearson, commander at Prescott, noted that the trading licences granted between the United States and Upper Canada were the instances of the introduction of enemy agents into "a strongly disaffected part of the province, the Counties of Leeds and Grenville and township of Bastard." The result, he said, was that the enemy know of "*all* our movements and military dispositions."[13]

Thus, Joel Stone probably was not a crank, sensitive though he was on the loyalty question. Actually he was especially well informed as he was appointed in February 1812 by Isaac Brock as one of the commissioners for the Johnstown district to exact the oath of allegiance from suspicious persons.[14] In his various official capacities (JP, commissioner of oaths, colonel of the militia) he was involved in pursuing judgment in at least two major cases of disloyalty in the local area. In August 1812, he registered an affidavit, as justice of the peace, concerning Jonathan Stevens of Bastard township, which adjoins Leeds and Lansdowne, who had observed "that he was not indebted to the King for anything – and that what property he had, he had bought with his money that he brought from the States and that Government had not given him one pence and said God damn them."[15] Then, in November 1813, Stone, as a JP, issued a warrant for the arrest of one Libeous Armstrong for suspicion of treason and effected in the same operation the arrest of David Kilbourn, his son, and one Clark Kittle.[16] Kilbourn, of Kitley township, was a thorn in the loyalist side and as late as 1820 Stone was still collecting evidence against him, in particular a deposition that on 18 January 1813 Kilbourn and one Joel Dunbar had led a private meeting in Bastard township at which they framed a roll of the names of American sympathizers, "so that when the United States come here, they should know their friends."[17]

Intriguing though such instances are, they are too scattered to permit any firm generalization concerning the loyalty of the population in the local area, nor do the seizures of the lands of enemy aliens and of treasonable subjects tell much. Under provi-

---

13 Lieutenant-Colonel Pearson to Colonel Foster, 7 February 1814, in PAC McDonald-Stone papers.
14 The warrant from Brock, 27 February 1812, is in PAC, McDonald-Stone papers, no. 795–796.
15 Affidavit witnessed by Joel Stone, 6 August 1812 (PAC, McDonald-Stone papers, no. 806).
16 The warrant of 27 November 1813 and an appendix by the executing officer is found in Hawke, 68–9.
17 Oath sworn before Benjamin Simon (?) (PAC, McDonald-Stone papers, no. 849).

sions of 1814, inhabitants of the United States who in any way received grants of land or inherited it in Upper Canada and who withdrew from the province without licence after 1 July 1812 were to be considered aliens and incapable of holding lands within the province.[18] The medieval practice of attainting treasonable subjects was invoked (although that word was not used) and in March 1814 a commission of nine local worthies was set up for the Johnstown district to seize property of treasonable persons as well as of departed aliens. Several of the members' names are already familiar: Joel Stone, Solomon Jones, David Jones, William Fraser, Thomas Fraser, and Stephen Burritt.[19] In the entire Johnstown district approximately sixty estates were seized (almost all from departed aliens). In Leeds and Lansdowne township only four persons lost their property, involving roughly eleven hundred acres.[20]

3

The problem with details of seized estates, reports of detected disloyalty, and attacks by various authorities is that they all involve instances of gross disloyalty and as such are cases of deviant behaviour. Ideally, one would like to discover some equivalent of an opinion poll which would show how the Leeds and Landsdowne populace felt about the war and the demands made upon them, but of course no such poll exists.

A very revealing "proxy," however, does, in the form of information on desertion in the militia. The militia can be thought of as a representative "sample" of the local populace since virtually the entire adult male population up to middle age was enrolled. Their behaviour is revealing. Writing in 1818, John Strachan claimed that in Leeds county during the war "nearly three hundred militia men deserted to the Enemy."[21]

This is certainly a shocking claim and one easy to discount since Strachan was strongly opposed to "the promiscuous introduction" of

18 About fifty proclamations for seizures under the alien lands acts are found in Upper Canada Land Papers, Box 2, folder 7 (Queen's University Archives). There is none for the local area, but the papers are obviously very incomplete.

19 Proclamation of 24 March 1814 carried in the *Kingston Gazette*, 4 May 1814.

20 See "Alien Estates Forfeited to the Crown, 1819" (AO, RG 1, ser. A-IV, 16); "Duplication of ... Inquisitions made of Aliens" (AO, RG 22, 05/120/12); and the original inquisitions (AO, RG 22, ser. 3-C, Box 1); *Eleventh Report of the Bureau of Archives for the Province of Ontario 1914*, 221–2.

21 John Strachan to Colonel Harvey, 22 June 1818, quoted in George W. Spragge, ed., *The John Strachan Letter Book: 1812–1834* (Toronto: Ontario Historical Society 1946), 166.

settlers from the United States into Upper Canada and was perhaps inclined to exaggerate the difficulties their settlement involved. If, however, one reduces the inflamatory phrase "deserted to the Enemy" to merely "deserted," Strachan should be credited at least with recognizing a serious problem. "Returns of Deserters" exist for three of the companies of the second Leeds Regiment and these can be compared to the nominal strength of the respective units.[22]

Company commander	Strength 4 June 1814	Deserters (from 1 July 1812)
William Jones (Battalion Company)	41	6 (a/o 3 February 1814)
Duncan Livingstone (Battalion Company)	46	14 (a/o 26 February 1814)
Ira Schofield (Flank Company)	38	11 (a/o 27 December 1814)
Totals	125	31

Thus, in the companies for which we have evidence a desertion rate of 24.8 percent existed and in the élite flank company it was almost 29 percent. Well might Colonel Joel Stone lament to the authorities in Kingston that "so many desertions and vile elopements have taken place."[23]

The great value of the information on desertion rates is that they are derived not from what people said but from what they actually did. Desertion in these instances should not be interpreted as meaning that the individual militiamen left Upper Canada to join the enemy or even that they sympathized with the American side. Rather, desertion should be taken as meaning that these men did not find it worth their time to join the war. Rather than turn out for parade and duty they stayed at home, harvested their crops, and looked to their own business. They voted with their feet and marched not to the militia's drummer but to their own.[24]

22 Compiled from "Returns of Deserters in Capt. Jones Company 3 February 1814," "Returns of Deserters from Capt. Livingstone's Company 26 December 1814," and "Return of Deserters from Capt. Schofield's Company 27 December 1814," "Return ... 4 June 1814" (all items in AO, Stone papers).

23 (Draft) Joel Stone to Colonel Vincent, 5 June 1813 (Stone papers, Queen's University Archives).

24 One piece of interpretation that should *not* be engaged in is drawing any inference from the notations in the two desertion reports which indicate that the deserters in Livingstone's and Schofield's companies were "American born." This phrase is meaningless in the context of the time, for the majority of the adult population was American-born. What one needs to know is when and why the specific deserters came to Upper Canada, and that information is not available.

Nevertheless, even if desertion was not "desertion to the enemy" the impact must have been prodigious. If one employs the desertion rate as a public opinion poll, roughly one-quarter of the local population refused to have anything to do with actively prosecuting the war against the United States. Moreover, this figure probably seriously underrepresents the actual disapproval of the war by the locals, for desertion from even a local militia unit could cause difficulties for the individual who dropped out. One wonders, therefore, if the war had the approval, let alone the active support, of even half of the population.

4

The actual behaviour of the men who served in the militia has as background the argument in the preceding chapter that the economic system can be understood as unabashedly atomistic and selfish and that in this local society the number and extent of group activities were distinctly limited. The corporate concept had not invaded business activities and a sense of collectivity did not characterize local civic agencies. Local government, like local business enterprises of the time, can best be interpreted as a series of short-term contracts valid only as long as they served the interests of the allied parties. Concrete bargains, not abstract loyalties, determined communal affiliations. It will become clear that the war did not in any significant way alter the economic and social game or change the way in which civic compacts were formed.

Far from being willing to accept the war of 1812 as a cause that rightfully commanded communal loyalty, many locals, including men of the most distinguished loyalist families, treated attempts to prosecute the war as a violation of the social contract. For example, when in November 1813 the government introduced martial law as a means of controlling rapidly rising food prices and especially as a means of forcing the farmers to send produce to the army garrisons, the locals were resentful, the more so because they made a good living selling to both sides. Livius P. Sherwood, the representative for Leeds county, successfully moved in the Legislative Assembly "that the proclamation ... declaring martial law to be in force throughout the Johnstown and Eastern Districts as far as related to the procuring of provisions and forage, was and is arbitrary and unconstitutional and contrary to and subversive of the established laws of the land."[25]

Similarly, local citizens used civilian judicial means to offset

25 Cruikshank, 41.

military practices which they found unacceptable. As a result of a clash with one of his chief militia officers, Joel Stone found himself at least twice being sued in the local court of requests, once by the officer himself and once by some of the men in that officer's company.[26] This use of the court of requests was canny, for such courts were set up in most townships for the collection of small debts and it thus set at polar extremes the practice of militia law as set down by the governmental authorities and the local social contract with its own concept of equity. By suing Stone for back pay in a civil court the insubordinate militiamen were able to offset the demands for loyalty and discipline coming from the central authorities. Understandably, these suits rankled Stone (their actual disposition is not known), as did the earlier suit against him by Major William Read with the assistance of one of the old loyalist Breakenridge family.[27] Especially vexing was a court of requests judgment that required him to return ten pounds, more or less, of fine money that he had taken from insubordinate men under this command.[28] He was further required to pay fifteen pounds to a deserter by the district court in Brockville.[29] On the other hand, the magistrates refused to help Stone collect fines through the civil courts which he had levied on deliquent militia men.[30]

Even after the war Stone was chased through the courts, as far as the District Courts and King's Bench, for his wartime enforcement of military orders. As late as 1816 he was sued in district court by Dr George Breakenridge, who had been surgeon to Stone's regiment, by his attorney Daniel Jones, Jr (two older loyalist families than Breakenridge and Jones could not be found) for having compelled under military law the doctor to attend a general court martial in Kingston in April 1814.[31]

Each of these instances involves the opposition of centrally imposed discipline to local civic practice, of "national" ideology to accepted local custom, and of abstract concepts (province-wide

26 (Draft) Joel Stone to Captain Lorand, 13 March 1814 (Stone papers, Queen's University Archives); (draft) Joel Stone to Nathaniel Coffin, 27 March 1814 (Stone papers, Queen's University Archives).
27 Benoni Wiltse to Joel Stone, 3 July 1813 (Stone papers, Queen's University Archives).
28 (Draft) Joel Stone to Nathaniel Coffin, 21 November 1816 (Stone papers, Queen's University Archives).
29 (Draft) Joel Stone to Captain Lorand, 13 March 1814 (Stone papers, Queen's University Archives).
30 (Draft) Joel Stone to Nathaniel Coffin, 27 March 1814 (Stone papers, Queen's University Archives).
31 Stone to Coffin, 21 November 1816.

"loyalism" and the concept of military discipline) to the prevailing concrete bargains of local life. In using legal instrumentalities to defend their local rights, the citizens of Leeds were pitting law against loyalism.

Another set of actions which indicates that the locals were not willing to give up their individualism for corporate sensibility is found in the chronic state of indiscipline in the militia: a 25 percent desertion rate indicates an endemic problem, and those who did serve were often contumacious. In July 1813, ten men of the second regiment of the Leeds militia were court martialled for refusing to obey the colonel's orders, because "They considered them contrary to Law and unjust."[32] In February 1814, another set of men, fourteen in number, had to be court martialled and fined a total of £26 10s.[33] In March 1814, Stone was apprised of the circulation by some militia men of "a very mutinous writing called a petition" but could not get hold of it.[34]

The most intriguing instance of bad discipline occurred late in the war, when some troops and loyalists broke into Colonel Joel Stone's property. The details are unclear (only part of the relevant correspondence survives), but on the night of 10 November 1814, the militia men and others broke into Joel Stone's barn and he experienced considerable loss of property. This nearly broke Stone's spirit. He suggested to the authorities that he could stand it no longer and that, under the existing circumstances, it might be necessary for him to give up his property in Gananoque and go elsewhere. The authorities responded by offering to pay his losses and authorizing him to have his property protected by the military authorities.[35]

Much of the trouble in the militia came not from nameless marauding and insubordinate men in the ranks but from persons of high social standing who had impeccable loyalist credentials and served as militia officers. One of the most striking cases of this sort involved Benoni Wiltse, an early loyalist whose large family was centred in Yonge township, with some of his offspring settled in Leeds and Lansdowne township. Wiltse had a successful career in the militia, at least for a time: he began as a captain in a flank

---

32 Benoni Wiltse to Joel Stone, 19 July 1813 (PAC, McDonald-Stone papers, no. 866).
33 Note by Joel Stone, dated 4 February 1814 (Stone papers, Queen's University Archives).
34 Stone to Coffin, 27 March 1814.
35 See two letters of Nathaniel Coffin to Joel Stone, each dated 19 November 1814, one marked "private," the other an official communication (Stone papers, Queen's University Archives).

company, was promoted major, and eventually became lieutenant-colonel, the second ranking position in the entire regiment.[36] He was at heart a believer in strong discipline and in 1810, early in Stone's tenure as colonel, urged him to put disciplinary law "in full force" and the ungoverned "in subordination."[37] Wiltse stayed loyal to Stone in the face of difficulties raised by Colonel James Breakenridge, commander of the first regiment of the Leeds Militia, first (and only) lieutenant of Leeds county, and loyalist par excellence. In July 1812, Stone had Wiltse send a party of his men to Kingston to pick up some arms. Wiltse himself did not accompany them but went to Brockville. There he encountered Colonel Breakenridge who, though he had no jurisdiction over Wiltse, publicly reprimanded him for following Stone's order without first receiving Breakenridge's permission. According to a report made to Stone by a third party, "Breakenridge abused him [Wiltse] publicly, damned his and your authority and said that he would teach you better."[38]

When a man of Wiltse's disciplinary temperament and loyalty to his colonel began to reject militia discipline it was a matter of considerable moment. Wiltse did so not because of any personal difficulties but because he felt that the local economic structure was being upset by militia rules. In April 1813, he wrote to Stone protesting plans to call up the militia during spring planting time. "Give me leave to remark," he wrote, "of the certain calamity that must befall us if the Militia are thus continued to be cawled [sic] from their families ... If they are cawled [sic] one month or six weeks from their farms they can put no spring grain in the ground." And, he concluded, "families must inevitably suffer the Famine."[39] (Adapting militia discipline to local economic realities was no new idea: the previous fall, the local regular army commander had permitted most of the militia in the St Lawrence counties to go home for the harvest.)[40]

This was the beginning of a breach between Stone and Wiltse and seems to have begun a serious deterioration in militia discipline. In June 1813 Colonel Stone, believing that his militia regiment was becoming more and more negligent, sent out an order to Lieutenant-Colonel Wiltse to order a court martial. This was done so half-heartedly by Wiltse that it did not produce the desired effect. When,

36 Irving, 51–2.
37 Benoni Wiltse to Joel Stone, 6 June 1810 (PAC, McDonald-Stone papers, no. 761).
38 William Jones to Joel Stone, 14 July 1812 (PAC, McDonald-Stone papers, no. 797).
39 Benoni Wiltse to Joel Stone, 9 April 1813 (AO, Stone papers).
40 McKenzie, 59–60.

in October of the same year, an order from headquarters was received to assemble the whole militia, the result was that only seventy men turned out, which is to say that two out of three refused orders. Stone had them rounded up, but the greater proportion redeserted. In December 1813 Stone convened a meeting of his officers, but far from stemming the tide of indiscipline it only made things worse. Wiltse and Stone had words and Stone finally demanded that Wiltse leave the meeting. Stone not only ordered more courts martial but instigated a special session of the civil magistrates to examine persons accused of harbouring deserters. According to Stone, the special session soon discovered that many of the older people of the district – fathers and mothers and other heads of families – were leading the youth astray by their bad example and counsel, that is, parents were encouraging their children to desert, hardly an indication of a popular war. (Nor can the fact that Colonel James Breakenridge and others threatened to proceed against this special session "for extortion" be taken as an indication of popular enthusiasm for the effort.)[41] Matters came to a head with Wiltse when, in mid-March 1814, Stone ordered his men out on an alert and Wiltse treated the orders "with contempt" (to use Stone's words). Thereupon Stone had Wiltse arrested.[42]

5

If the behaviour of the citizenry in the second regiment of the Leeds militia confirms chapter 2's thesis that local civic contracts were short-term, self-interested, and non-ideological the behaviour of the militia men also confirms the atomistic economic model. The incorruptibility of the rules of local civic life and the demands of "loyalism" were shown by a stubborn refusal to suspend the local rules for the national purpose, and the economic behaviour of the individuals was so strong that the military events actually were bent to accord with the way the local economic game was played. To put it simply, sacrifice was to be avoided and, if possible, one tried to do well out of the situation.

Not all of these efforts were honest. For example, the men of the Leeds militia who at war's end refused to return their government-issued blankets were following their own economic interest, not the

41 Stone's troubles are detailed in Joel Stone to Sir Gordon Drummond, n.d. (PAC, McDonald-Stone papers, no. 70).
42 (Draft) Joel Stone to Captain Lorand, 13 March 1814 (Stone papers, Queen's University Archives); (copy) Joel Stone to Gordon Drummond, 13 March 1814 (PAC, McDonald-Stone papers, no. 905).

practice of public probity.[43] In all likelihood the men who broke into Colonel Stone's barn in the fall of 1814 were engaged as much in simple theft as in expressing a rejection of militia discipline, and the regiment's adjutant who was "not able to account" for sixty odd pounds of the militia fine money paid to him was caught with his hand in the till: that was a large sum, much too large to have simply been misplaced.[44]

One reason for the locals' ready desertion from the militia was the necessity of tending their farms. If they did not, they would face severe deprivation (as Wiltse had pointed out), but if they did tend their crops, they would (as no one needed to point out) make a large profit. Food prices rose sharply during the war and farmers held back provisions and forage so as to drive prices even higher. In particular, they were reluctant to supply the garrisons, believing that higher prices could be obtained later on from the civilian population. Thus, as mentioned earlier, martial law finally had to be declared in the Eastern and Johnstown districts in the winter of 1813–14 in an attempt to force the farmers to provision the garrisons. Lieutenant-General Drummond rescinded martial law late in January 1814, believing that as soon as the winter roads were well formed the farmers would sell, but later in the spring he found that the farmers who supplied Kingston were withholding their hay and demanding an exorbitant price.[45]

The farmers were selling their goods in these times of high profits mostly to the other members of the civilian population, especially those living in towns, and to the Upper Canadian garrisons, when forced to by fiat or when finally paid a high enough price. We do not know (and probably never can know) how much went to the enemy, or, indeed, how much came from the enemy to the Upper Canadians: one estimate is that near the end of the war two out of every three soldiers on the Canadian side were eating beef provided by Yankee entrepreneurs.[46] The supply routes north and south across Lake Ontario were well developed and smuggling was an accepted form of livelihood for some of the most solid loyalist families. Also, during the war a number of trading licences with the

43 (Draft) Joel Stone to unnamed, 23 January 1815 (Stone papers, Queen's University Archives).

44 (Draft) Joel Stone to Nathaniel Coffin, 15 April 1815 (Stone papers, Queen's University Archives).

45 Cruikshank, 40–1.

46 Berton, 23. See also H.N. Miller III, "Smuggling into Canada: How the Champlain Valley Defied Jefferson's Embargo," *Vermont History* 38 (1970): 5–21; "A 'Traitorous and Diabolical Traffic': The Commerce of the Champlain-Richelieu Corridor During the War of 1812," *Vermont History* 44 (1976): 78–96.

United States were issued which gave every opportunity of keeping the *sub rosa* trade routes alive.[47] The most intriguing implication concerning local smuggling activity involves Charles Jones, who after his father's death early in 1812 became the chief businessman in the empire of the bedrock loyalist clan. Jones was said to have raised a company of provincial dragoons during the 1812 war but then to have gone away out of danger to Halifax. Interestingly, one Guy Burnham, formerly clerk in one of Jones's stores, went over to the enemy at about the time of Jones's leaving the province and operated a cross-border goods smuggling operation. Once the war was over, Charles Jones came home – by way of the United States. He was soon a justice of the peace and once again a distinguished citizen, despite the fact that he publicly decried the alleged tyranny of the administration and especially that of General Gordon Drummond.[48]

The bending of the war to fit local economic rules is clearly shown in the participants' refusal to be paid in intangibles. They were not to be satisfied with having served an ideological purpose; they wanted money. After the Forsyth raid, Dr James Schofield, leader of a loyalist clan that had come to the rear of Leeds and Lansdowne township in 1795, treated four wounded Upper Canadian soldiers and sent the government a bill, although his son Ira was captain of the same regiment's flank company. At least some of the wounded had served under his son, and another son, James, was employed by the government's commissary department at Cornwall and attached to the forces as a physician and surgeon. A third son, Peter, also a medical doctor, was a member of the College of Physicians and Surgeons of the State of New York when the war broke out and served as a surgeon in the United States Army before returning to Leeds county at the war's end, where he practised medicine and was a respected justice of the peace.[49] Such men demanded pay not in ideology but in coin of the realm.

The clearest case of an individual demanding to be requited for his national service by money was that of Joel Stone. His seeking recompense is important in itself, for as colonel of the second regiment of the Leeds militia he was the ranking individual in the local loyalist force. It is also important because it helps to validate some of the inferences drawn earlier concerning Stone and his regiment. The material indicates that Stone was not a loyalist

47 Cruikshank, 41.
48 (Draft) Joel Stone to Nathaniel Coffin, 21 November 1816 (Stone papers, Queen's University Archives).
49 Leavitt, 61; Hawke, 66.

fanatic, that he was not willing to set aside concrete personal interest for an abstract cause, and, thus, that he was not a maverick by local standards of ethics and economics. The troubles that he had with his troops cannot be imputed to his being a loyalist zealot amidst an agnostic population but rather as endemic to the social structure and values of the entire group with which he was dealing. In other words, the trouble had stemmed not from Stone but from the incompatibility of strict loyalty with local values.

Stone's quest for compensation began as a result of the American raid on Gananoque of September 1812. He asked at various times for roughly £35 for destruction of a storehouse by the American raiders and for another £50 for trucks broken by the enemy and a leather bellows destroyed. He received £75 6s. 9d.[50] Then, as a result of his property having been ransacked in November 1814 by, as he phrased it, "troops, sailors, mariners, boat men and wagon drivers," he estimated damages at £269 5s.[51] The government was responsive to his claim although the exact amount of payment is uncertain.[52] Stone also wanted to be recompensed for the expenses he had incurred in various courts martial and especially for attending a general courts martial in Kingston from 4 to 15 April 1814.[53] Moreover, he submitted a claim for being on militia duty (for "active service" pay in modern terminology), from 2 July 1812 to 15 April 1814 inclusive, for £210 10s. 1d.[54] In this claim Stone was cutting a very fine edge indeed and he was blocked by Colonel Cartwright, who insisted that Stone had not been ordered on active duty at Gananoque and had been "no more on duty than any other colonel of militia in the province." Stone had to settle for pay and allowance for only thirty-one days, and a lump sum of £100 to cover his courts martial and other expenses.[55] Stone's response was less one of gratitude than of bathos. "I cast my eyes to the right and left. Destruction and loss of almost all comforts of life and prosperity stare me in the face."[56]

50 (Draft) Schedule of Losses," n.d. (Stone papers, Queen's University Archives); Hawke, 66.

51 "Schedule of Losses."

52 See two letters, Nathaniel Coffin to Joel Stone, 19 November 1814, and C.L.L. Foster to Joel Stone, 3 December 1814 (Stone papers, Queen's University Archives).

53 (Copy) Joel Stone to Nathaniel Nichol, 26 December 1814 (AO, Stone papers).

54 See PAC, McDonald-Stone papers, no. 892.

55 Nathaniel Coffin to Joel Stone, 9 April 1815 (Stone papers, Queen's University Archives). Ultimately Stone received £130. See Stone to Coffin, 25 November 1819 (Stone papers, Queen's University Archives).

56 (Draft) Joel Stone to Nathaniel Coffin, 15 April 1815 (Stone papers, Queen's University Archives).

One must be suspicious of Stone's accounting. A schedule of losses which he sent to General Gordon Drummond after the unfortunate November 1814 episode included an estimate of over forty pounds for a board fence taken and burned and over ninety-two pounds for rail and slate fences burned,[57] exhorbitant sums considering that Stone owned a sawmill and had access to a virtually unlimited supply of cheap timber. Stone's practice of increasing his estimates of losses without any itemized accounting creates doubt that he was merely seeking compensation. He at first claimed £353 0s. 3¼d. in direct war losses[58] but then raised this to £1,300[59] and then to £1,550.[60]

Stone's motives, to avoid personal financial sacrifice and probably to make a profit from his war losses, are more important than the actual official disposition of his claims, which remains clouded. He was given some remuneration for the actual property damage done in 1814; he received thirty-one days' active duty pay and one hundred pounds for additional expenses; he was indemnified by the government against having to repay to it fine monies which he had used for his own "subsistence";[61] and in the fall of 1821 he was given a grant for his service from Crown waste lands.[62] (Where and what these were is not specified; Stone denominated twenty-two hundred acres of distant "wild lands" in his will[63] and the bulk of these well may have been rewards for his militia service.) Impercipient as Stone's motives were in dealing with his alleged losses, there is no doubt that in his trade with the army authorities he fully intended to turn a profit. He had a nice little trade with the King in viands to headquarters staff[64] and probably proferred other articles as well: at war's end he claimed to be owed somewhat over £106 for "supplies sent."[65]

Thus, war or no war, even the local militia colonel continued to

57 "Schedule of Losses."
58 Ibid.
59 Joel Stone to Sir Peregrine Maitland, quoted in Hawke, 70–1.
60 (Draft) Joel Stone to Nathaniel Coffin, 21 November 1816 (Stone papers, Queen's University Archives).
61 "Report of the Select Committee on the Petition of Col. Joel Stone" (AO, Stone papers).
62 See (draft) Joel Stone to Nathaniel Coffin, 31 December 1821 (AO, Stone papers) and (draft) Joel Stone to Livius P. Sherwood, 1 January 1822 (AO, Stone papers).
63 The will is most conveniently available in Hawke, 103–5.
64 Several letters in the Stone-Coffin correspondence make passing reference to Stone's providing fresh produce. See, for example, Nathaniel Coffin to Joel Stone, 19 November 1814 (Stone papers, Queen's University Archives).
65 "Schedule of Losses."

be an entrepreneur. He was vigilant above all to prevent any potential pecuniary loss that might be entailed by his national service. In his attitudes Stone was typical of the citizens of Leeds and Lansdowne township. They were expected to serve in a war; some did and some refused, but, whenever possible, they made the war serve them.

6

"The War of 1812 was unique among wars. Two of the former participants both seem to think that they won it. And the British, who were quite as much involved as Canadians, have forgotten that it ever happened."[66] Richard Preston's remark hints at the real importance of the war in Canadian history: what actually happened was soon obscured and what people wanted to believe prevailed. There are few points upon which historians of central Canada are in such close agreement and none on which they are so persuasive as in the argument that the war of 1812 was crucial in creating a firm sense of Canadian identity. Arthur Lower's classic statement is that "as a factor in the building of the Canadian nation, it is hard to see how it can be outranked by other experiences."[67] As such a factor, it was a feat of cultural levitation equalling the illusionary transcendence of the hanging gardens of Babylon.

Out of the war of 1812 came a set of intertwined beliefs that were at once an Upper Canadian patriotic mythology, a justification of extant patterns of economic and civic morality, and an ideology that implied certain general political-constitutional positions. That the actual events of 1812–14 were so distorted as to be virtually unrecognizable is irrelevant; what counts is that the historical events were malleable and could be fashioned into a past that could be used.[68]

66 Richard A. Preston, "The First Battle of Sacket's Harbour," *Historic Kingston* 11 (1963): 3.
67 Arthur R.M. Lower, *Canadians in the Making: A Social History of Canada* (Toronto: Longman, Green and Co. 1958), 173.
68 For the following discussion of post-1814 beliefs and mythologies, these are valuable: David V.J. Bell, "The Loyalist Tradition in Canada," *Journal of Canadian Studies* 5 (1970): 22–3; Carl Berger, *The Sense of Power: Studies in the Ideas of Canadan Imperialism, 1867–1914* (Toronto: University of Toronto Press 1970), chapter 3, "The Loyalist Tradition," 78–108; J.M. Bumsted, "Loyalists and Nationalists: An Essay on the Problem of Definitions," *Canadian Review of Studies in Nationalism* 6 (Fall 1979): 218–32; Jo-Ann Fellows, "The Loyalist Myth in Canada," *Canadian Historical Association: Historical Papers* (1971): 97–111; Keith Walden, "Isaac Brock: Man and Myth" (MA diss., Queen's

The patriotic mythology which grew out of the war of 1812–14 was evolutionary in the sense that it changed during the course of the nineteenth century and eventually became enclosed in a larger loyalist myth that stretched back to the founding of Upper Canada. In its early form, the myth centred upon the heroism of the war years. That is important, because for the patriotic myth to be usable in the two or three decades that followed the war, it had to be ecumenical, that is, inclusive. It had to serve an Upper Canadian population that had experienced the war but the bulk of whose members were not United Empire Loyalists. To insist on United Empire loyalism as a pre condition for patriotic memorialization would have been divisive. Instead, the war became a bonding myth bringing together United Empire Loyalists, late loyalists, and former Americans who arrived at any time prior to 1812 and did not actively take the American side in the war. As time passed, it came not to matter that (as in Leeds and Lansdowne township) a large proportion of the militia had deserted, or at least had mutinied at one time or another; instead, old "veterans" talked about how they had been in things together, and their children believed them, for the ears of children, of whatever age, are naturally credulous of their parents' words.

Of course, the mythic version of the events of 1812–14 was strongly revisionary in its use of historical data, for much of the real story of the war was not germane for patriotic purposes or, worse yet, downright humiliating. Thus the patriotic mythology shifted the focus of attention in military matters from the British regulars to the Canadian militiamen and from the militia's general untrustworthiness to its heroic episodes. In this regard the figures of Sir Isaac Brock and the York Volunteers, his premier militia unit, were central. In the patriotic myth Brock and his men became a symbol of the virtue of the men of all Upper Canada, heroic, self-sacrificing, and victorious. Concerning the civilian population a subsidiary theme emerged, that during the war of 1812 the general population had

University 1971); S.F. Wise, "Colonial Attitudes from the Era of the War of 1812 to the Rebellions of 1837," in Canada Views the United States: Nineteenth-Century Political Attitudes, ed. S.F. Wise and Robert Craig Brown (Toronto: Macmillan 1967), 16–43.

The next chapter will return in detail to the behaviour of the inhabitants of Leeds and Lansdowne township. Here it is sufficient to note that the general characteristics of post-1814 patriotic mythology and loyalist myth-making which are discussed in the text prevailed in the local area as well. Thaddeus W.H. Leavitt's History of Leeds and Grenville (Brockville: Record Press 1879) is an omnium gatherum of material, reproduced virtually unedited from scores and scores of local sources, many of them of quite early date.

suffered hardship for their ideals and that this suffering was not an historically isolated event but of a piece with the long tale of virtuous hardship that began with the first United Empire Loyalist settlers.

The emphasis in the patriotic myth both upon the virtue and upon the suffering of the faithful is particularly relevant in relation to the economic and social structure of the province, for it implicitly provided justification for a marked economic, civic, and social advantage for individuals who had arrived before the war over those who came later. The case of Leeds and Lansdowne township clearly indicates that early arrivals in the economic, civic, and social game had a distinct edge, and by the time the war of 1812 was over they had a vested interest in continuing to play the game by the existing rules. In effect, a syllogism evolved.

1 Virtue deserves to be rewarded and suffering to be compensated.
2 The loyal populace of Upper Canada both suffered and was virtuous.
3 The loyal populace therefore deserved reward.

When it became clear in the decades immediately after the war that the earlier settlers were doing very well indeed, especially in comparison to the immigrants who began to arrive in increasingly large numbers after 1815, then the train of logic was extended.

4 The economic, civic, and social game provided the loyal persons of 1812 (and their heirs) with their deserved reward for virtue and justified compensation for their suffering.
5 Something which dispenses justice truly is, by definition, just.
6 The existing economic, civic, and social arrangements are therefore morally justified, even though they might seem at first glance to be tilted unfairly against new immigrants.

Such an argument (never put so starkly, of course) had its greatest force when invoked by officers, such as Jarvis, Ridout, and Robinson, who had served with Brock's legendary York Volunteers, but the same manner of thinking was operative in towns and rural townships throughout Upper Canada and served to help explain why one lawyer rather than another obtained a court sinecure, why another man was appointed a magistrate, or why still another had an inside edge in obtaining civic building contracts. This is relevant to understanding what an immigrant who arrived after 1815 faced: he encountered not only an established way of doing things that placed

him at a disadvantage but a mythology which justified morally the advantage earlier arrivals had over him.

The patriotic myths surrounding the years 1812–14 implied at last the creation of an empirically demonstrable political-constitutional ideology, whose precepts, however, were vulnerable. Two ideological axes were important. It is not clear that the general population during the war of 1812 was very strongly anti-American but the enshrinement of Upper Canadian patriotic heroes required an opposing pole and thus a rejection of American cultural values and political structures. This fit nicely with the justification-of-privilege aspect of the patriotic mythology, for if one were virtuously opposed to American evils the notable American vices of democracy and egalitarianism had to be resisted. A pro-British political posture was also implied, and this was accentuated as the myths of the war of 1812 evolved. Imperial ties and the symbols of monarchy increasingly were revered, in no small part because of their superiority to the strident factionalism and barren political forms of the republic to the south.

The Britishness of the emerging mythology fit well with the nature of the post-1815 immigration, which came mostly from the British Isles. Statistically, one can talk about a recolonization of Upper Canada after 1815, for the proportion of the populace native to the North American continent dropped as larger and larger waves arrived of immigrants who had no direct experience of North American life and whose most direct cultural contacts were overseas. Common allegiance to British symbols made it easier than it otherwise would have been for the immigrants to adjust to their new surroundings and simultaneously made it more likely that the Upper Canadians would accept the newcomers.

Ironically, it was the Britishness, the allegiance to British symbols, and indeed the very loyalty implied in the patriotic mythology, that eventually undercut its usefulness as a justification of the privileged position of the pre-1815 residents. The myth was vulnerable to attack from inside. As a protection against the demands of those immigrants who pointed to American democratic practice as a precedent to follow, the patriotic mythology was effective: it pinpointed as evil the American scheme and justified not following it. But against those new arrivals who accepted the symbols of imperial Britain and were willing to swear loyalty in all degrees and forms it was much less effective.

Most immigrants from the British Isles could claim to be loyal, and one group in particular had a history of hyper-loyalism, the

Protestants from Ulster and some of the Anglo-Irish Protestants from elsewhere in Ireland. In fact, one could scarcely find a more vociferously loyal group anywhere in the empire. They also had, however, a predilection for political radicalism, although not for outright democracy. The Irish Protestants arrived with a fairly wide experience of participation in civil government (it was the Catholics who were kept from full political participation in the homeland), a knowledge of how to use political institutions to further the interests of the individual and of the group, and experience in organizing voluntary societies, ranging from political pressure groups to paramilitary bodies. They were also hungry for land and for economic advancement. All this meant that in Upper Canada they would be virtually unstoppable. In later chapters it will be seen that in Leeds county it was these ultra-loyalists, not the American democrats, who eventually broke down the walls with which the earlier settlers tried to protect their privileges.

Finally, if the reader will grant that a group of people can have an "intellectual history" in the sense of evolution of what the bulk of the people think and how they think it, the myths which evolved out of the war of 1812 are important sign posts in the intellectual history of Upper Canadians. The patriotic myths imply a new collective sense and an emerging abstract manner of conceptualizing the polity: the loyalist community was presented as a province-wide group, not merely as one's immediate neighbours. Paradoxically, this communal and abstract mythology was used to justify maintenance of the pre-war economic, civic, and social system, which was based on concrete bargains (not abstract loyalties) made by individuals. As evidence of ways of thinking, the practices of the pre-war settlers and the patriotic mythology with which they justified their position were fundamentally incompatible.

CHAPTER FOUR

The Local Irish
Revolution, 1816–1849

I

If one places a piece of polarized glass (such as in an ordinary pair of sunglasses) at right angles to another piece, the resulting image is virtually opaque. If one stacks three or more such pieces of glass at various angles to one another, no light whatsoever passes through. The evaluation of the changes wrought in the township of Leeds and Lansdowne as a result of the immigration from the British Isles after the Napoleonic Wars is like that: there are a number of filters which, although not misleading in themselves, produce a great blackness when used uncritically in relation to each other. The perspectives must be aligned so that they all share the same axis. The result, like that of two properly aligned polarized lenses, will be an undistorted image. The historical portrait, of course, will not be as bright as we would like, but it never is: historians, like the early Christians whom the Apostle Paul so earnestly tried to console, must be content to see through a glass, darkly.

One lens through which the historian can view the effects of immigration on the compact society of Leeds and Lansdowne township consists of a set of data that highlights the continual and progressive improvement in the community, especially in material well-being considered at the macro level. As was discussed in chapter 1, from 1816 onwards extensive migration from the British Isles to British North America was a pervasive fact. From at least 1825 (when the first data are available) the Irish comprised the bulk of the migrants to British North America, and in all probability they had done so since 1816.

As one would expect, given the fact that Leeds and Lansdowne township had a considerable quantity of unpatented land (see chapter 2, map 8), it experienced a population surge based largely upon new immigrants. As figure 1 indicates, this surge consisted not

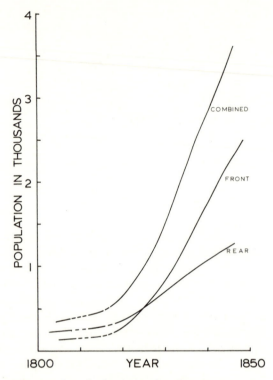

Figure 1 Population growth, 1800–50

of a sudden boom, followed by stasis, but of a sustained increase from the end of the Napoleonic Wars to the mid-century.[1] It is, however, as late as the 1842 census before one can obtain a reasonably reliable account of the place of birth of the people of Leeds and Lansdowne township. This reveals that slightly over 37 percent of the population at that time was foreign-born. If one adds to this an estimate of the number of children in families headed by foreign-born parents, then probably two-thirds to three-quarters of the population was either born abroad or the offspring of foreign-born parents. The Irish were the largest group: close to 19 percent of the local population had been born in Ireland and nearly 43 percent were either Irish-born or children living in families headed by either one or two Irish-born parents.[2]

1 In figure 1 and figures 2–5, individual annual irregularities are averaged in the graphing procedure. The actual raw data on population are found in Appendix A.

2 The ethnic composition of the population is discussed in detail in the text. The limitations on the 1842 data are discussed in the introduction to Appendix C.

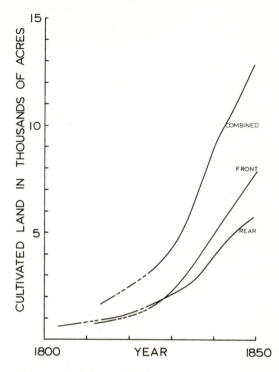

Figure 2 Cultivated land, 1800–50

When one applies certain indices of material well-being, such as the assessed numbers of horses, milch cows, horned cattle, and the amount of land assessed as cultivated, a series of impressively upward-bending curves results.[3] Seemingly, settlement was taking place smoothly and the local economic system was expanding apace with immigration.

2

Yet another set of data might appear to indicate that settlement was far from smooth for the new immigrants and indeed that severe impediments made it very dificult for them to obtain an economic foothold in the township. These can be seen as becoming operative in the late 1820s. The numbers of immigrants represented a social pressure and, when blocked, almost any pressure can become explosive. It is not surprising that in the early 1830s the London government began to demand information from specific localities

3 The raw data for figures 2–5 are found in Appendix B. The limitations on the data are set out in the introduction to that appendix.

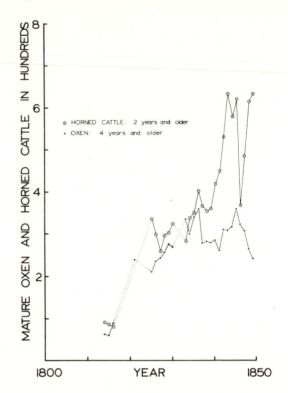

Figure 3 Mature oxen and horned cattle, 1800–50

on its North American colonies. In the papers of the clerk of peace for the Johnstown district is a circular from Downing Street dated 5 March 1831, requiring information for a return to the imperial House of Commons on migrants to the several British North American colonies.[4]

A primary impediment to the influx of new settlers was the harsh physiography of the township. The Frontenac axis of the Precambrian Shield dips into Leeds and Lansdowne township and distinctly limits the amount of usable land. Rock knobs, some bare and others covered with shallow soil, alternate with beds of clay. These clay blocks are suitable for farming, although they present serious drainage problems. Only a few deposits of loam soil exist and most of these are also limited by drainage difficulties. The distribution of soil types is indicated in map 10. This depiction of soil types can be

4 Circular of 5 March 1831 in AO p. G. 22, ser. 7, Johnstown District, "Sundry Municipal Papers," Box A.

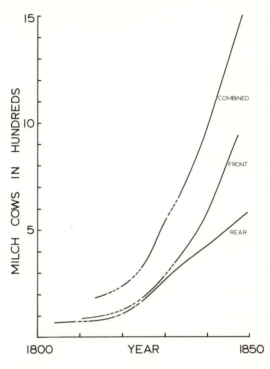

Figure 4 Milch cows, 1800–50

translated into an approximation of soil suitability for agriculture, as is found in map 11. Of necessity, this approximation is based upon modern data (no equivalent survey exists for the early 1830s) and is only a rough indicator: ox- or horse-drawn implements were able to work shallow soils that defy present-day tractor-drawn technology, so that land which now is abandoned to bush was at one time marginally productive agriculturally. Nevertheless, rock is rock and workable clay or loam was the most desirable land then as now.[5]

To this primary physiographic impediment one can add a second one, based on legal realities. By 1830 most of the good land had been patented and seemingly this was an obstacle to the settlement of new migrants. The plausibility of this argument is obvious when one compares the two maps of soil and agricultural suitability with the data on map 8 in chapter 2, which covers land patented through

5 In addition to the sources cited on maps 10 and 11, see L. J. Chapman and D. F. Putnam, *The Physiography of Southern Ontario*, 2d ed. (Toronto: published for the Ontario Research Foundation by the University of Toronto Press 1966). The whole volume repays study, but see especially 336ff.

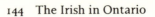

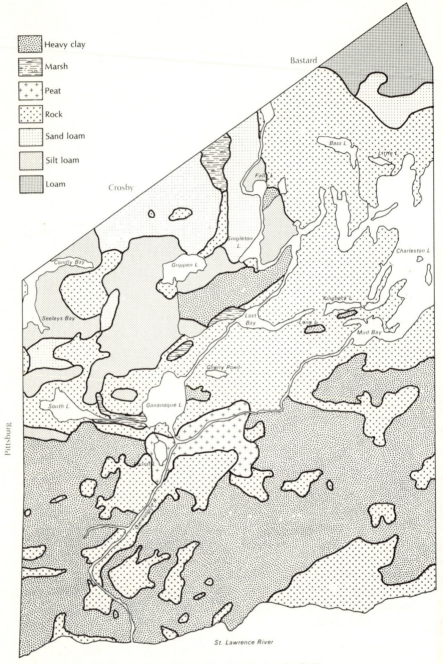

Source: Simplified from Environment Canada. Soil Capability for Agriculture. Kingston 31C. 1:250,000

Map 10 Soil types, simplified modern classification

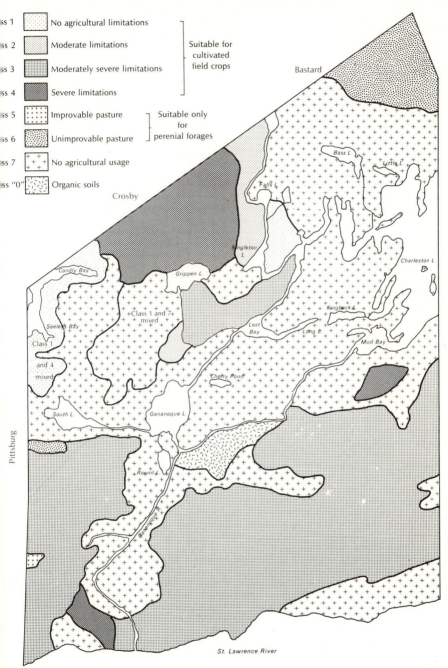

ss 1 No agricultural limitations
ss 2 Moderate limitations   Suitable for cultivated field crops
ss 3 Moderately severe limitations
ss 4 Severe limitations
ss 5 Improvable pasture   Suitable only for perenial forages
ss 6 Unimprovable pasture
ss 7 No agricultural usage
ss "0" Organic soils

Bastard
Crosby
Bass L
Little L.
Falls L
Charleston L.
Ingleton L.
Condly Bay
Grippen L.
Kingbeck L
+Class 1 and 7+ mixed
Seeley's Bay
Lost Bay
Long L
Mud Bay
Class 1 and 4 mixed
South L.
Gananoque L
Cherry Pond
Pittsburg
Round L.
Gananoque R.
Yonge
St. Lawrence River

Source: Simplified from Ontario Soil Survey, Report no. 41, Soils of Leeds County

Map 11 Soil suitability for agriculture, simplified modern classification

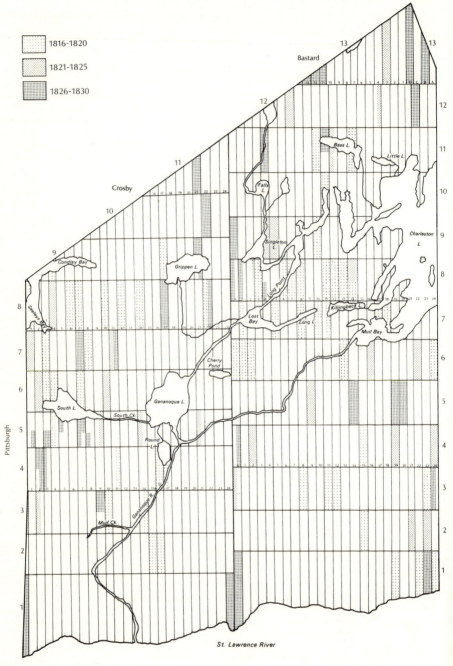

Map 12 Date of land patenting, 1816–30

Source: Abstract Index of Deeds

1815, and the information on map 12 below, covering patentings from 1816 to 1830 inclusive. It would be natural to conclude that not much unpatented land was left that an immigrant might want.[6]

A complex of three additional impediments – the ownership of quantities of patented land by speculators, the existence of clergy reserves and of Crown reserves of unpatented land – further reduced the land available to new immigrants, or so it seems. The first of these inhibitors, the speculators, is a vexed matter in the historiography of Upper Canada. The denunciation of land speculators by contemporaries was so vivid that historians sometimes have accepted the description without questioning the reality. Speculators were condemned both for withholding land from the market, and for releasing it at too high a price when they finally did sell. It is hard not to be carried along by the cry of Susanna Moodie, whose first experience with land speculators took place in the early 1830s: "Oh, ye dealers in wild lands – ye speculators in the folly and credulity of

6 The reader may have noticed that a plausible impediment to settlement in Leeds and Landsdowne, the gradual increase in the difficulty of the legal requirements for patenting land after the Napoleonic Wars, has not been mentioned. As far as the province as a whole is concerned, this is a controversial topic, as there may have been a deliberate attempt to inhibit landholding and thus create a surplus of labour. (See especially Leo A. Johnson, "Land Policy, Population Growth and Social Structure in the Home District, 1793–1851," *Ontario History* 63 [1971]: 41–60, reprinted in J.K. Johnson, ed., *Historical Essays on Upper Canada* [Toronto: McClelland and Stewart 1975], 32–57.) However prescient Johnson's observations may be for the Home district, I can find no demonstrable effect in the specific eastern Ontario township here under study. Instead, one confronts the highly visible "impediments" discussed in the text. Local realities – geological, economic, etc. – not central policies, were prepotent.

One does need to be cognisant of the changes in governmental land policies. The standard works are Lillian F. Gates, *Land Policies of Upper Canada* (Toronto: University of Toronto Press 1968) and G.C. Patterson, "Land Settlement in Upper Canada," in *Sixteenth Report of the Department of Archives for the Province of Ontario* (Toronto: 1921). Especially relevant are the details of developments leading to the abolition of free grants to immigrants in 1826 and the considerable reduction of grants to privileged classes of residents, such as United Empire Loyalists, militia men, and officials in 1837. Actually the changes of 1826 and 1837 were not as great as they appeared, as, even in the era of so-called free grants, considerable fees of various sorts were required (for example, in 1819 nearly seventeen pounds in fees were paid on lots of two hundred acres), and, despite the reduction in grants to privileged persons after 1837, such grants were abolished completely only in 1851.

On the process which an immigrant went through to acquire land see James Strachan, *A Visit to the Province of Upper Canada in 1819* (Aberdeen: James Strachan 1820), Appendixes 1–3. See also the Finding Aid for the RG I series in AO.

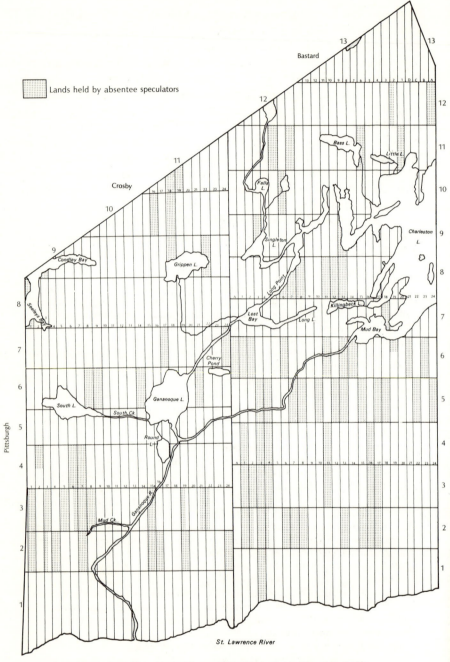

Lands held by absentee speculators

Source: Archives of Ontario, Court of General Session-Johnstown District, "Sundry Municipal Papers", Box B, Folder, "Treasurer's Returns of Absentee Lands, 1829", with corrections from Abstract Index of Deeds.

Map 13 Lands held by absentee speculators

your fellow men – what a mass of misery and of misrepresentation productive of that misery have ye not to answer for!"[7] Despite the apparent importance of land speculators, historians have developed no method of identifying them which could be applied over the entire province and which would be useful over significant stretches of time. Definitions have ranged from the disastrously simple-minded equation of land speculator with large landholder to the sophisticated multi-dimensional "motivation and scale" analysis of R.W. Widdis,[8] which requires more information than is available for many of the early townships in Upper Canada. For Leeds and Lansdowne township in the late 1820s and early 1830s, however, we possess a reasonably accurate contemporary talley of speculative lands in the form of the district treasurer's returns of land held by absentees who were eight years or more behind on their taxes, and this information is presented on map 13. Not all such absentees were necessarily speculators (a few may eventually have settled in the township and farmed their land) nor all resident landholders non-speculators (small farmers sometimes improved and farmed a piece of land with the intention of reselling it), but it is not unreasonable to suggest that most of these lots were being held not for farming purposes but for eventual resale.

Speculative activities affected only land that already was "in circulation," that is, land which was part of the market economy and which would be transferred once a threshold price had been reached. Land in the clergy and Crown reserves, however, was kept out of the market system and thus was a potentially greater impediment to settlement. No matter how much money an immigrant had in his purse, the land was inaccessible unless official policy made it available. The clergy reserves in the front of Leeds and Lansdowne township are shown on map 14. As if readily apparent, these reserves in Leeds and Lansdowne township did not follow the perfect checkerboard pattern which prevailed in much of Upper Canada, indicating that the reserves were not laid out until a good deal of land had been patented in the late 1790s.[9] Thus the clergy reserves were concentrated back from the St Lawrence in the

7 Susanna Moodie, Roughing it in the Bush (London: Richard Bentley 1852), x.
8 "Motivation and Scale: A Method of Identifying Land Speculators in Upper Canada," Canadian Geographer 23 (1979): 337–51.
9 Gates incorrectly states, "In Upper Canada the chequered plan was not deviated from except for those townships which had been fully or partially located before 1791. In such cases reserves were set aside in other townships or in blocks in the centre of townships, or in the rear concession." Lillian Gates, "The Heir and Devisee Commission of Upper Canada, 1797–1805," Canadian Historical Review 38 (1957): 21.

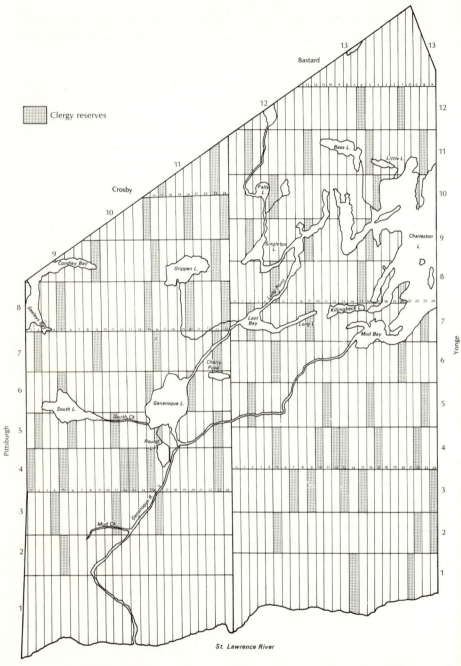

Source: Archives of Ontario, Crown Land Papers, R.G. 7, Ser. A-IV, vol. 32, "Crown and Clergy Reserves, returned to the Canada Company 1824, with corrections from R.G. 1, Ser. C-II-3, vol. 4, no. 4, "Schedule of Clergy Reserves, Johnstown District, 1828", and Abstract Index of Deeds

Map 14 Clergy reserves

inland tier of concessions towards which the immigrants from the British Isles would naturally look for land.[10]

Similarly, the Crown reserves, shown on map 15, were, with the exception of a few parcels, set back from the front. Prior to 1827 these lands were allocated to settlers under the so-called free lands policy and thereafter they were disposed of chiefly by sale (although certain privileged persons still could obtain land "free," that is, without direct charges but with the payment of various legal fees to the government). There were many fewer restrictions upon the government in disposing of the Crown reserves than upon the custodians of the clergy reserves in dealing with the lands entrusted to them, but the Crown reserves were by no means a free-market entity. Whether or not the various lots were available to new immigrants was a matter of official policy and thus the reserves were a potentially very strong roadblock to settlement in any specific locale.[11]

The possible cumulative impact of these three major potential impediments to settlement of new migrants in the township (the activity of speculators and the existence of Crown and clergy reserves) is indicated in map 16 which is an overlay of those three factors. When these are combined with the geological limitations of the township it would seem that by the late 1820s a barricade had been erected which would make difficult the reception and assimilation of significant numbers of immigrants from the British Isles.

Finally, one must mention the Canada Company. The company was not a direct impediment to settlement like the potential barriers detailed already, but rather a barrier to potential relief. The Canada Company, founded in 1823, effectively had a first option to purchase Crown reserve lots as they became open, provided that the lots were not leased and had been surveyed before 1 March 1824. Potentially, therefore, the company stood between new immigrants and those Crown and clergy reserves which their custodians decided to sell. The company charter prohibited the firm from paying more than 3s. 6d. for land, although it could, and often did, pay less.[12] In the case of Leeds and Lansdowne township, the company had a return

10 The standard work on the clergy reserves is Alan Wilson, *The Clergy Reserves of Upper Canada: A Canadian Mortmain* (Toronto: University of Toronto Press 1968). A convenient précis is his *The Clergy Reserves of Upper Canada* (Ottawa: Canadian Historical Association Booklets 1969). See also his "The Clergy Reserves: 'Economical Mischiefs' or Sectarian Issue," *Canadian Historical Review* 42 (December 1961): 281–99.

11 A useful general discussion is J. Howard Richards, "Land and Policies: Attitudes and Controls in the Alienation of Lands in Ontario during the First Century of Settlement," *Ontario History* 50 (1958): 193–203.

12 For the development of the company see Clarence Karr, *The Canada Land Com-*

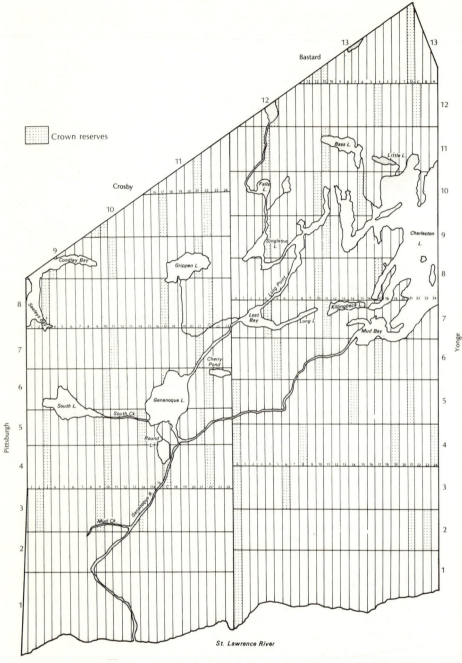

Source: Archives of Ontario, Crown Land Papers, R.G. 7, Ser. A-IV, vol. 32, "Crown and Clergy Reserves returned to the Canada Company, 1824", with corrections from Abstract Index of Deeds.

Map 15 Crown reserves

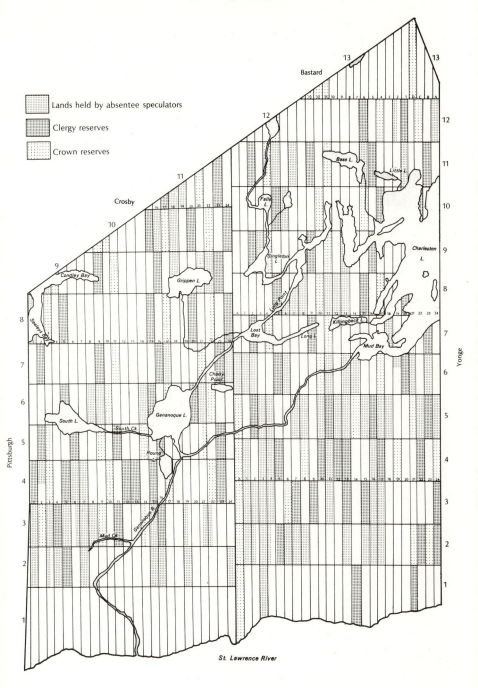

Map 16 Impediments to settlement

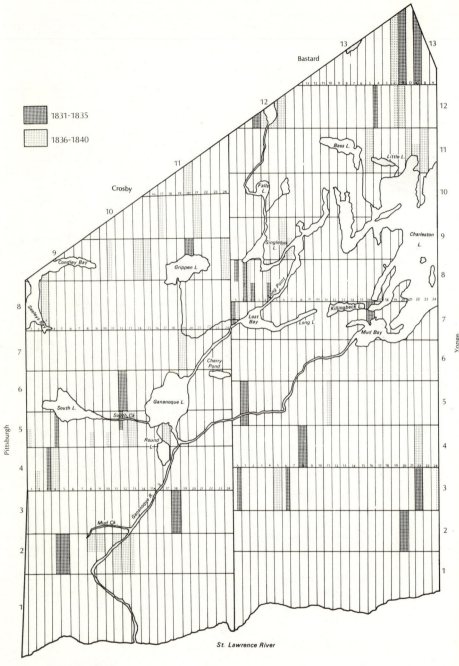

1831-1835

1836-1840

Bastard

Crosby

Pittsburgh

Yonge

St. Lawrence River

Source: Abstract Index of Deeds

Map 17 Date of land patenting, 1831–40

compiled in 1824 of all the Crown and clergy reserves and from that list decided which lands it wanted.[13]

3

Yet another lens reflects on our previous perception of the potential impediments to settlement in Leeds and Lansdowne township and may show how accurate or how distorted that viewpoint was. Momentarily this will seem confusing, but eventually, when all the various lenses are aligned properly, the difficulties will be resolved.

The legal arrangements and speculative ventures described earlier actually existed, but they were not necessarily important, much less prepotent in the local setting. Despite the number of potential impediments to settlement which existed in the late 1820s, the land records of the township show that a considerable number of new patents were taken out during the 1830s and 1840s. These are detailed in maps 17 and 18.

The Canada Company did not play much of a part in this activity and private individuals predominated. Indeed, the Canada Company's activities in the township evinced three characteristics. First, as map 19 indicates, they exercised their option to purchase relatively few of the reserves that were open to them.[14] Second, considering that they had compiled an inventory of land in 1824, they were quite late in actual selection and patenting of the lots. Undoubtedly the company officials had more pressing matters in their major land tracts to take their attention, but within the local context they seem to have been more lackadaisical than avaricious in their approach. Third, the company showed remarkably bad judgment in the selection it made. Much of the land it acquired was virtually rock and a good deal of the rest was under water. Whatever the intent of the Canada Company's investment policies (and in the local context they can be judged only as incompetent or incomprehensible), the company certainly did not interfere with new settlers finding farm land.

As for the Crown reserves, from the later 1820s onwards the new immigrants had to pay the government for the land, but this proved

---

pany: The Early Years, an Experiment in Colonization 1823–43 (Toronto: Ontario Historical Society Research Publication no. 3 1974).

13 AO, Crown Land Papers, RG 7, ser. A-IV, 32, "Crown and Clergy Reserves returned to the Canada Company, 1824."

14 In comparing map 19 with maps 14 and 15 the reader may have noticed that the Canada Company acquired three pieces of land that were not on the earlier inventory of reserves. Either the earlier inventory was incomplete (the most likely explanation) or the company purchased the land in an unusual fashion.

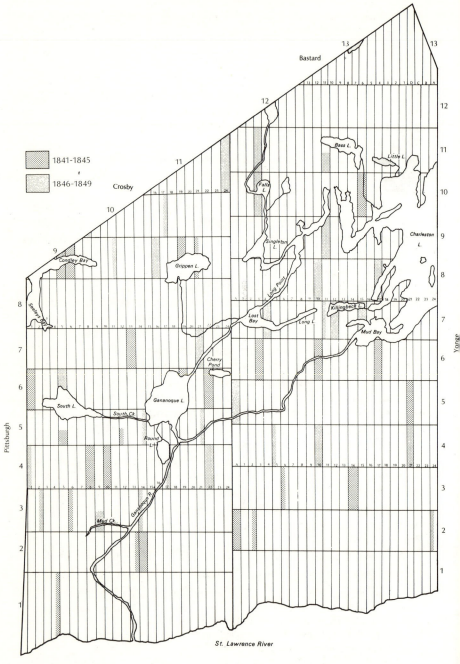

Source: Abstract Index of Deeds

Map 18 Date of land patenting, 1841–9

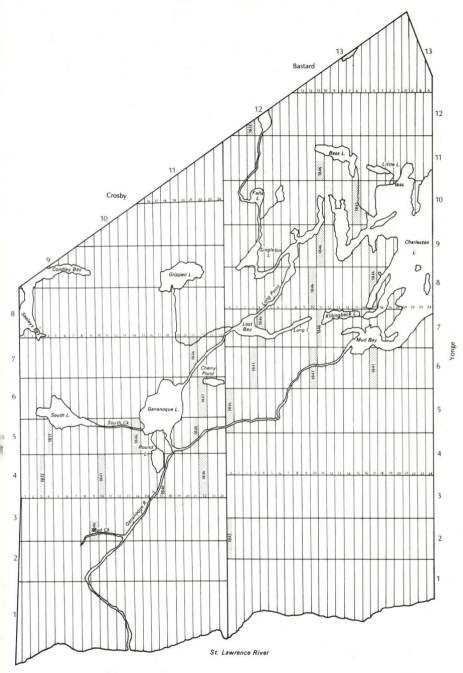

Source: Abstract Index of Deeds

Map 19 Lands patented by the Canada Company through 31 December 1849

no insuperable impediment. The data for maps 12, 15, 17, 18, and 19 reveal that of the sixty-four lots of Crown reserves in 1824 only seven remained unpatented by the end of 1849 and, of those seven, only one was a full two hundred acre lot. The rest were either half lots or small lots bordering on lakes, streams, or township boundaries. The equivalent of eighteen of the sixty-four Crown reserve lots went to the Canada Company (which, as already stated, chose land badly), so that approximately 60 percent of the Crown reserve lots actually were patented by private individuals, and this somewhat under-states the case: private individuals tended to acquire full lots and those with the best agricultural potential. The small, flooded, desperately rocky lots tended either to go unpatented or to be acquired by the Canada Company. If the patent data are any guide, the acquisition of the Crown reserve lots by private individuals did not take place in a single great rush but was spread over the time from the late 1820s to mid-century.[15]

Judging the effect of the clergy reserves upon settlement is more complicated. If one compares the plotting of the clergy reserves as of 1824 (map 14) with the information on land not patented before mid-century (map 20), one can easily (albeit wrongly) infer that the reserves actually were a serious blockage in the land system: only slightly over 11 percent of the clergy reserves had been patented by mid-century. Nevertheless, this does not mean that the reserves

15 The available data on prices paid for the Crown reserves are too sketchy to be trusted. The problem is that although the government officials often tried to auction land, they also sold it by private treaty at varying reserve prices. The government's own records do not inspire much confidence. For instance, a sur-vey of Crown and clergy reserves for each township, made in 1838, stated that there were no Crown reserves left in Leeds and Lansdowne, although land regis-try data clearly indicate that this was wrong (AO, Crown Land Papers, RG 7, ser. A-IV, 56, "Land in Upper Canada consisting of each townships of Crown and Clergy Reserves quarterly granted and vacant, 1838"). A responsible journalist writing in the mid-1840s reported that the price for Crown lands in Leeds and in Lansdowne was 8 shillings per acre (William H. Smith, Smith's Canadian Gazetteer [Toronto: H. and W. Rowsell 1846], 96 and 97).

Although certainly it would be interesting to know the price of each lot, the information would actually be irrelevant to the point at issue, for we know that the land indeed was purchased. This indicates (1) that the purchaser some-how acquired the capital to make the purchase, which is to say that, however straitened financially he may have been, the purchase was within his means, and (2) that, whatever the price, the acquisition of the land was judged to be a wise investment. Whether the purchaser was right is another matter entirely. The point is that we can deal here with actual behaviour and do not have to speculate about the relative attractiveness to settlers of various investment alternatives or about whether, from their perspective, land prices were perceived as too high. Their actual behaviour, the purchase of the land, obviates the need for any such speculation.

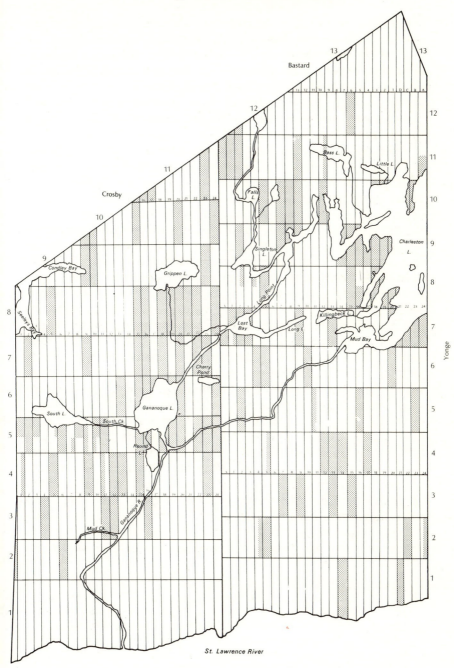

Source: Abstract Index of Deeds

Map 20 *Lands not patented as of 31 December 1849*

stood as a barricade to settlement. The assumption which has pervaded the North American land-holding attitudes is that the natural and best arrangement of rural economy is for each farmer to own and to occupy his own ground, but the British agricultural norm of the period was to separate ownership of the land from use and occupancy. The new settlers from the British Isles were well acquainted with the practice of tenant farming and the leasing of the clergy reserves to farmers was not repugnant to them.

From 1811 to 1834 the clergy reserves were rented on twenty-one-year leases with rents set at seven-year intervals. By contemporary leasing standards in the British Isles this was an unusually long period and it provided sufficient certainty of occupancy to permit a farmer to clear and improve his land with the knowledge that he would reap the profits in terms of agricultural produce. The annual rental payments were graduated so as to keep the burden to the tenant relatively low in the first seven years of his farming and then to increase as, presumably, his agricultural income increased: leases made after 1811 were set at the equivalent of 4s. and 3s. 4d. per acre per year for the first seven years, rising to 6s. and 9s. 4d. in the second seven-year period, and to 8s. and 1s. 10d. in the final seven years.[16] Far from inhibiting the influx of new migrants, such arrangements were facilitatory. Long leasing on such terms permitted a new settler to acquire control of a piece of land without necessitating heavy capital investment. He was therefore able to put his money into livestock and implements and to rise out of the subsistence economy more quickly than if he had been forced to purchase the land. For many new arrivals, the choice was not between leasing and buying but between leasing and becoming a wage labourer. Thus for a new settler of limited means the clergy reserves were not a barrier to success as a farmer but actually were an avenue.[17] Not surprisingly, then, the clergy reserves in Leeds and Lansdowne township were well leased.[18] Of course the attractions to a new settler were even greater if he could simply squat on the land and pay no rent at all. In 1835 this was said to occur on the great part of the

16 See Gates, *Land Policies of Upper Canada*, 198–9.
17 For an excellent American study establishing the economic rationality and efficiency of leasing over purchase in certain situations, see Donald L. Winters, *Farmers without Farms: Agricultural Tenancy in Nineteenth Century Iowa* (Westport, Conn.: Greenwood Press 1978). See also his article, "Tenant Farming in Iowa, 1860–1900: A Study of the Terms of Rental Leases," *Agricultural History* 48 (January 1979): 130–50.
18 See, for example, AO, RG 1, ser. A-VI-5, 1, "Inspectors Report. Johnstown District Clergy Reserves 1822–27." Numerous similar reports are found in the series.

reserves in the Johnstown and Eastern districts,[19] although probably it mostly took place in the inland townships.

Sale of lots from the clergy reserves was a matter of some argument. For a time in 1824 it seemed that the Canada Company would be granted a purchase-option on any reserves it wanted. It surveyed the local reserves and determined that it would like to acquire twenty-four parcels involving forty-five hundred acres.[20] Its acquisition of clergy reserves was blocked by political efforts on behalf of the Anglican Church, but in 1827 tenants were given the privilege of buying their land by private treaty. A further act of 1834 extended the tenants' private-treaty privilege and threw open to public auction those lands not taken up by the leaseholders. In Leeds and Lansdowne township, however, very few − slightly over 11 percent − of the land parcels in the clergy reserves had been taken over and patented by mid-century, chiefly because the system of leasing the clergy reserves was so advantageous from the settler's viewpoint. Between 1827 and 1830 the average price of clergy land sold in the province was 15s. and during the lifetime of the 1827 act averaged 13s. 4½d.[21] Even considering that a purchaser was given ten years' credit, a tenant would have to set aside annually several times the amount of cash which he previously had been accustomed to pay in rent. A sensible tenant would not buy the land he occupied until his lease ran out, and the standard lease was for twenty-one years. Even though the leasing system was discontinued in 1834, the average time left on a lease would have given the typical tenant until the mid-1840s before he had to decide whether or not to purchase. Of course, there was also the inevitable lag in the patenting process, even when tenanted land was purchased. Thus the process of transfer to private hands muddled slowly into the 1850s, until finally the secularization of 1854 promised to end the problem entirely. A second reason why so relatively little land was patented from among the reserves is that many of the lots were in less than desirable locations and presumably were not judged worth the going sale price. In some cases, this was perhaps exacerbated by the timber having been stripped: the Johnstown district was reported to have suffered particularly from timber-stripping and abandonment of clergy lots.[22]

This brings us to the question of the actual effect of land

19 Wilson, "The Clergy Reserves," in CHR, 295.
20 AO, Crown Land Papers, RG 7, ser. A-IV, 32, "Crown and Clergy Reserves returned to the Canada Company, 1824."
21 Gates, Land Policies of Upper Canada, 211.
22 Ibid., 211.

speculators. It is hard to define which piece of land was held by a speculator and which was not, but the individual plots of land indicated on map 13 can be denominated with a high degree of probability as speculative, since they were held by non-residents who had not paid their taxes for eight years and more. That is precisely the behaviour one would expect of a speculator, to hold the land but put off paying any charges on it as long as possible and preferably only when the land is sold and cash is in hand. The significant point about these local speculation activities is that the price of local land had not risen enough by the late 1820s to make it worthwhile for the speculators to sell. However, two land-law changes improved things immensely, the ending of free land grants in 1827 and new leases on the clergy reserves in 1834. These changes meant that all the land of the township became part of the same market system, just when the great waves of immigrants of the 1830s were arriving in Upper Canada.

Without question, the land speculators wanted to sell. From the late 1820s onwards the local newspapers were full of advertisements by local speculators trying to unload their lands throughout the Johnstown district. Among them were the local magnates Jonas Jones and Charles Jones and the big-time gambler George Mallock. Sales were far from easy, however, and the speculators had to offer credit to the purchaser (ranging from eighteen months to several years) in order to sell the properties.[23]

Sell they did: fewer than one-eighth of the speculative lots of 1829 were still being held at mid-century.[24] It is, however, difficult to determine whether the lands were overpriced. This is in part because the prices given on the Abstract Index of Deeds are not sufficiently comprehensive or specific to be trustworthy. We know the general price range from other sources: in 1831 wild lands seized by the sheriff in the township were selling at 10 shillings an acre,[25] and the few Crown reserves left in the 1840s were open at 8 shillings an acre.[26] Yet, even if we knew all the prices paid for land purchased

23 See, for example, the *Brockville Gazette*, 13 March 1829, 4 September 1829, and 26 February 1830. The advertisements were ubiquitous in any local paper of the period.

    A useful general discussion of credit land purchase is David P. Gagan, "The Security of Land: Mortgaging in Toronto Gore Township, 1835–95," in *Aspects of Nineteenth Century Ontario: Essays Presented to James J. Talman* (Toronto: University of Toronto Press 1974), 136–55.

24 Derived by comparing the source for map 13 with all transactions listed in the Abstract Index of Deeds.

25 *Appendix to Journals of the Legislative Assembly of Upper Canada 1831*, 142.

26 Smith, 96–7.

from speculators, the question of overpricing would be misplaced, for such a judgment would require a knowledge of alternative investment possibilities open to new settlers and this is well beyond the state of economic historiography of the period. We do know, however, that the lands were purchased. Approximately 30 percent of the speculative lots passed into other private hands by direct sale during the 1830s and approximately 36 percent in the 1840s.[27] This indicates that, whatever the price actually was, in the judgment of a large number of contemporary settlers the lands offered a fair return on investment and were obtainable within the terms of the credit facilities open to them. By their acquisitional behaviour contemporary purchasers indicated that the lands were not overpriced, however much they may have complained when in their cups.

It is noteworthy that the much dreaded sheriff's sale of rural folklore most often affected land speculators, not serious settlers. Of the parcels designated as speculative on map 13, somewhat over 22 percent had been seized by mid-century for sale by the local sheriff as a consequence of non-payment of local taxes.[28] This makes a startling implication about the profitability of land as an investment. Far from being the low-risk, high-profit venture it so often is said to have been, speculative land had downside possibilities – even when it was free land obtained before 1827. In permitting their lands to be seized by the sheriff, the speculators in Leeds and Lansdowne township were implictly acknowledging that the carrying charges on the land exceeded their hope of eventual income from its sale. The carrying charges were only the legal land registry fees which had been incurred when the land had been obtained from the Crown and the annual local taxes, usually a few shillings per lot. When the owners of 22 percent of the speculative lots let them go under the sheriff's gavel rather than maintain these mild carrying charges, they were graphically indicating that in this particular township the rewards of land speculation in many cases were not merely nil but actually negative.

4

In presenting the perspective on the settlement process in Leeds and Lansdowne township through three separate and contradictory lenses, one is not being perverse but is raising at the level of local process several of the key issues that concern historians of central Canada in this period. The period from 1815 to the mid-1830s in

27 See n24.
28 Ibid.

Upper Canadian history is analogous to the Dark Ages in European history. As with classical Rome, historians know a good deal about the loyalist era, but suddenly thereafter records become thinner and the light much dimmer. On a township level, however, one can employ the data of specific local events to align the three lenses properly so that some light does indeed filter through. The focal years for aligning our three seemingly contradictory lenses must be the early 1830s and the axis of alignment shall be determined by the Irish settlers who, in the early 1830s, became agitated and organized and eventually turned the local society upside down. Specific local personalities and finite local grievances are crucial to understanding the social revolution of the 1830s.

As a whole, the settlement process as it affected all settlers, not merely the Irish, was remarkably rational. As indicated by map 8 in chapter 2, the land first patented (in the decade 1796–1805 inclusive) was chosen because of locational factors (proximity to the St Lawrence River and, in the rear of Lansdowne, to the alleged iron sites). Thereafter, the sequence of patenting followed, albeit crudely, one determined chiefly by the agricultural desirability of the land. (Compare the pattern indicated by the post-1805 data on map 8 in chapter 2 and that on map 21 below with the data on soil type and agricultural suitability in maps 10 and 11 in this chapter.) This confirms Thomas McIlwraith's work which suggests that in occupying land the bulk of the early settlers had little regard for roads in choosing land settlement sites, but instead operated from other bases of selection,[29] in the local case, land quality as far as it could be determined in advance of settlement. McIlwraith found that farmers were able to subordinate apparent ease of communication to other factors in choosing land, in large part because of the practice of using sleighs in winter to deliver market goods. At Yonge Mills, near Brockville, for instance, he found that well over half of the annual quantity of wheat delivered arrived in winter. The chief commercial crop in the Johnstown district, wheat, did not require that a farmer have year-round access to a market but merely that he be able to deliver his crop to a buyer at least once a year.[30] Since this was always possible, given the good sleighing conditions each winter, settlers were able to select their land with productivity paramount in mind. Further confirmation that a rational sequence occurred in the selection of land by new settlers and that this

29 Thomas F. McIlwraith, "The Adequacy of Rural Roads in the Era before Railways: An Illustration from Upper Canada," *The Canadian Geographer* 14 (1979): 358.
30 Ibid., 357.

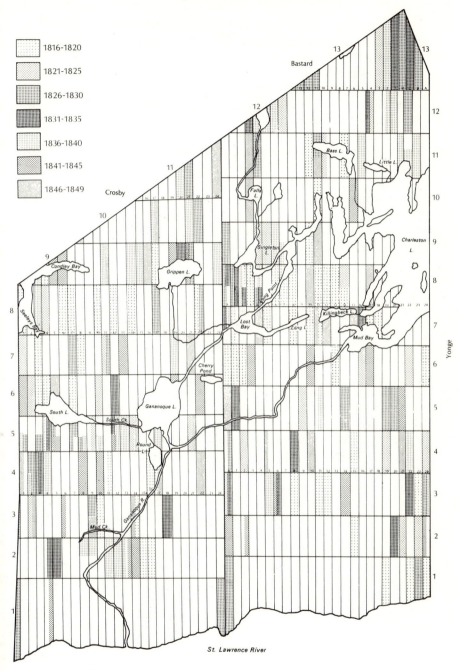

Source:Abstract Index of Deeds

Map 21 Date of land patenting, 1816–49

rationality was based upon agricultural suitability is found by comparison of the map of agricultural quality with that of land left unpatented as of 31 December 1849 (maps 11 and 20 respectively). If one removes from consideration those unpatented parcels which were part of the clergy reserves and which, as explained earlier, were delayed in being patented (approximately 45 percent of unpatented parcels), the residual was largely part-lots or lands that had little agricultural value, being either under water, marshy, or unspeakably rocky. The pattern of unpatented land in the fifth concession of Leeds, the area between Gananoque Lake and Grippen Lake in Leeds, and the strips of lands left unpatented around Charleston Lake and near Lost Bay, Singleton Lake, and other small lakes in Lansdowne all testify to the good sense of the immigrants. Whatever else they may have been, in selecting and settling farm land the successive waves of new settlers were not fools.

5

The local Irish were the largest component in a broad stream of immigrants who settled in the township of Leeds and Lansdowne after the end of the Napoleonic Wars. The magnitude and composition of that stream, however, were not defined until the census of 1842, quite late (although not too late) for our purposes. The aggregate census data show that the population roughly doubled between 1816 and 1824 and that it doubled again by 1835.[31] Undoubtedly, some of this growth came from natural increase on the part of the population settled in the area in 1816, and perhaps from the in-migration of individuals who previously had settled in other places in the Canadas. The probability is, however, that most of the increase stemmed from immigration from outside British North America. The real question is not if the external immigrants and their offspring came to predominate in the township but when.

Table 6 indicates the birthplaces of the township's population as determined in 1842.[32] Like all such tallies, it understates the degree of Old World influence, since all children of the foreign-born were counted as native Canadians so long as their parents had touched

31 See Appendix A for the annual census data. There are no complete figures for 1816, but on the basis of the full data for 1815 and the partial data for 1816 one can impute an 1816 figure of 556. If the reader does not wish to accept this, then he may simply use the 1815 data. The basic point made in the text concerning the magnitude of population increase is affirmed in any case.
32 Unless otherwise stated, the data for 1842 referred to in the text are taken from the manuscript census of 1842, found in AO. The processing of the data is mine.

TABLE 6

Birthplaces, Population of Township of Leeds and Lansdowne, 1842

	Front No.	%	Rear No.	%	Entire township No.	%
NATIVES OF CANADA						
French origin	44	2.0	23	2.4	67	2.1
British origin	1,203	55.4	690	73.3	1,893	60.8
Subtotal	(1,247)	(57.4)	(713)	(75.7)	(1,960)	(62.9)
FOREIGN-BORN						
Naturalized citizens born abroad:						
England	83	3.8	15	1.6	98	3.2
Ireland	459	21.1	125	13.3	584	18.7
Scotland	136	6.3	2	0.2	138	4.4
Continental Europe	1	0.1	4	0.4	5	0.2
United States	166	7.6	83	8.8	249	8.0
Subtotal	(845)	(38.9)	(229)	(24.3)	(1,074)	(34.5)
Aliens born abroad not yet naturalized	81	3.7	0	0.0	81	2.6
TOTAL	2,173	100.0	942	100.0	3,115	100.0

Source: AO, 1842 census manuscripts

these shores before the children's birth. The foreign-born and their children made up the bulk – two-thirds would be a conservative estimate – of the local population in 1842. This point is made clear if one considers the Irish in isolation. If one goes through the manuscript census data and adds to the Irish-born all those children born in Canada who were resident in families in which either one or both parents had been born in Ireland, one obtains the following crude index of Irish ethnicity:

	Front	Rear	Entire Township
Total Irish persons	960	375	1,335
As percentage of total local population	44.2%	39.8%	42.9%

Of course one cannot apply a precise "multiplier" based on these Irish figures to other groups (if for no other reason than that the children of ethnically mixed marriages are included in the Irish figures above), but one can safely argue by analogy that in any realistic assessment of the cultural origins of the people the entire foreign-born population must be multiplied to take into account their Canadian-born offspring.

Reworking of the 1842 data allows us to push them back in time to shed light on an earlier period. Specifically, the census-takers asked those born abroad how long they had been in the country. As was the case with so many peripheral items in the pre-1851 census, this one was sometimes ignored, occasionally answered inaccurately, or the response recorded illegibly. Nevertheless, if one interprets the response to mean "how long did people *say* they had been in the country?" then one can make use of the following tally of the years of residence of those Irish-born adults who responded to the question and whose response is legible on the returns:

0–5 years	97
6–10 years	79
11–15 years	62
16–20 years	46
over 20 years	67

The average time spent in the country was 12.0 years. These sketchy data should not be overread, but they do imply that about half the members of the largest local immigrant group, the Irish, were already in Canada in 1830.[33] Since the population of the township roughly doubled between the end of the Napoleonic Wars and 1824 and had, using the 1816 imputed base, quadrupled by 1835, a reasonable speculation is that the post-war foreign immigrants and their offspring became numerically dominant sometime in the years between 1825 and 1830.

This suggestion is confirmed quite dramatically when one turns from quantitative data to narrative material. Beginning in 1830 and continuing for the next six years, the immigrant Irish ran amok, or at least so it seemed to the representatives of the old economic and social order. This eruption is exactly what one would expect if, just prior to 1830, the Irish had become aware that the foreign-born and their offspring were a majority locally, that they, the Irish, were the largest component of the immigrant culture, but that the local establishment was blocking their rightful economic, political, and social progress.[34]

33 Two potentially self-cancelling sources of bias in the data may be mentioned: (1) arriving in the country and settling in the township of Leeds and Lansdowne may have been separated by a considerable time lag in many cases, but (2), on the other hand, there doubtless were early Irish settlers in the township who had out-migrated or who had died before the 1842 census was taken. As suggested in the text, the data should not be overread.

34 The account which follows in the text of the local Irish upsurge is both detailed in narrative and nasty in its details. Two volumes might be of use in keeping it in perspective. One is Evelyn Purvis Earle, *Leeds the Lovely* (Toronto: Ryerson

6

The key figure in the local Irish eruption was Ogle R. Gowan, surely one of the most insistent figures ever to stride across the Upper Canadian stage.[35] His father was a prominent Wexford landowner, but, as a younger (and probably illegitimate) son, Ogle became a "squireen," one of the caste most despised in Ireland, the "half-mounted gentry." Many of the Anglo-Irish ascendancy were content to remain in the countryside, acting as part-time agents for various landlords and as attenuated dependents of their own families, lording it over the Catholic peasantry but never being fully accepted by the real gentry. Gowan, though only half-mounted, tried to make his own living, or at least his own fame, in Dublin, and he did so through exploiting his family background. County Wexford was among the areas which had suffered worst from Catholic depredations in the 1798 Rising and, indeed, the Gowan family home had been burned. His father was one of the earliest local Orangemen and young Ogle had been named for his godfather, George Ogle, who was one of the grand masters of the Orange Order in Ireland. Young Ogle himself joined the Order in 1818. In Dublin, he made money and fame from the rancid underside of the

Press 1951). This is the work of a local enthusiast and it emphasizes the more romantic aspects of Irish settlement. It has some delightfully evocative passages. The second volume is the sometimes underrated Durham Report, in its observations on the rise of the "emigrant" party (Lucas edition, 2: 153ff.). Durham's arguments about the emigrant party may or may not be applicable to the whole province, but they fit the Leeds and Lansdowne situation nicely. (1) He asserted that an emigrant party arose, with its origins in the heavy migration that began in 1825–6 (he used "party" in the contemporary British sense of an interest group or coalition, not in the modern sense of political party, although such interest groups often did act in politics). (2) He noted that the newcomers did not coalesce into a distinct party for quite a time after their arrival, but (3) that they were precipitated into a substantial unit by (a) a desire to assimilate the Upper Canadian political system closer to United Kingdom standards and (b) a desire to have removed the disqualifications and discriminations they experienced. (4) In the election of 1836 the newcomers from the British Isles effectively won their points. Incidentally, Durham adopted contemporary imperial usage and employed "British" to describe all migrants from the British Isles. This included the Irish, who, in fact, comprised the bulk of the migrants to Upper Canada.

35 Hereward Senior's discussion of Gowan in the DCB is the best available. There is also valuable information in Senior's "Ogle Gowan, Orangeism, and the Immigrant Question, 1830–1833," *Ontario History* 66 (1974): 193–206. See also Walter McCleary, ed., *History of the Orange Association in the Dominion of Canada, No. 1: One Man's Loyalty* (Toronto: Committee on Orange History 1953).

Anglo-Irish character: he wrote pamphlets against the Roman Catholics and published a small anti-Catholic paper, *The Antidote*. During these years Gowan cultivated the Orange system and when, by act of the Westminster parliament, the Orange Order was dissolved in 1825, he became an "assistant grand secretary" for a benevolent society which was a surrogate for the Order, designed to keep the network together while remaining just barely within the law. Why Gowan decided to emigrate to Upper Canada is unclear, but he arrived in 1829 with a wife, seven children, and two servants, a handsome, clear-featured, aggressive twenty-six-year-old, possessed of monumental self-assurance and a deep instinctive knowledge of the drives, fears, and hatreds of his fellow Irishmen.

Within a year of his arrival, Gowan, now ostensibly a gentleman farmer from Brockville but actually a fulltime organizer and agitator, was in the centre of several troubles. Gowan operated as the hub of three concentric circles of agitation, national, provincial, and local. His national prominence came through his founding role in the Orange Order in British North America.[36] Orange lodges had sprung up in British North America well before Gowan arrived, but they were local occurrences, formed by various regiments of imperial soldiers stationed in the Canadas or by pockets of local Irish emigrés. They served as local social clubs, not as part of a formal network.[37] Gowan changed that. Soon after settling in Brockville, he began sounding the opinions of Orange sympathizers and on 1 January 1830 the Grand Orange Lodge of British North America was founded at a meeting held in the Brockville courthouse. Failing to attract a royal duke as titular head, Gowan became the Grand Master. With remarkable energy and organizational ability, he tied together the extant local Orange lodges and expanded the network throughout Ontario and Quebec. By 1833 he had issued warrants creating ninety-one lodges in Upper Canada and eight in Lower.[38] Membership in the British North American

36 The standard study of the origin of the movement is Hereward Senior, *Orangeism in Ireland and Britain 1795–1836* (London: Routledge and Kegan Paul 1966). Senior continued the story in *Orangeism: The Canadian Phase* (Toronto: McGraw-Hill Ryerston 1972). A more analytic study is *The Sash Canada Wore: A Historical Geography of the Orange Order in Canada* (Toronto: University of Toronto Press 1980). For an Orangeman's view of the Order's origins, see Leslie H. Saunders, *The Story of Orangeism* (Toronto: The Grand Orange Lodge of Ontario West 1941).

37 See Hereward Senior, "The Genesis of Canadian Orangeism," *Ontario History* 60 (1968): 13–29.

38 Cecil J. Houston and William J. Smyth, "The Spread of the Loyal Orange Lodge through Ontario, 1830–1900" (paper presented at CHA annual meeting 1978), 4.

colonies was claimed to be over ten thousand, most of them in Upper Canada.[39] This number rose continually and by 1860 the Order claimed over one hundred thousand members,[40] a number which, although doubtless inflated, indicates that the Order was a major national phenomenon.

Since the Brockville area was Gowan's home, the Orange movement had considerable adherence in Leeds county. Houston and Smyth's plotting of the residences of the grand lodge executive and grand committee members in 1833 shows that most of them came from within a twenty-mile radius of Brockville.[41] In the vicinity of Brockville, several lodges were granted warrants, the most important for our purposes being in Leeds and Lansdowne township: the lodges in Gananoque and Lansdowne were both formed by 1833.[42] In the light of the eventual clash of the Leeds county Irish with the existing political establishment, it is worth noting that there was a backlog of tension between Orangemen and the local worthies dating back to 1823. In that year, when the Orange lodges were merely individual units, not part of a national network, an attempt to ban them had been introduced into the Upper Canadian legislature. Charles Jones, one of the two members for Leeds, spoke in favour of the ban. When the vote on the second reading was evenly split, the second member for Leeds county, Livius P. Sherwood, as speaker had the casting vote, which he threw against the ban. This does not mean that Sherwood was favourably disposed to the Order – indeed, in the debates no one defended it – but merely that it seemed inexpedient to try to control the Orangemen with legislative monitions.[43]

If forging the Orange network was an achievement on a national scale, Gowan's activities in the legislative assembly for Upper Canada and later for the parliament for the united Canadas had

39 Hereward Senior, "The Character of Canadian Orangeism," in *Thought from the Learned Societies of Canada, 1961* (Toronto: W.J. Gage 1961), 177–89.

40 Cecil Houston and William Smith, "The Ulster Legacy," *Multiculturalism* 1 (1978): 10.

41 Houston and Smith, *The Sash*, figure 2, 31.

42 See the map mentioned in note 41 above. And in McCleary, *One Man's Loyalty* (9), it is mentioned that in 1832 the Orangemen from Gananoque had to cancel their accustomed walk, so presumably it was established by 1831, if not before. Thaddeus W.H. Leavitt, *History of Leeds and Grenville* (Brockville: Brockville Recorder 1879), 139, says Lodge No. 26 in Lansdowne is one of the oldest in central Canada, and its number indicates that it was founded by 1833 at the latest. The Orange lodge in Lansdowne officially came to an end on 13 July 1982 (*Gananoque Reporter*, 23 June 1982).

43 On the bill and debates see Senior, "The Genesis of Canadian Orangeism," 16–18. See also Senior, "Orangeism Takes Root in Canada," *Canadian Genealogist* 3, no. 1 (1981): 14–15.

province-wide reference. He was in the house off and on from 1834 until his retirement in 1861, at which time contemporaries had given him the soubriquet "the father of the house." His parliamentary activities often had a sharp local reference. Gowan, like any good politician, understood that any wider fame was contingent upon keeping his local constituents happy. In particular, the immigrant community, his natural constituency in Leeds county, needed help in obtaining clear titles to land, and he took upon himself responsibility for dealing with the often recalcitrant officials in Toronto. At first he did this himself, but in late 1835 he deputed his cousin James R. Gowan, then resident in Toronto, to act as agent for those Leeds county petitioners of whom he approved. The instructions to James from Ogle Gowan are worth reading in detail, for they indicate what Gowan was doing to obtain the adherence of the Leeds county immigrant community.

My object in writing to you at present is to ascertain from you if you could do for me the land business which might otherwise require my presence in Toronto ...

There are many good loyal old country people in this part, who would all support me, if they had their deeds, and a great many of them are entitled to their deeds, and only need some friend, who would take the trouble to produce them for them and I think it a pity to leave them without their titles ...

There is some trouble in procuring a deed. In the first place I will have to send you the location tickets and settlement duties certificate; these you will have to take then to Radenhurst [an official in the surveyor general's office] who will file them and give you a description, which you then take to the Attorney General's office, where you obtain a fiat, which you take to Mr. Cameron's office (the provincial secretary) where the deed is engrossed and the great seal affixed. If you mention to Mr. Cameron that the deed is for me, I think he will send it over to the government house and get his excellency's signature for you. Lastly you take it to the attorney general whose signature will complete the deed. There will be no charge for all of this, but if there is I will forward it to you. If you say you can do this for me, I may occasionally trouble you upon the subject, and at any time you want to make a search in the surveyor general's official, if you mention to Mr. Thornhill it is for me, he will do it for you, free of charge. Also, if you should have business at Mr. Baine's office (secretary to the clergy corporation) if you tell Mr. Baines it is for me, he will do anything in his power for you.[44]

44 Ogle Gowan to James Gowan, 20 November 1835, AO, Gowan papers.

Cousin James agreed.[45] The document shows that Gowan had been doing this service for long enough to be conversant with all the details, that he seems to have been on close terms with at least three of the officials engaged in the legal process, and that they were in some ways indebted to him or at least favourable to his cases. The indebtedness which an immigrant would feel to Gowan is obvious, but it is not so obvious that Gowan was being doubly effective politically: he was not only bonding the immigrant to him but was actually creating his vote, and thus his own political future, for title to land was requisite for the franchise.[46] (That Gowan picked up parcels of land for himself both by patenting and by buying land from the patenter should surprise no one.)[47]

All Gowan's activities had some local reference, but for the purposes of this study the most important were his election campaigns for the legislative assembly. Although these campaigns were initiated by an official call to elect members for the Upper Canada assembly, in practice the series of elections held in Leeds county in the 1830s was really about control of the local political power structure. Provincially called elections were the arena but the fight was local. In the local electoral structure there were three seats in the legislative assembly to fight over, one for Brockville, which does not require our attention here, and two for the county of Leeds proper. There were more factions than spoils, so that conflict was endemic. The two most established families were the old loyalist and very Tory ones stemming from two separate Jones clans, the descendants of Solomon Jones and his two brothers, and those of Ephraim Jones.[48] In the narrative which follows, Charles and Jonas Jones, sons of Ephraim, are the most important. A third loyalist

---

45 (Draft) James Gowan to Ogle Gowan, 27 November 1835, AO, Gowan papers. The first document came down from Ogle to James Gowan in a letter of 9 December 1835 (AO, Gowan papers).

46 On the rural franchise requirement see Graeme H. Patterson, "Studies in Elections and Public Opinion in Upper Canada" (PHD diss., University of Toronto 1969), v–vii. This thesis also has an insightful discussion of several Leeds county elections.

47 Locally, for instance, part of lot 13 in concession 5 of Leeds township and all of lot 12 in concession 7 of Lansdowne township.

48 For want of a better term, the two Jones clans and the Sherwoods and their associates are described as Tories. This does not mean that they were Tory in the narrow sense of political party as understood in our own time. As S.F. Wise has said, "It is impossible to disagree with [G.M.] Craig's contention that 'party' in anything but the most embryonic sense, was not a factor in Upper Canadian elections. The evidence for any substantial degree of province-wide party organization, even in 1836, simply does not exist." (S.F. Wise, "Tory Faction-

family, the Sherwoods, was consequential, though of diminishing influence. In addition, another old loyalist family, the Buells, was important in local political contests, for it fought for the "reform" viewpoint with considerable vigor. The most important of this clan at the time was William Buell, editor of the *Brockville Recorder*. The dominant families in Leeds and Lansdowne township, the Landons in Lansdowne and the Stone-McDonald interests in Gananoque, did not run for provincial office and, perforce, the representation of Leeds and Lansdowne township was fought as part of the battle for control of Leeds county.[49]

When an election was called for 1830, Ogle R. Gowan, not one year off the boat from Ireland, came forward as a candidate. This was not so ill-considered as it must have appeared at the time, for we now recognize the demographic shift which immigration from the British Isles, and especially from Ireland, had caused in the late 1820s and we now know how effective Gowan had been in forming the Orange network.[50] Further, the election provided a tactical opportunity that might be exploited: only one of the sitting

---

alism: Kingston Elections and Upper Canadian Politics, 1820–1836," *Ontario History* 57 [1965]: 205.)

The following comments by Wise indicate that the term "Tory" nevertheless has a socio-political meaning that makes it a valid concept to use concerning the 1830s: "If Upper Canad[ian] conservatism lacked uniformity and homogeneity, this is only another way of saying that it was an alliance of groups, with different interests and outlooks. It is possible to express the nature of the alliance in several ways. A Tory of the time would certainly have said that conservative leadership came from the 'respectable classes' in the community. In this sense, Toryism was the political expression of the province's small upper class, the people who considered themselves the natural leaders of society." "The core of Tory support was in the eastern counties, the area of major Loyalist settlement, and in the towns, especially Kingston, Brockville, York-Toronto, Niagara and London." "The Tory 'party,' then, was a quasi-official coalition of the central and local elites united for the purpose of distributing honours and rewards to the politically deserving." The quotations are from S.F. Wise, "Upper Canada and the Conservative Tradition," in *Profiles of a Province: Studies in the History of Ontario* (Toronto: Ontario Historical Society 1967), 24, 21, and 27 respectively.

49 On local power alignments, Elva M. Richards, "The Joneses of Brockville and the Family Compact," *Ontario History* 60 (1968): 169–84, is especially valuable. Professor Ian MacPherson has kindly permitted me to see his manuscript, "The Buell View: Building a New Order in Brockville, 1830–1850," which is very illuminating on the local power structure. A revised version is at present in press (Belleville: Mika Publishing Co.) under the title *Matters of Loyalty*.

50 There were over forty lodges affiliated with the Orange network as early as 1830 and eleven of these were in Leeds, Grenville, or Frontenac counties. (MS record book, "Records of the L.O.L. of British North America," in National Orange Archives, Toronto.)

members, William Buell, was running and, although his seat could be taken as safe, there was an opening for the other Leeds seat. In the light of Gowan's later hyper-loyalism, it is important to recognize that he wanted to be elected more than he wanted to be elected on any particular principle. At first he hoped to be accepted by the reformer Buell as a *de facto* running-mate and thus to be returned virtually unopposed, but the Buells had a candidate of their own, Mathew Howard.[51] Gowan went ahead anyway. In the era before strict party politics evolved, the practice was for a series of meetings to be held in various spots in the county and each meeting (usually claiming to be non-partisan) nominated candidates. The nominations were not binding but were crudely indicative of popular feeling. Gowan, realizing that he would have to fight the Buells, announced himself as something of a backwoods Tory, thus permitting at least a tolerant relationship with Henry Sherwood, who was the candidate favoured by the old loyalist Tories. More significantly, Gowan clearly identified the social constituency for which he spoke: at a meeting at Lamb's Pond (Elizabethtown township, Leeds county, now called New Dublin) which endorsed his candidacy, a resolution was passed stating that "as there are three representative seats for the county [two for the county proper and one for Brockville] ... we are decidedly of the opinion that one of these three should be an Irishman," adding, ominously, "a measure the concession of which we deem necessary to ally the rapidly increasing spirit of national animosity ..."[52] At a meeting about a week later for the backwoods townships of Burgess and Elmsley, it was resolved that, as the majority of the population of the township "are Europeans by birth and education, we conceive that if a European Canadian of equal talents and integrity can be found, he should possess a peculiar claim upon our sympathy and support."[53] The meeting then endorsed the old loyalist Sherwood and the new Tory Gowan. In the actual election, the reformers Buell and Howard were elected for Leeds county but Gowan ran ahead of Sherwood, had only seventy votes fewer than the poll leader, Buell, and was just fourteen votes behind Howard.[54] The handwriting was on the wall, but the established families were slow to react.

Gowan's next step was logical (in matters of ambition he was as

51 Senior, "Ogle Gowan, Orangeism and the Immigrant Question, 1830–1833," 195–6. See also reports in *Brockville Recorder*, 21 September 1830.
52 *Brockville Recorder*, 28 September 1830.
53 *Brockville Recorder*, 12 October 1830.
54 DCB, William Buell; Hereward Senior, "Ogle Gowan, Orangeism and the Immigrant Question, 1830–1833," 198.

logical as he was relentless) for he used a by-election in neighbouring Grenville county in 1831 to turn his shotgun entente with
Ephraim Jones's descendants into a formal alliance. Late in 1830 he
cooperated with the Joneses in trying to form a set of "independent
clubs" with the idea of uniting old loyalists and Irish Protestants and
Catholics against the distant but frightening alarm of William Lyon
Mackenzie.[55] This effort was not notably successful, nor was the
Leeds Patriotic Club founded in early 1831 under the presidency of
the loyalist George Breakenridge, with Gowan as a vice president,[56]
but in these connections Gowan was establishing his own loyalty
and, *mutatis mutandis*, that of his Irish followers. Of more practical
importance, when asked in 1831 to run in the neighbouring county
of Grenville in a by-election forced by the death of Edward Jessup, he
declined.[57] This was shrewd, for Grenville county had a higher
proportion of old established families than did Leeds. Gowan's
future lay with the emerging immigrant majority in Leeds, and in
fact he told one meeting that if an election were now held in Leeds
he would win by a majority of five to one.[58] Instead of pushing
himself forward in Grenville, he worked energetically for Jonas
Jones,[59] whose candidacy, however, was unsuccessful.

Gowan, like the immigrants whom he represented, was always
in danger of being labelled subversive, which he and they certainly
were in wishing to shoulder aside some of the established holders of
power. They were not, however, disloyal to the constitution. Thus,
the tour of William Lyon Mackenzie through eastern Upper Canada
in the autumn of 1831 was a perfect stage-set for Gowan, allowing
him to make a great show of holding his own meetings or, when
possible, debating Mackenzie in person. It was particularly important that Gowan (and by implication his Irish followers in eastern
Ontario) put as much distance as possible between himself and the
Orangemen of Mackenzie's York constituency, and, in reaction to
the Orange signatures on Mackenzie's "York requisition," Gowan
intoned, "Oh how the heart sickens and the blood recoils at the idea
that even one Irishman could be found who, false to his country, his
religion and his God, has veered about and united with the Yankee
junto of hypocrits, traitors and knaves who hold their seditious

55 Senior, "Ogle Gowan, Orangeism and the Immigrant Question, 1830–1833,"
   199.
56 *Brockville Gazette*, 26 January 1831.
57 Gowan's letter of 4 November 1831 is found in the *Brockville Gazette*, 10 November 1831.
58 *Brockville Recorder*, 3 November 1831.
59 Richards, 180.

meetings at York, and fulminate from thence their poison through the province."[60] One can almost hear the old loyalist families, the various Joneses and the Sherwoods, sighing in relief and murmuring that, though our local Irish may be savages, at least in the heel of the hunt they are loyal.

The appearance of Mackenzie was doubly useful for Gowan, as not only could he trumpet his own and his followers' loyalty, but the Buell family and their electoral associate Mathew Howard were affiliated with Mackenzie, although not associated in detail with all his policies. Gowan had no scruples about tarring the Buells with the radical brush. He charged them with trying to keep Mackenzie away from areas of immigrant (read Irish) settlement and with trying to keep the Irish, even the Catholic Irish whom they were said to champion, "in the dark." A bitter controversy raged for months in the Brockville papers.[61]

Early in 1832 Sir John Colborne, lieutenant governor of Upper Canada, called for local initiatives in the formation of "emigrant societies" to help settle new arrivals in the country. This raised directly an issue that was crucial to virtually everyone in the province, the more so because local newspapers were watching with baleful eye the progress of cholera throughout Europe. The *Brockville Recorder* (26 January 1832) noted that "the frightful disease was extending its progress in England" and warned that "there is too much reason to apprehend its introduction into this country, perhaps next summer with the emigrants from the old country." Various vested interests naturally used the concept of emigrant societies to further their own purposes, in some instances to promote a political viewpoint and in others to promulgate pro- or anti-immigration views. For example, in the nearby constituency of Lennox and Addington, two reform assemblymen cannily used the emigrant society meeting of 16 February 1832 to pass resolutions favourable to Mackenzie's views and to discountenance migration of the poor to Upper Canada: "there is a class of people whom we have no desire to see transferred to the Province. We mean the profligate and abandoned, and the helpless inmates of poor houses who, if here, would rather add to the calendar of crime and the amount of misery than otherwise.[62] Obviously, an immigrant leader such as Gowan had to contain such feelings, especially because he had led his local followers into the anti-reform camp. He was not,

60 The text is from a meeting held at the Methodist Episcopal church, Brockville, reported in the *Brockville Gazette*, 10 November 1831.
61 MacPherson, 140.
62 Resolutions printed in *Brockville Recorder*, 29 March 1832.

however, in full control: when an emigration society meeting took place at Burritt's Rapids (in Grenville county) on 22 February 1832, Gowan was frozen out. He was present but was not elected to the executive management committee. Charles Jones was chosen president and the tone of the meeting was thoroughly anti-immigrant, although (as one would expect with Charles Jones as president) anti-reformer as well.[63]

When in mid-March 1832 a large emigrant society meeting was planned for Brockville, it was crucial to Gowan that the anti-reformers be strong and that he himself gain a prominent position to protect the interests of his Irish followers. Before the meeting, two events had further inflamed matters: news arrived that the assembly of Lower Canada planned to place a head tax on immigrants and Mathew Howard, reform member for Leeds, published a letter that opposed, however gently, pauper immigration.[64] It was not a big step for Gowan and his followers to identify pro-reform and anti-Irish sentiments as coterminous and the emigrant society meetings as a potentially dangerous platform for each. Gowan therefore packed the Brockville meeting, and a wild and indecorous affray it was. The meeting apparently began in the Brockville courthouse and turned into a name-calling contest between the Buells and the Irish and some of their loyalist allies. Buell stated, "Mr. Gowan can speak with so much eloquence that he could turn this assembly to be either government men or rebels," and he may have been nearly right. But when Buell, having failed to make his disapproval of the meetings and especially of Sir John Colborne sufficiently heard, walked out with his followers to hold a counter-meeting in the Methodist church, Gowan seemed to abandon eloquence and turned to violence. "Let traitors hold meetings in holes and caves if they wish," he cried, "but they shall never again hold one in this county. Follow me and we will drive them out."[65] Fortunately for the public peace, the reformers, whom Gowan denominated "Yankees," prudently had dispersed before his mob arrived.

Gowan now was near full stride, for he had affirmed the bonding power of sheer Billingsgate and he had tested and vindicated the efficacy of disruption and threat of violence. During the summer and autumn of 1832 Gowan was relatively quiet; he was in ill health, and, in any case, the populace was universally concerned

63 *Brockville Recorder*, 29 March 1832.
64 Senior, "Ogle Gowan, Orangeism and the Immigrant Question, 1830–1833," 203.
65 *Brockville Gazette*, 29 March 1832.

with the cholera which struck in early summer.[66] The next year, however, he took up his old ways. In March of 1833 the two representatives for Leeds county, William Buell and Mathew Howard, convened a meeting at Farmersville (now called Athens) in Yonge township, on the subject of the demerits of the Anglican Church establishment in Upper Canada and the inadequacy of public education. Andrew Norton Buell, brother of William, began the meeting, but before a chairman could be chosen Gowan and a body of his supporters arrived. Accounts vary, but it seems that a great furor arose over the chairmanship and that the Irish, who were armed with "shileleaghs," beat up the reform party's chairman and generally turned the meeting into a shambles.[67]

At this meeting and at a grand procession held in Brockville later in the same month, Gowan not only had at his side the representatives of old loyalist Tories (David Jones, Charles Jones, and Henry Sherwood joined in the Brockville procession) but he also tried, with some success, to attract Irish Catholics to his van.[68] His hatred of the reformers, it seems, was ecumenical.

The Irish-Gowan alliance with the old Tories was only one of expedience, and the two sides eyed each other like two crabbit bears in a cave. The alliance had to come apart and when it did the Irish attempted to shove aside not only the Buell-reformer forces but the two Jones families and the Sherwood Tories as well. Although virtually inevitable in its dissolution, the entente with the two Jones families and the Sherwoods ended in a most unexpected way which had little to do directly with politics. At this time, Gowan had an Orange friend and outrider, a "Captain" James Gray, who was

66 On his health, see McCleary, 9.
    The cholera epidemic, in both its provincial and local dimensions, is covered in C.M. Godfrey, *The Cholera Epidemic in Upper Canada, 1832–1866* (Toronto: Secombe House 1968) and Geoffrey Bilson, *A Darkened House: Cholera in Nineteenth-Century Canada* (Toronto: University of Toronto Press 1980). On the British background of the epidemic see Robert J. Morris, *Cholera 1832: The Social Response to an Epidemic* (London: Croom Helm 1976) and Michael Durey, *The Return of the Plague: British Society and the Cholera, 1831–32* (Dublin: Gill and Macmillan 1979).
    The local papers, especially the *Brockville Recorder*, charted the epidemic locally with considerable care. Of course the epidemic was tragic, but for anyone who savours ironies, a letter in the *Recorder* of August 1832 is worth noting: eight prisoners in the debtors' ward of the Brockville gaol pleaded to be let out as they were certain that cholera had come to be lodged in the gaol walls. Among the eight were the names of two scions of two of the oldest loyalist families, James Breakenridge and W.H. Sherwood.
67 *Brockville Recorder*, 14 March 1833, and MacPherson, 142–3.
68 MacPherson, 143–4.

particularly obnoxious to the old established families. It was Gray who, with Gowan, had convened a meeting at Smiths Falls in December 1832 as a preliminary to petitioning the lieutenant governor of Upper Canada "for the purification of the magistracy of this District."[69] Gray and Jonas Jones were at dagger-points because Jonas served as the local agent for a London firm that was prosecuting Gray for debt. Gray publicly insulted Jonas and his family, calling him, among other things, a liar and a coward, and when, in January 1834, barns, stable, and sheds on Jonas Jones's farm were burned, Gray was imprisoned without bail.[70]

Gowan was instinctively loyal to his friend but he also used the occasion to turn the central government's attention to the established hegemony in local government. At one point in the imbroglio, Gowan and two of his other associates were bound over by the quarter sessions to answer a charge of conspiracy against Jonas Jones.[71] Gowan charged in a letter to Sir John Colborne that when he had tried to interfere to protect Gray's just interests Jonas Jones had used the testimony of an inmate of a local whorehouse as the basis of a conspiracy charge. The government, he told Colborne, should protect the local citizenry from the tyranny and oppression of "the American party,"[72] as he labelled the two Jones families and the Sherwoods. He must have felt some satisfaction when later in the year Adiel Sherwood, the sheriff, was required to pay £7 10s. damages to Gowan for seizing and damaging a printing press under the impression that it belonged to James Gray![73]

These events, which at our distance in time seem to be merely parish comedy, were deadly serious to contemporary participants, and they precipitated in Gowan and his Irish followers the determination to go ahead on their own in the approaching general election called for the autumn of 1834. In the event, Gowan's tactics proved to be audacious, brilliant, brutal, and successful, and at least temporarily he and his immigrant followers shoved aside both the Buell reformers and all the old Tory families.

His first step was to try to reduce the effective number of seats for Leeds county from two to one, by convincing the attorney general of Upper Canada, Robert S. Jameson, a gentleman recently over from England, to stand for Leeds. A government candidate such as Jameson was in theory above mere petty politics; he ran as a

69 *Brockville Recorder*, December 1832.
70 Richards, 180–1.
71 *Brockville Recorder*, 22 February 1834.
72 Ogle Gowan to Sir John Colborne, 10 February 1834, quoted in Richards, 181.
73 *Brockville Recorder*, 29 August 1834.

government candidate, not as a party man. Jameson accepted the invitation although he loftily indicated that he would be unable to visit the constituency.[74] It was a measure of Gowan's growing power that a senior government official would stand, if not with him, at least at his invitation. In inviting Jameson, Gowan was engaging in a double or nothing gamble. Assuming that Jameson won a seat (and, although not automatic, this was a strong probability), then, if Gowan took the second seat, both sets of Leeds county families, the reformers and the Tories, would be out and the Irish would dominate the political scene. The danger was that Gowan was doubly vulnerable: if he lost to either set of old families, he would be completely eliminated.

His second tactic was to have the government change the designated spot of voting in Leeds county from Farmersville in the southeastern quadrant of the county to Beverly (now Delta) located in Bastard township, well to the rear of the long-settled riverfront townships.[75] To understand what Gowan was doing one must realize that the electoral arrangements of the time were both vulnerable and visible. Electors cast their votes publicly at pollings which lasted several days and in which electors had the privilege of voting twice, albeit not for the same candidate. The Irishmen who supported Gowan were particularly efficient at gang fighting and, both in the Old World and the New, organized their factions with a skill which bordered on the military.[76] In fact, it was reported that in the spring of the preceding year, 1833, Gowan had held a meeting in New Dublin at which his Irish followers went through the early stages of forming their own paramilitary corps.[77] The report may have been a little hysterical, but the potential of Irish organized violence was real in a county in which the Orange lodges were strong. Moreover, Beverly was a perfect piece of ground on which Gowan could fight, for it was an active Orange centre and the local justice of the peace, Joseph K. Hartwell, was an Orangeman.[78]

In dealing with the Irish threat, both the reformers and the Tories

---

74 *Brockville Recorder*, 4 July 1834.

75 Senior, *Orangeism: The Canadian Phase*, 25.

76 There is a considerable historical literature on Irish factions and secret societies, but both the substance and the flavour of Irish rural violence can best be obtained by reading the contemporary stories of William Carleton, "The Party Fight and Funeral," and "The Battle of the Factions," found in his *Traits and Stories of the Irish Peasantry*, which went through several editions in the nineteenth century.

77 *Brockville Recorder*, 25 April 1833.

78 MacPherson, 148.

were at times naive. The reformers, in late 1833, had flirted with the idea of an alliance with Gowan. Andrew Norton Buell informed his brother William that "Gowan seems coming around to the liberal side and perhaps with a little management might be brought full over ... What would you think of a union between the Canadians [meaning the reform party] and the Irish and allowing G. to go in at the next election under strong pledges? Might it not allay the bitter feeling now existing between them and tend to draw them to support the course of reform?"[79] Andrew pondered the subject further, however, and decided "to go the whole length if practicable in the good old cause of reform," by which he meant that they should run two pure-reform candidates in the 1834 election.[80] This was just as well, as any attempt to bind Gowan with "strong pledges" would have been as effective as an attempt to harness the wind. A.N. Buell, though, discarded a Gowan alliance chiefly because he underestimated the Irishman: reform meetings throughout Leeds county held early in 1834 (including one in the front of Leeds and Lansdowne) condemned the conduct of the Upper Canadian assembly and extolled Mackenzie, and Buell believed that, as far as Gowan was concerned, the Gray affair had "put a damper on his expectations ..."[81]

The old loyalist Tories were equally naive. They too saw the 1834 election as a chance to rid the county of Gowan's influence, and they were all too willing to accept the advice of the Beverly magistrate J.K. Hartwell, a friend of the Charles Jones family, that Gowan had recognized that both he and Attorney General Jameson could not win and that by securing Jameson's election Gowan would then be in line to receive a political plum in some other district. Therefore, it was argued, the best thing to do was to ensure Jameson's election and the best way to do this was for all the "magistrates and their loyal Canadian population" to hold back from voting until the Gowanite force was spent and then "plump" (that is, use only one of each elector's two available votes) for Jameson.[82] Whether or not Hartwell intentionally was acting as

---

79 A.N. Buell to William Buell, 12 December 1833, PAC, MG 24 B75.
80 A.N. Buell to William Buell, 29 December 1833, PAC, MG 24 B75.
81 A.N. Buell to William Buell, 28 January 1834, PAC, MG 24 B75.
82 See quotations of letters from J.K. Hartwell to Charles Jones, 5 May 1834, in Richards, 181. Richards also paraphrases a further letter of approximately the same date from Hartwell to Jones. The dating of this second communication is vexed, but Richard's reasons for dating it close to the 5 May letter are convincing (182 n42).

cat's-paw for Gowan (he probably was), the effect was the same: the old Tory voters decided to hold back their votes.[83]

Then Gowan pounced, swiftly, crudely, and perfectly. The poll, which took place in Beverly, opened with the usual speeches by each candidate and with opposing groups massing around the hustings like teenage gangs in a schoolyard. There were minor scuffles. Most voters hung back, only slightly more than two dozen electors voting on the first day. On the second day of the poll several supporters of the reform ticket of Buell and Howard were hit, kicked, and had their clothes ripped, and some took some small knife wounds as they tried to vote: Gowan's men had surrounded the entrance to the hustings. The reformers tried to have the returning officer, Adiel Sherwood, keep order, but he held that his authority was good only on the hustings proper and not around them (a strange assertion given that he also was sheriff for the county, but his family was strongly anti-reformer). The magistrates present did little or nothing. On the third and fourth days the same tactics continued, with Gowan's Irish supporters intimidating the reformers who wished to vote and the old Tories, because of their ill-conceived theory of hanging back and then plumping against Gowan at the end, stayed away. Buell and Howard became convinced that they could not break through the line of Irish shillelaghs and after the fourth day retired. With the reformers out of the fight, it was too late for the old Tories to do anything as Gowan and Attorney General Jameson were now far ahead, both over two hundred votes ahead of the nearest rival. Amazingly, Leeds county's seats were held by the attorney general for Upper Canada and by Ogle R. Gowan, Irish demagogue.[84]

7

Gowan and his Leeds County Irregulars had won a significant victory. Just five years after he had stepped off the boat from Ireland, they had shoved aside the old family politicians, both reformer and

83 Richards (182) suggests that Hartwell was duped. This is possible, but he was an Orangeman and slightly later came out unambiguously for the Gowan-Jameson candidacy (see MacPherson, 148–9). Hartwell could have been playing either or both sides of the game.

84 The fullest reports of the electron disturbances are found, not surprisingly, in the *Brockville Recorder*, 10 and 17 October 1834, and 7 November 1834. These accounts obviously were far from disinterested, as the paper was strongly pro-reform. The facts beneath the rhetoric, however, seem to have been accurate and were confirmed by subsequent governmental investigation.

anti-reformer, in Leeds county. This victory was obtained by foul means and in the future Gowan and his Irishmen had to share the spoils of power with the old guard, but a dramatic realignment of the local power structure had occurred. This county-wide political restructuring owed a good deal to Gowan's tactics but was fundamentally a result of the demographic and economic changes occurring in the county – of which the earlier data presented for the front of Leeds and Lansdowne township are a synecdoche. Gowan was important, but, had he not existed, he would have had to have been invented.[85]

The reallocation of power consequent upon immigration from the British Isles was dramatic but not revolutionary. What *was*

85 The reader will have noted that the discussion of the local political *aufruhr* centres on Gowan, not the earlier figure, Robert Gourlay. Although fascinating in itself, the career of Robert Gourlay as it affected Leeds and Lansdowne township was ephemeral. It neither caused significant social change nor was effective locally in representing the emerging social furies. The contrasting response among the local people who centred around Lansdowne and those whose life revolved around Gananoque is interesting, however. As one might expect, the town of Lansdowne in 1818 was much less prosperous than Gananoque, for it was not on the St Lawrence and it lacked significant water power, which Gananoque had. The town was dominated by the Landons, a family which was more efficient at producing children than wealth. Oliver Landon, the first settler, had arrived with six sons and in 1818 had in his patriarchate nine sons, six sons' wives, nineteen grandsons, twelve granddaughters, as well as three daughters of his own, each of who had two children. The report for the township of Lansdowne was prepared by four Landons and six other settlers and is found in Gourlay's *Statistical Account of Upper Canada Compiled with a View to a Grand System of Emigration* (London: Simpkins and Marshall 1822) 1: 502–7.

But the leaders of the wealthier Gananoque establishment blocked Gourlay's work in Leeds township, and he had to settle for publishing a mostly topographical survey provided by the Reverend William Smart of Brockville (see *Statistical Account* 1: 516–17). A meeting of the local establishment, chaired by Joel Stone and including Charles and John S. McDonald, actually had met to draft a detailed reply to Gourlay's questions but they then suppressed the document. (Fortunately, the original was preserved and was reprinted by Leavitt, 128–331.) Details are lacking on the suppression, but surviving evidence makes it abundantly clear that Stone deeply abhorred Gourlay and his views. In a draft of a letter of 21 July 1818 to Colonel Nathaniel Coffin he added, and then crossed out, a line which said that in his own trouble, "I do now and sincerely hope to continue to thank the Lord of All for one important consolation (viz. that I hope to be able to retreat (if necessary) without becoming a Gore or a Gourleysite." (Queen's University Archives, Stone papers.) Stone distrusted the followers of Gourlay and among his surviving papers is a memorandum listing persons in the township of Kitley who favoured Gourlay (n.d., in Stone papers, Queen's University Archives). That it was Stone who caused

revolutionary was a fundamental change in the way the local society worked and in the way people thought about it. As discussed in detail in chapter 2, the behaviour of individuals in Leeds and Lansdowne township in the loyalist era could be adequately explained through a system of individual contracts defining social, political, and economic life and human relations conceived not in abstract but in concrete terms. After the war of 1812, a new way of thinking began to permeate the population of earlier settlers. The emerging loyalist mythology noted in chapter 3 introduced an abstract and communal facet into their outlook, even while it attempted to justify the earlier settlers' privileged position in the everyday, concrete, competitive economic world.

The change was paralleled by the way in which the new immigrant community evolved. The flood of new peoples changed the scale of every local society to which they came. After a certain threshold is passed, one can no longer know everyone in the community, individual social contracts become harder to negotiate, and they can no longer be enforced chiefly through community consent. Thus eventually political contracts (and later economic and social ones) come to be negotiated collectively. The banding together of the Leeds county Irish is a beautiful, almost laboratory case of how the corporate activity of individuals who perceived themselves as a group evolved and how, through collective action, they came to dominate the local scene.

The change was part of a true intellectual revolution, which occurred at the everyday level. People came to conceive of their society and to understand their position in it abstractedly. They saw themselves as members of collectivities which existed irrespective of the membership of any specific individual. This ability to think of society in abstract terms is a fundamental prerequisite to the development of ethnic interests, of religious denominations, of large-scale business activities, and for those two singular characteristics of the "modern" world, nationalism and social class allegiance.

It is not surprising that the collective consciousnesses of the earlier loyalist settlers and of the Irish immigrants were incompatible: what is surprising is how surely the Irish won.

---

the Leeds township report to be withheld is clearly implied in a letter of Gourlay to the *Kingston Gazette*, dated 12 June (published 16 June 1818), in which he told of a steamboat trip to Prescott: "By the way I called on Col. Stone at Gananoque, a worthy gentleman who had also withheld a statistical report from me."

8

Ogle Gowan can scarcely have been surprised when the validity of
the 1834 Leeds election was called into question or when the
committee appointed by the reform-dominated assembly to investi-
gate the matter declared his and Jameson's election void. (The date
of the unseating was 14 February 1835.) New elections were called for
early March 1835 and Gowan again fastened on violence as his main
tool of persuasion. Sir John Colborne, in exercising his prerogative
to set the place of the election, tacitly helped the Gowan-Jameson
ticket by again selecting Beverly, the Orange centre and site of the
previous violent exercise in representative government. The candidates in this March 1835 by-election were essentially the same as
before: two reformers and two Gowanites, with the old Tories
staying out. In theory the election was to last six days, with sixteen
to seventeen hundred potential votes to be cast by 800 to 850
electors. There was no need for all that voting: on the first day of
actual polling the supporters of Gowan and Jameson rioted so badly
that the election had to be stopped. In the mélée the local patriarch
Jonas Jones was severely wounded in the head while attempting to
restore order, a wound which was a suitable metaphor for what was
happening to the old family Toryism which Jones represented. No
further polling being possible, the returning officer certified Gowan
and Jameson as elected. Gowan's Irish supporters had indeed put in
a good day's work.[86]

It had, however, a nasty aftermath. (I do not count as tragic the
case of the owner of Lewis's Tavern in Beverly who, finding the reformers and the Gowan forces about to destroy his inn in a brawl,
saved it by yelling "fire!" and thereby emptying the premises.)[87] A
group of Buell supporters, having been beaten at the polls (in more
than one sense), found their way to the tavern of a reform sympa-
thizer, one James Philips, about three miles north of Beverly (at a
site now called Philipsville). They drank for a while and left just in
time to run into two Gowan supporters on the road and forcibly take
the white campaign ribbons from their opponents. The Gowanites
then went for help and brought ten or twelve sled loads of supporters,

---

86 The March 1835 Leeds county election is covered with more detail and detachment in the Kingston papers, *The British Whig* and the *Kingston Chronicle
and Gazette*, than in the Brockville papers. See the *Chronicle* issues of 14 February 1835, 18 February 1835, 28 February 1835, 4 March 1835, 7 March 1835, 11
March 1835. See also the *British Whig* issue of 2 February 1835, 9 February 1835,
19 February 1835, 2 March 1835, 9 March 1835.
87 *Kingston Chronicle and Gazette*, 11 March 1835.

said to be mostly non-voters from Lanark county. Intimidated, the reformers hid in a gully while the Gowan men began to destroy the tavern. Philips, the unfortunate owner, finally could take the vandalism no longer and led a rush to save his tavern. In the fight that followed, Philips went berserk, wielding his wooden claymore like a demented dervish. When the battle was over, it was found that Philips had clubbed to death one Edward Rusic, a Gowan supporter.[88]

Gowan's and Jameson's election, like their first victory, was declared void by an investigatory committee of the provincial assembly and in mid-April Leeds county was again without representatives.[89] In the months that followed, meetings were held in most townships in the county, including one in Gananoque for the front of Leeds and Lansdowne township which denounced the "tyrannical and unjust conduct" of the assembly in unseating the two immigrant favourites.[90]

Ironically, the trial for murder of the tavern-keeper James Philips did more to clean up Leeds politics than did the assembly's investigation of corrupt election practices.[91] Attorney General Jameson had a strong personal stake in the judicial proceedings (he had, after all, been on the same ticket as Gowan) and prosecuted the case himself. So persuasive was the evidence about the disorder in Leeds county that a conviction was impossible,[92] but the Philips case at least had the effect of focusing attention upon Leeds throughout the province. Thus it was easy for Andrew Norton Buell, brother of the wronged candidate William Buell, to draw up an act for yet another Leeds county election to fill the two seats declared void. This act was shrewd. Instead of a single husting, it declared that the poll, set for March, should be taken in four different places in the county: Coleman's Corners (now Lyn), Beverly (now Delta),

88 MacPherson, 152–3.

89 *Kingston Chronicle and Gazette*, 11 April 1835, 15 and 16 April 1835; *British Whig*, 6 April 1835, 13 April 1835.

90 *Kingston Chronicle and Gazette*, 8 August 1835. The quotation is from the Gananoque protest meeting. Its tone was typical of that of a dozen meetings held in the county on the same issue.

91 I owe this point to the shrewd discussion of the Philips trial in MacPherson, 153–4.

92 After his acquittal Philips remained active in politics and was a vice-president for the Johnstown district on the reform "Committee of Vigilance and Management." After the failure of the 1837 rebellion he went to the United States and he returned with the invading force in November 1838. In the Battle of the Windmill, an affray in which Ogle Gowan was one of the commanding offcers, Philips was killed.

Smiths Falls, and Gananoque. This would make intimidation of the voters more difficult. Mobility of electoral gangs from one district to another was cut by requiring that people in specific townships vote at specific polls. The Gananoque poll, for instance, was only for the electors of Leeds and Lansdowne township. Rioting and similar disruptive behaviour were defined as a "high misdemeanour" and were to be prosecuted. Each poll was under the supervision of a local notable: Gananoque's was under John McDonald, former partner of the late Joel Stone and the most economically powerful person in the area.[93]

Gowan protested.[94] He knew that unless he formed an alliance with the hated old Tories (the Joneses and Sherwoods) he could not defeat the Buell reform ticket except by Irish violence. The attorney general, Robert Jameson, had decided to keep clear of the Leeds election this time, so someone was needed to run alongside Gowan. Jonas Jones wished to do so, but Gowan was not yet ready to work with Jones (the ashes of the Gray case were still warm) and he supported J.D. Fraser of north Leeds for second spot. At a Tory meeting, Fraser defeated Jonas Jones, leaving Gowan the undisputed Tory leader in the county[95] but vulnerable to the reformers if the old Tories should sulk rather than vote. In the event, the election went smoothly, which is to say that the new arrangements prevented Irish violence, and the reformers won as the following table indicates.[96]

	Gowan	Fraser	Buell	Howard
Gananoque	92	81	68	67
Smiths Falls	167	167	145	143
Coleman's Corners	170	167	220	215
Beverly	86	74	165	168
	515	489	598	593

These figures confirm our earlier speculation that in Leeds and Lansdowne township, which voted at Gananoque, the Irish had become predominant. The data further suggest, however, that there

93 The full text of the bill is given in the *Brockville Recorder*, 23 December 1835. *British Whig*, 9 March 1836, and *Kingston Chronicle and Gazette*, 12 and 16 March 1836.
94 See his letter to the *Kingston Chronicle and Gazette*, 23 March 1836. *The Chronicle*, which had earlier supported Gowan, refused to run most of the letter as being "abuse without argument."
95 MacPherson, 154–5.
96 *Kingston Chronicle and Gazette*, 2 April 1836. See also *British Whig*, 6 April 1836.

was a distinct limit to Irish power. Native-born Canadians of the reform persuasion would not join the Irish, who seemingly were more Tory than the old Tories, and the old Tories would not work with the Irish unless a reasonable partnership were hammered out. Gowan, in a letter written to the electors of Leeds soon after his defeat, acknowledged all of these facts, albeit not entirely gracefully. He explained that he had dropped out of the election as soon as it had become clear "that a certain influential and respectable family party in Brockville had determined on not voting." By this he almost certainly meant the large Jonas and Charles Jones connection and he identified clearly his source of support: "to the Old Countryman of the county I feel a debt of gratitude ... and for the few, but faithful Canadians, who nobly adhered to the principle of their immortal Sires, I entertain those sentiments of grateful pride and satisfaction which every truly British heart must feel for a brother Briton."[97] In other words, chiefly the Irish had voted for the Gowan ticket. Gowan now recognized that to dominate in Leeds, he must admit into partnership, at least as juniors, the old family Tories.

Sir Francis Bond Head was appointed lieutenant governor of Upper Canada late in January 1836 and soon after the Leeds by-election he called a general election for the summer of 1836. The electors of Leeds county could have been forgiven for suffering from a surfeit of their local brand of representative government, two general elections and two by-elections in the space of three years. Gowan was pleased to have a chance to overturn his recent defeat and Bond Head's announcement breathed new life into the old Tory families, the Joneses and the Sherwoods. They, like Gowan, had been effusive in welcoming Bond Head as lieutenant governor and he in his turn was sensitive to their predilections. In particular, he declared, to their obvious advantage, that Leeds county would return to a single hustings system and that Beverly (that Orange stronghold) would be the site of the polling. Moreover, Joseph K. Hartwell, Orangeman, incompetent justice of the peace, sometime friend of the Joneses, and sometime friend of Gowan, was selected as returning officer.[98] So unfair did his appointment seem that William Buell and four Tory magistrates petitioned to have Hartwell removed, but to no avail.[99] Even more important, however, from the Tory viewpoint, Gowan and the Jonas Jones group of old Tories

97 *Kingston Chronicle and Gazette*, 20 April 1836.
98 MacPherson, 155–6.
99 *British Whig*, 9 June 1836, and *Kingston Chronicle and Gazette*, 11 June 1836.

made their peace: Gowan and Jonas Jones would run as Tory candidates[100] against the Buell ticket of reformers. From the Gowanite viewpoint, this situation was a great improvement over that of the preceding election: now the Irish had an alliance with an old Tory family and the election was taking place on a single husting at a site where they knew they could intimidate their opponents through violence.

And the old Tory–new Irish, Jonas Jones–Ogle Gowan ticket won handsomely, by a margin of roughly 180 votes each over the reformers.[101] The Buells intended to protest the election because of the violence used against them, but the assembly returned at the general election was overwhelmingly Tory and such a petition would have been a fool's errand.[102]

Although it was not clear at the time, Gowan and his Irish followers had won almost everything. Jonas Jones was appointed to a choice judgeship in 1837 and his vacated seat made a one-seat by-election necessary in 1837 to choose someone to sit alongside Ogle Gowan. The Buell family, the local bulwark of the reformers, chose to withdraw from politics and instead of putting forward their own candidate preferred to support a "moderate conservative."[103] For the time being, the reforming wing of the old loyalist families was politically dead.

As for the old Tory families, although in 1837 the sons of Ephraim Jones effected a compromise with Gowan that permitted their splitting local patronage,[104] they had no strong personality to put forward in the race for Jonas Jones's vacated seat. The three candidates turned out to be that well-known political aspirant Joseph K. Hartwell, Benjamin Tett, a relative newcomer with no following, and James Morris, originally from Lanark county. To Gowan, it seemed not to matter greatly who sat beside him and Morris was chosen, as much with support from the old reformers (since in their view he was the least extreme alternative) as from Tories.[105] Morris became a long-serving member but in no sense a rival to Gowan. The Gowan-Jones coalition finally and permanently unravelled early in 1838 and the central government acknowl-

100 MacPherson, 156.
101 Brockville Recorder, 1 July 1836.
102 MacPherson, 157. On intimidation by Orangemen at the polls see also Kingston Chronicle and Gazette, 3 December 1836.
103 MacPherson, 157.
104 Richards, 183.
105 MacPherson, 162; British Whig, 22 July 1837; Brockville Recorder, 3 August 1837.

edged the prepotence of Gowan by permitting his opinions to override those of the Joneses in matters of patronage.[106] As one of Gowan's supporters said in 1838, "have we not literally annihilated the family compact in this district?"[107] Indeed they had.[108]

9

Dramatic figure though he was, Ogle R. Gowan was less a cause of the rise of the Leeds county Irish than an effect. His political skills

106 Richards, 183.

107 Letter in the *Brockville Recorder*, 4 July 1838, quoted in Richards, 184.

108 The reader may have noticed that in this book the term "family compact" is not used, except in direct quotations. This is because I am an agnostic on whether it has much explanatory power as a historical concept. A considerable number of able and diligent scholars have employed the term, but very very few have tried to define it with any rigour.

The key to evaluating the usefulness, or alternatively the uselessness, of the idea of a "family compact" is the fundamental recognition that it did not exist, that is, there has not been found any written concordat, such as, say, the *magna carta* between the king and barons among the Upper Canadian ruling caste. And there has been no proof that formal, considered, and binding unwritten agreement was reached by members of that same caste. This is natural, since the "family compact" is an heuristic fiction by which one attempts to conceptualize a complex pattern of human behaviour, a pattern which was not based on written contracts or complex and binding verbal agreements but upon small pieces of actual behaviour, carried out from day to day over a long period of time among many interacting individuals. Thus, the term "family compact" serves the same purpose as a hypothetical construction in the social sciences or a metaphor in the humanities. To assess the "family compact" as an heuristic device is no different than judging any similar concept. To be useful, the device should be (a) historically apt, that is, as little dipped in anachronism as possible; (b) accurate, in the sense that the factual statements it implies are verifiable by the canons of historical scholarship; (c) comprehensive, in that it will relate clearly and in a verifiable fashion all the pieces of data to one another; (d) non-tautological; and (e) necessary – there is no need for the heuristic fication if another concept or set of concepts does the job more efficiently.

The great virtue of the "family compact" as used in the historical literature, it seems to me, is that as a concept it was employed by contemporaries, at least as early as the 1830s. It was used in 1833 by William Lyon Mackenzie (see C.P. Lucas, ed., *Lord Durham: Report on the Affairs of British North America* [Oxford: Clarendon Press 1912] 2: 148 n1). The term certainly was in common usage before the Lord Durham's report made it a permanent part of the historical vocabulary, and it cannot be said to be anochronistic.

Matters of factual accuracy and comprehensiveness must be judged in detail by specialists in the field. Suffice it to say here that there are specific factual assertions tied to the concept of the "family compact" that must be verified before the concept is applied in an historical argument. Among these

and drastic methods hastened their rise, but the Irish were a precondition of his career rather than *vice versa*. To a degree unusual among political leaders Gowan came to personify his followers, to encapsulate their experiences and aspirations, and to symbolize their social migration and interaction with their New World society. Gowan's local career after the 1836 election stands for the metamorphosis to respectability which his Irish followers, individually and severally, underwent.

---

are the following factual statements by Lord Durham himself (see Lucas 147–8), namely that the individuals in the "compact"

1 were linked by party interests;
2 were also brought together by personal ties;
3 but had few actual family connections;
4 acquired permanent authority over the government;
5 possessed almost all the highest public offices;
6 maintained legislative influence by predominating in the legislative council;
7 parcelled out the smaller patronage posts throughout the province;
8 controlled the bench, the magistracy, the higher offices of the Anglican Church, and most of the legal profession;
9 acquired nearly the whole of the waste lands of the province;
10 controlled the chartered banks;
11 belonged mostly to the Church of England;
12 were mostly born in North America.
13 In addition, one can add as factual assertions normally associated with the compact the list of names compiled by William Lyon Mackenzie and incorporated by J.C. Dent (see the very interesting discussion by Robert E. Saunders, "What Was the Family Compact?" *Ontario History* 49 [1957]: 165–78, especially 168ff.).

Each of these factual assertions and their relationship to one another must be verified before the concept of "family compact" is deemed acceptable in historical scholarship. It is possible that an investigator may disprove certain of the factual assertions and discover others but still wish to use the idea of "family compact." If so, however, he must spell out explicitly and precisely what factual assertions and interrelationships are implied by his now-modified use of the "compact."

From a non-specialist's point of view, it appears that often (but by no means always) the concept of "family compact" is used in historical explanations in illogical fashion. At its simplest this takes the form of the implied syllogism.

(a) the family compact had patronage and power;
(b) so-and-so had patronage and power;
(c) therefore so-and-so was a member of the family compact.

That, of course, fails, as one needs a distributed middle term for the argument to be valid.

More pernicious, however, is the tautological use of "family compact," as a label simultaneously for the distribution of power and patronage (i.e., an effect) and for the cause of that distribution. For examples which show that the concept can be employed non-tautologically, see David Gagan, "Property

Gowan, like his followers, became at least semi-respectable. After several unfortunate attempts at journalism, he founded the successful *Brockville Statesman* in 1836; he became active in local politics, especially after the municipal reforms of 1842; in 1844 and 1847–50 inclusive he was warden of the counties of Leeds and Grenville;[109] and in parliament he was scrupulously loyal in outlook. In fact, in 1836–7 he framed a militia bill which was more rigorous than anything the old loyalists would have dared: the bill made every physically able male from sixteen to sixty liable to bear arms and prescribed an annual period of active duty for élite companies, the death penalty for desertion, and strict courts martial for speaking disrespectfully of the monarch or the royal family.[110] Scant wonder, then, that local newspapers could suggest that one of the chief charges that could be leveled against Sir Francis Bond Head was that he suffered an undesirable intimacy to exist between

<hr />

and 'Interest': Some Preliminary Evidence of Land Speculation by the 'Family Compact' in Upper Canada, 1820–1840," *Ontario History* 70 (March 1978): 63–70; and John Clarke, "The Activity of an Early Canadian Land Speculator in Essex County, Ontario: Would the Real John Askin Please Stand Up?" *Canadian Papers in Rural History* 3 (1982): 84–109.

Finally, one may wonder whether the heuristic fiction of the "family compact" is really necessary; does it help to explain something that is not better explained in other ways? Frederick Armstrong and Colin Read in their individual studies of the London and Western districts have each pointed to the existence of district and township oligarchies and, in Armstrong's words, "looking even deeper, a more obscure gathering of luminaries was to be found in each township." (Frederick H. Armstrong, "The Oligarchy of the Western District of Upper Canada, 1788–1841," *Historical Papers, 1977,* 87. The entire article repays close reading, especially 87–102. See also Colin Read, "The London District Oligarchy in the Rebellion Era," *Ontario History* 72 [December 1980]: 195–209.) It would be extremely interesting if scholars were to view these local élites not as excrescences devolved upon local communities by the central power-broker but as evolutions of the several local social systems. Were this true, the acquisition of local patronage positions would not be perceived so much as creating local élites as ratifying them. That the social and economic evolution of the township of Leeds and Lansdowne can be explained adequately without reference to the "family compact" suggests that the concept may be, from the viewpoint of historical explication, a largely redundant overlay. But one case can only be indicative; scores of local studies are needed before generalization is possible.

109 DCB, Gowan; Leavitt, 54. The details of Gowan's local political activities are not germane here. They are conveniently available in primary source in the compilation by William Jelly, *A Summary of the Proceedings of the Johnstown District Council 1842–1849* (Brockville: Council of the United Counties of Leeds and Grenville 1929).

110 See *Brockville Recorder,* 23 December 1836 and 6 July 1837.

himself and Gowan, a charge founded on Gowan's hyper-loyalism, not on any visible condescension on Bond Head's part.[111]

The seal on Gowan's loyalty and the validation of his local importance and increasing respectability was his being made a captain and later a lieutenant-colonel in the second regiment of the Leeds militia (Joel Stone's old regiment), which encompassed the men of the front of Leeds and Lansdowne township. His captaincy legitimized a standing he already had obtained by paramilitary activity: as tensions rose, but even before the attempted Mackenzie coup of 1837, Gowan had raised a corps of 140 men called the "Brockville Invincibles" and said to consist entirely of Orangemen. This voluntary militarism on Gowan's part is not surprising in view of the report in 1833 that he was organizing a paramilitary body in Leeds to use against his opponents and in view of the tactical and programmatic aspect of his election violence, involving as much disciplined and calculated intimidation as mayhem. The corps was assimilated into the militia as the Ninth Provincial Battalion and eventually Gowan led it into battle.[112]

Before then, however, he was given command of a company of the Queen's Own Rifles which participated in an attack on Hickory Island on 22 and 23 February 1838. This battle was of virtually no military importance but was significant in the development of the local mythology of loyalty. Hickory Island lies less than three miles below Gananoque and was used by a group of Americans as a base for an intended attack of Kingston. Their plans became known, however, and when the Upper Canadian forces assembled most of the Americans hied off.[113] It was not much of a victory, to be sure, but it permitted the local Irish to present themselves as helping to save their new homeland from the dangerous Yankees.

Of more military consequence was the Battle of the Windmill, near Prescott in Grenville county, in mid-November 1838. For that engagement, Gowan was back in charge of a unit consisting of Protestant Irishmen, the Ninth Provincial battalion. The attack on Prescott was intended to be one of several coordinated efforts in an invasion of Upper Canada, but because of sloppy seamanship on the invader's part its practical result was that approximately 160 American and Canadian radicals landed at the wrong place and eventually found themselves surrounded in a stone windmill which had stone outbuildings and stone fences around it. Thus the

111 *Kingston British Whig*, 1 June 1837, quoted in *Brockville Recorder*, 8 June 1837.
112 DCB, Gowan; McCleary, 39; Senior, *Orangeism: The Canadian Phase*, 31–2.
113 DCB, Gowan; Leavitt, 51; McKenzie, 72. For interesting bickering among the victors after this battle see *Brockville Recorder*, 13 March and 5 April 1838.

invaders had no chance of attacking Prescott but were very hard for the Canadian counterforces to ferret out. The invasion began on Sunday, 11 November. On Monday, word of it spread, Gowan brought down two companies from Brockville to reinforce the corps already at Prescott, and other companies soon followed. An attack on the invaders failed on Tuesday. Only on Friday did an artillery detachment and three twenty-four-pound guns arrive from Kingston, and the invaders were finally driven into submission.[114] In retrospect, the victory of ten corps of Upper Canadians[115] (comprising perhaps fifteen hundred men) over fewer than two hundred surrounded opponents was not exactly heroic, especially considering that it took almost a full week for the counterattack to succeed. Some genuine courage, however, was shown, with undoubted loss of life, injury to body, and the makings of great folklore, such as the report that one of the prisoners was carrying a list of the names of leading Prescott citizens who were to be hanged after the town was taken. There was also a memorable victory parade in which the American prisoners were led through Prescott tied in single file to a rope, to the edification of the loyal populace. They then were taken by boat to Kingston, where a second victory parade was conducted.[116]

Ogle Gowan, now Lieutenant-Colonel Gowan, was twice wounded and was mentioned in despatches. His provisional battalion had eight rank and file men wounded and for its services was given the name of Queen's Royal Borderers.[117]

Hereward Senior, a student of the Orange Order, has taken as accurate Gowan's suggestion that throughout the province nearly half the militia volunteers were Orangemen,[118] and he shrewdly suggests that "the rebellion had, in a sense, naturalized Orangeism."[119] One need not restrict this suggestion to Orangemen: the 1837 rebellion and subsequent invasion naturalized all immigrant Protestant Irishmen, whether or not they were members of the Order. Locally, membership in the militia and participation in the affrays at Hickory Island and at the Windmill did for these Irish immigrants what participation in the war of 1812 had done for post-loyalist arrivals in Upper Canada: it gave them a chance to prove their loyalty and thereafter to participate in a bonding myth

114 Leavitt, 45–51; McKenzie, 71–3.
115 See Leavitt, 51 for the list of corps.
116 McKenzie, 73.
117 DCB, Gowan; Leavitt, 51; McCleary, 43.
118 Senior, Orangeism: The Canadian Phase, 31.
119 Senior, "The Character of Canadian Orangeism," 180.

that enshrined their sacrifice and validated their full participation in all privileges of the society. The Protestant Irish had won their place in the political power structure by tough and often nasty dealing, but, just as the dirtiest piece of parchment can receive judicial authority by the affixing of the Great Seal, so the Irishmen's new-found reputation for loyalty to their young Queen Victoria validated their claim to be fully loyal. It also legitimized their holding what they already had seized.

The legend of Ogle R. Gowan and his loyal Irishmen was consequential even if, like all myths, it was less than historically accurate. Gowan himself reminds us of this point in a letter to his cousin James describing two wounds he received in the Battle of the Windmill, "You ask me, or rather express a hope, that my wounds, ... are not serious. I received two wounds, both (Thank God) slightly, one a little below the hip, from a bayonet, when the right wing (which I had the honour to command) charged the ruffians, who were entrenched behind a stone wall. One inch further to the right would probably have finished me ... the other wound is in the side of my knee and was given by a ball fired from one of the windows of a stone house as we advanced to drive in the doors. Neither caused me any serious pain ..."[120] The first wound described above is fascinating. Perhaps one could sustain such an injury in a frontal confrontation with a bayonet, but it is difficult to imagine how, and in his own newspaper, *The Brockville Statesman*, Gowan permitted the following to be inserted: "As we advanced many of our gallant men fell, among whom was the brave Lieutenant Johnson, of the 83rd. The ruffians were so securely planted behind the stone fences, that they stood the charge to the last minute. Col. Gowan received the bayonet of one of the brigands in the left hip, [hence Gowan's reference in the letter to his cousin of the disadvantageous effect if the wound had been further to the right], at the moment they forced him and his men to retreat."[121] All of this is a circumspect way of saying that Gowan's chief wound came from a bayonet in the buttock, received after turning to flee from the enemy.

From such thin threads is the tapestry of heroism woven.

10

If, as suggested earlier, it is true that Ogle Gowan's breakthrough in political and social standing was a metaphor for the radical

120 Ogle Gowan to James Gowan, December 1838, quoted in McCleary, 43.
121 Quoted in Donald McLeod, *A Brief Review of the Settlement of Upper Canada* (1841; reprint, Belleville: Mika Silk Screening 1972), 258.

upgrading in status of the Irish immigrant community in Leeds county, one should expect this to be shown most particularly in their economic position. The 1842 census for Leeds and Lansdowne townships provides us with an opportunity to examine just how well the Irish were doing. In the agrarian economy of the time certain litmus-like indicators revealed each household's economic position: the amount of land owned; the amount cleared; the production of certain crops that often were sold for cash, particularly wheat, and to a lesser extent, barley; the production of the dietary staple, potatoes; and the possession of livestock, in particular cattle, sheep, and hogs.[122] (Protestant and Catholic Irish are lumped together in the discussion which follows because at this early date there were not enough Catholics to provide a statistically valid "cell.")

In order to obtain a clear reading on the position of Irish versus non-Irish in an agrarian setting it is necessary to focus on the rear of Leeds and Lansdowne township. This area was a district of its own for statistical purposes, although not for the purposes of municipal government, and was almost entirely rural. (The front must be excluded from purely agricultural comparisons of immigrant groups, as it contained the manufacturing centre of Gananoque and the commercial town of Lansdowne, whose populations were large enough to distort any agricultural comparisons.)[123] A reworking of the 1842 manuscript census data indicates that there were 179 households in the rear of Leeds and Lansdowne, sixty-nine of which had at their head either one or two persons who were Irish-born.[124] (For the sole purpose of convenience these are denominated as "Irish" households in the discussion which follows.)

Examining first the information on land-holdings as presented in figure 5, one discovers that the Irish were anything but disadvan-

122 Imperfections in the local data make it impossible to work with either the production of oats or the possession of horses, both of which are also useful indicators of agricultural wealth.

The reader may notice that I have not presented "distress indicators," that is, certain crops which, if grown in quantity, usually indicate hard times or perduring poverty. The chief of these indicators, buckwheat, was produced in such low quantities (only 110 bushels in the entire rear of Leeds and Lansdowne in 1842) as to be virtually non-existent. The other indicator, the growth of flax in quantity usually points to endemic poverty and oversupply of labour but can not be used reliably as a poverty indicator in Ontario until near the end of the nineteenth century. In any case, none was grown in Leeds and Lansdowne in 1842.

123 The manuscript data are found in AO.

124 The imperfections in the questionnaire and collection of the 1842 census data preclude defining the ethnic category in any other way. See the introduction to Appendix C for a discussion of the problems with the 1842 data.

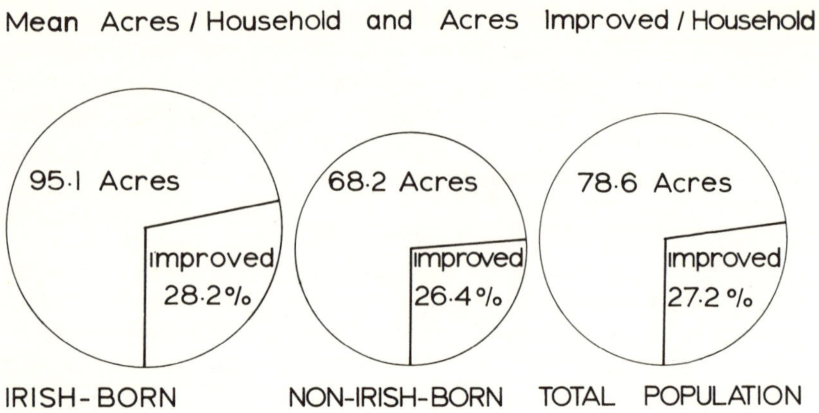

Mean Acres / Household and Acres Improved / Household

| IRISH-BORN | NON-IRISH-BORN | TOTAL POPULATION |

95.1 Acres — Improved 28.2%

68.2 Acres — Improved 26.4%

78.6 Acres — Improved 27.2%

Figure 5 "Ethnic" comparison of landholdings, rear of Leeds and Lansdowne, 1842 census

taged. On average, Irish households held more land than did their non-Irish counterparts, they had more acres cleared, and, despite having more raw acreage, actually had a higher proportion of their lands cleared.

As for crop production, here too the results are striking. As the accompanying table indicates, the Irish were much more committed to growing the main cash crop of the time, wheat, than were the non-Irish. This suggests that they were deeper into the cash economy than were their counterparts and probably had more disposable cash income. Barley, grown both for malting and for livestock feed, was relatively downplayed. Interestingly, the number of winchester bushels of potatoes grown by Irish and non-Irish households was nearly identical, suggesting that not much dietary difference existed between groups: everyone ate large quantities of potatoes.

The last table deals with the possession of farm animals. Livestock in the rural economy were both an indicator of accrued wealth and also a means of future production. The livestock data are not dramatic. The average Irish household had slightly fewer neat cattle than did the non-Irish but not markedly so. (One suspects that the relatively lower production of barley among the Irish is related to their having fewer cattle; everything else being equal, instead of feeding barley to cattle they preferred to grow

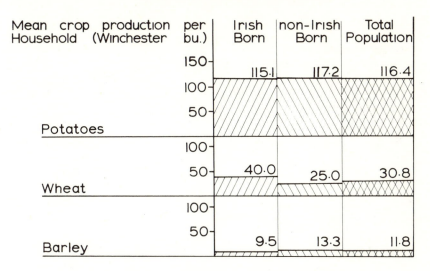

Mean crop production per Household (Winchester bu.)	Irish Born	non-Irish Born	Total Population
Potatoes	115.1	117.2	116.4
Wheat	40.0	25.0	30.8
Barley	9.5	13.3	11.8

Figure 6 "Ethnic" comparison of crop production, rear of Leeds and Lansdowne, 1842 census

wheat and obtain cash directly.) The Irish predilection for raising hogs and their relative dislike of sheep, which is shown in figure 7, is probably a direct result of their experience in the homeland. Virtually every Irish small farmer kept at least one pig, but only large landlords kept sheep, so the immigrants had no experience with them. The livestock data should not be overinterpreted; they suggest a rough equivalence of the average Irish and non-Irish households.

Indeed, the import of all of the agricultural data is very simple: the Irish households did economically as well as, or better than, the rest of the population, most of which was native-born. Clearly, the Irish were adaptable to the North American agricultural environment and also overcame whatever discrimination there was against them. Given the state of Upper Canadian agriculture at the time, they may not have been good farmers, but they were as good as everyone else.

11

If the rear of Leeds and Lansdowne township in 1842 provides an admirably clean laboratory in which to view the economic as-

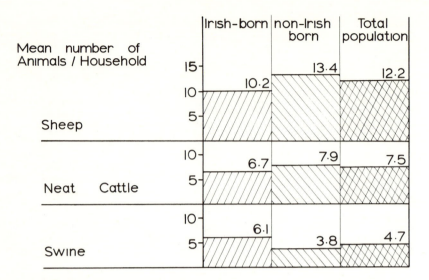

Figure 7 "Ethnic" comparison of livestock production, rear of Leeds and Lansdowne, 1842 census

similation of the Irish in a virtually pure agrarian setting, the front of the township in 1842 provides us with another setting: the mixed economic structure in which farming predominated but in which there was one modest market centre (the town of Lansdowne) and one larger mercantile, nascent-manufacturing town, Gananoque. In this mixed and more complex economic environment, what position did the Irish obtain?

When one takes tallies, the apparent occupation of the head of all households in which one or both of the parents were born in Ireland and for which information on occupation was given, one secures the following results as against the entire population of the front of the township (a total of 326 households):

Occupation	"Irish" households (N = 160)	All households (N = 166)
Farmer	51.9%	47.2%
Labourer	20.6	23.0
Skilled trade	20.6	22.7
Merchant	3.1	3.4
Professional	.7	.9
Spinster	3.1	2.8
	100.0	100.0

The two profiles are roughly similar, although the Irish were more likely to be supported by farming than was the general population and slightly less apt to earn a living by employment in the skilled trades. The Irish cohort was less apt than the general population to depend upon unskilled labour as their source of income.

CHAPTER FIVE

The Irish and the New Rural Order, 1849–1871

I

"Sub-infeudation" is a term which is alien to Canadian history. It is the coin of medieval historians, who use it, in the strict sense, to mean the creation of a set of small feudal subtenancies and, in a more general way to refer to the complex infilling of a feudal society with people and institutions, such as occurred in Wales under the marcher lords or in Connaught under the Norman barons. In the second, broad, sense, the concept of sub-infeudation provides a useful analogy or metaphor for what was taking place in Leeds and Lansdowne townships in the third quarter of the nineteenth century. The society was being filled in. As with the many subtenants in a fully articulated feudal society, the ever increasing number of local inhabitants came to hold the means of livelihood on similar terms one with another, and, as in feudal social order, there was only a small number of individuals of high economic and social status.

This chapter will discuss a process that was in a sense the sub-infeudation of an Ontario township. The use of this medieval – and thus resolutely pre-industrial – metaphor is intended to emphasize that most of the social changes that occurred in this period were not a function of industrialization. Industry did emerge in the area and this will be discussed in the next chapter; but the industrialization of Gananoque, the chief village in the locality, did not determine the fundamental nature of the township's infilling but only tinctured that character. The large-scale in-migration of newcomers would have fundamentally changed the nature of local society, whether Gananoque had remained an old-fashioned mercantile village (as did Lansdowne, the other major village in the front of the township) or had begun, as actually was the case, its transformation to an industrial town.

The sub-infeudation of the local area involved several simultaneous processes. Fundamental to all other layers of change was the marked increase in density of population. This led to a concentration of governmental, legal, and administrative agencies upon ever decreasing physical areas. In governmental activities professionalization occurred, as local government began to be transformed into a set of more efficient and more impersonal activities. The increased population also made possible a fourth characteristic, increased reticulation in virtually all forms of voluntary social activity, and led to a marked speciation in religious aggregations. The increasing articulation of networks of communication meant that all activities, economic and interpersonal, could be carried on more quickly within the local area and that there was greater and speedier access to individuals and businesses whose locations previously had not been conveniently accessible. Economically, this facilitated the transition from wheat culture to full-scale mixed commercial farming. None of the processes was entirely limited to the period 1849–71 and one must necessarily make references to their antecedents in the early 1840s and in some instances even in the 1830s.

Like so many developments in social history, cause and effect here circle back on themselves like a snake in an early Celtic manuscript. The immigrants to the township, together with the increasing numbers of offspring of the earlier settlers, by their very numbers changed the entire scale of local society and set in train the processes outlined above; but the new citizens in adapting to this world of flux not only altered local society but inevitably were themselves changed by its evolution. After discussing the changing local social and economic structure, one must necessarily ask, how well did the Irish adapt to this ever-new world?

2

Human numbers, the Procrustean bed of social history, are rarely dramatic but often determinative. The fecund shift in the local society is clearly indicated in the 2.6-fold population expansion between the early 1840s and the beginning of the 1870s:[1]

1 Derived from manuscript census of 1842 and 1848 in AO and from the printed aggregates: *Census of the Canadas, 1851–52* 1: 16–17; *Census of the Canadas, 1860–61* 1: 62–3; *Census of Canada, 1870–71* 1: 30.

Total Population

	Front of Leeds and Lansdowne township	Rear of Leeds and Lansdowne township	Combined
1842	2,173	942	3,115
1848	2,639 (?)	N/A	N/A
1851	N/A	N/A	4,722
1861	N/A	N/A	6,814
1871	5,780	2,363	8,143

The maddening holes in the above data result from the lack of an extant copy of the 1848 census for the rear of the township, and, for 1851 and 1861, from the vexing decision of the census officials to rearrange the boundaries of data collection. If, however, one accepts for a moment their decision to cut the united townships on a north-south axis (instead of east-west as was the procedure before and after those two censuses), one finds the following:[2]

	Leeds township	Lansdowne township
1851	2,283	2,439
1861	3,709	3,105

Here, two seemingly pertinent observations are worth attention because of their actual *irrelevance* to the point at hand. During this period the rate of population growth in the united townships of Leeds and Lansdowne actually was slowing: this is clear if one charts the rate of increase over roughly decade-long intervals. (A true rate of decennial increase is not obtainable since there was no adequate census in 1841 and, in any case, the dates of census day moved around for 1851, 1861 and 1871; still, for our purposes the data are adequate.)[3]

Period	Percentage of increase over base
1832–42	66.8%
1842–51	51.6%
1851–61	44.3%
1861–71	19.5%

2 *Census of the Canadas, 1851–52* 1: 16–17; *Census of the Canadas 1860–61* 1: 62–3.
3 For the raw data for 1832, see Appendix A.

A second observation is that almost inevitably the proportion of foreign-born inhabitants dropped while correspondingly the proportion of native-born Canadians grew. Given below are the native-born inhabitants of the townships of Leeds and Lansdowne[4]

	Number of native-born Canadians	Percentage of total population
1842	1,960	62.9%
1851	3,301	69.9%
1861	5,088	74.7%
1871	6,506	79.9%

These two observations are not relevant at this point (although they will be germane later in my argument) because the sub-infeudation process was triggered by the local society's reaching a certain threshold level. This threshold had nothing to do with rates of population growth or with the place of birth of the inhabitants but with the relationships of the population pool to the space which it occupied. Once it was passed, the local society began undergoing a set of transformations that were much more than merely quantitative: by the early 1870s the entire quality of local life was transformed.

3

Contemporary local residents were keenly conscious that, consequent upon population growth, the scale of life was changing. One of their first indications was the focusing of governmental agencies onto a smaller geographic area than previously had been the case. They readily accepted the opportunity afforded them by the general reforms in local government which passed the legislature in 1849 and welcomed the split of the previously united township of Leeds and Lansdowne into two separate municipalities. One of these, the front of Leeds and Lansdowne township, took in the first five concessions of Leeds and the first six of Lansdowne. The other, the rear of Leeds and Lansdowne township, consisted of the inland

4 See chapter 4, table 6, and Census of the Canadas, 1851-52 1: 16-17; Census of the Canadas, 1860-61 1: 62-3; Census of Canada, 1870-71 1: 358. In these and the preceding tables I have, of course, added Gananoque (a separate census entity) to the figures for the front of Leeds and Lansdowne in order to give comparability with the earlier data.

areas.[5] The extent of these two jurisdictions was roughly comparable (58,885 acres in the front, 45,551 in the rear).[6] This development effectively doubled the apparatus of local government in the area.

This change at the lowest level of government, the township, confirmed a trend that first had been evinced earlier at the district level. Even after the awesomely large Johnstown district of loyalist times was shrunk in the 1820s by removing the Bathurst district, it was too large. A royal proclamation of 19 March 1842 hived off townships north of the Rideau, North Gower, Marlborough, and Montague, and most of the townships of Burgess and Elmsley also were transferred to the Bathurst district.[7] This left the Johnstown district coterminous with the area which became the United Counties of Leeds and Grenville when in 1850 counties replaced districts as the unit of second-tier government.[8]

The real concentration, however, came at the township level, closest to the people, and in the Johnston district the amalgamated neighbouring township to Leeds and Lansdowne, Yonge and Escott, was divided, first in 1853 into the separate townships of the front of Yonge and Escott and the rear of the same,[9] and then in 1859 into a further separation of the front of Yonge from the front of Escott.[10]

The other notable characteristic of the shift in local government came in the population centres. Brockville had become a self-governing village in 1832[11] and a town in 1849,[12] and within the new municipality of the front of Leeds and Lansdowne one soon heard discussions of the need for the settlement of Gananoque to have a municipal government that would concentrate solely on its own affairs and leave the rural areas to the township government. After a good deal of argument concerning the merits of incorporation (predictably hinging on whether or not local rates would rise), the

5 12 Vict. c. 99; J.D.W. Darling and W.H. Wallace, *Sketch of the Early History of the Front Concessions of Lansdowne and Thousand Island Group* (Gananoque: privately printed 1925), 7. The change was not entirely without opposition. See the *Brockville Recorder*, 19 April 1849 and 3 May 1849.

6 Jesse E. Middleton and Fred Landon, *The Province of Ontario – A History, 1615–1927* (Toronto: Dominion Publishing Co. 1927) 2: 1155.

7 Affidavit of Johnstown district clerk, James Jessup, in AO, RG 22 ser. 7, 59-D, "General Quarter Session, Johnstown district, Sundry Municipal Papers."

8 12 Vict. c. 78.

9 16 Vict. c. 226.

10 22 Vict. c. 82.

11 2 Wm. IV, c. 17.

12 12 Vict. c. 81.

village of Gananoque became an incorporated municipality in January 1863.[13]

From the standpoint of the suggestion made earlier that the sub-infeudation of the area was a phenomenon largely completed by 1871, the significant fact is that none of the three relevant boundaries differs today from those set in the period under study: the limits of the United Counties of Leeds and Grenville are the same as those set under the municipal government act of 1849; the municipalities of the front of Leeds and Lansdowne and of the rear of Leeds and Lansdowne are the same as determined in 1849, and Gananoque remains a separate entity. There was a "separation movement" in the later 1850s, pressing for both Leeds and Grenville to be full-fledged rather than united counties, but nothing came of it.[14] Under the press of population increase, the local citizens had recognized the need to alter their governmental boundaries but, being sensible and indeed hardminded, when they found them suitable, they did not waste their time on further alterations.

Not only were the geographic foci of the various levels and agencies of government concentrated, but a major qualitative change occurred in the nature of township and county government. It will be recalled from chapter 2 that the characteristics of the original JP system of local government had been: an admixture of judicial and governmental functions undertaken by the general court of quarter session in the Johnstown district; a dependency upon individual citizens accepting their obligations as part of myriad individual social contracts; a structural weakness at the township level – since township meetings were infrequent and very limited in their powers and individuals took on the unpleasant local tasks (especially poundkeeperships and constableships) often only under threat of fine and a dominance of amateur government both at the township and the district level, in the sense that there were very few officials actually paid to function as fulltime local government officials. Government was a sideline usually and unpaid.

Sub-infeudation changed that and local government moved several steps in the direction of professionalism. In 1842, for example, the judicial and the administrative functions of local government agencies were separated. The justices of the peace continued to be appointed by the central government and to meet as

13 For details of Gananoque's development see chapter 6.
14 See the *Brockville Recorder*, 12 and 26 March, 1857. Most of the impetus came from residents of Grenville County.

the court of general quarter sessions (the name "quarter" was dropped in 1868). The JPS still were the court of primary jurisdiction for minor matters and they were not professional in the sense of their being solely trained lawyers, but now they were at least functionally specialized, dealing only in law, not in civil administration, a major stage in legal evolution.[15] According to the Honourable William Morris, the first person to hold the wardenship of the Johnstown district after these changes occurred, the justices of the peace were glad to be rid of their administrative responsibilities, "as no part of their public duty was felt to be so onerous and so obnoxious to animadversions."[16] They now were quite happy to be able to concentrate on preserving the public peace.

The other half of the arrangements for local governance, the administrative, were radically altered. By a two-stage process involving acts effective 1 January 1842[17] and 1 January 1850,[18] local government ceased to be based primarily on the network of central government patronage and local social contacts and became elective. Local governmental officials were still for the most part citizens who undertook administrative positions as part-time civil obligations, but they now were functionally tied directly to their constituencies through a formal constitutional mechanism.

The two-tier system that had emerged by 1850 of elected township councils and elected district councils implied a degree of functional democracy. So too did the village councils created under the 1849 act and the Gananoque village which was incorporated in 1863. Details varied slightly according to the level of government, but fundamentally in each government unit resident freeholders or householders formed a body corporate with all the usual powers attached to incorporation: possession of a corporate seal, the right to sue or be sued, and the privileges of purchasing property and appointing corporate employees. Each township, village, or district elected a council and this council chose its own head, a warden or reeve. These new arrangements were far from being Jacobinical, but they did represent what the chief historian of nineteenth-century

15 I am grateful to Ms Kathy Shepherd, curator of legal records in AO for her help in tracing the changes in the court of general session. For general background, see J. Jerard Bellomo, "Upper Canadian Attitudes towards Crime and Punishment (1832–1851)," Ontario History 64 (1972): 12–26.

16 Address of Hon. William Morris, Warden of Council," 8 February 1842, AO, RG 21, "Johnstown District," 1842 (3).

17 4 and 5 Vict. c. 10.

18 12 Vict. c. 79, 80 and 81.

local government has called "the culmination of a long struggle for 'home rule' at all levels of local government.'[19]

The new local governments were nothing if not serious about their assigned tasks. The criteria of financial efficiency and accountability were the foremost theme in the inaugural address of the first warden of the Johnstown Council, the Honourable William Morris. At the convening meeting of council, 8 February 1842, he explained that "complaint had long been made in various parts of Upper Canada, whether just or not it is not necessary now to inquire, that the Justices [of the Peace under the old system] in the expenditure of the district revenue, were not guided by that scrupulous regard for economy which in the opinion of many, the interests of the people at large required at their hands."[20] Morris went on in this vein at great length and with each paragraph it became clear how greatly the new style, with its emphasis on accurate accounting and value for money, differed from the days when JPS had been appointed by the provincial authorities under the belief that the justices, like English squires in similar positions in the home country, would control local affairs by a judicious mixture of social superiority and gentlemanly firmness.[21] When, on 1 January 1850, the new council for the United Counties of Leeds and Grenville replaced the Johnstown district council, the serious tone continued. Meticulous minutes were kept, so detailed that in the twentieth century a clerk of the council could produce two good-sized books from the

19 J.H. Aitchison, "The Municipal Corporations Act of 1849," *Canadian Historical Review* 30 (1949): 107. The thesis underlying Aitchison's interpretation of the 1849 "Baldwin Act" fits well with the argument being presented here. His view is that before the reforms of the 1840s the districts were inherently unstable political units as the direct consequence of their size. Thus, concentration of local governmental activities on smaller physical areas was a prerequisite for the functional improvement in their operation.

20 "Address of Hon. William Morris." See n16 above.

21 Morris's emphasis upon new-style administrative efficiency is all the more significant for his having been appointed as warden of Johnstown by the central governmental authorities. Afraid of too much democracy and innovation, they had kept in the Crown's hands the powers of appointing the warden, clerk, and treasurer of each district. By 1846, however, it had become clear that the various councils were quite competent for this task and therefore it was bestowed upon them. See William Jelly, ed., *A Summary of the Proceedings of the Johnstown District Council, 1842–49* (Brockville: Leeds and Grenville Counties Council 1929), 5. For a list of the local wardens, from 1842 to 1878 inclusive, see Thaddeus W.H. Leavitt, *History of Leeds and Grenville* (Brockville: *Brockville Recorder* 1879), 54–5.

records.[22] In some years these minutes actually were printed and distributed, as were bound copies of council by-laws, in most cases in a quality of typography that put to shame that being used for debates and papers of the provincial government.[23] Such seriousness of purpose could lead to ludicrous self-importance, as when the Leeds and Grenville council graciously informed his excellency the Governor General that in their opinion all the British possessions in North America should be united and the Union of Upper and Lower Canada dissolved.[24] (One wonders if they did not subsequently see themselves as the fathers of Confederation.)

Neither the municipality of the front of Leeds and Lansdowne, nor the council of the village of Gananoque went in for elaborate printed records,[25] but the same seriousness, verging on self-parody, is found in the early minutes of the Gananoque council, whose first priority seems to have been to guard their dignity by procuring "a proper corporate seal."[26] One of the prices paid for the new seriousness in local government was that the township and village elections sometimes served as a simulacrum of the larger political divisions in society, electors choosing their township and village officials according to national stances that were quite irrelevant to local affairs.[27]

For all their earnestness, the county, township, and village councils were concerned chiefly with two matters, schools and roads, and everything else was peripheral. Schools will be discussed later. Here, the matter of the roads is instructive, for the way

22 Jelly, ed., *A Summary, 1842–1849* and *A Summary of the Proceedings of the Council of the District of Johnstown and the Council of the United Counties of Leeds and Grenville, 1842–1942* (Brockville: Leeds and Grenville Counties Council 1943).

23 See, for example, *Minutes of the Municipal Council of the United Counties of Leeds and Grenville* (Brockville: David Wylie 1854); *By-Laws of the Municipal Council for the United Counties of Leeds and Grenville passed at their Session, held at Brockville, in Jaunary and March 1850* (Brockville: Wylie and Sutton 1850); *By-Laws of the Municipal Council of Leeds and Grenville, passed at the Session held in Brockville in June 1851* (Brockville: D. Wylie 1851).

24 The item is found in draft in AO, RG 21, "Johnstown District," 1855 (7). The original apparently was sent to other municipal councils. Replies were noted as received from Stormont, Waterloo, and Carleton councils.

25 In the case of Gananoque there were, in fact, complaints about the lack of published records. *Brockville Recorder*, 5 January 1865.

26 OA, RG 21, SEC. A (uncatalogued), "Minutes of Proceedings of the Municipal Council of the Corporation of the Village of Gananoque," 19 January 1863.

27 For evidences of the intrusion of provincial and national issues upon the local politics of the front of Leeds and Lansdowne and Gananoque, see the *Brockville Recorder*, respectively, 15 January 1863 and 5 January 1865.

in which roads came to be handled indicates an important halfway stage in the evolution of professional government. Under the old JP system of local administration most roads were maintained by statute labour, that is, the appointment in each township of several overseers of roads and highways who apportioned the work to the local residents. Major works were undertaken without competitive bidding or precise advance specifications and often were done by an interested party: the early bridge over the Gananoque River put up by Joel Stone comes to mind (see chapter 2). That example contrasts sharply with the way in which the Leeds and Grenville council acted when they determined in 1855 to put a newer bridge across the river on the site of the old structure in the village of Gananoque. This time they set down a contract of fourteen copperplate pages of specifications to be met by the professional contractor who took on the job.[28] On another major project, the projected "Gananoque and Rideau Railway Company," the Gananoque council, when it voted ten thousand dollars in a complex debenture issue, seemingly showed that it had moved light-years away from the era of conscripting the inhabitants and their horses for maintaining communications.[29]

Yet the evolution was more mixed than those instances might indicate. Professionalism infiltrated local governments but it did not become dominant overnight. For instance, the Gananoque village council very early in its existence, in 1863, provided for the commutation of road labour in the town, that is, residents now paid a money fee rather than actually give of their labour,[30] but in the neighbouring countryside the people of the township of the front of Leeds and Lansdowne still appointed the traditional overseers of the roads and highways who maintained the concession roads in the old manner. In 1861 there were fifty overseers of road divisions in the township.[31] The South Lake road is a nice case in point, for it shows the varying styles of dealing with roads, none of them very successful. This road was the main artery north out of Gananoque, heading through the front of Leeds and Lansdowne township and thence to Seeleys Bay in the rear (it is now found, in a slightly improved version, as Highway 32, reputedly the shortest King's Highway in Ontario). This twisting, muddy, waterlogged, rock-strewn passageway served as a standard for judging other local roads, and when the editor of the *Gananoque Reporter* wanted to

28 The contract is in AO, RG 21, "Johnstown District," 1855 (5).
29 "Minutes, Village of Gananoque," 26 May 1871 and 1 July 1871.
30 Ibid., 7 July and 8 December 1863. See also 13 August 1867.
31 *Gananoque Reporter*, 27 February 1861.

explain how bad the highway from Brockville to Kingston was he simply stated that it was as bad as the road to Gananoque from South Lake.[32] The people in the township were notoriously opposed to improving roads, the *Reporter* said, and one could not go more than three miles an hour on a horse on South Lake road. Nevertheless, the locals "would rather plod on through the mud and mire, wearing out horse, using up vehicle, exhausting patience and retarding business."[33] Eventually the situation became so bad that the township council for the front of Leeds and Lansdowne had to do something more than merely refer the matter to the overseers of the roads. In the late 1850s they had voted fifty pounds to fix the road from Gananoque to the railway station and South Lake, a step towards professionalization, one might think, as cash rather than actual labour was involved. According to one source, however, the reeve of the township had himself appointed head of the project, pocketed the money and did little, so that in 1861 wagon wheels were tumbling over raw stones. Similarly, the council appointed a man, said to be a political friend of the council members, to replace the bridge over the end of South Lake and paid him cash. Instead of building the bridge at a safe distance above the inadequate old one, he built it alongside so that in the spring water was three or four feet over one end![34]

The merchants of Gananoque who needed a good communication route to the north first responded to this situation by trying to pressure the rural township council by convening a public meeting to discuss macadamizing portions of the South Lake road.[35] This accomplished little. After Gananoque was incorporated, D. Ford Jones, factory owner and reeve of the new village, convened in November 1865 a meeting of the leading citizens and put to them the proposition that a joint stock company should be formed to make a macadamized or gravel road running north as far as Haskins Corners in the rear of Leeds and Lansdowne. The people did not care for this and only a few were willing to take any stock.[36] That having failed, the next year the Gananoque council took matters in its own hands and let a tender for macadamizing the portion of the South Lake road leading out of the village.[37] Four years later, when the notorious bridge at South Lake again needed fixing, the village

32 Ibid., 31 October 1860.
33 Ibid., 27 February 1860.
34 Ibid., 17 April 1861.
35 Ibid., 12 December 1860.
36 *Brockville Recorder*, 30 November 1865.
37 "Minutes, Village of Gananoque," 28 June 1866.

council voted one hundred dollars to the rural council to help them with the task.[38]

A wise historian has taught us that historians can learn as much from historical comedy as from tragedy.[39] The laziness, veniality, ambition, and hard-eyed business acumen that affected the progress of the winding South Lake road reminds us that change in attitudes towards government, like the very process of sub-infeudation of which these evolving attitudes were a part, was uneven; the new professional ways overtook the old in patches, breaking out here and there, and finally consolidating their pattern like swatches of grass coming out from beneath the snow in the spring sun. Most civic officials still were citizens performing their civic function on a part-time basis, and certainly this was not the era of scientific management. Individual deals and eccentric practices still remained (and still do, as anyone who has dealt with poundkeepers, fence viewers, or livestock valuers in the present-day township will testify). With sub-infeudation, however, had come the men with accurate minute books, detailed methods of financial accounting, and a knowledge of debentures and of how to let a least-cost contract. The progress of marcher lords such as these could only be delayed, not stopped.

4

Concurrent with the increasing concentration of agencies of civil administration occurred a reticulation of voluntary associations. The local landscape was crisscrossed with an ever-infilling web of clubs, lodges, churches, and temperance societies, many of which were themselves part of a province-wide network of associate societies. Lines of affiliation arose among the temperance societies in Gananoque, Brockville, Kingston, and Smiths Falls, between Orange lodges in the front of Leeds and Lansdowne township and the rest of the United Counties of Leeds and Grenville, and between the various Catholic and Protestant churches and their coreligionists in their respective dioceses, conferences, or circuits, so that eventually many social telegraph lines crisscrossed the local area where previously few had existed.

At the upper and middle end of the social scale were the fraternal lodges, the most important being the Masons and the Odd Fellows.

38 Ibid., 22 August 1870.
39 The observation is Sir Lewis Namier's. For an extended example of this all too rare genre of historical writing, see Lewis P. Curtis, *Chichester Towers* (New Haven: Yale University Press 1966).

The former had a long history in central Canada (the first lodge was formed in Kingston in 1794) and there were lodges in Kemptville, Merrickville, Farmersville, Smiths Falls, as well as in Brockville, Kingston and Gananoque. These fit into a network covering both Ontario and Quebec and embracing in 1856 forty-one lodges.[40] The Odd Fellows were more important locally by virtue of their having a very vigorous Gananoque chapter, Lodge 201. The affiliational network of the Independent Order of Odd Fellows was not as firm as that of the Masons, for at mid-century the Canadian lodges, which previously had been part of "the American Unity," were cut adrift and left to manage for themselves.[41]

Also significant were the Mechanics' Institutes, which despite their name hardly provided fare for the working classes but served as combinations of reading room, lecture forum, and sometimes debating society. (Although apparently the Institutes seem to be a colonial descent of Lord Brougham's Society for the Diffusion of Useful Knowledge – the much derided "Steam Intellect Society" – it is worth noting that, given the Irish predominance in the area, they closely resembled the "Reading Societies" that had emerged in the north of Ireland in the late eighteenth century.)[42] During the third quarter of the nineteenth century these Institutes were formed in various places in Leeds and Grenville counties such as Merrickville, Prescott, Brockville, and Kemptville; the first to be incorporated was at Merrickville in 1857.[43] The Gananoque Institute, of uncertain date, was flourishing by 1860. To celebrate the coming of the year 1861, its members rented a hall on New Year's Eve, draped it with Union Jacks, and had a night of speeches, songs by the town's glee club (including the euphonious "I Love the Banging Hammer"), and community singing of some carols and "Go Tell Aunt Rhoda."[44] The Gananoque Mechanics' Institute kept close ties with that in Brockville and when in 1861 the Brockville group sponsored a

---

40 See William J. Dunlop, ed., *The First One Hundred Years: A History of the Grand Lodge, A.F. and A.M. of Canada in the Province of Ontario, 1855–1955* (Toronto: Grand Lodge 1955), passim. Grand Lodge news was of sufficient importance to demand reporting in the local press, for example, *Brockville Recorder*, 25 October 1851.

41 *Brockville Recorder*, 20 March 1847 and 7 March 1850.

42 For a discussion of these Irish forerunners of the Mechanics' Institutes see Donald H. Akenson and W.H. Crawford, *Local Poets and Social History: James Orr, Bard of Ballycarry* (Belfast: Public Record Office of Northern Ireland 1977), 22–3, 74–80.

43 Ruth McKenzie, *Leeds and Grenville: Their First Two Hundred Years* (Toronto: McClelland and Stewart 1967), 212.

44 *Gananoque Reporter*, 2 January 1861.

"Mechanics Festival" a strong representation of exhibits from Gananoque was included.[45]

Two threads run through the development of most of the voluntary societies in the local area. First, the societies represent an energetic, sometimes almost manic, effort to overcome the loneliness, the distance between people, that had prevailed in the early days of settlement. Second, there was a latent but powerful desire to smooth down the roughest edges of a harsh society, to make gentler – and in some cases genteel – the way people acted. This process of course was not limited to the local area, or indeed, even to North America,[46] but its local referents are unmistakable.

In this latter regard the social activities of the local churches are instructive. In their activities (mostly motivated by a need to raise funds for building purposes) the churches introduced a new social vocabulary and spread a new social style amongst the general population. Foreign loan-words such as "bazaar" and "soirée" became part of the local vocabulary,[47] and innumerable church tea parties combined good works with refined gossip.

Some of this new social control involved nothing more than the discipline and agreement necessary in any group activity. The Gananoque Glee Club and the town brass band, both lively in the early 1860s,[48] can be seen as activities of this sort. And semi-spontaneous activities, such as the town picnic[49] and a celebrated boat race between Gananoque and Kingston,[50] probably involved no more discipline than everyone turning out to the event in good humour. On the other hand, some of the internal discipline of the voluntary groups could be quite heavy-handed: in 1861 the local Catholic priest took out an advertisement in the Gananoque paper, listing in a black box nine column inches long the names of defaulting subscribers to St John's church and the amount they owed. The advertisement ended with the motto "Let the rising generation hand this down to their offspring."[51]

Nevertheless, the increasingly reticulated voluntary social network implied a degree of social control by the middle and upper

45 Ibid., 30 January 1861.
46 For a description of a similar process occurring at roughly the same time in Ireland, see Donald H. Akenson, *Between Two Revolutions: Islandmagee, Co. Antrim, 1798–1920* (Toronto: P.D. Meany Co.; Hamden, Conn.: Archon Books; Dublin: Academy Press 1979), especially 99–118, 145–70.
47 See *Gananoque Reporter*, 26 September 1860 and 15 January 1862.
48 Ibid., 2 January 1861 and 16 July 1861; *Brockville Recorder*, 27 July 1865.
49 *Gananoque Reporter*, 21 August 1861.
50 *Brockville Recorder*, 27 July 1865.
51 *Gananoque Reporter*, 30 January 1861.

orders over those lower on the scale. Through lodges and churches genteel values were expected to percolate downwards. Thus "The Learned Blacksmith," a celebrated lecturer of the time, in 1861 was brought to the Wesleyan church for a public performance. His topic was "The Highest Law of Missions and Commerce," and he argued that free trade was a "powerful agent in the work of civilizing and evangelizing the world." When not enough citizens turned up to hear this medley of capitalism and Protestantism, the editor of the local paper chided the villagers and reminded them that "the only way in which first class lecturers can be induced to visit a village like ours is to give them crowded houses.[52] Obviously, the Learned Blacksmith was not a threat to the social order. In contrast, at only its second full meeting after incorporation, the Gananoque village council passed a by-law relating to the licensing of circus riders,[53] apparently under the apprehension that unless properly controlled such people could mesmerize a congress of locals, with unguessable consequences.

The Volunteer militia which was centred in Gananoque and drew from the surrounding rural area is an interesting case. Although in theory part of the national defence force, in reality it was another local voluntary social association. In a society where many men were very accomplished with firearms, and some quick to use them, it was very useful to enrol as many strong yeomen as possible, to introduce them to a minimum amount of discipline, and, most important, to bond them together as part of a group. At the head of the local militia inevitably was a substantial member of the community, and most officers were solid citizens. None of that was new; it was as true in 1820 as in 1860. What was new, however, was the introduction of a clublike activity, competitive shooting. This sport swept the country during the 1860s, with Canadian teams under gentry captains being selected to shoot in the British Isles and Europe. The Gananoque Volunteers, like many similar units in the province, joined with local gentlemen and sponsored shoots. In November 1863, for example, the locals held a shoot open to all comers with two hundred dollars in prizes and the special prize of a revolving rifle to be shot for by all Volunteers in the riding.[54] To their credit, the local Volunteers did not go so far in underscoring the implicit connection between the practised use of firearms and social discipline as did the Kingston Rifle Association, which earlier in the

52 Ibid., 13 March 1861.
53 "Minutes, Village of Gananoque," 31 January 1863.
54 *Brockville Recorder*, 12 November 1863.

same year advertised that their shoot was to be distinguished by "a running man target," which they boasted was the first of its kind ever tried in Canada.[55]

The ever more articulated voluntary social network implied that a good deal of latent social control was invoked by the substantial citizens. Things, however, did not necessarily go smoothly for the solid burghers and their allies among the large farmers, and there was often a comic nature to their own newly acquired gentility. There is a pure unholy joy in watching the pompous "Warden's Supper" of 1859 – an occasion when the representatives of the various townships on the Leeds and Grenville counties council met to dine and toast themselves, the Queen, and other worthies – turn into a bun fight. Instead of setting an example of public decorum, the councillors entered into a slanging match over whether the editor of the *Monitor*, the conservative paper in Brockville, had been going "round with the begging box," and the various toasts were interspersed with name calling. Hogarth would have done wonders with the scene.[56] And the devil and all his minions can only have laughed as the Gananoque Presbyterians bickered at a soirée in March 1852. In that instance there was a difference of opinion about whether it was sinful to have a few tunes played on the piano at such an occasion. The argument was sharp enough for its reports to be carried as news in the *Brockville Recorder*.[57] The question of music continued to bedevil the local Presbyterians and almost a decade later their annual soirée was once again disrupted by a dispute on the topic when the remarks of one of the clergy concerning the proper form of congregational singing in church differed from those of some of the laymen present.[58] At times it seemed singing a sweet song unto the Lord was not easy.

The litmus case in indicating the connection between the emerging voluntary social network and the perceived need for social control is the temperance movement, for in the local area leadership came unmistakably from the privileged in society and it was their values that were being preached to those below them on the social scale. A great flood of words has been written about the question

55 Ibid., 22 October 1863.
   To be sure, the clublike bonding of the rank and file volunteers to their officers did not last forever. Two years later, the men were briefly in an uproar because they were owed pay for sixteen days' drill at half a dollar a day, which they believed had stuck in the officers' pockets (*Brockville Recorder*, 9 March 1865).
56 *Brockville Recorder*, 20 October 1859.
57 Ibid., 23 March 1852.
58 *Gananoque Reporter*, 13 March 1861.

and it is well to underscore three simple facts about alcohol in the predominantly rural environment of central Canada. First, drink was necessary for survival. Just as alcohol was the swiftest ticket out of the Manchester slums for the proletariat of the industrial revolution, so it was the surest, quickest way for the isolated farmer, the bush worker, and the village claustrophobic to escape his environs. The long hours of manual labour, often alone or in the company of the same small family group, day in and day out, the omnipresent silence when out of doors, the cramped quarters indoors, especially in December, January and February, all dictated that a person sometimes had to hear a fair and enspiriting musik, conveyed to him by alcohol.[59]

Second, as late as the 1860s Ontario farmers were reported commonly trading a portion of their grain for whiskey.[60] This was only natural, as the milling industry was functionally integrated with distilling and there was a commercial conduit from farmer to alcohol-distiller. It made great financial sense for the farmer to get his liquor this way, for by buying it in quantity at wholesale rates he was avoiding the markup of the spirit grocer or tavern keeper. Annual per capita consumption of spirits in Canada, calculated in 1869, was well over a gallon a year for every man, woman, and child, and this included only legally manufactured spirits: home-distilled liquors, beers, wines, and ciders were not included.[61]

Third, alcohol was undeniably the proximate cause of trouble. Farmers, hired labourers, their sons, and their spouses, people who often drank for relief, went to war with fist, club, gun, or knife against whoever had the bad fortune to be near them. The early temperance advocates were not mere bluenoses; they had a wealth of personal experience that demonstrated to them that the consumption of spirits and the potential breakdown of the social fabric were intimately related. A few examples from the front of Leeds and Lansdowne township will suffice to make the case as far as the context of this local study is concerned. About two miles below Gananoque there was a very rough rural drinking establishment, "The Sheban House," where disorder was commonplace. The

59 An unsympathetic but informed discussion of early pioneer drinking habits, with reference to the later period as well, is the Reverend M.A. Garland and J. J. Talman, "Pioneer Drinking Habits and the Rise of the Temperance Agitation in Upper Canada prior to 1840," *Ontario Historical Society: Papers and Records* 27 (1931): 341–64.

60 Graeme Decarie, "Something Old, Something New ... Aspects of Prohibitionism in Ontario in the 1890s," in *Oliver Mowat's Ontario*, ed. Donald Swainson (Toronto: Macmillan 1972), 157.

61 Ibid.

regulars at the house in the mid-1860s included several Yankee "skedaddlers" (men who came to Canada to avoid military service in the American Civil War) and several local hard cases, mostly farmers but including a shoemaker who when drunk hollered like a mad bull and on occasion had to be bound hand and foot to keep him from killing anyone with whom he came in contact. A common night's entertainment involved a fight in which a man was driven or jumped through a window to save himself from being half-murdered, and on another evening five or six men began to fight with sticks and clubs, one of the combatants being battered senseless and another badly hurt.[62]

This kind of drink-related violence was not kept within the walls of dram establishments. A man named Malowing who had come down the Gananoque River on a scow in mid-May 1865 berthed it above the village and went to sleep. About two in the morning seven or eight local drunks leapt on board, consumed as much of his bread and pork as they could, destroyed the rest, and then continued on their spree.[63] Similar incidents could be multiplied by the score: the local polling in an 1860 election was marked by staggering drunks and a free fight in the street; a proper young lady, walking home, was knocked down by two speeding drunks on horseback; four or five young rowdies fell upon two rivals and beat them with sticks;[64] and they can be found in every township in the district and in every year in the middle two quarters of the nineteenth century.

At mid-century serious attempts were begun locally to gain control of the use of spirits, and it is not accidental that the rise of the temperance societies corresponded so closely to the period of sub-infeudation of local society, with its emphasis upon a gentling of manners and human relationships. There were two fundamental ways to attack the drink problem, depending upon one's idea of causality. If one viewed alcohol as the midwife, not the originator, of the problem, then one attacked the problem by removing the reasons that people drank. If the boredom, loneliness, and frustrations of rural life had been taken as the cause of the drink problem, then conceivably contemporaries could have reacted to it by trying to strengthen the social alternatives to getting drunk. The evolution of the voluntary social structure, which we already have described in this period of sub-infeudation, could have been accelerated by

62 *Brockville Recorder*, 9 March 1865 and 23 March 1865.
63 Ibid., 18 May 1865.
64 Reports of the instances referred to are found, respectively, in *Gananoque Reporter*, 17 October 1860 and 11 September 1861; *Brockville Recorder*, 23 March 1865.

those who were worried about the social disruption caused by alcohol abuse.

Instead of adopting this analysis and the strategy of control dictated thereby, contemporaries believed that alcohol itself was the causal agent in the drink problem and that to alleviate the problem one had to attack the use and availability of the drug itself. The first temperance society in Upper Canada was formed in Bastard township (which abuts on the rear of Lansdowne township) in 1828.[65] Other localities in the Johnstown district followed suit: Merrickville in 1830, and Brockville and Yonge township in 1832.[66] Halting attempts were made during the 1830s at founding a provincewide temperance society,[67] but it was only in the late 1840s and early 1850s that a strong body emerged. This was the Sons of Temperance, with its offshoots the Daughters of Temperance and the Cadets of Temperance, which grew steadily during the next four decades. The Sons had more than five thousand members in 1882 and with ten thousand were still growing in 1893.[68] Gananoque and Brockville opened two of the first (perhaps the very first) lodges of this temperance order in 1847 and 1848.[69] The new organizational vigour of the temperance movement coincided with the changing of its ideological base from temperance to complete abstinence, although confusingly the name "temperance" was retained.[70]

The most interesting feature of the local Sons of Temperance was the leadership. John Lewis McDonald, a grandson of Joel Stone and with his two brothers an heir to both the Stone estate and that of his father who had been the first merchant prince of the area, was extremely active, proselytizing widely for the society. In the summer of 1849 he presided over a public meeting for the promotion of the society at Coleman's Corners (now Lyn) involving the assemblage of men and women from Gananoque, Brockville, and

65 Garland and Talman, 352.

66 *Brockville Recorder*, 15 March 1832; McKenzie, 90.

67 Garland and Talman, 353.

68 Malcolm G. Decarie, "The Prohibition Movement in Ontario, 1894–1916," (PHD diss., Queen's University 1972), 7.

69 Decarie cites Brockville as having the second lodge in Canada, formed in 1848. There is some confusion about the Gananoque unit. A Sons of Temperance lodge is reported extant there in 1847 (*Brockville Recorder*, 20 March 1847), but in March 1850 the Gananoque lodge is reported to have been celebrating its first anniversary (*Brockville Reporter*, 7 March 1850).

70 Decarie's entire thesis repays reading, charting as it does the ideological development that began with temperance, moved to abstinence, and then to prohibitionism.

even Ogdensburg, New York, with the men in full regalia. According to newspaper reports, five to six hundred people assembled in a rural grove and took the pledge to abstain totally from all intoxicating drinks.[71] The local society had as other prominent leaders Messrs George Mitchell, successful carriage maker and precentor of the Presbyterian church in Gananoque, William Brough, general and produce merchant and a Scot who had bought the village's main milling and mercantile business, A. Britton, factory and sawmill owner, and Robert Brough, manufacturer. To their number was added the presiding presence at one early anniversary celebration, William Stone McDonald, grandson of Joel Stone and a factory owner and land speculator.[72] Obviously, the views and goals of the Sons, Daughters, and Cadets of Temperance were congruent with those of the township's more successful citizens.

In promotion of total abstinence the society did provide some degree of alternate social activity – brass bands and lodge regalia enlivened special occasions – but mostly the intent was to control the drink problem by moulding public opinion so that alcohol consumption was reduced. Eventually the temperance people hoped to make drinking intoxicants socially unacceptable, and when that quixotic attempt failed many temperance enthusiasts advocated total prohibition by legislative decree.[73] The zenith of prohibitionism was a long distance in the future, however, and in the short run the temperance forces contented themselves with using their powers over local government bodies to make access to spirituous liquors more difficult than otherwise would have been the case. For example, under the old justice of the peace system of local government there had been in the front of Leeds and Lansdowne seven licensed spirit dealers in 1833;[74] the corresponding

71 *Brockville Recorder*, 14 June 1849.
72 See list of platform party in *Brockville Recorder*, 7 March 1850.
73 I cannot find local data on attitudes towards prohibition, but one can only be struck with the results of the Ontario government plebiscite in 1894 which showed that about 65 percent of rural voters favoured prohibition, an amazing success for temperance forces. (See M.G. Decarie, "Paved with Good Intentions: The Prohibitionists' Road to Racism in Ontario," *Ontario History* 66 [1974]: 15 n2.) Given that Gananoque and its rural catchment area were in the vanguard of the early Sons of Temperance movement, it would not be surprising if they had also been ahead of the rest of the province in their conversion to prohibitionism.
74 AO, RG 22, ser. 7, "Johnstown District, Register of Inn-Keepers, 1833–41."

figure for 1853, after the elective county council form of government was in action and after the Sons of Temperance were well established, was four,[75] despite the increase in population. The same determination to limit access to spirits was shown in the newly formed Gananoque village council's by-law in February 1863 for the licensing of shopkeepers and other sellers of liquors.[76]

It has been convincingly argued that in its later stages (the 1890s and thereafter) the anti-alcohol movement became both anti-urban and racist in the sense of being anti-immigrant.[77] In the Leeds and Lansdowne area during the third quarter of the nineteenth century neither characteristic held. Alcohol abuse demonstrably was a serious rural problem, not an urban one to be pointed at with disdain by virtuous farmers. Further, the foreign-born in the township did not form a social sediment which could be associated with drink and disorder; actually (as will be discussed later in this chapter) the foreign-born farmers were more successful and thus higher on the rural economic scale than were native-born Canadians.

By its very nature any local opposition to the spread of the anti-drink movement left little mark upon the historical record: the man who wants to have a jar in peace does not sign a petition, have a parade, or form a lodge, but merely takes the lid off the family crock and puts his feet on the hearth. Thus the remonstrance of several citizens of Leeds and Grenville county against by-law 194, "To Provide for the preservation of the Public Morals of the United Counties of Leeds and Grenville, 9 November 1860," is noteworthy. This by-law had allowed individual citizens to prosecute on behalf of the county other individuals for breaking the spirit laws and could be used not only against licence violations by tavern owners but against individuals who were publicly drunken. In protest against this enactment, thirty people signed a petition, "As a great deal of *dissatisfaction* and *ill will* is arising in some of the *townships* of the said United County, by the *ultra* members of the *Teetotal Abstainer Societies*, on behalf of the *County* corporation on *suspicion* ... [and are] not particular whether the parties are guilty or not as they can take shelter under the by-law and throw the *costs* on the *counties*, which amounts to nothing more than prosecuting morally those who may differ from them in opinion." The petition-

75 *Brockville Recorder*, 17 March 1853.
76 "Minutes, Village of Gananoque," 26 February 1863.
77 See the Decarie articles and thesis cited above.

ers wanted a removal of the right of private prosecution and also desired (rather in self-interest, one suspects) precise definititons of what constituted a drunken person and illegal tippling![78]

In the phrase "prosecuting morally those who may differ from them in opinion" the petitioners raised the ethical issue that must be resolved again and again in any non-totalitarian society, the conflict between the desires of the majority and the rights of the minority. This question, however, was not one which the social leaders of the township recognized or consciously addressed.

5

During the third quarter of the nineteenth century, as part of the process that has been denominated as sub-infeudation, religious structures crystallized into a form which they have held virtually unchanged to this day in Leeds and Lansdowne township.[79] These religious developments shared many of the characteristics of the evolutional government and of local voluntary associations. As population grew, the individual churches tended to concentrate their activities on ever smaller geographical areas, to introduce more and more fulltime professional leaders, and to multiply their ties with congregations of coreligionists elsewhere in the province in systems similar to the reticulated social networks of the various lodges. This process involved the additional reagent of increasing theological denominationalism and thus there occurred a type of evolution similar to that amongst evolving *genera* in the animal kingdom which stem from the same ancestor: speciation.

As S.D. Clark notes, in the early days of settlement a person's choice of religious affiliation "tended to be determined by the availability of agencies of good fellowship" There was a "tendency of many frontier settlers to shift from one religious persuasion to another, differing at times widely in direction and form of church government." Clark explains that this "reflected the impermanency of religious organization and the willingness of the individual to

---

78 AO, RG 21, "Johnstown District," 1861 (1), "Petition of Certain Inhabitants, 15 October 1861."

79 For general descriptions of the religious situation in the province before 1850, see M.A. Garland, "Some Phases of Pioneer Religious Life in Upper Canada before 1850," *Ontario Historical Society: Papers and Records* 25 (1929): 231–47, and John S. Moir, "The Upper Canadian Religious Tradition," in *Profiles of a Province: Studies in the History of Ontario* (Toronto: Ontario Historical Society 1967), 189–95.

participate in whatever religious resource was available."[80] John Strachan in his "Ecclesiastical Chart" of 1827 (admittedly not an infallible source) listed only five fulltime clergymen in the Johnstown district even before the size of the district was pared down.[81] Congregations often shared a building and indeed the same service. In the rarest cases Catholics and Protestants worshipped together, as occurred in Kingstown prior to 1808 when, having no congregation of their own, the Catholics attended the Anglican liturgy.[82] Much more common was sharing of common service among Protestant denominations. In Gananoque the Presbyterians and the Wesleyans had a close relationship. The first church was built on land willed by Joel Stone (a Methodist), at the expense of the Honourable John McDonald (a Presbyterian), and both groups used the church at various times and for a while had a "union sabbath school."[83] So difficult was it to obtain a clergyman in the early days and so undifferentiated were denominational feelings among many Protestants that in 1806 the Presbyterian congregations of Yonge, Elizabethtown, and Augusta (the neighbouring townships to Leeds and Lansdowne) had temporarily converted themselves to Dutch Reformed in the hope of acquiring a clergyman from the Dutch Reformed Church in the United States![84] The most common form of religious cooperation, however, was in the shared use of a secular building for religious purposes. The Gananoque schoolhouse, built in 1816, was "free for all denominations" for Sunday worship.[85]

All this changed, not overnight nor in a simple linear trend, but piecemeal. In the 1850s a watershed was passed and full-fledged religious speciation took place. In operational terms, the characteristics of this speciation as it concerned any given denomination were the formation of a congregation that was concentrated in a small enough geographical area for any of its members to attend

80 S.D. Clark, *Church and Sect in Canada* (Toronto: University of Toronto Press 1948), 167.
81 Also, itinerant clergy based in Kingston helped to serve the Johnstown district. Arthur G. Doughty and Norah Story, eds. *Documents Relating to the Constitutional History of Canada, 1819–1828* (Ottawa: King's Printer 1935), 375–6.
82 Kathryn M. Bindon, "Kingston: A Social History, 1785–1830," (PHD diss., Queen's University 1979), 173–4.
83 H. William Hawke, "Religious Life in Gananoque – Yesterday and Today" (unpublished paper in the possession of Mrs Janet Harding, Gananoque), 5, 7; and Hawke, "Early Religious Life in Gananoque" (unpublished paper, also in the possession of Mrs Janet Harding), 3. Hawke's work assimilates a good deal of that done by the late Miss Edith McCammon.
84 McKenzie, 82.
85 Ibid., 88.

service without the necessity of overnight travel; the holding of weekly services; the appointment of a fulltime clergyman who, although he might do some "missionary work" in backwood areas, was chiefly responsible for ministering to the local congregation; and a church that belonged to the individual congregation, was intended primarily for religious usages, and was wholly under the local group's control. For religious speciation to be judged to have occurred in any specific locality, several congregations demonstrably must have acquired these characteristics.

If, in attempting to chronicle the religious speciation of the township of Leeds and Lansdowne, one looks at the census data concerning religious affiliation, one is struck by two points. The census authorities were remarkably cavalier in the manner in which they analysed religion. They changed categories in each succeeding census and this, combined with their vexing altering of the geographic units, means that these data are of little direct value in pinpointing the characteristics of local religious evolution. At the aggregate level, however, denominational affiliations did not change very much over time. The key groups in 1842 were the Church of England, the various Presbyterians and Methodists, and the Roman Catholics, and this held true thirty years later.

In practical terms, the key question in charting the progress of religious speciation is when did each congregation put up a stone church of its own? This "stone church test" is not suggested frivolously: such an investment was made only if regular weekly services were held and only if a substantial number of parishioners could regularly attend. A virtual concomitant for this level of investment was the appointment of a fulltime clergyman. For the historian, therefore, church construction is a convenient index of several related phenomena.[86]

The cases of the Church of England and of the Roman Catholic Church are absolutely clear. (Here "Anglican" is employed as a convenient synonym for the so-called Church of England, even

86 In a fascinating article, "The Dominion of the Lord: An Introduction to the Cultural History of Protestant Ontario in the Victorian Period," *Queen's Quarterly* 83 (Spring 1976): 47–70, William E. de Villiers-Westfall points to a general change in architectural taste among Protestant denominations in the third quarter of the nineteenth century: crudely put, they increasingly adopted a "medieval" style of building. This is exactly what happened with the three Protestant denominations in Gananoque when they built their new stone structures (the Catholic stone church was replaced, so one cannot comment on its character). Westfall's point is that the new architecture implied not only a stage in each group's economic and social development but a cultural one as well.

TABLE 7

Religious Affiliations, Leeds and Lansdowne Townships

	Church of England	Various Presbyterians	Various Methodists	Roman Catholic	Other creeds	No creed given	No religion	Not accounted for	Total population
1842									
Front of Leeds & Lansdowne	506	433	423	300	53			458	2,173
Rear of Leeds & Lansdowne	220	45	236	45	101			295	942
Townships combined	726	478	659	345	154			753	3,115
1851									
Leeds Township	647	383	428	358	292	175			2,283
Lansdowne Township	751	289	695	189	191	324			2,439
Townships combined	1,398	672	1,123	547	483	499			4,722
1861									
Leeds Township	1,269	658	740	725	144		173		3,709
Lansdowne Township	1,047	436	1,097	194	141		190		3,105
Townships combined	2,316	1,094	1,837	919	285		363		6,814
1871									
Front of Leeds & Lansdowne (incl. Gananoque)	1,315	1,080	2,003	1,114	138	121	9		5,780
Rear of Leeds & Lansdowne	978	159	889	108	203	26	0		2,363
Townships combined	2,293	1,239	2,892	1,222	341	147	9		8,143

Sources: Derived from manuscript census of 1842, AO; Census of the Canadas, 1851–52 1: 52–3; Census of the Canadas, 1861–2 1: 142–3; Census of Canada, 1870–71 1: 130–3

though, strictly speaking, use of the term is anachronistic.) Despite their forming the largest denomination in the townships of Leeds and Lansdowne, the Church of England adherents were not well served until the 1850s, having to make do before that with missionary clergy who most often were centred in Kingston. Nevertheless, they formed regular congregations and in 1839–40, in the town of Lansdowne, completed a modest frame structure (replaced in 1878).[87] Two years later, a classic Ontario white frame church (still in use) was put up in the countryside in the rear of Leeds and Lansdowne, the superb joinery being carried out by an English craftsman.[88] But the two townships lacked a fulltime clergyman and Gananoque, the largest population centre, was very poorly served. There the local congregation met at various times in an old school house, in a disused chapel, and in the Odd Fellows' building. The turning point came in October 1854, when the Reverend John Carroll was licensed as a travelling missionary for Leeds county, with his residence in Gananoque. His presence catalysed the congregation and, working to plans which he drew up himself, they set about constructing a permanent church which was completed in 1858. As a student of church architecture, the Reverend Mr Carroll was an amateur, but a gifted one, and the resulting building was (and still is) an impressive conflation of native building materials, warm sandstone, hand-rubbed hardwood, and ecclesiological symbols from the Old World: the influence of the Camden Society is unmistakable. From his base in Gananoque, the Reverend Mr Carroll served Anglican congregations as far west as Kingston Mills and as far north as the township boundary.[89] The church's architectural excellence should not blind one to the fact that the local Anglican congregation spanned a wide social spectrum and was not on the whole wealthy. The church's building committee was not being lachrymose when it described itself as representing "a poor congregation."[90] The local social establishment tended to be Presbyterian or Wesleyan Methodist.

The chronology of the Roman Catholic body is similar to that of the Church of England, although made slightly more complicated

87 Allan J. Anderson, *Diocese of Ontario (Anglican Church of Canada): Archives: Preliminary Inventory, 1980,* 149. This corrects Leavitt, 60.

88 See the historical sketch of the church in the *Gananoque Reporter,* 23 July 1980.

89 *Ninety Years in the Service of Christ* (Gananoque: privately printed 1948) and *Christ Church, Gananoque, Ontario* (Gananoque: privately printed 1957). I am grateful to the Reverend B.H. Lindsey, Rector of Christ Church, for providing me with copies of these items.

90 *Christ Church, Gananoque, Ontario,* 8.

by a two-stage evolution. Like the Anglicans, the Catholics were first served by missionary priests and the early congregations had no fixed or appropriate place of worship, individual homes having to suffice. In June 1846, however, Gananoque and area were raised from a mission to a full parish, with the appointment of its first resident priest. He stayed only six months (and indeed priests spun through Gananoque with great speed in the early days: eight between 1846 and 1874), and it was left to his successors to construct in 1847 a stone church dedicated to St John the Evangelist and complete in 1853 a stone rectory for the priest to reside in. Up to this point the Roman Catholic and Anglican evolutions were remarkably alike. The Catholics, however, did not build, or overbuild, with quite the degree of confidence of the Anglicans, with the result that their facility increasingly was inadequate and in 1889 they sold one stone edifice and built a larger one. Nevertheless, from 1853 onwards, in the case of the Catholics, and from 1858 for the Anglicans, both denominations were supplied with fulltime clergy and both possessed physical symbols, substantial buildings, which testified to their respective congregations' permanence within the community.[91]

In their societal effects, the local Roman Catholic Church and Church of England were similar not only in their chronology but also in their ecclesiastical polity. Catholics and Anglicans shared a sense of religious geography that stemmed from the undivided Christian Church of pre-Reformation days. Each denomination conceived of its religious world as an administrative network comprising individual parishes administered in an hierarchical system, involving bishops overseeing dioceses and archbishops superintending provinces. This diocesan system, with its administrative and organizational presuppositions inherited from the Old World, fit perfectly into the New World in this period of sub-infeudation. Neither the Anglican nor the Catholic administrative hierarchies had any trouble in frequently dividing their dioceses and parishes into smaller units as population increased (thus paralleling the concentration of governmental units in secular society) or in keeping the various parishes bound together in a diocesan network (thus parelleling the reticulation of voluntary secular social groups). Hence, the Anglicans were part of an ever strengthening

91 On Catholic development see Sister Mary Faustina, "The Christian Community of St. John the Evangelist, Gananoque, Ontario (in Retrospect)" (unpublished paper in Gananoque Public Library) and L.J. Flynn, *The Story of the Roman Catholic Church in Kingston, 1826–1976* (Kingston: Archdiocese of Kingston 1976), 266ff.

diocesan network: in 1785 they were under the Bishop of Nova Scotia; in 1793, a separate Quebec diocese was formed which included what is now Ontario; in 1839 Upper Canada became a diocese, and finally in 1862 the diocese of Ontario, comprising eastern Ontario, was set up.[92] The same process held for the Catholics: the originally massive territories of Bishop MacDonnell were redefined in 1826 when the new diocese of Kingston, taking in the whole of Ontario, was created; in 1841 the diocese of Toronto was separated out, and in 1847 the diocese of Bytown was hived off.[93]

In contrast, the Baptists, the one significant local denomination which had little sense of territoriality and structural hierarchy. adapted very badly to social change. Among the early settlers in the rear of the townships of Leeds and Lansdowne and in neighbouring Bastard and Kitley were a considerable number of Baptists. Most were of American background and they were associated with the pioneer adventurer, early industrial speculator, and religious charismatic, Abel Stevens. The census data concerning the Baptists are not very revealing. (Indeed the number for 1842 is so clearly unreliably low and that for 1851 so suspiciously high that it was necessary to include the Baptists under "other creeds" in table 7.) For the two years in which one can place trust in the census data, 1861 and 1871, Baptists comprised in each instance 3.7 percent of the combined populations of Leeds and Lansdowne townships.[94] Much more revealing is what happened to their congregations. One was founded in the front of Leeds and Lansdowne at Gananoque in 1819 with a membership of thirty-five and another in the eighth concession in the rear of the township with an average membership of about fifty in the 1835–50 period. In common with other Baptist

---

92 Anderson, *Diocese of Ontario*, preface.
     For other material reflecting at least indirectly on the in-filling of the Church of England's structure, see Allan J. Anderson, *The Anglican Churches of Kingston* (Kingston: privately printed 1963); Katherine Greenfield, "Reference Sources for the History of the Church of England in Upper Canada, 1791–1867," *Journal of the Canadian Church Historical Society* 9 (September 1967): 50–74; John S. Moir, *The Church in the British Era: From the British Conquest to Confederation* (Toronto: McGraw-Hill Ryerson 1972); John S. Moir, *Church and State in Canada, 1627–1867* (Toronto: McClelland and Stewart 1967); H.C. Stuart, *The Church of England in Canada, 1759–1793: From the Conquest to the Establishment of the See of Quebec* (Montreal: privately printed 1893); J.J. Talman, "The Position of the Church of England in Upper Canada, 1791–1840," *Canadian Historical Review* 15 (1934): 361–75.
93 Flynn, 22–40.
94 The Baptist census data are from the same sources as table 7.

congregations in the united counties (most notably at Delta in Bastard township and also in rural Augusta township), the Baptists did not grow, had a difficult time obtaining qualified clergy, and were not able to build substantial houses of worship. Writing in 1879, Thaddeus Leavitt reported that the Baptist congregation in the rear of the township had been materially diminished in numbers;[95] in 1880 the Gananoque Baptist Church ceased to exist.[96]

In the front of Leeds township, the intertwined histories of the Free Presbyterians and the Wesleyan Methodists illustrate the way in which early cross-denominational symbiosis gradually gave way to denominational speciation. Until the mid-1830s neither group had a regular clergyman (although the notable Reverend William Smart of Brockville did try to serve Presbyterians). In 1835 the first Methodist preacher was stationed in Gananoque,[97] and in 1837 the Presbyterians appointed their first resident cleric.[98] Early in the 1830s (the precise date is uncertain) a frame church had been built for the Methodists on land bequeathed by Joel Stone and with funds donated largely by the Honourable John McDonald. The Presbyterians rented this building for Sunday morning services and the Methodists held theirs at night. Prudently, the Methodists used the rent paid by the Presbyterians to build another wooden church, this one being completed in 1836. This left the Methodist Wesleyans with one church of their own and one building to rent out to the Presbyterians. Unfortunately, the Presbyterian congregation grew faster than the Methodist, so the two congregations agreed to switch

95 Leavitt, 63.
96 McKenzie, 84–5. The fate of the Baptist congregation in Delta, Bastard township, encapsulates the contrasting history of the Baptists and the Anglicans. In 1811 the Baptists began to build a church but were unable to afford to complete it. An agreement was struck with the Anglicans whereby they completed the building and both congregations shared it (McKenzie, 85). Ultimately, in 1864, the Baptists went under and the Church of England took over the church building (Anderson, *Diocese of Ontario*, 153).
97 For a résumé of the earlier history of the Gananoque congregation, see *Kingston Chronicle and Gazette*, 1 February 1837.
98 For the data on Presbyterian and Methodist church development which follows in the text, I am indebted to Mrs Blythe Roberts "History of Presbyterianism in Gananoque," originally prepared as a presentation to the St Andrew's Church, November 4, 1974, and graciously lent to me by the author, and to Clifford Sine, comp., *Grace United Church 1836–1936: Historical Sketch* (Gananoque: privately printed 1936), found in the MS collection, Gananoque Public Library, as well as to the two Hawke items mentioned earlier. Hawke also produced *Grace United Church, Gananoque, Ontario, Canada, 1836–1975.* (Gananoque: privately printed 1975). This is drawn from his other pieces.

churches, and this they did for a period of ten years. Then, as the Methodists' number began to grow rapidly, the two congregations went back to sharing a church, this time the larger one.

This cooperation should not be confused with ecumenism. It was not a syncretistic relationship. Both parties understood that cooperation was merely a way-station to full denominational differentiation. The threshold of full religious speciation was reached in 1851 when the Presbyterians began to build St Andrew's church, a formidable stone structure that was ready for worship in 1855. (Note the similarity in timing to the Catholic and the Anglican developments.) The land was donated by the Honourable John McDonald and large gifts were made by the family of W.S. McDonald and George Mitchell, the latter two names already familiar from discussion of the temperance movement. This church was made the more impressive by the addition of a Sunday School building and the erection of a gallery, completed in 1871. These structures remain to the present time the functional centre of Presbyterians in the township. That the dates of the Presbyterians' building program, beginning in 1851 and ending in 1871, so closely coincide with the era of sub-infeudation should surprise no one.

The evolution of the Wesleyan Methodists reached the stage of masonry walls, heavy buttresses, and stained-glass windows just at the end of the era of sub-infeudation. In 1871 their old frame building finally was declared out of date and it was sold to a man who moved it and turned it into a store and residence. The new cornerstone was laid in 1871, and in March 1873 the Wesleyans, like the Catholics, Presbyterians, and Anglicans before them, had their own religious citadel. (This building was gutted by fire in 1980, but so strong was local attachment to its architectural lineaments that the congregation rebuilt a new church within the old shell.) All these denominations in their outward building programs were proclaiming an inward conviction, less sacred than social, stating, we have fully arrived and here we shall stay.

Clearly the Methodists and the Presbyterians were successful locally, and they, like the Catholics and Anglicans, stood in sharp contrast to the failing Baptists. Like the Anglicans and Catholics, the Methodists and Presbyterians possessed a religious polity that adapted efficiently to an era of increasing geographical concentration and social reticulation in the secular world. The Presbyterian concept of a religious network – church sessions, presbyteries, and synods – and the Methodist arrangements – congregations, circuits, and connections – were just the opposite of the Catholic and Anglican ones. In the Methodist and Presbyterian networks, power

was conceived as flowing upwards from the congregational level, whereas the traditional systems of the Catholics and Anglicans understood power as flowing downward, from the Godhead through the bishops and clergy to the people. The differences, however, did not matter. Both systems worked, and worked well, for in an era of rapid social evolution both systems provided for religious analogues to secular change, permanent local associations of believers, served by professional personnel, and tied to coreligionists elsewhere in the province by an efficient network of religious affiliation; and all this became ever more effective in the early 1870s when both Presbyterians and Methodists started joining into more efficient networks the previously divided factions within their respective denominations.[99]

The Christian churches in Leeds and Lansdowne townships had, and intended to have, an impact on the way people acted in everyday life. A fundamental principle of Christianity, after all, is that a knowledge of eternal values makes one less apt to be swept away by the ravages of greed, lust, and violence (and, if the desires of those good ladies running all those fundraising bazaars and tea parties were known, incivility, unpunctuality, and stinginess might also be added to the list). The modulating effect of religion upon a rough population was considerable and the values promulgated more often were those of the established middle and upper classes than of the backwoods or backstreet poor. But once one has admitted that religion was instrumental and consequential in gentling and maintaining the social order, one has reached an

99 One thinks of the union of the Wesleyan and the New Connexion groups but especially of the joining of eight previously split Presbyterian factions in 1875.

For general information on the evolving Methodist polity, see Eula C. Lapp, *To Their Heirs Forever* (Picton: privately printed 1970), which details the origin of Methodists in eastern Ontario; J. Malcolm Finlay, "The Nature of Methodism in Upper Canada in the Mid-Nineteenth Century, with particular reference to the Christian Guardian" (MA diss., Queen's University 1956), which is valuable on liturgical aspects; and George F. Playter, *The History of Methodism in Canada* (Toronto: Anson Green 1862), for a contemporary description of the polity.

On the Presbyterians, see Lawrence Kitzen, "The London Missionary Society in Upper Canada," *Ontario History* 59 (1967): 39–45. The Society, although non-denominational, effectively founded Presbyterianism in eastern Ontario by the appointment of the Reverend William Smart who had his headquarters in Brockville and served Gananoque in the early years. See also William Gregg, *History of the Presbyterian Church in the Dominion of Canada, from the Earliest Times to 1834*, 2d ed. (Toronto: Joseph Perry Clogher 1905), and John S. Moir, *Enduring Witness: A History of the Presbyterian Church in Canada* [Don Mills: Presbyterian Publications Board 1975 (?)])

evidentiary *cul de sac*: exactly who was affected by religion, how deeply, and how widely that effect spread are questions towards whose answer the available evidence does not permit us to march.[100] The best one can do is note that in an era of relatively limited resources, of long and hard days of labour or difficult travel, many, many local residents gave time, money, and immense devotion to establish their respective churches on a permanent basis.[101] Whatever one's personal viewpoint about religion – opium of the people or balm of the soul – it was a medicine that many people found effective.

6

In studying local societies it is well to remember that, despite the community's strong (indeed, often excessive) sense of identity, much of its life was influenced by the development of technologies, by governmental policies, and by the vagaries of market systems which were determined far outside the local boundaries. That fact is so obvious as to be a truism. Yet the new technologies and changing marketing systems which affected rural life in Leeds and Lansdowne townships in the third quarter of the nineteenth century served as a confluence and not as a diversion of the stream of social events that I have labelled sub-infeudation.

In communications, for example, a quick and graphic way to summarize the confluence of demographic growth, improvement in all modes of transport, and changes in central governmental attitudes towards the facilitation of personal communication is to use the postal system as a surrogate. The speed, cost, and convenience with which a person in Lansdowne could get in touch with a relative in Brockville or the ease with which a merchant in Gananoque could place an order with a supplier in Kingston or a miller in Lyndhurst contact a farmer in one of the back concessions are all examples of the considerations which, taken together, helped define the degree and pace of social integration.

100 For an all too rare study of the relation of religion and social-gentling, see Peter Russell, "Church of Scotland Clergy in Upper Canada: Cultural Shock and Conservatism on the Frontier," *Ontario History* 73 (June 1981): 88–111.

101 Although the focus of this study is necessarily local and concerned with how the churches fit into a specific local context, it is worth noting that in hundreds of local parishes the churches of Ontario had to adapt themselves to a rapidly evolving society and thus the natures of the religious denominations themselves were altered. For an introduction to some of these changes see John S. Moir, "The Canadianization of the Protestant Churches," *Canadian Historical Association: Historical Papers, 1966,* 56–69.

The earliest mail routes affecting Leeds and Lansdowne townships necessarily followed either the Lake Ontario–St Lawrence system or the rudimentary roads which skirted the waterfront. Around the year 1810 (the exact date is uncertain) one local, Peter Cole, provided a service of sorts: at least monthly he trudged to Kingston and there picked up the mail from Toronto. Then he proceeded to Montreal passing through the front of Leeds and Lansdowne on the way. In Montreal, he picked up the mail intended for Toronto, which frequently had accumulated for a full month and weighed sixty pounds, and then he made his way back to Kingston. He was said to be able to make the round trip in fourteen days.[102] Soon thereafter, the war of 1812 made regular mail connections along the riverfront necessary, and a set of postal relay stations in Leeds county was set up in Brockville, "Halleck's," Mallorytown, and Gananoque. The Gananoque relay station was known as "Dragoon's Stables." These were part of a long string of relay stations, usually located at roadside taverns, and by changing horses a rider could take mail between Montreal and Kingston in twenty-four hours.[103]

After the war, Gananoque became in 1817 a permanent post office, thus becoming part of a network with the most important office in Upper Canada, Kingston (f. 1780), and the leading offices in the Johnstown district, Brockville (f. 1811 as "Elizabethtown" post office) and downriver Prescott (f. 1814). In Leeds county new modes of postal communication emerged more slowly. Beverly (now Delta) had a service by 1828, Portland by 1833, Yonge by 1833, Newboro by 1836, and Westport by 1841.[104] Frequency of delivery increased gradually. In 1837, for example, a daily mail boat covered the Prescott-Kingston corridor[105] and a decade later improvements in the service made it possible for anyone who could get a letter to Brockville to have it taken to Perth or Smiths Falls (daily service), to Farmersville, Beverly, Portland, Newboro, or Westport (thrice-weekly service), or to Bytown (thrice-weekly).[106]

The real changes, however, came rapidly and were part of the whole sub-infeudation process. Map 22 gives the dates of the

102 Max Rosenthal, "Early Post Offices of the Brockville-Gananoque Area," BNA Topics 20 (July–August 1963): 188.
103 Ibid.
104 Frank W. Campbell, Canada Post Offices, 1755–1895 (Boston: Quarterman Publications 1972), passim. Here, and on the map which follows in the text, I have excluded the brief false start made in Unionville (1831–3).
105 Brockville Recorder, 28 December 1837.
106 Ibid., 1 July 1847.

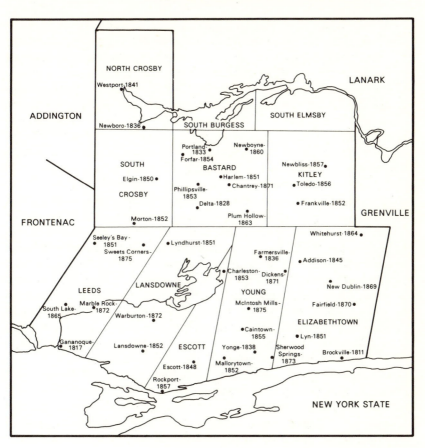

Map 22 *Permanent post offices, Leeds county, to 1875*

establishment of all post offices in Leeds county. No less graphically than a map of a successful military campaign it provides visual confirmation that Leeds and Lansdowne townships were becoming part of an ever more finely woven social web.

Mid-century marks not only a quantitative expansion in facilities for postal communication but a marked upgrading in their quality. Prior to 1851 the mail service was diabolically bad (although along the Kingston–Montreal corridor delivery between postal stations was faster than it is today). Various investigations found that some postmasters charged more than the legal amount for mail, that others opened communications and read them, and that newspapers were apt to be delivered unwrapped and well

thumbed. It was a major initiative when, under authority of the London government, the various provinces took over the post office in 1851. Subsequently, in 1867, the post office of the Dominion of Canada further amalgamated and integrated the system.

Immediately following the 1851 reorganization, postal rates dropped, from an average of 9d. per letter to a uniform 3d. The result of lowered rates was that the number of letters delivered in British North America rose by over 50 percent in the first year. Delivery became swifter, as it now became possible for the sender to prepay his letters and thus reduce handling time: previously letters were paid for by the recipient. This was not an overnight revolution, as traditionalists and penny pinchers still refused to buy stamps, but the practice grew. Nationally, the number of post offices in British North America rose graphically, from 601 in 1851 to 855 in 1852 and 2,336 in 1867.[107] The local inhabitants were fully conscious of these new developments and aware of the advantages which increased postal communication offered: in the spring of 1852, at the very moment when the postal system in British North America was being so radically improved, the Leeds and Grenville county council petitioned the legislature to take the improvements to their logical conclusion and to set up a system of "Ocean Penny Post applicable to all parts of the Empire, especially the British Isles."[108]

When one turns from noting how pieces of paper were passed about to considering how heavy goods and individuals themselves moved, the themes running through the era of sub-infeudation are substantial displacement of water with land transport and a general increase in speed, whatever mode was involved. The Lake Ontario–St Lawrence River traffic is a good example. In 1817 the first steamboats were introduced into the bottom lower end of the Lake Ontario basin[109] and they gradually supplemented and eventually replaced sail and manpowered boats as a means of transporting goods and people. As early as 1823 the *Charlotte*, a river steamboat, sailed down each Saturday from Kingston to Prescott, stopping at Gananoque and Brockville on the way and returning to Kingston on Sunday.[110] This provided a weekly delivery service for merchants

107 William Smith, *The History of the Post Office in British North America, 1639–1870* (Cambridge: Cambridge University Press 1920), especially 143 and 263–76. Also useful is his chapter "The Post Office, 1763–1841," in Shortt and Doughty, 4.

108 AO, RG 21, "Johnstown District," 1852 (4), petition of 7 May 1852.

109 Arthur L. Johnson, "The Transportation Revolution on Lake Ontario, 1817–1867: Kingston and Ogdensburg," *Ontario History* 67 (1975): 199.

110 *Kingston Chronicle*, 16 May 1823.

but of course was inoperative for the winter months, as with all water transport in Upper Canada.

Marine trade and travel were not so much an Upper Canadian affair as international: the lake is a basin, and maritime trade does not follow land borders. Thus, in 1831 the *Great Britain* began to steam every five days from Niagara to Oswego, New York, then on to Kingston, Brockville, and Prescott. The ship provided luxury cabins and presumably cargo space as well.[111] Leeds township gained its own regular service in 1832 when a local syndicate built the *William IV*, a paddle wheeler. The vessel did general cargo and passenger hauling around the Ontario basin and eventually became part of a line of boats that went from Prescott to Toronto, collectively providing daily service from Prescott, with intermediate stops along the way. In its slowness and fuel consumption the *William IV* was a symbol of the relative inefficiency of early marine travel: its ratio of fuel cost to earnings was 56 percent, while a modern boat runs under 15 percent and an old propeller-driven steamship something in between.[112] In the forties and through the mid-fifties marine enterprises multiplied and prospered, but the relative decline of Kingston in the late 1840s,[113] combined with the economic crisis of 1857–8, drove out all but the most efficient local boat lines. Most of these switched from the inefficient paddle-wheeler to propeller-driven vessels, but even these ships found it hard to compete with the speed and cost-efficiency of the newly emerging railway network. Except for the very heavy cargo trade, by Confederation lake transport was in serious decline.[114]

The other major maritime corridor in the area – the Rideau Canal – is of more interest for its construction history than for its military or economic importance. Nevertheless, the canal was not without economic significance and, within the context of this study, it had some peripheral effects. By the mid-1840s a regular circuit had

111 McKenzie, 137.

112 "A Saga of the St. Lawrence," in *Thousand Islands Sun* (Alexandria Bay, New York), 12 June 1980.

113 See Duncan L. McDowall, "Kingston, 1846–54: A Study of Economic Change in a Mid-Nineteenth Century Canadian Community (MA diss., Queen's University 1973), passim; D.J. Pierce and J.P. Pritchell, "The Choice of Kingston as the Capital of Canada, 1839–41," in *Canadian Historical Association; Historical Papers* (1929), 57–64; R.A. Preston, "The History of the Port of Kingston," *Ontario History* 46 (1954): 201–11; and R.A. Preston, "The History of the Port of Kingston," *Historic Kingston* 3 (1954): 3–25. For a useful general discussion of Kingston's development, see Donald Swainson, "Chronicling Kingston: An Interpretation," *Ontario History* 74 (December 1982): 302–33.

114 Arthur L. Johnson, "The Transportation Revolution," 199–209.

emerged, Kingston-Ottawa-Montreal, served by thirty small steam-boats and this expanded in the 1850s, carrying passengers and drawing heavy goods barges.[115] Merchants and farmers in the front of Leeds and Lansdowne, being within this triangle, could use the service quite conveniently. Equally important, timber, first in the form of rafts of squared timber and later as sawed planks carried on barges, could be brought from the interior down to Kingston and then floated to Gananoque where it served as the raw material for several of the manufacturing plants. Although the Rideau was of some economic consequence, only Seeleys Bay in the far northwest-ern corner of Leeds township was in the area served directly by Rideau steamer and barge. Most of the rest of Leeds and Lansdowne township can be considered only as part of a vague "Rideau canal transport hinterland."[116] Had the canal come through the centre of Leeds township (as had been a possibility)[117] the story would have been different.

In any case, the introduction of railway technology completely changed the communications network of the local area, and it would have done so wherever the canal was located. The introduc-tion of the railways did to water transport what, in our own time, the introduction of the motor car eventually did to railways, and the railway more than any other mode of communication charac-terized the era of sub-infeudation.

115 McKenzie, 140. For an excellent discussion of the economic, as distinct from the military significance of the Rideau system, see V. Alan George, "The Rideau Corridor: The Effect of a Canal System on a Frontier Region, 1832–1895," (MA diss., Queen's University 1972).

116 See the maps in George, 65 and 125. This peripheral impact contrasts sharply with the effect in core-corridor areas. For a useful contrast to the weak and diffuse impact in the townships of Leeds and Lansdowne, see Max and Virginia Martyn, *The Story of the Lower Rideau Settlement: Merrickville, Burritt's Rapids and District* (Merrickville: Merrickville Historical Society 1976).

117 There were various alternatives (see George, figure 2), the most feasible being the use of the Gananoque River as the outlet for the southern twenty miles of the Rideau system. In 1826, citizens of Bastard township and the rear of Lansdowne township effectively tried to pre-determine the path of any canal by mooting a joint stock company to make the Gananoque River navigable as far as Beverly (*Kingston Chronicle*, 18 August and 29 September 1826). For readable recent histories of the Rideau system, including early con-struction alternatives, see *History of the Rideau Waterway* (Toronto: Depart-ment of Energy and Resources Management 1970), and Mary Beacock Fryer, *The Rideau: A Pictorial History of the Waterway*, ed. Adrian G. Ten Cate (Brockville: Besancourt Publishers 1981). A useful history of the political and administrative aspects of construction, based on a 1970 Yale PHD thesis, is found in George Raudzens, *The British Ordnance Department and Canada's Canals 1815–1855* (Waterloo: Wilfrid Laurier Press 1979).

In January 1851, a meeting was held of the inhabitants of the front of Leeds and Lansdowne township with the idea of encouraging the construction of a railroad from Prescott to Toronto and thence on to Hamilton. Two of the three local men who headed the meeting – the Honourable John McDonald, William Brough, and William Stone McDonald[118] – were individuals whom we have met earlier as leaders of the local temperance movement. This was not coincidental; the changes occurring in the period of sub-infeudation were related. The local élite's desire to gentle the society by encouraging temperance was the obverse side of a coin whose reverse was the promotion of economic development. The meeting also shows a very early awareness by local leaders of the inadequacy of water transport for their purposes and the need for greater speed and frequency of land communication. The Grand Trunk Railway did not receive its charter for the Montreal-Toronto corridor until 1853, but early in 1851, the locals knew that a railroad would come at least as far as Prescott from Montreal, and they jumped in early to try to ensure that it would extend far enough to benefit them. The civic leaders of the front of Leeds and Lansdowne township were notably prescient in recognizing the potential of the new communications system, and they were intense (much more than their neighbours) in lobbying for its development. The locals in the township passed resolutions stating that they were willing to incur their proper share of the railway debt through the issue of debentures by the county council; but at that time the Leeds and Grenville county council not only was chary of the idea of debentures but refused even to send delegates to a "Grand Provincial Railroad" conference held in Kingston in February 1851.[119]

The railroad, the legendary Grand Trunk, eventually was built. It reached Brockville in mid-November 1855 and provided a daily service to Montreal, taking at first six hours. Soon Lyn, Mallorytown, Lansdowne, and Gananoque Junction (four to five miles north of the town of Gananoque itself) were joined. Some of the most difficult construction engineering on the entire road to Toronto was encountered between the Gananoque River and Kingston, but the run from Montreal to Toronto was complete by late October 1856.[120]

That took care of the most important communication vector,

118 *Brockville Recorder*, 23 January 1851.
119 Ibid., 23 January and 13 February 1851.
120 Ibid., 22 November 1855, 6 March 1856, 30 October 1856; McKenzie, 141. As noted in the text, the Gananoque Junction stop was between four and five miles north of Gananoque itself and therefore not as convenient to villagers as

east-west, but the north-south one was another matter. A charter had been granted in 1850 for the Bytown and Prescott railway service and by fits and starts, partly caused by engineering difficulties, partly by financial problems, the line reached first Kemptville in 1854 and then Bytown. Sometime in 1855 it was renamed the Ottawa and Prescott Railway. The line had chronic financial problems and went into receivership in 1861, was sold in 1865, and then reorganized as the St Lawrence and Ottawa Railway Company in late 1867. Nevertheless, by 1870 when Parliament was sitting, it was operating two trains equipped with Pullman cars daily.[121]

More immediately useful to the people of Leeds and Lansdowne township was the development of the Brockville and Ottawa Railway, chartered in 1864, for its connection with the Grand Trunk was considerably more convenient than the Prescott-Ottawa one. Like the Ottawa and Prescott line, however, its construction was littered with engineering problems, financial shortages, and dashed expectations. The line reached Carleton Place in 1859 and virtually stopped there. It went bankrupt in 1864, was financially reconstructed, and eventually amalgamated with the Canada Central Railway which in turn was subsumed by the Canadian Pacific in 1881.[122] Not a glorious history certainly, but, with luck, goods and travellers could go from Leeds and Lansdowne townships to the vicinity of Ottawa in one or at most two days and also could tie into several other railroad lines covering the interior of the province.[123]

---

they wished it to be. Eventually in 1884 a tiny short-line, the "Thousand Islands Railway," was built connecting the village and the Grand Trunk. It had only two stops, besides the village and the Grand Trunk depot, a cemetery and a cheese factory. Unlike most railways, it made a decent profit well into the twentieth century (between 8 and 15 percent on its capital investment) and the Canadian National (which succeeded the Grand Trunk) continued to operate it as a distinct subsidiary until 1958 ("Short Rail Line just a Memory," *Whig Standard*, 7 June 1978). For a comparison, see Duncan McDowall, "Roads and Railways: Kingston's Mid-Century Search for a Hinterland, 1846–1854," *Historic Kingston* (1975), 52–69.

121 C.C.J. Bond, "Tracks into Ottawa: The Construction of Railways into Canada's Capital," *Ontario History* 57 (1965): 126; McKenzie, 153–4.

122 Bond, 127, 130; McKenzie, 142. The early vicissitudes of the railway are reported, often in quite amusing terms, in the *Brockville Recorder*, in 1856–9 inclusive, as the paper had a crotchet about the project. Especially see the issues of 14 February, 20 March, 22 May, 10 July, 7 August, 25 September, 27 November, 4 December, 11 December, and 18 December 1856; and 5 February, 19 February, 5 March, 19 March, 26 March, 16 April, 23 April, 27 April, 7 May, 21 May, 28 May, 23 June, 30 June, 17 September, and 5 November 1857; and 14 January, 29 July, 9 December 1858, and 13 January 1859.

123 On the province-wide network, see W.H. Breithaupt, "The Railways of Ontario," *Ontario Historical Society: Papers and Records* 25 (1929): 12–25.

7

Where did the Irish fit in the process of sub-infeudation? The period of social change in Leeds and Lansdowne township began roughly at mid-century, just at the time when the unhappiest waves of the Irish diaspora were arriving in the New World. In Brockville and Kingston, as the two opposed poles which marked the periphery of the Leeds and Lansdowne cultural system, the newspapers note three facets of local reaction to the Great Famine: the people were very well informed about events overseas, were quite sympathetic to the sufferers, but were not entirely pleased to receive the new immigrants from Ireland into their own area. Both the Brockville and Kingston papers carried detailed stories, issue after issue, about the potato famine. The Brockville Odd Fellows lodge, in voting relief funds for the distressed overseas, showed, in addition to a sense of charity, a degree of sophistication about the Famine that even most modern historians would do well to note. They recognized what is too often forgotten, that the potato famine was not solely an Irish famine but a disaster affecting all potato-dependent regions in the British Isles. Hence, of their £107 15s. for Famine relief, £77 15s. went to the Irish and £30 to the starving Scots highlanders.[124] It was easier, however, to help the distant destitute than to accept them into the local area, particularly given the immediate health risk the immigrants posed. The *British Whig* of Kingston reported in August 1847 that the city was for some time almost deserted by the country people who were afraid of "the emigrant disease." Editorially, the paper continued, "What is to be the end of the barbarous policy now pursued of pouring to the extent of from 80,000 to 100,000 of the famished and the diseased population of downtrodden Ireland into this province in one season we cannot tell. Sickness now prevails extensively both in town and country."[125] One result of the aforesaid "barbarous policy," if such it was, was the need to bury in Kingston about fourteen hundred Irish immigrants who died of typhus in Kingston in 1847.[126] The intertwining of accurate information, sympathy for the destitute overseas, and resentment of the presence of immigrants when they did arrive in Canada is quite natural and was made the more so because Canadians had spent much more than had the Americans on Famine relief – five times

124 *Brockville Recorder,* 25 March 1847.
125 *British Whig,* 21 August 1847.
126 These remains were re-interned in September 1966 with due ceremony and with the presence of the Irish ambassador, and a plaque was affixed (*Whig Standard,* 6 September 1966).

more in 1847 according to a modern source[127] – but had been encumbered with almost all the sick and dying because of the American refusal to accept immigrants with ship fever. Not surprisingly, feeling against Irish immigration ran high.

One might expect that the Irish immigrants who finally fetched up on the hard soil of Leeds and Lansdowne township would be ill-adapted to prosper, if for no other reason than that they had been through a dispiriting and deeply exhausting experience and had to enter a local community there which was experiencing a rapid social evolution. The ennervation of the Irish might easily be contrasted to the synergistic character of the social changes involved in sub-infeudation, in which each strand of change reinforced and energized all the others: thus one has a ready-made explanation for the failure of the Irish.

As a group, however, the Irish who settled in the rural parts of the local area and took up farming *did not* fail. They did not do less well than the average farmer; they did better.[128]

This startling fact must be examined. Initially, we should examine the number and proportion of Irish-born as given in table 8 (as was the case in table 7, the frequent shifting of aggregate census units makes a simple clean table impossible of attainment). The Irish-born percentages are not indicative of ethnicity; they signify

127 Oliver MacDonagh, in R. Dudley Edwards and T. Desmond Williams, eds., *The Great Famine: Studies in Irish History, 1845–52* (Dublin: Published for the Irish Committee of Historical Sciences by Browne and Nolan 1956), 372.

128 In the discussion that follows, I do not wish the reader to think that I am accepting the increasingly fashionable attitude among some historians of Ireland, who downplay to the point of secondary importance the consequences upon Irish society of the Great Famine. One can gain a feel for this attitude most effectively by reading back issues of *Irish Economic and Social History*, a journal of admirably high standard, for the most part, that serves as the forum for the new social and economic historians of Ireland. Their impatience with the use of the Famine by previous generations of historians – as an Urcause of virtually everything that happened in the second half of the nineteenth century in Ireland, with little precision given to intervening causal variables – is justified. But the weakness of the explanatory system tying the Famine to later social changes in Ireland does not mean that the Famine itself as an event was of secondary importance. Actually, it was of epochal importance, which is exactly why it is so hard to tie to the concise intervening variables and to the finite effects that those historians trained in the social sciences prefer.

Thus, the success of the Irish in adapting to rural life in Leeds and Lansdowne township does not mean that in reality the Famine was a minor trauma to those who emigrated under its stress; their pain was great and the Irish national trauma real, and merely average success would have been notable. Locally their actual above-average achievement is genuinely triumphal.

only that a person was an immigrant from Ireland. Ethnicity is a broad concept and confusion with place of birth can prove intellectually disastrous, for it leads to underestimating the existence and significance of an ethnic cohort.[129] With this caution in mind, it appears, first, that there was a concentration of the Irish-born in the front of Leeds and Lansdowne in 1848, immediately after the onslaught of the Great Famine (we have no comparable data for the rear).[130] Second, this bunching did not last long and by 1851 the proportion of Irish-born in the combined townships of Leeds and Lansdowne was slightly less than it had been in 1842. In this instance, the "step-wise" process of Irish immigrant migration from the seaports to the front townships and, for many, further inland appears to have taken place quickly.[131] Third, although the actual number of Irish-born immigrants in the combined townships of Leeds and Lansdowne did not decrease between 1851 and 1871 – which is to say that for each Irish immigrant who left the township or died a new one took his place – the Irish-born proportion of the population continually declined. Another way of putting this is to say that Irish immigration into the township continued after the famine but not proportionally as quickly as the rise in the native-born population. The native-born percentages in the combined townships rose continually, as is shown in the data for 1842, 1851, 1861, and 1871: 62.9 percent, 69.9 percent, 74.7 percent, and 79.9 percent respectively.[132] Fourth, as the Irish-born immigrants dimi-

129 Surprisingly, David Gagan in his otherwise very sophisticated work *Hopeful Travellers: Families, Land, and Social Change in Mid-Victorian Peel County, Canada West* (Toronto: University of Toronto Press 1981) makes this error (see especially 106–7). Thus, virtually all his conclusions about ethnicity have to be treated with a touch of skepticism. Lest this point seem overly harsh, let me add that Gagan's book, flaws and all, seems to me to be the most stimulating piece of Canadian rural history presently in print; and his overall argument is convincing.

130 The 1848 census of the front of Leeds and Lansdowne should not be overread, although it is adequate for the point made in the text. I calculate that there could have been as much as a 4 percent error in the aggregates. (Compare the 1848 manuscript census in AO with "Return of the inhabitants of the front of Leeds [and Lansdowne] 1848," also in AO.)

131 The concept of "step-wise migration" is at present being developed and tested by Dr Darrell A. Norris of the Historical Atlas of Canada. See his article, "Migration, Pioneer Settlement, and the Life Course: The First Families of an Ontario Township," in *Canadian Papers in Rural History*, ed. Donald H. Akenson 4 (1984) 130–52.

132 Derived from manuscript census of 1842 (AO); *Census of the Canadas, 1851–52* 1: 16–17; *Census of the Canadas, 1860–61* 1: 62–3; *Census of Canada, 1870–71* 1: 130, 358–9.

TABLE 8
Irish-born in Leeds and Lansdowne Townships

	Total population	Irish-born	Irish-born as percentage of total population
1842			
Front of Leeds and Lansdowne	2,173	459	21.1
Rear of Leeds and Lansdowne	942	125	13.3
Township combined	3,115	584	18.7
1848			
Front of Leeds and Lansdowne	2,639 (?)	710	26.9
Rear of Leeds and Lansdowne	Not available		
Township combined	Not available		
1851			
Leeds township	2,283	399	17.5
Lansdowne township	2,439	453	18.6
Townships combined	4,722	852	18.0
1861			
Leeds township	3,709	467	12.0
Lansdowne township	3,105	465	15.0
Townships combined	6,814	932	13.7
1871			
Front of Leeds and Lansdowne twp (excluding Gananoque)	3,760	438	11.6
Gananoque Village	2,020	185	9.2
Subtotal, Front of Leeds and Lansdowne twp	5,780	623	10.8
Rear of Leeds and Lansdowne twp	2,363	230	9.7
Townships and Gananoque Village combined	8,143	853	10.5

Sources: Manuscript censuses of 1842 and 1848, AO; *Census of the Canadas, 1851–52* 1: 16–17; *Census of the Canadas, 1860–61* 1: 62–3; *Census of Canada, 1870–71* 1: 130, 358–9

nished as a proportion of the total population they were not in this period succeeded by any new immigrant group. The residual percentage left over after one has taken account of the Irish-born and of the native Canadian-born declined regularly, from 18.3 percent to 12.1 percent, 11.6 percent, and finally to 9.6 percent in the

successive census years.[133] This means that, coincident with years of sub-infeudation, the community was becoming increasingly indigenous. Finally, employing the 1871 material as our only accurate datum point, it is clear that the Irish-born immigrants were not drawn disproportionately to the proto-industrial village of Gananoque: in fact, they made up a slightly smaller percentage of the population of Gananoque than they did of the rural hinterlands.

One wants to know more than these aggregate numbers tell us. One wonders how well the Irish-born did in relation not only to economic indicators (although these are very important), but in relation to the whole social process of sub-infeudation. Here there is a conceptual difficulty: in the third quarter of the nineteenth century, the townships of Leeds and Lansdowne no longer can be studied as a simple and unified entity. The townships were segmenting and differentiating along conflicting axes. In civic matters, the townships were split from 1850 onwards on an east-west axis. The front of Leeds and Lansdowne townships formed one entity and the rear of Leeds and Lansdowne townships another. A second split, less formal, was on a north-south basis and this was a commercial divide. Both the townships of Leeds and of Lansdowne had mercantile centres (Gananoque and Lansdowne respectively), each of which was the base point of a north-south road. The census authorities in 1851 and 1861 effectively recognized the importance of the two north-south commercial axes and, instead of following actual municipal boundaries, collected their material on the basis of the nominal townships which ran north and south.

Here, like a biologist shifting magnification on a slide, it is well to concentrate on one of the two commercial divisions, either Leeds or Lansdowne township, and do a farmer-by-farmer survey, looking at the characteristics of the Irish immigrants and the general population in detail. Of the two possibilities, Leeds township is the obvious choice because this will lead smoothly to the next chapter's examination of the Irish in the proto-industrial town of Gananoque. The particular slide which we wish to view under the microscope is the agricultural census of 1861 for Leeds township. This census was taken long enough after the Great Famine in Ireland to allow sufficient time for any famine-forced migrants to the township to have settled in and to have become economically integrated into the society, facts that permit valid comparisons between the

133 Derived from the same sources as listed in the preceding note. Each census had one or two individuals included in the residual who were in the not-known category. This makes no difference to the point at hand.

Irish-born and the other inhabitants. This particular census (in contrast to those of 1851 and 1871) has the advantage of expressing the value of agricultural land and buildings, implements, and livestock in terms of currency, and this makes possible the aggregating of farm items so as to determine the total "worth" of each farmer.[134]

Actually, as applied to agriculture, the 1861 census was two censuses.[135] The census takers completed a person-by-person social inventory of each home religion, place of birth, occupation, and so on, and then did a more comprehensive inventory of farmers. It is not difficult to link the information on these two censuses, but thereafter one must make a discimination so as to reduce slightly the number of persons on the agricultural census by removing those households whose heads were only living on a farm but making their livelihood elsewhere (on the outskirts of Gananoque several individuals "commuted" to daily factory work). One must also delete individuals (such as bushworkers and hired men) who, though holding an acre or so of land as noted on the agricultural census, were not farmers. Then one recalculates all the totals for this now-revised agricultural census. The result is a farm-by-farm census of every farmstead in Leeds township which was managed as an economic (as distinct from a merely residential) unit. Each farmstead was effectively an independent commercial venture and one can justifiably compare the success of these ventures with each other.

We have 319 such farmsteads, representing what today would be called "fulltime farm enterprises." These can be identified according to the place of birth of the head of the household. Within the context of this study, one then can ask key questions: in this particular community, did the native Canadians and the immigrants face different problems; among the immigrants, were the

---

134 It is fair to ask how accurate the estimates were of livestock, implements, etc., when made in terms of currency. Professor Marvin McInnis of Queen's University, who has worked extensively on the 1861 agricultural census on a province-wide basis, informs me that he ran an accuracy check by comparing the total value of livestock reported in the census to the number of livestock multiplied by exogenously reported prices per head. He found a correlation of .94, which is very high indeed.

135 For the instructions to enumerators, see the Peel County History Project, *Annual Report Year II*, 104–8. The census date was 14 January 1861. For amusing comments on the ferocious weather that hit the province at that time and its effect on the enumerators, see the Peel County History Project, *Annual Report: Project Year One, 1971–72*, 66.

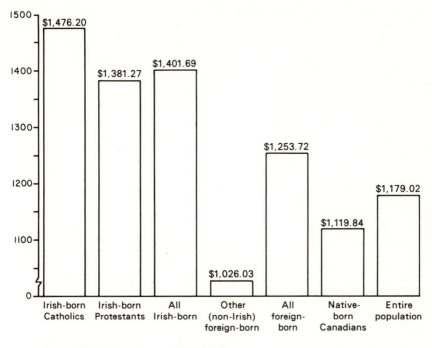

Source: Manuscript census of 1861 (PAC)

Figure 8 Average cash value of farm (land and buildings), by head of household's place of birth

Irish-born distinguished by either marked success or failure; and did the Irish Catholic immigrant constitute a separate economic caste? The answers to these questions are presented in figures 8–11, and they are disquieting, or at least surprising.[136] They tell us that, within this particular community, the immigrants really were more successful at running fulltime farm enterprises than were the Canadian-born; among the immigrants the Irish-born were more successful than the non-Irish; the non-Irish immigrants were less

136 For reference, the raw number of farms, by head of household's background are as follows: Irish-born Roman Catholic, 20; Irish-born Protestant, 74; subtotal of all those born in Ireland, 94; non-Irish-born immigrants, 61; total of all immigrants (that is, all foreign-born), 155; native-born Canadians, 146; unknown or illegible, 18; total number of farms, 319. The total cash value of the entire 319 farms was $376,107; the total cash value of implements was $20,474; the total value of livestock (including horses) was $86,774; and the combined total capital value of all the farms was $483,355.

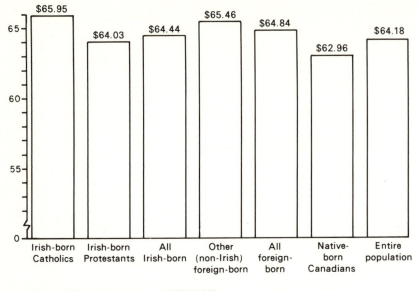

Source: Manuscript census of 1861 (PAC)

Figure 9 Average cash value of farm implements, by head of household's place of birth

successful than were the Canadian-born; and, among the Irish immigrants, the Roman Catholics rated higher on all indices of success than did the Irish-born Protestants.

Thus, in 1861 the order of economic status among the fulltime farmers of the front of Leeds township was Irish Catholic immigrants, Irish Protestant immigrants, native-born Canadians, non-Irish immigrants.

By modern lights, this ethno-economic stratification is so perverse as to demand scores of questions, but these all boil down to two: how do we explain this situation, or how do we explain it away?

To explain it away, a cheap – and unacceptable – move would be to suggest that Leeds township is merely a random variation and not worth any further attention. That would be true if the case were being presented as a representative sample of the Irish experience in the New World, but that is not what we are doing here. Instead, we

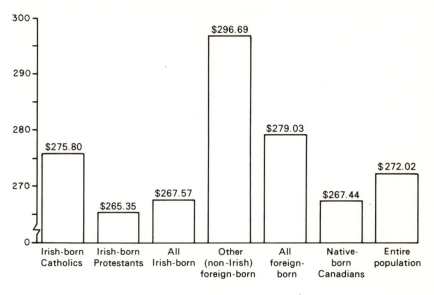

Source: Manuscript census of 1861 (PAC)

Figure 10 Average cash value of livestock (including horses), by head of household's place of birth

are dealing with a 94.4 percent "sample" (there were some farm enterprises whose owners were of unknown background) of a discrete statistical universe which existed as part of that integrated and complex local social system which was described in detail earlier in this chapter. These farmers were not statistical phantoms, and presumably their situation and behaviour can be explained by the same principles of cause and effect, and by the same methods of documentation, argumentation, and explication which prevail throughout the realm of historical rhetoric. A simple analogy will make this clear. Although the "history" of one individual has no statistical significance in the development of any theory concerning human nature generally, the writing of biography is an accepted form of historical study and one which follows quite strict canons of evidence: individuals lived; historians therefore deal with them. Similarly, this community existed. It was a fact; it cannot be wished out of existence; it must be explained.

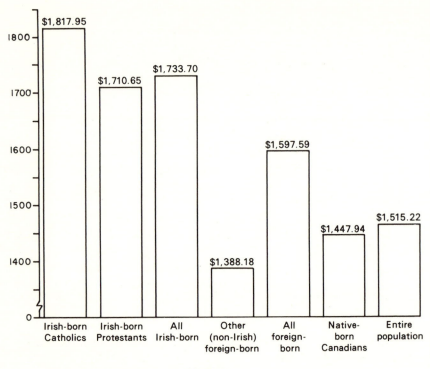

Source: Manuscript census of 1861 (PAC)

Figure 11 Average total cash value of farm enterprise, by head of household's place of birth

8

It is possible that the mode of agriculture that developed locally in this period of sub-infeudation was particularly suited to the propensities and abilities of the Irish-born; but, if so, the social and technological attributes of this particular group of Irish immigrants were very different from those usually depicted. The farmers of Leeds township were a long way from "spade-and-Lumper" husbandry. In the third quarter of the nineteenth century they were evolving into successful mixed-farm operators, raising livestock and, most notably, running a sophisticated dairy products sector. That the evolution had already passed the wheat-mining phase is easily seen in the production of wheat, both fall and spring, reported

in the combined townships of Leeds and Lansdowne (the smallest reliable geographic unit one can find in the various reports) for the years 1851, 1861, 1871. Production rose from 41,366 bushels reported in 1851 to 105,675 ten years later and then dropped radically to 39,077 bushels in 1871.[137] Precisely when the break away from wheat towards mixed farming occurred is indeterminate, but the general crash of 1857 probably had a direct local impact and from that date one can justifiably view mixed farming as being in the ascendant.

The local area had never depended upon wheat to the extent that parts of western Ontario had, but it had been the key cash crop. Now livestock became the form in which most farmers marketed their agricultural surplus and locally coarse grains and corn were grown chiefly to feed to the animals rather than as cash crops. The basis for conversion to the kind of mixed farming that emphasized livestock production had been laid even before the depression of the late 1850s by a steady cattle trade to the United States, for which Gananoque served in winter months as a major crossing point.[138] The Reciprocity Treaty with the United States, which became effective in the spring of 1855, confirmed the local inclination to trade with the states, especially in livestock, and the American Civil War reaffirmed it by intensifying demand.[139]

A second form of livestock-oriented mixed farming came to rival the production of animals for meat: this was the dairy industry, whose development came chiefly in the 1860s. In 1865 an anonymous Gananoque resident, "Junius", chided the farmers of the surrounding area for selling their milch cows to the Americans for twenty-five to fifty dollars apiece when it had been calculated that each of the cows of a good farmer averaged thirty-five dollars a year in cheese and did this year after year.[140] This letter of "Junius" points to the fact that in the late 1850s and early 1860s a new cheese-making technology was imported directly into Leeds county; the

---

137 Derived from *Census of the Canadas, 1851–52* 1: 28–9; *Census of the Canadas, 1860–61* 2: 42–3; *Census of Canada, 1870–71* 1: 24.

138 Robert L. Jones, *History of Agriculture in Ontario 1613–1880* (Toronto: University of Toronto Press 1946; reprint, 1977, 182) cites the *Canadian Agriculturalist*'s July 1852 report that "In Hastings County in 1851 the 348 cattle shipped to the United States by steamer were but a fraction of those driven through to cross the St. Lawrence at Kingston or Gananoque."

139 For comments on Civil War-created demand on livestock locally, see *Brockville Recorder*, 1 June and 29 June 1865, specifically the comments of "Junius," an anonymous Gananoque resident, discussing prices in the front of Leeds township.

140 *Brockville Recorder*, 1 June 1865.

settling of P.W. Strong, an American, in Farmersville in 1865 gives a very precise date to this new importation. Previously, the thirty miles or so around Brockville had been known as excellent butter-making areas, and the advent of the cheese factory was a quantum leap into a related form of farming, because for such a factory to succeed there had to be a reliable and sufficient supply of milk within easy year-round transport distance of the factory.[141] Immediately, Leeds county farmers took to the new form of marketing their crops, by turning grains, pasture, and corn into milk and thence into cheese. At century's end, Leeds had the largest cheese production of any county in Ontario, a striking fact considering the poverty of its soils.[142]

The whole dairy industry, however, not only cheese-making, became the rival of raising livestock for meat as the final product of the local farmers. The cheese industry was introduced so late in the period under discussion in this chapter (1849–71) that only one industrial cheese factory was in full operation in the front of Leeds township by the 1871 census,[143] a far cry from the time, another twenty years on, when there would be one and sometimes two cheese factories on each concession road. In the 1850s and 1860s another form of dairy production, butter-making, already was fully established, and this form was important both in itself and as an important transitional state to full-scale cheese factories. In general, butter-making in Ontario had a deservedly poor reputation, but there was one exception. For about thirty miles around Brockville a rich sweet butter was produced as a local speciality and sold well in the northern United States, its quality overcoming the price disadvantage which tariffs on butter involved. By 1865 Brockville district butter had become well known in the United Kingdom and continued to sell there well into the 1880s.[144] The manuscript agriculture census for the front of Leeds township for 1871 shows that most local farm enterprises involved butter-making. The total

141 See Donald Cochrane, "A Brief Description of the Agricultural Development of Upper Canada to 1867," First Annual Agricultural History of Ontario Seminar, *Proceedings,* 29.

142 See Earl Haslett, "The Growth and Decline of the Cheese Industry in Ontario, 1864–1924," Third Annual Agricultural History of Ontario Seminar, *Proceedings,* 68–85. Of course it is the new technology that is here important. There had been a small but thriving domestic cheese industry before this. From Gananoque in 1845 over 24,000 pounds of cheese had been exported (Donald Cochrane, 29).

143 Manuscript census of 1871, "Schedule No. 6 – Return of Industrial Establishments" for front of Leeds township (PAC).

144 Jones, 262.

output was a significant amount, 44,365 pounds, an average of about 195 pounds a year for each producer, well beyond mere domestic production[145] Of course not all of these producers intended their product for the Boston or New York city carriage trade or for the United Kingdom; some were producing for the Kingston-Gananoque-Ottawa market.

Not every farmer in Leeds township took to mixed agriculture, livestock production, and dairying with an equal degree of avidity or facility, and there were still a few virtual subsistence farmers left. In general, however, there was an impressive degree of commercial sensitivity among local farmers and, especially in dairying, an extraordinary willingness to embrace technological change. Local farmers took to the new products of the period with enthusiasm: in 1871, the 202 fulltime farmers in the front of Leeds township owned between them a total of 132 fanning mills, fifty-five reapers and mowers, fifty-five horse rakes, and eighteen threshing machines.[146] A telling item appeared in the *Brockville Recorder* in 1865 concerning a court case in Gananoque in which a farmer who had been caught smuggling a threshing machine from the United States had been held not responsible for making payment to the seller. "This is of some importance to the public at large to know," the paper intoned. Certainly it was if, like this local farmer, one was keen to smuggle into the area the latest United States farm inventions.[147]

If one erased the name of Leeds township from the farm data just discussed and read to a group of agricultural historians the characteristics and date of the farm enterprises just adumbrated, what would they think? They would note the direct evidence of acute commercial adaptivity and of marked receptivity to technological change; they would also note the shrewd way in which the cash cropping of wheat was replaced by more complex marketing chains, involving livestock and dairy products; they would remember that the topography of the area was not very hospitable to farming and that the soils were second-class at best and would infer that the people were notably frugal in being able to build up a sophisticated commercial farming system upon such a thin base. If asked to guess what country they were dealing with they would choose amongst several reasonable possibilities and select, perhaps, Switzerland. They would not be likely to guess that this was a township in eastern

145 Manuscript census of 1871, "Schedule No. 5 – Live Stock, Animal Products, Home-made Fabrics and Furs," for front of Leeds township (PAC).

146 Manuscript census of 1871, "Schedule No. 3 – Return of Public Institutions, Real Estate, Vehicles and Implements," for front of Leeds township (PAC).

147 *Brockville Recorder*, 9 February 1865.

Ontario in which Irish immigrants were the predominant agricultural group.

9

It is obvious, then, that the quickly evolving agricultural structure of Leeds township was not easily worked into by the Irish immigrants, but certainly there was nothing wrong with the way they adapted to their corner of the New World. Irish immigrants did better in commercial farming than did native-born Canadians, and it would be easy to assume, misleadingly, that something was wrong with the native-born. In the travel literature of Ontario, a fairly standard complaint among British visitors was that the native Canadians were very inferior farmers.[148] This judgment almost invariably was the product of the visitors' failure to understand that the conditions of Ontario farming were not the same as those of the British Isles, where a generally mild climate and a high ratio of agricultural labour and capital to land prevailed. R.L. Jones, in his standard history of Ontario agriculture, accepted this viewpoint for the third quarter of the nineteenth century and evolved a racial succession theory of agricultural development: the native Canadians were good at breaking the forest but, when the real farming was to begin, moved into the bush and were replaced by immigrants from the British Isles who were better equipped in skills and knowledge to meet the demands of improving agriculture.[149]

This familiar kind of racist thinking, based on assorted imperceptive contemporary reports, was once applied to the Irish to explain why they could not possibly be good farmers in the New World and now is directed against the native-born Canadians. Such prejudice is unacceptable. Aside from the general repulsiveness of racialist explanations of human behaviour, we are here dealing with a specific local environment and must remain true to our commitment of using this local study to contribute to valid future generalizations. We need to discuss, however tentatively, the existence of a set of economic and social filters that, as related to commercial farming in the township, were more permeable by a certain type of immigrant than by native-born Canadians.

148 For an analytic discussion see Kenneth Kelly, "The Transfer of British Ideas on Improved Farming to Ontario During the First Half of the Nineteenth Century," *Ontario History* 63 (1971): 103–11. Also relevant is the same author's "Notes on a Type of Mixed Farming Practiced in Ontario during the Early Nineteenth Century," *Canadian Geographer* 17 (1973): 205–19.
149 Jones, 53–62.

10

One logical intervening question must first be dealt with: was the difference between the immigrants and the native-born only a matter of place of birth, or was it a fundamental difference of ethnic behaviour? Here, one must use the census for 1871, the first year in which ethnic data were collected, and simultaneously make another shift in the scale of analysis to the front of Leeds township. Once again this is similar to a biologist changing the magnification on a microscope as he endeavours to keep in sharp focus the individual activities of his specimen culture.

At first the new slide is opaque and reveals nothing relevant to the question posed above. This is because in a small population one cannot hold place of birth constant and simply measure ethnicity. At first look, the ethnic group that had been in the area the longest – the English with their United Empire and late-loyalist roots – were the least prosperous as commercial farmers and the latest arriving groups, Irish-born Roman Catholics (and the relatively few Scots) were the best off. This observation, however, reflects only recency of in-migration, not ethnicity.

A more meaningful question, however, asks, among people of Irish ethnicity, did those born in Canada regress toward Canadian-born standards or were they as economically successful commercial farmers as those born in Ireland? This question permits us to make a comparison within the single largest ethnic group in the commercial farming sector (125 fulltime farms in the front of Leeds were run by individuals of Irish ethnicity in 1871, of whom thirty-four were Roman Catholic) and it allows us to discriminate in their case between ethnicity and place of birth as alternate explanatory factors. The results are summarized below.[150]

It is reasonable to conclude that ethnicity was not crucial and that some social or economic mechanisms relating to immigrant or non-immigrant status were the pivotal (although not necessarily exclusive) causal factors. Apparently these mechanisms filtered like semi-permeable membranes in the animal world, making it easier for some individuals to pass successfully into commercial farming and less easy for others. In the discussion that follows, one must keep in mind two possibilities, that the "filter" was a simple screen, letting immigrants into successful commercial farming

150 Derived from manuscript census of 1871, Schedule No. 1, "Nominal Return of the Living," Schedule No. 4, "Return of Cultivated Lands, of Field Products and of Plants and Fruit," and Schedule No. 5, "Live Stock, Animal Products, Home-made Fabrics and Furs," for front of Leeds township (PAC).

	Irish-descended Catholics		Irish-descended Protestants		Irish-descended both faiths	
	Born in Canada	Born in Ireland	Born in Canada	Born in Ireland	Born in Canada	Born in Ireland
Land occupied	119.18 acres	115.43 acres	95.13 acres	100.64 acres	99.77 acres	105.65 acres
Land cultivated	56.36 acres	59.43 acres	54.15 acres	57.98 acres	54.58 acres	58.47 acres
Horses over three years old	1.55	2.26	1.89	2.02	1.84	2.10
All milch and horned cattle (excluding oxen)	8.18	9.96	7.39	9.18	7.54	9.44

rather more easily than native-born Canadians, or that, as a social screen, it had a double function and also sorted out within each group (immigrant or non-immigrant) according to ability: possibly it sent the "best" immigrants into commercial farming and tended to turn chiefly the "handicapped" native-born Canadians into the same sector.

11

A person, immigrant or non-immigrant, set up farming in Leeds township in the 1850s and 1860s either by inheriting land or buying it. Except for scrap parcels, the days of free land were over. When the Ontario Agricultural Commission of 1880–1 collected information about early settlement patterns it asked when each municipality "could be said to be all settled?" The answer for the front of Leeds and Lansdowne was 1857 and for the rear 1845–50.[151] These dates are of course approximate, but they mean that in the third quarter of the nineteenth century, since land was no longer a free good, agriculture required a considerable capital investment. The 1861 census data showed that in Leeds township the average commercial farm and its buildings were worth $1,179.02. A beginning farmer could start with a smaller or less valuable holding, but he had to stock his operation and buy equipment and implements, so that probably one thousand dollars is a reasonable estimate of minimum initial investment for a commercial farm in the area. How an

151 Ontario Agricultural Commission, *Report of the Commissioners 2, Appendix B*: 291.

individual acquired this sum – by borrowing, saving, inheritance, or a mixture of all three – is irrelevant: local farming was no longer a pioneer activity but a business and it followed commercial rules.

Plenty of local land was available if one were willing to pay the price. A good deal of speculation was engaged in by locals, buying and selling or patenting and selling the few remaining unclaimed lands, but this speculation was different from that of the 1820s–1840s: now it was informed speculation. Gone was the old United Empire Loyalist business of taking a gamble on distant wild lands. Now speculation was done mostly by local businessmen, large farmers, and lawyers, not by absentees. Collectively these speculators acted as a mechanism for passing land on to new owners. As the Famine took hold, they became aware of the wave of new buyers descending upon their province from the British Isles: as early as mid-1847 an advertisement in the *Brockville Recorder* called the attention of "farmers and others" to the fact that a certain Brockville estate agent had "a regular correspondence with the old country" and that he had "excellent facilities for the disposal of farms or lands to emigrants and capitalists."[152]

The major speculators (or land-intermediaries, if one prefers a value-free term) were local worthies: William S. McDonald, grandson of Joel Stone, factory owner and strong supporter of temperance and Presbyterianism; James W. Parmenter, a Gananoque grocer on his way to going broke; and Thomas Dempster, an Irish-born farmer with a flare for investment. The most important name, however, was also the most familiar, the Honourable John McDonald whom we already know as the patriarch of Gananoque and probably the richest man in the village. McDonald's land operations were chiefly (but not entirely) in the front of Leeds township and they developed in three phases. In the early 1840s he purchased clear title to large portions of the Joel Stone estate from the chief heirs. In 1847 and 1848, just as the Irish migration was in full spate, he disposed of most of the farm lands (keeping several village lots). In many instances he took back mortgages, thus facilitating the creation of new commercial farming enterprises. McDonald thereafter specialized in a form of speculation that he had begun in the late 1840s, buying farms on the open market (in rare instances he still was able to patent the odd piece of empty land) and reselling them at a profit. Sometimes he took back a mortgage as part of the transaction and thereby provided the capital for someone to enter commercial farming. A search through the Abstract Index of Deeds for the front

152 *Brockville Recorder*, 3 June 1847.

of Leeds township reveals that between 1847 and 1859 McDonald was involved in transferring to new owners twenty-nine parcels of farm land,[153] and these are only the recorded transactions. Undeniably, McDonald made a good deal of money in these dealings, but to recognize this fact is not to deny him his right to profit. He did well and thereby new aspirants to farming in the township were enabled to better themselves. Without any irony whatsoever, the *Gananoque Reporter* noted upon his death in 1860 that he had owned large tracts of land in Leeds, Lansdowne, and Pittsburgh townships, "and from the nature of this business, being brought into intimate contact with all classes of people, he was personally known to almost every man and woman in these counties, a great many of whom remember him to have been the first with whom they became so acquainted and the first with whom they transacted business after coming to this country."[154]

The collective impact of the activities of the land-intermediaries, such as the Honourable John McDonald, W.S. McDonald, J.W. Parmenter, Thomas Dempster, and the scores of one-shot sales by farmers retiring from the enterprise or selling to move west meant that land was readily available for anyone with either credit or the money in hand who wished to start commercial farming. The most graphic evidence of the way in which the locals were enabled to put even the most marginal farm land to use is indicated in the fact that in 1860 the township of the front of Leeds and Lansdowne was 40 to 50 percent under some form of forest cover. In 1880, less than 10 percent was under such cover. [155] In fact, clearing for commercial agriculture had gone too far and threatened to unbalance the local ecostructure.[156]

12

There were, then, a ready supply of commercial farm land in the locality and a strong demand for it, but was this market in itself discriminatory against native Canadians and advantageous to immigrants? In terms of timing, it was. The release of big blocks of land from the old Joel Stone estate by the Honourable John McDonald in 1847 and 1848 was a fortunate (if not entirely

153 Abstract Index of Deeds, AO.
154 *Gananoque Reporter*, 26 September 1860.
155 Kenneth Kelly, "The Changing Attitude of Farmers to Forest in Nineteenth-Century Ontario," *Ontario Geography* 8 (1974): figures 1 and 2.
156 Kenneth Kelly, "Damaged and Efficient Landscape in Rural and Southern Ontario 1880–1900," *Ontario History* 66 (1974): especially 7–10.

fortuitous) piece of timing for Irish migrants. In the first two years of the Famine particularly, many Irishmen of modest means emigrated. Typically these were industrious small farmers with anything up to two hundred pounds; they would cut their grain crop one day, sell it the next, and be off to the New World as quickly as possible, with money in their pockets and their landlords looking for the rent. [157] For people like that, the Honourable John McDonalds of this world were a godsend, making land available at just the right time to benefit both McDonald and the immigrant who had money to invest in a commercial farm. In one way the immigrants had an advantage over the Canadian-born in that they were sufficiently numerous to stimulate the creation of a land market in response to their appearance in the locality. This almost certainly is the case in Leeds and Grenville county in general and in Leeds township in particular. The potential farm buyer with native Canadian background was not so well served: he saved his money and presumably entered the market not in concert with his fellows but on his own. Thus, the native Canadian demand was less visible (being spread over time, rather than bunched in a few years), and no special local market was set up to satisfy it.

These considerations of timing, however, explain only to a small degree the relative prosperity of the immigrants as compared to native Canadians in the local commercial farming scene. The success of any individual in commercial farming was largely a function of two variables, his propensity for capital accumulation and investment and his personal ability, in the widest connotation of that word, meaning his level of ambition, physical fitness, quickness to adapt to technological change, and shrewdness of eye for the commercial economy. Each of these variables, however, was affected by circumstances.

Among the band of Irish migrants who were able to enter commercial farming (and this group, not the entire Irish population, is the relevant one), it well may have been the immigrant, not the resident, who was relatively advantaged in capital accumulation and investment. The Irish farmer who sold out and came to Canada, either before the Famine or in its early stages, may have had enough cash to buy land upon arrival or he may have had to work at various jobs until he had enough to purchase a farm in the New World. How he got the money is irrelevant: he may have put forward the full thousand dollars or so that he needed to set up in

157 For an evocative quotation making this point, see MacDonagh, in Edwards and Williams, 326.

farming or he may have put down half and paid off a mortgage in ten years (more generous terms than that are rare). What does count is that the Irish migrant did not owe: he came to the New World with a clean slate. If he wished – and many did – he could send a remittance home, but the amount was always set by himself, at a level suitable to his own pocket and conscience. Legally, he was free to put as much as he wished of his own yearly earnings into building upon his agricultural enterprise.

This is in sharp contrast to the native Canadian who inherited a farm from his parents. In the third quarter of the nineteenth century in localities where the land was "filled up" it became the general practice to lumber the chosen heir to the family farm with the duty of taking care of his widowed mother (if she survived) and unmarried sisters (if any) and paying either a lump sum or making several years' annual installments to his brothers as representing their fair share of the family farm. David Gagan in his pioneering study of Peel county (a locality which like Leeds and Lansdowne townships was filled up roughly by mid-century and which underwent social sub-infeudation during the third quarter of the nineteenth century) states that " it is probably not too wide of the mark to suggest that the real costs of inheritance under the system represented, on the average were the equivalent of at least three years' cash income from a hundred acre farm. Whatever the actual costs, they were often more, in any case, than the now land-poor second generation could afford of its own meagre assets."[158] Thus, in many cases, arriving with a clean slate was better than having to ransom hostages from a previous generation. In such instances, it was easier for a foreign migrant to build up his farm than for the native-born, as he had more of his income available for investment in livestock, implements, land, and improvements.

Further, commercial farming served as a "test" for both immigrants and native-born Canadians, but with two very different grading scales. The Irish migrant who made it into commercial farming in the area had left Ireland in all probability with his family intact as a working unit,[159] and had left not because he and his family were starving to death but because of his recognition (in the pre-Famine years) that his lot was limited in Ireland or (in the early days of the Famine) that a massive economic disaster was sweeping

158 Gagan, 53–4. For a useful comparative perspective on Gagan's work, see Mark Friedberger, "The Family Farm and the Inheritance Process: Evidence from the Corn Belt, 1870–1950," Agricultural History 57 (January 1983): 1–13.
159 See MacDonagh in Edwards and Williams, 328–9.

the country. He journeyed to Canada and encountered a physical environment about as alien to his previous experience as the far side of the moon, yet he managed to wend his way to an emerging mixed-farming area and to bring with him enough financial resources (perhaps earned on this side through several years' work as a hired labourer) to enter this style of commercial farming. Merely to enter mixed farming in this locality, the migrant had to have passed an extraordinarily difficult set of "examinations" that permitted only the ablest to enter.

In contrast, the favoured son of an indigenous farm family needed no other talent to acquire the farm than the ability to maintain a benign relationship with his father until the old man died and the farm was passed on. On the surface, the test of getting into mixed farming in the area was the same as the immigrant faced but in terms of ability the entrance threshold was much, much lower. The native had to pass no tests of commercial acumen, or prove an ability to understand and adapt to massive technological changes, or have any driving ambition to farm in the area. Is it any wonder then that the native Canadians as a group competed less effectively in the mixed agricultural economy of this locality than did the hard-winnowed immigrants who, like some of Darwin's species, had won a battle of survival of the fittest even before they took off their first crop in the township?

Once stated, all this seems so obvious that it hardly bears comment. It is possible, however, that yet another set of discriminations occurred within the native-born population. These related to the particular locale, where Gananoque, beginning roughly at mid-century, rose as a proto-industrial centre. This will be discussed in detail in the next chapter, but suffice it to say that there were commercial-industrial opportunities (not mere manual labour) for the sharp local lad who kept his eyes open, bided his time, and then jumped from the farm into the office of an up-and-coming firm. These kinds of openings would be invisible to the immigrant passing through the village, especially if he had his heart set on farming, but someone brought up in the area and tied into the local gossip network would know about good jobs opening up before a stranger and could seize the main chance. Just possibly, the local economy attracted the brightest young native-born residents to the prospering village of Gananoque and left the least able behind to take over the parent's farm.

Should that indeed have been the case, then the filters which controlled entry to and success in commercial farming in this particular locality were double filters: they sorted the most able

immigrants *into* commercial farming and filtered the most able native-born Canadians *out*.

13

There are points, nevertheless, at which this argument has some weaknesses. We are dealing with a specific locality at a specific period in time, and it is incontrovertible that herein the Irish immigrants did better than the native-born Canadians in this rapidly evolving mixed-farming sector. It is also undeniable that the Catholic Irish immigrants did better than the Protestant Irish. In the case of both Protestants and Catholics, ethnicity as such was not important but place of birth was crucial. The children and grand-children of Irish ethnicity slipped back towards the level of native-born Canadians.

What is missing? For one thing, the argument cannot explain, person by person, why this particular group of able and capital-possessing migrants from Ireland came to this specific area. Of course, in general terms it was exactly what they wanted: commer-cial, not bush, farms were available, and the area already had a base population dominated by people of Irish background. Indeed, if one takes the fact that well before mid-century the Irish were the largest local group, then the sociological maxim that the greatest determi-nant of present migration is past migration seems apposite.[160] This would be especially important for the Catholics: the Catholics in the area were very successful from the 1830s onwards and it would be natural for ambitious immigrant Catholics to settle among such a group of co-religionists.

Further, although it is certainly reasonable to see the Irish migrants who finally set up in commercial farming in this area as winners of a Darwinian survival examination, it cannot be proved: they may conceivably have been merely lucky, although that is doubtful.

Least strong is the conjectural discussion of relative debt-loads for immigrant and native Canadians in the mixed farming sector (the point about the Irish migrant having no legal obligations in the homeland stands, of course). This is because the 1851 census for the

160 "Once it is well begun, the growth of such a movement is semi-automatic: so long as there are people to emigrate the principle cause of emigration is prior emigration." William Peterson, "A General Typology of Migration," *American Sociological Review* 23 (1958): 263.

front of Leeds and Lansdowne is lost,[161] and without it a debt-census of the entire population for the period of sub-infeudation cannot be made. Thus, the conclusion drawn by David Gagan in his study of Peel county, concerning the system of inheritance which became prevalent among native-born Canadians when a locality became "filled up," has been applied. His case seems convincing but whether it is applicable to other filled-up townships is a matter of judgment.

14

This chapter began with a discussion of the social ramifications of sub-infeudation and now at the end we return to three institutional matters that directly impinged upon the Irish and their relative success or failure in the locality: institutional religion (in particular the Anglican Church), the school system, and the Orange Order. In this era of sub-infeudation, the three institutions made it considerably easier for the Irish immigrants in general (and Protestants especially) to settle successfully in the rural society than otherwise would have been the case. Moreover, these institutions helped the Irish to adjust more than they helped other immigrant groups.

The religious census of the townships of Leeds and Lansdowne was summarized in table 7 and the religious composition of the population was as follows (only the major denominations are included).

	Anglican	Various Presbyterians	Various Methodists	Roman Catholic
1842	23.3%	15.3%	21.2%	11.1%
1851	29.6%	14.2%	23.8%	11.6%
1861	34.0%	16.1%	27.0%	13.5%
1871	28.2%	15.2%	35.5%	15.0%

Obviously the Church of England (for which "Anglican" is here

161 The reader who is familiar with PAC's listing of available manuscript census material will be surprised by my statement: the material for the front of Leeds and Lansdowne township is listed as being held by PAC and, indeed, as available in microfilm. The listing is in error. When I brought up the possibility that PAC indeed might not hold the material it thinks it does, Mr Thomas A. Hillman, their expert on census material, graciously spent several days checking to find out what the case actually was. His conclusion is that the listings are wrong and that PAC never has held a copy of the manuscript 1851 census for the front of Leeds and Lansdowne; he has no idea where it could be but believes that it is irretrievably lost. Should any reader actually find it, I would be grateful if he would write to me.

employed as a synonym) was central, for it was the largest single denomination in the period from 1842 to 1871. (The various Methodists had a larger membership in 1871, but this was split among factions.) The Anglican Church has been grossly misunderstood in Canadian historical writing, at least as it operated on the parish level, and the misunderstanding has its roots in a failure of historians to study its transatlantic background. Specifically, three fundamental errors have obscured the actual ground-level impact of the church, particularly among the Irish.

The first of these stems from the basic misconception that in the first seven decades of the nineteenth century something called the "Church of England" existed in the home country. In fact, on 1 January 1801, as part of the Act of Union of Great Britain and Ireland, a religious merger had occurred when what had previously been the Established Church of England and Ireland became "one Protestant Episcopal Church, to be called the United Church of England and Ireland," and this union continued until Irish disestablishment on 1 January 1871.[162] In practice, the two formerly separate churches continued largely to operate independently, both in administration and in theological terms. The Irish church was much more "puritan" in its outlook than was the English branch and much more austere in its liturgy. By accepting at face value the title "Church of England" in Upper Canada, scholars have missed the point that the Canadian branch was as much an outgrowth of the Irish Established Church as it was of the English.[163]

This point was made as long ago as 1938 by J.J. Talman, who showed that, of the ninety-one Anglican clergymen serving in Upper Canada in 1841, thirty-two were born in England, thirty-one in Ireland, three in Scotland, fifteen in Upper Canada, and the rest

162 One does not have space here to establish the factual basis of the points made in the text covering the church in the homeland, but the reader will find them in Donald Harman Akenson, *The Church of Ireland: Ecclesiastical Reform and Revolution, 1800–1885* (New Haven and London: Yale University Press 1971), passim. See also, *The Life of John Travers Lewis, D.D., First Bishop of Ontario, "by his wife"* (London: Skeffington and Son n.d.).

163 We do not as yet have ethnic breakdowns on the various religious denominations in Canada. The preliminary national sample for 1871 done by Darroch and Ornstein suggests that nationally the Anglican Church was 22.6 percent of Irish ethnicity and 34.3 percent of English ethnicity. In the strong Irish areas of eastern and western Ontario the Irish element doubtless was much higher and the English element lower, whereas in the centre of Ontario the English element probably was magnified. An understanding of the nineteenth-century religious situation requires not merely national, or even provincial, breakdowns, but analyses by major subreligions within each province: in all probability, the patterns of religious ethnicity varied greatly, subregion by subregion.

in a variety of places. At the parish level the Irish-born clergy were the single largest group, as several of the Englishmen were employed at Upper Canada College. Further, the largest single supplier of clergymen for Upper Canada was Trinity College, Dublin: in 1841 no fewer than nineteen, and possibly twenty-four, Trinity, Dublin, men were serving in the province as compared to thirteen to nineteen Cambridge men (several of whom were schoolteachers) and only ten or twelve Oxonians. Schooled in a single low-church tradition and often interrelated by marriage, Trinity College, Dublin, clergy were a phalanx which largely determined the low-church stance of Anglicanism in Upper Canada. The seal of their dominance in western Ontario came in 1857 when the Bishopric of Huron was created and Benjamin Cronyn, a low-churchman from Trinity, Dublin, was chosen as the first bishop.[164]

At the other end of the province, in eastern Ontario, the Irish clergy were nearly as prepotent. In 1861, what had previously been the Archdeaconry of Kingston became the diocese of Ontario and the man whom the eastern Ontario clergy and laity elected as founding bishop was John Travers Lewis. He was thirty-seven years old, rector of St Peter's, Brockville, Irish-born from the parish of Blarney in Cork, a graduate of Trinity College, Dublin, and a former curate at Newton Butler, county Fermanagh. His ideas of church discipline were distinctly Irish: he had studied under the Reverend Dr Elrington, editor of the works of that most Irish of divines, James Ussher, Archbishop of Armagh. Ussher, not Laud, stood as the theological godfather of the Anglican polity in eastern Ontario and Lewis's longtime occupancy of the bishopric (until 1900) meant that the Irish imprint was very deep indeed.[165]

At the parish level, Rossington Elms, the Anglican missionary who did the pioneer work in Leeds county in the late 1820s and early 1830s, was an Irish immigrant.[166] More important, the cleric who presided over the Anglican church in Gananoque in the era of

---

164 J.J. Talman, "Some Notes on the Clergy of the Church of England in Upper Canada prior to 1840," *Transactions of the Royal Society of Canada*, 3 ser., sec. 2, 32 (1938): 62–3, 66. This is not to gainsay the fact that there was a high-church minority, stemming from the Oxford Movement in Upper Canada, but it was a small minority. See John Kenyon, "The Influence of the Oxford Movement upon the Church of England in Upper Canada," *Ontario History* 51 (1959); 79–94.

165 For a perceptive discussion, see D.M. Schurman, "John Travers Lewis and the Establishment of the Anglican Diocese," in *To Preserve and Defend: Essays on Kingston in the Nineteenth Century*, ed. Gerald Tulchinsky (Montreal: McGill-Queen's University Press 1976), 299–310, 383–4.

166 McKenzie, 77.

sub-infeudation was the Reverend John Carroll, a native of county Cork. He had come to Upper Canada in early adolescence and trained at Trinity College, Toronto. He was licensed first as a travelling missionary in Leeds county in 1854 and then, when the stone church was built in 1858, centred his work on Gananoque and Leeds township. Highly popular locally, the Reverend Mr Carroll stayed in this cure for the rest of his life; he died in 1881.[167]

All this meant that the Irish immigrant of Anglican persuasion entered easily into a religious system in which Irishmen were the largest single power bloc and the liturgy and theology very close to those of his old parish church in Ireland; locally he found a clergyman who was a permanent resident of the rapidly developing set of townships and who had direct experience of the Old Country and the problems of emigrants from it.

Another of the fundamental misconceptions concerning the Old World background is that the Anglicans in Ireland were an upper-class Ascendancy and thus the Anglican spiritual conduit to the New World was an irrelevance. In Ireland, the Anglicans were the largest Protestant denomination and, although it is true that the Ascendancy class in Ireland overwhelmingly belonged to the Established Church, the converse, that the Anglican Church was composed overwhelmingly of the upper classes, is not. The 1861 census of Ireland clearly indicated that a great number of Anglicans were of middling economic status (teachers, skilled artisans, minor civil servants, modest farmers) and that many were of lower classes (small farmers, domestic servants).[168] Of course, the number of Anglican peers and landed gentlemen who emigrated to British North America was limited; the real force of emigration among adherents of the Irish Established Church was the ambitious small farmer, artisan, or clerk who sought to better himself and his family's lot in the New World, and it was this sort of person to whom a familiar church polity could be of practical aid and spiritual comfort.

In Ulster the wide range of adherents of the Anglican Church was accentuated by the presence of the various Presbyterian groups.[169] The social boundaries between these groups and the Established

167 Christ Church, 8; Ninety Years, 3.
168 The most convenient summary of the 1861 Irish census is A. Hume, Results of the Irish Census of 1861, with a special reference to the condition of the Church of Ireland (London: Rivington's 1864).
169 A readable summary of Presbyterianism in Ireland is John M. Barkley, A Short History of the Presbyterian Church in Ireland (Belfast: Publications Board, Presbyterian Church in Ireland 1959).

Church were blurred but in general Presbyterians tended to draw from the social classes in the middle of the social spectrum, in large part because the voluntary nature of Presbyterian religious polity inclined it against acquiring too many poor adherents. Thus, in the north of Ireland, the Anglican Church tended to have a narrow band of upper-class support and then be encumbered with a large band of adherents from the lower end of the social scale. This was especially true in the English settled areas, such as county Armagh, and in the burgeoning industrial city of Belfast.

In Upper Canada, therefore, one should look behind the pretensions of the "Church of England" and recognize four facts: the Irish were the largest nineteenth-century immigrant group; most Protestants in Ireland were Anglicans; this numerical dominance was heightened by the Anglicans in Ireland almost certainly being overrepresented among the emigration-prone lower and lower-middle classes as compared to the Presbyterians; and the Anglican Church in Upper Canada had a strong Irish bias in its clergy. There are, therefore, strong possibilities that the Church of England in central Canada should be considered as much an example of cultural transfer from Ireland as from England and that, in any case, one of the church's most important latent social functions was to integrate Irish immigrants into a new society and to maintain for them and their offspring a set of religious and cultural values transported from the homeland. Obviously the examination of the hypothesis is well beyond the present study – I hope that social historians will someday explore the ethnicity of the Church of England's constituency in central Canada and the religious breakdown of all Protestants of Irish ethnicity – but locally its truth is indisputable. The diocese of Ontario was dominated by Irish clergy, the bishop was an Irishman trained in Dublin, the long-serving local priest was an Irish immigrant, and most of the Protestants of Irish birth were Anglicans: a reworking of the manuscript agricultural census of 1861 shows that 58 percent of all the commercial farmers in Leeds township (the group studied in detail earlier in this chapter) were Anglican.[170]

170 Derived from MS census of 1861 for Leeds township (PAC).
    The converse held true as well: not only were most local farmers Anglican, but around Gananoque most Anglicans lived on farmsteads, not in the village (Hawke, "Early Religious Life in Gananoque," 12). Concentration on the Anglicans does not slight either the Roman Catholics or the other Protestant groups. However, the transatlantic socially integrative effects of the Catholic and Presbyterian Churches have long been accepted and do not require extended comment. Not that the institutional history of all of these groups is well served. In particular, as John Moir has noted, "Scholarly works on the

15

The social gentling characteristic of the era of sub-infeudation not only involved religious agencies, temperance groups, and various voluntary societies but placed particular burdens upon the school system. One can admire the schools' being used in this manner (and speak of social assimilation) or dislike it (and talk of social repression and political indoctrination), but such judgments are irrelevant to an understanding of the social process. The "common" (that is, elementary or primary) schools were directed at turning out young citizens who were functionally literate, politically loyal, and socially cooperative, at least in the sense of respecting authority and being only moderately violent towards their fellows.[171] It was a commonplace for educational promoters of the time to equate educational advance with the lowering of crime rates. As one historian bitingly notes, the early educationist Charles Duncombe "started a fashion for quoting jail statistics which would flourish among educational promoters in Upper Canada for generations."[172]

The common school system, therefore, was a major cultural institution with which any group of immigrants had to cope. The schools provided a path into assimilation for the very young migrant and for the offspring of those born abroad. Simultaneously, the school system was a potential cultural wedge which could be forced between the migrant generation and the first generation born in Canada. Thus, the schools offered not only an opportunity but a

English-speaking Roman Catholic Church are ... virtually non-existent" (John S. Moir, "The Problem of a Double Minority: Some Reflections on the Development of the English-speaking Catholic Church in Canada in the Nineteenth Century," *Histoire Sociale/Social History* 7 [April 1971]: 53). As far as the Protestant denominations are concerned, the socially integrative value of the local Presbyterian church was somewhat limited *vis à vis* Irish immigrants, as its clergy in the period were drawn from Scotland. The Wesleyan Methodist Church in Gananoque also was of less value to the Irish, in part because of the transient nature of the methodist pastorate, in part because of the English-determined background of Wesleyanism.

171 Like any other system devised by man, the schools could be counter-productive in relation to their original intention. For example, in 1865 the school near South Lake bridge in the front of Leeds township was the cause of a case of assault and eventual conviction. This occurred because the older farm lads, who attended night classes, were terribly smitten with the young school mistress, and when she started to show partiality to one of their number he and his sister were stoned (*Brockville Recorder*, 6 April 1865).

172 Susan E. Houston, "Politics, Schools and Social Change in Upper Canada," *Canadian Historical Review* 53 (September 1972): 22–3.

great danger to the immigrants: it was important for the young to come to terms with the system and adopt the values and skills it taught, but if these values were too radically different from those of their immigrant parents the children well might be severed culturally from them. In this limited period (1841–71, but especially 1850–71) [173] the common schools system of Canada West was run in a way that caused the Irish migrants less cultural harm than any other social group in the society and, further, was so arranged that it was easier for the Irish migrant to deal with than for any other group.

Fundamentally the great Egerton Ryerson's school network was simply the transatlantic branch of the Irish national system of education. In curriculum and administrative structure the schools of Ontario were strikingly similar to those with which the Irish migrants were familiar before they left their homeland. Some of this near-congruence was the result of direct borrowing from Ireland by Canadian educators and some came from fortuitous decisions to solve similar problems by similar methods. From the viewpoint of the Irish migrant it did not matter: he already had had experience with a formal educational system which was very similar to that which his children entered and it held few terrors and no dangers for his family and to his ethnic identity. [174]

The curriculum is one example. When Egerton Ryerson assumed control, he found that the curriculum of the common schools in Canada West was not sufficiently defined by grade level and that they did not possess a set of suitable textbooks. American books were common, but these were undesirable because of their educational shoddiness and their political content. Ryerson's answer was to introduce a graded curriculum based upon what was generally recognized as the best set of textbooks in the English-speaking world, those of the Irish national system of education. A ban on American textbooks was promulgated in 1846 but was not fully enforced until 1859, presumably in order to give school trustees time to replace the American books as they wore out with the Irish

173 In particular, the 1850 school act (the "Great Charter" of the common schools) in crucial, but the preparatory measures of 1841, 1843 (the "Hincks" Act), and Ryerson's major act of 1846 are also important. The 1871 Schools Act so sharply changed the characteristics of the administrative system that it marks the end of an era.

174 The discussion of the Irish national system relies upon Donald H. Akenson, *The Irish Education Experiment: The National System of Education in the Nineteenth Century* (London: Routledge and Kegan Paul, and Toronto: University of Toronto Press 1970), passim.

ones.[175] The graded curriculum had to follow the sequential arrangement of the Irish texts, and so both the standards and the content of the curriculum followed the Irish precedent. Each year more and more Irish books replaced American ones and the system's content hewed closer and closer to the Hibernian line. For Irish migrants this was an incredible boon: the Canadian-born children of Irish-born parents entered a school system arranged in a way that their parents understood, and often the children used only slightly revised versions of the very same school books that their parents had studied in the Old Country. One could claim with considerable justification that in the Canadian schools of this era, Upper Canadians were being forced to conform to Irish standards rather than Irish to Canadian.

As established in Ireland, this curriculum had been hammered out with particular care so as not to offend any one of Ireland's major religious groups. The textbooks were interlarded with great bits of religiosity, but these were denominationally neutral. Each of the several school texts was thrice vetted, by the Reverend James Carlile on behalf of the Presbyterians, by Richard Whately, the Protestant Archbishop of Dublin, and by Daniel Murray, the Catholic Archbishop of Dublin. Anything that might have been unsettling to their respective constituencies was removed. Hence, the children of Irish ethnicity who used the books in Canada West were not apt to find anything that cut against their own religio-cultural background.

Extended discussions of the curriculum are available elsewhere;[176] here suffice it to say that the textbooks from Ireland were, first, highly moralistic, emphasizing honesty, respect for parents, and similar conventional virtues. Second, they contained a great deal of religious material, ranging from a paraphrase of the Judeo-Christian story of creation to a discussion of the meaning of salvation. All this, however, was presented with the doctrinal edges blunted, so that most Christian denominations would accept the material as fundamentally sound. Third, the political values inculcated were "west British," that is, they were loyal and Westminster-oriented rather than nationalistic or republican. These political

175 J. Donald Wilson, "The Ryerson Years in Upper Canada," in *Canadian Education: A History*, ed. J. Donald Wilson, Robert M. Stamp, and Louis-Philippe Audet (Scarborough: Prentice-Hall 1970), 219–20.
176 See Akenson, *The Irish Education Experiment*, 225–74. For a summary of the books' position in Canada West, see Harvey J. Graff, *The Literacy Myth: Literacy and Social Structure in the Nineteenth Century City* (New York: Academic Press 1979), 42–8.

values were the opposite pole to Irish nationalism, and in this matter the school system in Ireland was potentially in conflict with the values of the bulk of Irish people. In Canada West, however, this was not so: most of the Irish migrants to the province were Protestant and loyalist, and from what we know of the failure of nationalist movement among the Irish Catholics it appears that most of the Catholics who remained under the British Crown were willing to accept the consequent political allegiance. (The contrast to the Irish migrants in the American republic is striking.) Fourth, the curriculum not only provided functional literacy and numeracy but if a child were permitted by his parents to stay in school he eventually studied several subjects at a level that today is recognized as being "secondary education." Finally, it is worth noting that the curriculum contained a surprising amount of material on political economy. In particular, the values of nineteenth-century laissez-faire, the advantages of free trade, and the supposed inefficacy of trade union activity were included. This was largely the result of the influence of Richard Whately, the Protestant Archbishop of Dublin and the effective godfather of the Irish school system. Whately had the enthusiastic amateur's zeal for political economy (he had briefly been the Drummond Professor of Political Economy at Oxford) and he crammed paragraphs of political economy into the texts wherever he could.[177]

That the Irish-imported curriculum would not be greatly diluted by indigenous influences was guaranteed in the local context by the domination of the teaching professions by persons of Irish background: in the front of Leeds township in 1871, every teacher either had been born in Ireland or was born in Canada of Irish ethnicity.[178]

The Irish immigrant had the advantage of dealing with a familiar curriculum which had been tailored in the homeland so as not to offend his sensibilities, but he had a further advantage over members of other migrant groups in that he already knew how the schools worked as an institutional system and thus could bend the system more effectively to his own ends. In the homeland, the Irish primary school system was characterized by two dissonant, although not totally incompatible, administrative characteristics, extreme

177 The only modern biography of Whately is Donald Harman Akenson, *A Protestant in Purgatory: Richard Whately, Archbishop of Dublin* (Hamden, Conn.: published for the Conference on British Studies and for Indiana University by Archon Books 1981). See especially 165–205.

See also J.M. Goldstrom, "Richard Whately and Political Economy in School Books," *Irish Historical Studies* 15 (September 1966): 131–46.

178 MS census of 1871, "Schedule No. 1 – Nominal Return of the Living" (PAC).

centralization and extreme localism. Curriculum and policy were controlled from Dublin by a board of national education commissioners who gave grants towards teachers' salaries, books, and some capital expenditures of local schools. Each individual school was founded by local initiative, not by central compulsion, but on most matters local school managers dealt directly with the central authorities in Dublin: the "middle management" in the system was weak to the point of vapidity.[179]

This administrative architecture was remarkably similar to that which prevailed in Canada West from 1846 to 1871. In the former year Egerton Ryerson's common schools act set up a strong central authority that controlled curriculum, authorized textbooks, and tried to upgrade teacher qualifications. (It is not merely coincidental that in that year Ryerson had visited Ireland, France, and Prussia and in his report of that journey especially praised the work of the Irish and Prussian systems.)[180] It has, however, only recently become clear that the common school system in Canada West was simultaneously characterized by extreme localism. The very impressive scholarship of R.D. Gidney has shown that day-to-day management of the schools was controlled locally. Just as in Ireland, the actual powers of middle management were very attenuated. Although a mass of bureaucratic paper was pushed about, especially after 1850, Gidney's work clearly establishes that central policies had to be consonant with the wishes of the local management or become useless. Even after 1871, elements of localism remained strong: one can well understand the ironic understatement of a provincial minister of education who, in response to a demand by the general manager of Lever Brothers that a certain policy be instituted in the provincial schools, replied that "this Department does not hold the same relations to the different School Boards of the Province that a mercantile establishment does to the branch departments of its firm."[181] The Irish knew how to deal

179 For a préeis of the Irish educational structure, see Donald H. Akenson, "National Education and the Realities of Irish Life, 1831–1900," Eire-Ireland 4 (Winter 1969): 42–51.

180 Wilson, 216.

181 The following are very useful: D.A. Lawr and R.D. Gidney, "Who Ran the Schools? Local Influence on Education Policy in Nineteenth-Century Ontario," Ontario History 72 (September 1980): 131–43; R.D. Gidney and W.P.J. Millar, "Rural Schools and the Decline of Community Control in Nineteenth-Century Ontario," Fourth Annual Agricultural History of Ontario Seminar, Proceedings, 70–91; R.D. Gidney, "Making Nineteenth-Century School Systems: The Upper Canadian Experience and its Relevance to English Historiography," History of Education 9, no. 2 (1980): 101–16; R.D. Gidney, "Centralization

with a school system characterized by extreme centralism, extreme localism, and weak intermediate management long before their boats docked in Quebec City or Montreal.

On the local level it was clear from the very beginning that the inhabitants of Leeds and Grenville county were going to run a set of local schools in the way they wanted or there would be no schools at all. There was a local tradition of supporting education voluntarily. Under the leadership of Joel Stone and with the help, among others, of members of the McDonald family, a common school had been founded in Gananoque in 1815[182] and became eligible for grants from the government under the 1816 common school act. In 1826 a similar school was formed in Lansdowne, again with Joel Stone and the McDonalds among the leading patrons, together with several members of the founding family of that town, the Landons.[183] Elsewhere in the Johnstown district several common schools were formed by local citizens and aided under the 1816 common schools act: eighty-four common schools of one sort or another were in operation in the district in 1838.[184] The locals, however, would not be pushed, despite their favourable disposition towards supporting public elementary education. The 1841 common schools act was not at all to their liking, and despite the exhortations of their warden, the

and Education: the Origins of an Ontario Tradition," *Journal of Canadian Studies* 7 (1972): 33–47; R.D. Gidney and D.A. Lawr, "The Development of an Administrative System for the Public Schools: The First Stage, 1841–50," in *Egerton Ryerson and His Times*, ed. Neil McDonald and Alf Charton (Toronto: Macmillan 1978), 160–83; R.D. Gidney and D.A. Lawr, "Bureaucracy vs. Community? The Origins of Bureaucratic Procedure in the Upper Canadian School System," *Journal of Social History* 13 (Spring 1980): 438–57. The quotation is from Lawr and Gidney, "Who Ran the Schools?" 140.

182 For full details of the founding, see Frank Eames, "Gananoque's First Public School, 1816," *Ontario Historical Society: Papers and Records* 17 (1919): 90–105. For a listing of other schools in Upper Canada in the same era, see Frank Eames, "Pioneer Schools of Upper Canada," *Ontario Historical Society: Papers and Records* 18 (1920): 91–103.

Incidentally, the first school teacher (appointed 1815), the American John S. MacDonald, should not be confused with the Hon. John McDonald (var: MacDonald). John S. was not related to the local élite McDonald family, although he had in fact been a boyhood friend of Charles McDonald in New York State and later taught William Stone McDonald. After a time this John S. MacDonald became a land surveyor and one finds him in the land records as an active, although not big-time, speculator (See Eames, "Gananoque's First Public School," 27; Hawke, "Religious Life in Gananoque – Yesterday and Today," 18; and Abstract Index of Deeds, AO).

183 See indenture in Landon family papers (Queen's University Archives), item 16.

184 McKenzie, 100.

Honourable William Morris, they refused to accept the act's guidelines and consequently received no monies under it.[185] Revision of the education act in 1843 and amplification in 1846 fit local sensibilities (in particular by settling control of the institutions at the level of local school trustees), and they therefore became part of the provincial network.[186] The template for the years 1850–71 was set jointly by the great common schools act of 1850 and by the United Counties of Leeds and Grenville council affirming that the front of Leeds and Lansdowne township was one school district and the rear another.[187] Originally, each district had seven school divisions (which is to say seven schools) but this increased with the growth of population.

Although the locals accepted the provincial school monies they remained crusty and refused to be pushed too far by the provincial administration. In 1854 the *Brockville Recorder* reprinted a very funny correspondence between Ryerson and the trustees of the schools of the front of Leeds and Lansdowne township about the amount of £9 14s. 10½d. that was deficient in their previous year's accounts. The locals airily explained, "it is beyond the power of your Committee to give any explanation upon the several points complained of, for the reason that most of the sub-treasurers whose accounts it will be necessary to look over, live at too great a distance for your Committee to be able to communicate with them in time." Perhaps to encourage the orderly Ryerson to tear his hair more, they explained to him that actually it was very hard in rural areas to find people able to keep accounts at all.[188]

Because of the vagaries of local demography in Leeds and Lansdowne township, the common schools differed in one signal aspect from those in the homeland. The theory of the national educational system in Ireland was that it was non-denominational (emphatically not secular but non-denominational). By mid-century, however, that system had become denominational in practice. Of course, like so many words, "denominational" has a special meaning when applied to nineteenth-century Ireland. In contem-

---

185 "Address of Hon. William Morris, Warden of Council," 8 February 1842, AO, RG 21, "Johnstown District," 1842 (3); Jelly, ed., *A Summary of the Proceedings of the Johnstown District Council, 1842–49*, 4, 20, 35.

186 See Jelly, *A Summary, 1842–49*, especially 39, 43, 46, 79, and AO, RG 21, "Johnstown District," 1847 (4), "District Council ... Account of School Money in townships of Leeds and Lansdowne Front ... 3rd in 31st December 1846."

187 *By-Laws of the Municipal Council of the United Counties of Leeds and Grenville passed at their session held at Brockville in October 1850* (Brockville: Recorder and Advertiser, 1850), 7, by-law effective as of 1 January 1851.

188 *Brockville Recorder*, 19 October 1854.

porary Irish practice in matters such as appointments to governmental positions, access to government grants, and so on, there were only two denominations, Roman Catholic and Protestant. The fine lines between Protestant denominations were noted and then virtually ignored. Thus, in the sense of being either Protestant or Catholic, the Irish schools were denominational. Almost all schools were run by authorities (often the clergy) of a single faith who appointed teachers of that same faith and filled the school mostly with children of their own denomination. In effect, the schools were denominationally segregated. Egerton Ryerson liked the theory of the Irish national system of education more than the reality, and in Canada West he tried to prevent the development of the "separate schools," institutions whose roots preceded his own accession to power. Technically, separate schools were not solely Roman Catholic; there were some Anglican separate schools, although their number decreased year by year, and also a few separate schools for racial minorities. Nevertheless, it is fair to say that in the years 1850–71 the same distinction upon religious lines that prevailed in Ireland was being duly etched into the Ontario elementary school system.[189]

In the township of Leeds and Lansdowne, the great irony is that the Irish immigrants encountered two contradictory educational paradigms, each of which was in itself a conflict of appearance vs. reality. In Ireland they had experienced, or at least witnessed, an educational system that was non-denominational in theory but denominational in practice. But now, in their specific locality, they encountered a system of common schools that was denominational in theory (by the acts of 1841, 1843, and, especially, 1853, 1855, and 1863), but non-denominational in local practice! This occurred simply because at this time there were not enough Catholics to set up their own schools, and so Catholics and Protestants went to school together. The Catholic clergy in the area did desire separate schools – the parish priest in Brockville was petitioning for a

---

189 There is no advantage in rehearsing here the separate school controversy. The one suggestion that I would make is that historians pay attention to the pronouncements of the Synod of Thurles of 1850 and of Paul Cullen, Catholic Archbishop of Dublin. Cullen and this synod set the pace and tone in the English-speaking world for the agitation for *de jure* control of all educational institutions for Catholic children by the clergy of their own faith and articulated the basic case against the mixing in schools of Catholic and non-Catholic children. For a very thorough discussion of the separate school issue, see Franklin A. Walker, *Catholic Education and Politics in Upper Canada* (Toronto: J.M. Dent 1955).

separate school as early as 1851[190] – but in the rural areas it was impractical.

In Leeds and Lansdowne townships the Catholics did not sulkily accept the common schools but adhered to them with as much enthusiasm as did any one else. For example, in the rear of the township on Long Point, Daniel O'Connor, a large Catholic landowner who was recognized as the squire of the area, built a first-class stone school which became part of the common school network. The religious composition of the school was mixed and some, but not all, of the teachers were Catholics.[191] One of the probable reasons that the townships of Leeds and Lansdowne were so peaceful between Protestant and Catholic Irish (and this despite the history of Orange volatility on political matters) is that children of all faiths went to school together. Some indication that the schools could heal theological fissures was made in 1862 by the county council, which opposed the idea of letting the Church of England set up more separate schools. The council said that "Protestant children of all denominations have received together the blessings of a liberal and generous education and that they have been, and are, growing in united and friendly feeling devoid of sectarian prejudices."[192]

It is likely that in this era, before there was a large enough Catholic population to support separate schools, the lines of suspicion between Protestants and Catholics, especially those of Irish descent, were blurred if not totally erased by ecumenical schooling. The words of one of nineteenth-century Ireland's shrewdest and most generous bishops are applicable:

I do not see how any man, wishing well to the public peace, and who looks to Ireland as his country, can think that peace can ever be permanently established, or the prosperity of the country ever well secured, if children are separated, at the commencement of life, on account of their religious opinions. I do not know any measures which would prepare the way for a better feeling in Ireland than uniting children at an early age, and bringing them up in the same school, leading them to commune with one another

190 Brockville Recorder, 13 February and 20 February 1851.
191 Madeline O'Connor, Memory Turns a Dial (Kingston: privately printed 1980), 5–9.
192 Petition of United Counties of Leeds and Grenville Council to the Legislative Assembly, AO RG 21, "Johnstown District," 1862 (5). In this petition the Council acknowledged, slightly reluctantly, that they would, of course, honour their legal commitment to provide Roman Catholic separate schools where applicable.

and to form those little intimacies and friendships which often subsist through life.[193]

Those words were uttered in 1830 by James Doyle, Bishop of Kildare and Leighlin. Later in the century the Irish Catholic Church repudiated on theological grounds the idea of Catholics and Protestants sitting in school together and this same theology came to prevail in Canada West. Nevertheless, Doyle's social observation, that school integration well may lead to social amity, has a force that neither Cardinal Cullen nor Bishop de Charbonnel could obviate.

16

Of all the voluntary social institutions that blossomed in the era of sub-infeudation, seemingly the most directly beneficial to the Irish-born (albeit only to the Protestants) was the Orange Order.[194] The Order's work as an agency of economic integration of immigrants from the Old Country and as a source of jobs and business contacts in the New World is too well known to need recapitulation; equally, the importance of each local lodge as a social club and mutual-benefit society is now well recognized. Further, the extraordinary extent of the Orange network in the province is well known, with nearly one hundred thousand members by 1860.[195]

The real key, however, to understanding how useful the Order was to the Protestant Irish is to recognize that in Canada West it was not an Irish society. Unlike the St George's Society, the St Andrew's Society, and the (Catholic) St Patrick's Society,[196] the Orange Order was not an ethnic or national association, and this was the key to its strength. Although Irish in origin, the Order attracted non-Irish Protestants of all denominations to its membership and thus served as a "garrison of Protestantism and Britishness" and "a bulwark of colonial Protestantism."[197]

193 *Second Report of Evidence from the Select Committee on State of the Poor in Ireland*, 426–7, HC, 1830 (654), vii.

194 For a citation of the major works on the Order see chapter 1, n 46.

195 Senior, *Orangeism: The Canadian Phase*, 47.

196 The local St Patrick's society was founded in Brockville in 1859. Its chief public display was an annual march on St Patrick's Day which included a mass at the Catholic church. See *Brockville Recorder*, 22 March 1860, 21 March 1861, 19 March 1863, and 24 March 1864.

197 Houston and Smyth, 3.

In Leeds and Lansdowne townships the Orange Order was by far the largest lodge or club and individual lodges were thicker on the ground than were the houses of worship of any single denomination.[198] Monthly meetings provided an opportunity for men in a rural community to get together, go through a ritual affirmation of solidarity, smoke a few pipes, and drink some whiskey. The Order was best known for its July twelfth parades, usually held in a different town each year and certainly the high point of many a child's long dull summer. The July 1861 parade in Gananoque is a good example, viewed from the vantage point of a rural lodge, Lodge No. 23 at South Lake, about seven miles north of town. The brothers woke early, did their chores at four or five in the morning, and by six AM assembled at the lodge. There they had horses and carriages to take them to the village for the day's festivities. On the way south towards town they were joined by the men of Lodge No. 511; near the Grand Trunk railway bridge they picked up Lodge No. 912 and, another mile closer to town, Lodge No. 51, which was accompanied by the Gananoque Brass Band. Here they adopted marching order, as they were close to the village. Lodge No. 326 joined the procession and so did several bands; to some the procession seemed a mile long, although it scarcely can have been. The men perambulated the streets, then, hot and dusty, heard several speeches (the keynote address being by D. Ford Jones, the most important layman of the local Anglican church and owner of the Jones Shovel Factory, one of the village's largest employers), had a slap-up dinner and drinks, and eventually found their several ways home. All in all, a good day's outing for farmers and farm labourers and welcome distraction for the people of Gananoque.[199]

Always, however, behind the bands and the regalia and the excited young children and the yelping dogs and the dust and the hot sun was the dark potential of sectarian trouble. The marches, despite being adapted to Canadian conditions, still recalled the purpose of their Irish antecedent, marching about to show the Catholics who was boss. Thus, either explicitly or implicitly, newspaper reports of local Orange celebrations almost always took pains to make it clear that no sectarian disturbance was involved

198 I have not been able to find local lodge membership records for the period, so my comments here have only to do with lodges as distinct entities. I am grateful to Professors Hereward Senior and Cecil Houston for their advice in searching for the material that is available.

199 This is a paraphrase of an account by a member of the South Lake lodge in the *Gananoque Reporter*, 17 July 1861.

and that the parades were conducted in good order.[200] It was the dark wraith of sectarian cleavage, not actual violence, that marched in Orangeism, and it could not have been otherwise when membership was restricted to Protestants and when a member incurred an anathema should he marry a Catholic. This spectre can only have become virtually corporeal when in that same Gananoque parade of 1861 a band broke into "The Protestant Boys." Every adult along the parade route, Protestant and Catholic alike, must have known some variant of the words:

The Protestant Boys are loyal and true
They're fearless in battle and stout-hearted too.
The Protestant Boys are true to the throne and faithful and peaceful and easily so.

And so they bear and so they wear
The colours that floated on many a fray
When canons were flashing and sabres were crashing
The Protestant Boys can carry the day.

(traditional)

How deep anti-Catholicism ran among the Orangemen, let alone among the general Protestant population of Leeds and Lansdowne townships, is impossible to ascertain. The only aggressively anti-Catholic public institution (as distinct from the lodges, which were private) was the "No-Surrender Inn" at Charleston Lake. This was something of a monument as it had been one of Ogle Gowan's strongholds and it was there in 1844 that he had entertained the electors with an ox-roast after his victory of that year. The drink was free also and the event became part of the local folklore. In the 1850s the inn neatly combined anti-Catholicism (its motto harked back to the Protestant-Catholic wars in Ireland of 1688–9) with beady-eyed publicanism: "The undersigned [the owner, David Hamilton] ... informs his friends and the public generally that he still continues to keep constantly on hand at his old stand in Charleston a large supply of the following liquores ...: Common Whiskey; Morton's Proof Whiskey; Scotch Whiskey; Brandy; Gin; Rum; high Wines; temperance drinks; Greighon's premium beer; Wines; Peppermint etc. etc. ..." and also with solid Protestantism:

---

200 The clearest example is the *Brockville Recorder*, 14 July 1853, but reports for almost any year in any local paper substantiate the same point.

"No liquors sold on the Sabbath ... He also keeps on hand Dr. Booth's Celebrated Thomsonian Medicine ... and better than that he keeps a large and general supply of Bibles and Testaments from 6d to 2s for Testaments and 1s to 18s 9d for Bibles. These are from the Montreal Bible Society."[201]

Despite Orangeism in the local townships, there is no significant evidence of Protestant-Catholic tensions in this period giving rise to sectarian violence. Emphatically, this does not mean that there were not tensions, but in the documents of the period there are not sectarian incidents labelled as such. (It is conceivable but unlikely that a significant proportion of the arguments, fist-fights, and bar-brawls that were referred to earlier in the chapter were sectarian in origin.) Of course, there can also be quiet hostilities between groups of people which never reach the level of violence. It remains noteworthy, however, that at least a superficial veneer of tolerance and amity overlay whatever religious difficulties there were locally, making doubtful Arthur Lower's classic dictum, "The coming of the Irish completed the great Trinity of Protestant Upper Canadian or Ontarian hates: hatred of the 'Yankees,' hatred of the French, hatred of the Pope of Rome."[202] This opens the possibility that the Orangemen's ritual denunciations of the papacy had little or nothing to do with their Catholic neighbours. Locally, the Orangemen went through their anti-Roman rituals with all the solemnity of a politician deprecating governmental waste, while day by day they got along peacefully with the Catholics who lived on the next farm.

This interpretation fits well with what we know about the social composition of the Catholic population in Leeds and Lansdowne townships. In the rural areas the Catholics were a minority and posed no threat to the Protestant majority; Protestant and Catholic children were educated together in the common schools. The Irish Catholics were not a dangerous rabble: instead, they were on average more successful as commercial farmers than the Protestants and they were "respectable" in the full four-legged mahogany-table sense of that Victorian word.[203] In sum, depite the strength of Orangeism in religious relations, this locality had perhaps peace and certainly quiet.

201 Advertisement quoted by Curzon A. Lamb in article written in 1935 and quoted in entirety in Edna B. Chant, *Beautiful Charleston* (Belleville: Mika Publishing 1975), 16–17. See also 38–9.
202 Arthur M. Lower, *Colony to Nation*, 4th ed. (Toronto: Longmans 1964), 190.
203 Although I usually am wary of oral testimony, I take at face value the information given me by the late Madeline O'Connor, direct descendant of the first

Still, the Orange Order as an institution had a use for Irishmen related to cultural assimilation. It caused other ethnic groups, especially Englishmen and Scots, to adopt the Irish Protestant definition of colonial loyalism. In their study of the historical geography of Orangeism, Drs Houston and Smyth conclude that in Ontario the Order's membership was representative of the whole Protestant population. At mid-century it contained more Irish-born than any other immigrant group, but of course the Irish were the largest group in the general population. As the entire provincial population became increasingly Canadian-born, so too the lodges contained a higher and higher proportion of native Canadians.[204] In the absence of local records, one cannot directly show this fact for Leeds and Lansdowne townships, but indirectly one has confirmation that the Order bonded to its Irish base a much wider constituency. For example, the Leeds lodges' Orangemen's parade in Brockville of 1862 was turned into a general Protestant holiday: the ladies' sewing circle of the Presbyterian church (predominantly Scots in antecedent) announced a "grand strawberry festival" to go along with it and the ladies' society of the Wesleyan church held a bazaar as part of the Twelfth festivities.[205] Equally important, the lodges, which in rural areas were mostly composed of farmers and their labourers, grafted onto their membership elements of the long-established local elite. In the mid-sixties, for example, the county grand master for Leeds was Herbert Stone McDonald, son of the late Honourable John McDonald, once the richest man in Gananoque, and himself a rising Brockville lawyer and eventually a venerated judge. Other local notables held slightly less elevated offices.[206] Undoubtedly, these personages were less than totally sincere in their enthusiasms, but local social realities required that they adopt the postures and mouth the phrases of the Order's peculiar brand of Protestant colonial loyalism. If the behaviour and public political expressions of the local élite were affected by the Order, *mutatis mutandis* those of the rank-and-file members were more directly influenced.

Catholic squire, Daniel O'Connor, and herself a knowledgeable collector of local lore. She reported that in her father's day, 1850–90, the successful Catholics in the area spent Sunday being more sabbatarian than the Protestants: in good summer weather, they not only did no farm work, but sat out so that passers-by could see that they were virtuously unemployed!

204 Houston and Smyth, 91–6.

205 *Brockville Recorder*, 26 June 1862. The pattern of the churches' help in the festivities was a continuing one. See *Brockville Recorder*, 21 July 1870.

206 *Brockville Recorder*, 11 February 1865.

Thus, locally the Orange Order, like the Irish-based common schools and the Irish-influenced Anglican Church, changed entirely the connotations of "assimilation" as it occurred in this period of sub-infeudation, 1849–71. The Irish adapted to their new physical surroundings and assimilated with the existing society; but, because of the numerical prepotence and the singular institutional strengths of the Irish, the existing culture made an equally great adjustment. To a remarkable degree, it underwent assimilation to them.

CHAPTER SIX

Gananoque, 1849–1871: Yet Another Canadian Birmingham

I

Two separate reports from the *Brockville Recorder* of the 1860s introduce Gananoque in the third quarter of the nineteenth century. According to the editor, Gananoque was "fast becoming a Canadian Birmingham,"[1] but a Gananoque resident who wrote a column under the pseudonym "Junius" recalled that he had heard it said that Gananoque "was noted for its cordwood and bad whiskey."[2] Contradictory though these statements appear, both were correct: the village was developing a vigorous small-shop economy based on the presence of artisans and skilled factory hands, yet it still had a strong mercantile section (although its merchants certainly retailed more than bad whiskey) and was part of a larger local economy that was still dominated by agricultural production and resource-stripping, such as cordwood represented. That is why, in referring to Gananoque in earlier chapters, the term "proto-industrial" has been used. The village was not yet dominated by the manufacturing sector and the nature of production in Gananoque in this period was closer to classical domestic production by skilled artisans than to mass factory production by relatively unskilled workers. Because the evolution *towards* true industrialism is so important, one must be at pains not to overemphasize its rapidity. It is just as serious an error to disturb reality by magnifying this phenomenon so that its context is lost as it is to ignore or belittle it. Too often social historians, like proud fishermen holding their catch up close to the camera, have magnified their subject and thus lost its reality.

The metaphor used in the last chapter to describe the social and

---

1 *Brockville Recorder*, 15 October 1863.
2 Ibid., 9 February 1865.

economic development of the townships of Leeds and Lansdowne – sub-infeudation – was intentionally medieval. The term was chosen specifically to emphasize that in the total society of Leeds and Lansdowne the major changes in the society – increased population, professionalization of government, articulation of social networks, and speciation of religious denominations – were begun and largely carried forward in pre-industrial circumstances and that the evolution towards an industrial village happened within this larger context; it was not a primary cause of these developments. (That I am in good company in emphasizing the primacy of pre-industrial causes of many "modern" social changes should be clear to anyone familiar with the work of the *Annales* school.)[3] This allows us to escape from the domination of those economic historians (of whom David S. Landes is probably the best known) who, in dealing with "modernization," postulate the necessary and inextricable intertwining of such factors as demographic shifts, professionalization of government, and the creation of mass educational systems with industrialization.[4] Even in the hinterlands of Ontario, things were never that simple.

Gananoque in 1849 had 768 inhabitants: 109 men, 137 women, and 532 children.[5] That is as detailed as one can be: the 1851 census for the front of Leeds township, of which Gananoque was a part, has been lost.[6] The village was not incorporated until 1863, and so the 1861 enumerators were satisfied with making a list of the adult heads of households and the number in each family unit: 244 households, encompassing 1,340 inhabitants, were certainly a considerable increase over the preceding census.[7] By 1871 the village population was up to 2,020 residents.[8]

The civic-economic position of this burgeoning village within the larger study area, Leeds and Lansdowne townships, is presented visually in figure 12. At a fairly high level of abstraction one can think of Leeds and Lansdowne townships as being divided during the third quarter of the nineteenth century along two separate axes.

3 A particularly attractive recent example is Fernand Braudel's *The Structures of Everyday Life*, trans. Sian Reynolds (London: Collins 1981).
4 David S. Landes, *The Unbound Prometheus: Technological Change and Industrial Development in Western Europe from 1750 to the Present* (Cambridge: Cambridge University Press 1969). His admirably concise formulation of modernization is found on 6.
5 Freeman Britton. *Souvenir of Gananoque and Thousand Islands* (Gananoque: Gananoque Reporter 1001), 14.
6 See chapter 5, n 161.
7 "Village of Gananoque, 1861," Archives AO, MS 262, reel 4.
8 *Census of Canada, 1870–71*, 1: 133.

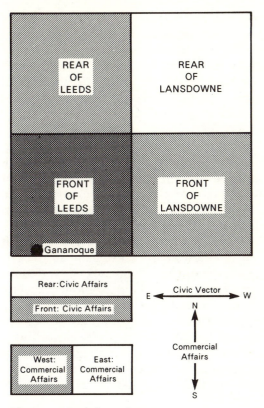

Figure 12 Social quadrants

One of these divided the front from the rear of the two townships in civic matters: from 1850 onwards the front of Leeds and Lansdowne townships was one municipal jurisdiction, the rear of Leeds and Lansdowne townships another. In economic affairs, however, there was a second axis, perpendicular to the civic one. This divided Leeds from Lansdowne township. Each had its own small "metropolis," Gananoque in Leeds and the unincorporated village of Lansdowne in Lansdowne township, and each of these had its own tiny satellite farther inland, Seeleys Bay and Lyndhurst respectively. The census organizers of 1851 and 1861 acknowledged the reality of this economic axis when they collected data not by civic unit but according to the economic division which ran north and south. Inevitably, the two perpendicular axes cut the township of Leeds and Lansdowne into four quadrants. Of these, the southwestern quadrant was important (being along the more developed St Lawrence River front and having the largest commercial centre

therein), and it was this sector on which the preceding chapter increasingly focused attention. The discussion in chapter 5 of the relationship of ethnicity and place of birth to success in farming, and particularly the "double-filter" hypothesis presented there, is therefore the specific context for examining the issues of place of birth, ethnicity, and occupational status in Gananoque village.

2

The rapid growth towards industrialization that took place in Gananoque in the third quarter of the nineteenth century rested on two pillars, one physical, the other social. The first of these was the Gananoque River. By no means an impressive watercourse – in places near the village it was no more than thirty yards across – the river was a perfect source of energy for a craft economy. It was easily controlled through a set of dams in the village and upstream, and the energy of the stream was converted first to running saws and gristing stones and later to propelling lathes, planers, and small forges. Eventually a complex method of regulating community access to this source of power developed which involved a sophisticated method of metering and distributing this kinetic energy.

The second pillar of the village was the McDonald family,[9] whose commercial antecedents stretched directly back to Joel Stone, first settler in the area.[10] The McDonalds were Americans from New

9 I have standardized the spelling of the family name as "McDonald," which most members adopted. For much of his later life, Charles Stone McDonald affected the spelling "Macdonald."

10 The summary of the McDonald family operation which follows in the text is my distillation of several sources. Fundamental to an understanding of the family is H. William Hawke's "The McDonald Family of Gananoque," an unpublished paper found in two versions, one in the Gananoque Public Library and the other in Queen's University Archives. See also Hawke's edited transcription of "Miss McCammon's Notes on the Early Days of Gananoque" (Gananoque Museum). The major manuscript sources are the McDonald family papers in Queen's University Archives, and the McDonald-Stone papers in PAC. The reports on the McDonald firms by R.G. Dun and Co are very revealing (Baker Library, Harvard University).

Various facts mentioned in the text are dated by reports in *Kingston Gazette*, 13 January 1818; *Kingston Chronicle*, 7 July 1826, 13 October 1826, 19 February 1831, 5 November and 19 November 1831; *Kingston Chronicle and Gazette*, 12 October 1833, 4 September 1835, 21 July 1838, 17 August 1839; *Gananooque Reporter*, 4 July 1860. Useful references are also found in Britton, 11–13; H. William Hawke, *Historic Gananoque* (Belleville: Mika Publishing 1974), 15–17, 27; Thaddeus W.H. Leavitt, *History of Leeds and Grenville* (Brockville: Recorder Press 1879), 60–1, 126–8; Robert L. Jones, *History of Agriculture in Ontario*,

York State and had a very quick eye for profit. The first of them to arrive in Gananoque, Charles, appeared in 1810. It was an opportune time, as Joel Stone had recently lost his only son and needed both solace and a business partner. Charles stepped in and soon he and Stone were in partnership. A year later he married Mary, Stone's only surviving child. In 1817 Charles's younger brother John (always known in later life as "the Hon. John," which serves as a useful way to distinguish him from other members of the family with the same name) joined the partnership, and in 1831 he married Henrietta Maria Mallory, granddaughter of Joel Stone's second wife and effectively Stone's ward. Eventually, three McDonald brothers and five sisters, all of the same family, migrated to Gananoque. The confusion this provides for the genealogists is prodigious. For the purposes of this study, however, the family tree can be simplified.

Leading members of the McDonald family

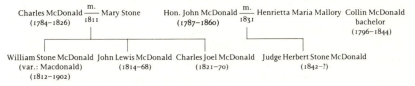

Of the first generation of McDonald businessmen in Gananoque, Charles seems to have been the most able. After his untimely death in 1826, his brother John became the senior member of the firm. By then he already had extensive land interests, but it was not until his marriage in 1831 that he set himself up as a squire and heir-apparent to the social hegemony of Gananoque. In 1831–2 he and his new wife built a superb regency house in a park setting just off the main thoroughfare of the village. (Recently restored, this fine building houses the town council and associated offices.) When Joel Stone died in 1833, John McDonald became the patriarch of the village. His position in the area was symbolized in his becoming "the Hon." John McDonald by virtue of being appointed a member of the Legislative Council of Upper Canada in 1839. Originally a Tory, he gradually became convinced of reform views. At first he took his political position seriously, but later lost interest: in 1848 he was

1613–1880 (Toronto: University of Toronto Press 1946; reprint, 1977), 135 n49; Norman McDonald, *Canada, 1763–1841: Immigration and Settlement* (London: Longmans, Green and Co. 1939), 341; Ruth McKenzie, *Leeds and Grenville: Their First Two Hundred Years* (Toronto: McClelland and Stewart 1967), 151; Ina G. Scott, *Yesterday's News: Today's History* (Gananoque: 1000 Island Publishers 1982), 47–52.

unseated because of non-attendance at two consecutive sessions. During the 1830s he was something of an entrepreneurial dynamo, being involved in canal building schemes and in companies which pioneered steamboat travel on the St Lawrence and Great Lakes system. In the 1840s, however, he increasingly turned to land speculation and playing the squire and left commercial details to his nephews. He was not averse, however, to collecting the hundred pounds annual salary as postmaster of Gananoque into the 1850s. There was in the first generation a third brother, Collin, who apparently was a lightweight. Although he arrived in Gananoque in 1818 and joined the family firm then, he was not made a partner until 1826, shortly before his brother Charles died. His much younger nephew, William Stone McDonald, not he, became the dominant force in the 1830s when the Hon. John McDonald's interests turned elsewhere. Eventually, in 1836, Collin withdrew from the partnership. He drifted to the United States and died in Cuba in 1844.

In the second generation, two sons of Charles McDonald came to the fore, William Stone McDonald and John Lewis McDonald. Of these, William was the cannier and more forceful, but even he did not have the foresight and toughness of his father. The family milling business continued to be large: in the mid-1840s it was manufacturing about thirty thousand barrels of flour a year using both Canadian and American wheat, and it was one of the largest mills, if not the largest, in Upper Canada. The radical revision of trade arrangements with the United Kingdom in 1846 sharply undercut the milling business and the McDonalds shrewdly sold off their milling and mercantile interests in 1848. William Stone McDonald continued milling and nail cutting in a much smaller way, but mostly he and other members of his family settled down to exploiting their inheritance in land, property, and water rights whose origin went all the way back to Joel Stone's successful prospecting for a fortune in the early 1790s.

For the sake of convenience, the important events in the history of the McDonald family enterprises are chronicled in table 9. Substantively, as concerns the village, the McDonald enterprises had four major characteristics. First, they pioneered the development of water power. Their acquisition in 1824 of Sir John Johnson's side of the Gananoque River gave them, when combined with Joel Stone's control over the other bank, complete control over its development and exploitation. Second, on their own behalf the McDonalds used this water power effectively. In the early years they had large amounts of timber, especially that suitable for ships'

TABLE 9
Chronology of McDonald Business Activities

1810–?	Unwritten partnership of Charles McDonald and Joel Stone.
1817–26	Firm of C. and J. McDonald. Partnership by Charles and his brother John. Brother Collin helps, at least intermittently, from 1818, but not as a partner.
1824	McDonalds buy Sir John Johnson's land; with Stone's land they control both sides of river. They lay out east side of river as a village.
1826	Build large grist and flour mill which later is described as largest in Upper Canada.
1826	Collin admitted to the partnership, under firm name of C. and J. McDonald and Co.
1826	Charles dies.
1833	William Stone McDonald joins firm.
1833	John Lewis McDonald apprenticed to firm.
1833	Joel Stone dies. His estate eventually filters to various McDonalds.
1830s	William Stone McDonald gradually takes over; Hon. John goes into politics and land speculation; Collin withdraws from partnership in 1836.
1840	William Stone McDonald begins pushing hard for village development.
Mid-1840s	Milling business declines sharply.
1847	Most of McDonald milling and mercantile interests sold to W. Brough.
1848	William Stone McDonald becomes sole proprietor of remaining milling and nail cutting business. His interest in affairs declines and by 1860 he is leasing mill to his son.
1850s	Family members go own way: land speculation and property management are biggest interests.
1860	Hon. John McDonald dies.
1860s	Water rights finally disposed of to newly created Gananoque Water Power Company.

spars and masts, floated down the Gananoque River to their sawmill where it was sawn and then marketed. More important, they built their massive flour mill in 1826 and carried on for two decades in that line of endeavour. Third, they were village-boosters. They were behind the first village survey of 1824 and the larger village plan of 1842. This boosterism became especially intense in the 1840s, as William Stone McDonald came to realize that for the family really to profit by its patrimony the village of Gananoque needed new industry. In 1840 he issued a prospectus designed to attract new industry which set out in detail the virtues of Gananoque's location, its abundant water power, and the extent of existing industries (the largest of which, like the water power, the McDonald family

controlled). He then specified which new industries would do particularly well, were they to move to the village.

TANNERY. To erect premises upon a scale sufficiently large to work to good advantage about 2500 Pounds would be required and to purchase Bark, Hides, &c. 5000 Pounds more. It is a business that pays well, and as Bark is becoming every year more difficult to be obtained in many parts of Canada, while here the supply would be abundant and Cheap, a good trade might be looked forward to for many years.

WOOLEN MILL. To set a small establishment in operation with a Building large enough to permit of subsequent extension would require about 1500 Pounds., as the works would be chiefly employed for Customers, a small Capital would suffice to carry on the Business, say 500 Pounds for the first year, after which a sufficient stock of Cloth would have accumulated for the supply of Future wants.

PAPER MILL. A mill of the best description could be erected for 3500 Pounds, and 1500 Pounds would suffice to carry on the business. Parties largely engaged in the sale of Paper, are of the opinion that there would be no difficulty in getting all the Paper made from such a Mill readily disposed of.

There are few places in America presenting greater facilities for the safe & profitable investment of Capital, it will be observed that the greater part of the Establishments enumerated are free from any speculative character, and their products being adapted to the wants of a rapidly increasing population, they possess every guarantee for permanence of which the nature of the undertaking will permit.

The Proprietor who has the control of the Water Power, and about 100 acres of the adjoining land, would treat with parties desirous of acquiring an Interest in the whole property, or those wishing to purchase Water Lots for manufacturing purposes of any description—For further information apply at Gananoque to W.S. MacDonald.[11]

A fourth aspect of the McDonald family influence offset in some degree their boosting of the village economy: in the 1850s and 1860s they did not manage their energy monopoly rights well. New industry did come in and old shops expanded into new factories, each of which required more and more water power. The McDonalds made their profit, but they were either unable or unwilling to work out the complexities of energy management. During the fifties and sixties one meets frequent complaints that the water supply for a certain firm was irregular, or that a shop near the top of the flume was allowed to nip the water intended for those down below, and so

11 Hawke, "The McDonald Family," (Queen's University Archives), 8.

on. Really efficient manufacturing required a dependable system of energy supply and an accurate method of metering. The best way of effecting these ends was to set up a producers' co-operative and this the local manufacturers tried to do. Dealing with the McDonalds was not easy, however. Both the Hon. John McDonald and his nephew John Lewis McDonald seem to have been impediments, and it was not until both were gone that things moved forward. John Lewis McDonald died in 1868 and in that year the local factory owners bought out the McDonalds' water rights and by act of the legislative assembly incorporated the Gananoque Water Power Company.[12]

This was a joint stock company and the amount of water that each factory owner could use was proportional to the number of shares which he held. To meter water usage effectively, the size of each factory's water wheel was proportional to the amount of water to which each enterprise was entitled. This did not entirely solve the energy problem: upstream landowners engaged in a twenty-year-long legal battle against the new village water company's tampering with water levels, and this ended with a court setting strict definitions of the permissible limits of high and low water levels. From 1868 onwards, however, the village industries ran on their own, not McDonalds', power.

3

If in Leeds and Lansdowne townships generally the third quarter of the nineteenth century was the era of sub-infeudation, this process had a referent that was specific to Gananoque: the village's economic structure moved from being proto-industrial right up to the threshold of becoming a true industrial economy. Two benchmarks in this process are the dissolution of the massive McDonald milling and mercantile firm in 1847, which coincided with the start of rapid expansion in several industries, and the freeing in 1868 of the major source of energy, waterpower, from the dead hand of Joel Stone's heirs. The details of these three decades of rapid economic evolution are difficult to obtain, largely because of missing census data, but one can chart the outlines by comparing an inventory of

12 The *Brockville Recorder*, 22 October 1863, stated that "for many years this water power was allowed to run to waste in consequence we believe of the owner's desire to obtain high prices for water privileges and his disinclination to sell ... Much of the property, however, has of late changed hands." Almost certainly the reference is to the Hon. John McDonald and the probating of his will and division of his property thereby (he had died in 1860).

Map 23 Gananoque in 1858. (From the National Map Collection, PAC)

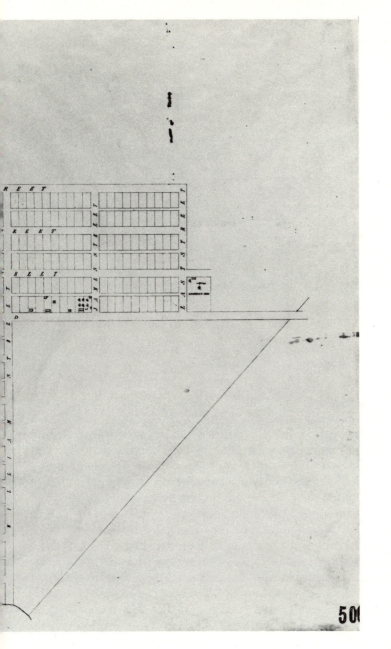

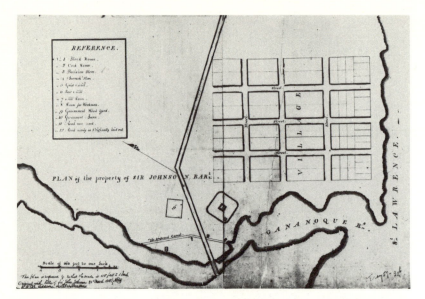

Map 24 Gananoque in 1818: a village plan before the McDonalds acquired Sir John Johnson's property. (From the National Map Collection, PAC)

village industries done by William Stone McDonald in 1848 and the manuscript census of 1871.

The former document has a curious history. It was compiled by W.S. McDonald apparently only for his own use and was buried in February 1848 in a sealed bottle that was deposited at the foot of a stone bank marking the boundary between his property and that of John L. McDonald. The bottle was dug up by workmen in 1874 and the inventory preserved. Its salient points are, first, that of the twelve major processing and manufacturing firms listed by McDonald four (three cereals mills and one sawmill) were for the processing of the raw products of the land or forest, and, second, that six of the firms were owned or managed by a McDonald or by someone who had married into the McDonald family.[13] The contrast to the 1871 census can hardly have been sharper (even granting that the two documents are not entirely comparable). The 1871 enumeration reveals that the industrial firms had turned sharply away from raw materials processing and were producing complex goods like car-

13 Hawke, "The McDonald Family," 8–9, printed inventory.

TABLE 10

Aggregate Summary of Gananoque Industrial Establishments, 1871

Number of industrial firms	49	
Capitalization:		
Total fixed capital	$ 201,200	
Total floating capital	132,785	
TOTAL	333,985	
Average capitalization per firm	$6,816.02	
Total number of employees	420	
Total wages paid, yearly	$ 113,760	
Average wage per employee, yearly	$ 270.86	
Aggregate annual balance sheet:		
Aggregate value of yearly output	$ 583,570	
Production costs:		
wages		$113,760
raw materials		284,735
sub-total, production costs	398,495	
Crude profit	$ 185,075	

Source: Compiled from manuscript census of 1871, Village of Gananoque, Schedule no. 6 "Return of Industrial Establishments," PAC

riages, shovels, and metal manufactured products. No industrial firms were owned by the McDonalds. Table 10 summarizes the situation in 1871 and should, of course, be read with the usual cautions (chiefly the reminder that firms did not draw up balance sheets in the nineteenth century in the same way and with the same precision as in the late twentieth). Within its limits, however, the 1871 census dictates certain clear conclusions. The first of these is the obvious one that the village now was completely caught up in an economic system that was fully and thoroughly capitalist. Second, the village industry as a whole was capitalized, that is, the firms represented the result of the accumulation over time of surplus funds which eventually were invested in industrial production. Third, on the surface it seems that, in aggregate, the industrial establishments were markedly rewarding. Granted, the aggregate amount of the village's industrial "crude profit" for the year, $185,075, was not pure gain: from it one could reasonably subtract as expenses of doing business the cost of selling the product, the costs of borrowing capital or of the owner's using his own (and thus foregoing income on lending it to others at interest), and a reasonable imputed wage to firm owners who worked in their own

establishment. That done, the residual net profit would be ascribable to either of two factors, a justifiable reward to those entrepreneurs in society who took considerable risks in starting new firms and developing new investments, or the capitalist's expropriation of the surplus value of his worker's efforts. This question of the "true"character of industrial profit is a methodological and ideological thicket into which the mere historian should not venture. Here suffice it to express the village industries' 1871 "crude profits" in three ways: as a percentage of aggregate output – 31.7 percent; as a percentage of total capital invested – 55.4 percent; as a percentage of total yearly wages paid – 162.7 percent.

Aggregates inevitably camouflage qualities and distributional matters. The overall figures, for instance, hide an important dimension of the Gananoque economic scene as it had evolved during the 1850s and 1860s: the burgeoning was largely in high-skill industries, such as the manufacture of agricultural implements, shovels, and forks, in foundry and machine shops, and in a spring factory and an axle manufactory. Workers in these industries, even the common factory hands, were skilled, often highly. This was not yet the day of the standardized factory with its dilution of skilled labour but rather a beehive of craftsmen, artisans, and skilled factory hands. They worked in complex chains of production, but each stage was dependent upon the skill of the individual craftsman. In line with the skilled nature of the work force, the factory managers seem to have been acutely technologically adaptive. (This same characteristic, it will be recalled, was found in the commercial agricultural economy in the surrounding countryside.) Local managers did not come up with any earth-shaking inventions but they were continually patenting small improvements and new products.[14] Indeed, given the dependence of most of the industries upon a limited water supply, the very existence of so many firms, all supplied with power for their shops through a maze of ducts, conduits, water wheels, and gearings, was in itself a monument to technological alertness on the part of their owners and managers.

Although there were six large firms (averaging forty-two employees each) which employed 60 percent of the village's industrial work force, most firms were quite small and had only a handful of employees. A good benchmark is a labour force of three employees: this, roughly, is the equivalent of the labour available on the average local commercial farm and thus provides comparability to

14 For examples of patents by Gananoque inventors, see *Brockville Recorder*, 10 May 1860.

the farm sector. Twenty-six of the forty-nine industrial establishments in Gananoque in 1871 (53.1 percent) had three or fewer workers.[15] Even the large firms were hardly behemoths: the largest employed sixty-six workers. All this explains why the locals were being apposite, not hubristic, in comparing their small industrial world to Birmingham, England, for here on the Gananoque River, as in that great industrial city, skilled workmanship, relatively small firms, and technological awareness prevailed.[16]

4

Was class a-borning? This question, taken to mean, was society becoming organized on the basis of social classes, dominates much of the recent social history written in Canada and the British Isles, and justly so. In terms of this study, the question can be phrased, did the industrializing economy of Gananoque produce a society which had clear levels of social class differentiation of which the villagers were themselves conscious? Necessarily, a class society implies the existence of two or more levels of individuals each of whom, as a group, shared some kind of relationship to the other class or classes. In a village like Gananoque, such relationships are devilishly difficult for the historian to uncover, in large part because the settlement was so small that a whole set of social patterns could have been understood and accepted without much evidence being set down in writing. That admitted, the indirect evidence that is available seems to suggest that the village was perhaps halfway, but no further, along the road to becoming a class-differentiated society and that this process was not complete until well after the termination date of this study, probably in the 1880s.

First, let us look at the village elders. During this period the local élite was changing. Previously, until roughly mid-century, it had consisted of the McDonald family with its many cousins and nephews. It was a ruling economic élite, though it certainly was not a class but a mercantile tribe. During the next two decades, the old mercantile money melded with the new industrial capital. The first town council chosen after the incorporation of the village met in January 1863 and serves as a window on the upper class of the

15 The industrial figures here and following are from the 1871 manuscript census, as cited in Table 10.
16 *The History of Birmingham* is found in three volumes. The second, subtitled *Borough and City 1865–1938* by Asa Briggs (London: Oxford University Press 1952) is especially good. The last half of volume 1 (Conrad Gill, *Manor and Borough to 1865*) is also relevant.

village. Incorporation was a big step for the village and election to this first council was a matter of some individual power and prestige. This fact, combined with the restrictions on qualifications for councillors and the restricted franchises for voters, meant that the electoral results would reveal at least the lineaments of the dominant class in the village. Under the relevant municipal act, councillors had to have freehold land worth forty dollars per annum or leasehold land valued at eighty dollars per annum, and this removed any Jacobin candidates. The franchise was restricted to male British subjects who were rated as proprietors or were tenants of a property valued at least at twelve dollars per year. These restrictions loaded the electoral scales against any demotic candidate.[17] In effect, this first prestigious election after incorporation gives us an opportunity to see who really counted in Gananoque.

Who was chosen? The senior figure was a representative of the old merchant caste, Herbert Stone McDonald, son of the Hon. John McDonald. He was very young, aged twenty-one, and very able: he received his MA from Queen's University at the age of nineteen. Within months of this election, he left Gananoque to form a law partnership in Brockville and to marry in 1864 into the prestigious Jones family, specifically that of David Jones, the registrar of Leeds county. In 1871 he became MLA for South Leeds (which included Gananoque) and in 1873 was appointed to a judgeship.[18] This young man was chosen to represent the McDonalds because by this time they were on the wane. One of his cousins, Charles Joel McDonald had taken his share of the Joel Stone inheritance and gone travelling in South America and China, among other places; a second, John Lewis McDonald, was content to live on his inheritance and, if anything, was averse to cooperating in local affairs; the third and most logical alternative was his cousin, William Stone McDonald, who had stayed in the village and who at least attempted to be a man of affairs. By the late 1850s, however, he was near the point where even his inherited property could not save him entirely from his lack of business acumen. In July 1860, the confidential informant for R.G. Dun and Company noted: "property all mortgaged to trust ... Always hard up. Is not bus[inesslike] and has no title to Cr[edit]. Is an hon[orable] man but deficient in sagacity. Never pays his

---

17 The electoral arrangements affecting incorporated villages at the time are admirably summarized in James Croil, *Dundas; or a Sketch of Canadian History* (Montreal: B. Dawson and Son 1861), 223–4.

18 Leavitt, 132.

notes."[19] Herbert Stone McDonald was the only presentable representative of Old Money in the village.

In contrast to the McDonald interests, James Turner represented the new merchant money among the town's power brokers. A Presbyterian, he had been born in Ireland in 1820 and emigrated to Canada with his father and four brothers in 1833. They were not poor immigrants even then: Turner Sr had purchased a farm for each of his five sons. James Turner moved to Gananoque in 1853 and at first had a store and residence in a single building, but as he grew successful he erected another building which included in its upper apartments the Odd Fellows Temple. His firm, besides retailing, sold cordwood to the Grand Trunk Railway for fuel and also was joint owner of a wharf. In his later years, Turner was prosperous enough to be able to turn over his various operations to his son and his two sons-in-law and thereafter spent his time on the village council and on the board of education, posts he held until his death in 1889. For an understanding of local society, it is worth adding that the Turner family was intermarried with another Lansdowne township Irish Protestant family, the Taylors, and George Taylor, a nephew of James Turner, worked for him, later became a partner, and still later became president of the Ontario Wheel Company. He was MP for South Leeds from 1882–1911 and for twenty-five years was chief whip of the Tory party.[20]

Robert McCrum was the leading local MD and the coroner as well.[21]

Directly representative of the new industrial promoters was Peter O'Brien, an Irish-born Catholic who seems to have come to Canada about the time of the Famine. He set up as a shoemaker in Gananoque in the mid-1850s and was reported by R.G. Dun and Company to be a "sober and hard-working man ... Steady and enterprising" with "a good deal invested in his business." He acquired various properties and by 1861 had started a stave factory while continuing his shoemaking firm. In 1863, the year he was elected to the town council, the Dun investigators reported that he was "a pushing, industrious fellow. Commenced on oo$ and has succeeded well." He had indeed, and sometime during the 1860s he

19 "Leeds Co., Canada West" 18: 89 (R.G. Dun and Co. MSS. Baker Library, Harvard University).

20 See MS census of 1871, "Schedule No. 1 – Nominal Return of the Living," 67 (PAC); Hawke, Historic Gananoque, 36–8, 69.

21 See The Leeds, Grenville, Lanark and Renfrew County Directory ... for the year 1859, 23.

moved from shoe and stave manufactory to ownership of a flour mill, with $14,500 in capital, an aggregate output of $40,000 a year, and a crude annual profit of $7,500.[22]

The most important of the new power brokers, D. Ford Jones, represented both old loyalist blood and new industrial wealth. Born in 1818, the eldest son of Jonas Jones of Brockville, he was educated at Upper Canada College before serving in mercantile firms in New York and then for a time in the firm of W.S. McDonald. In 1852 he and his American brother-in-law, Isaac Briggs, set up in Gananoque the St Lawrence Shovel Company which was renamed the D.F. Jones Shovel Co. in 1859 when his partner withdrew. Jones was a "pushing, close man," known for his honesty, but as with most entrepreneurs his business had its problems. In 1855 part of his factory burned, and in the early 1860s he was short of cash, in part because business was bad, in part because he had borrowed heavily to expand. Significantly, this was just the time that he decided to become civically active. In 1862, at the time of the Trent Affair, he either commanded or organized and commanded (sources vary) the Gananoque Field Battery. This enhanced his local status, which was already considerable, and he became a popular Tory politician, being elected an MP for the South Leeds riding in 1864. He did not stand for the next term but was elected again in 1874 and 1878. In 1871 he was sole proprietor of a business with a capitalized value of ninety thousand dollars, forty-eight men and seven boys on the payroll, and sales to hardware dealers throughout Canada worth eighty thousand dollars annually. Not surprisingly, his fellow inaugural councillors elected him reeve, a position he held for five years.[23]

Finally, one should mention Samuel McCammon, who, though not a councillor, was appointed clerk. At sixty-three dollars a year, his appointment was not a major benefice, but it indicates the cohesion of the local upper class. McCammon was born in County Tyrone in 1830 of Protestant family and had been brought to Canada as a virtual infant. Upon graduating from normal school in 1851 he

22 The quotations are from R.G. Dun and Co, "Leeds Co., Canada West" 18: 41 and 101. Other information is from the manuscript census for 1871, "Schedule No. 1 – Nominal Return of the Living," 99, and Schedule No. 6 – Return of Industrial Establishments," 11 (PAC) and *Gananoque Reporter*, 18 July 1860.

23 R.G. Dun and Co, "Leeds Co., Canada West" 18; 34, 39, and 89; Manuscript Census for 1871, "Schedule No. 6 – Return of Industrial Establishments," 1; *Brockville Recorder*, 4 June 1863, 18 June 1863, 25 June 1863, 17 September 1863, 7 January 1864, 4 February 1864; *Gananoque Reporter*, 4 July 1860; Leavitt, 98; Hawke, *Historic Gananoque*, 35, 70–1, 73. Several early account books of the firm are found in the Gananoque Museum.

taught for six years, during which period he made an advantageous marriage to Mary Jane Legge, a granddaughter of one of the five McDonald sisters who had followed their brothers from New York state to Gananoque and prosperity. Thus, as a shirttail relative of the McDonald family, he deserved taking care of and in 1858 he was appointed clerk of the division court at Gananoque. He got along well with the local power brokers and when the Field Battery was raised in 1862 he was appointed lieutenant and subsequently captain. Thus, when he was given the post of clerk to the new Gananoque corporation, both the interests of the old McDonald mercantile tribe and those of his militia commander, D. Ford Jones, were served. In addition to his court and village clerkships, McCammon began in 1863 a retail drug trade which he carried on until 1876, when he was chosen to manage the biggest operation in the village, the newly reorganized spring and axle factory.[24]

The first Gananoque village council was emphatically not a cabal of identically minded individuals: they fought among themselves, sometimes bickered along party lines, and argued over patronage appointments. There is, however, a sound, if indirect, indication that among the upper levels of society a structure and a consciousness of class had emerged. These councillors are a surrogate for a somewhat larger group which, for want of a better word, can be simply denominated the upper class. They were not distinguished by gentility of birth or, as in the days of the McDonald hegemony, virtually limited to one clan. They shared three things: relatively high economic status (shaky though their firms may have been at times), a functional identity (they were managers of capitalized enterprises), and a knowledge of who belonged and who did not. When expedient, they could run such bodies as the Gananoque village council like a club.

Further down the social ladder, the picture becomes cloudy. As noted earlier, most industrial establishments in the town had three or fewer workers, and even if one goes upward to ten or a dozen employees, one is still talking about a very *petit* bourgeoisie. The owners ranged from men like John Banfield, who in 1871 had a one-man, three-woman tailoring shop with a total capitalized value of $25.00, William Edwards with his four-man cabinet shop that turned out $3,000 worth of goods a year, George Mitchell, respected owner of a sash and door factory ("a very careful

24 Manuscript census for 1871, "Schedule No. 1 – Nominal Return of the Living," 60; Hawke, *Historic Gananoque*, 67–8; Leavitt, 176. Incidentally, it was Samuel McCammon's daughter Edith who collected much of the material Hawke later used in his own works.

Immigrant's reward: the home of Samuel McCammon, an Irish immigrant who married into the McDonald family and eventually became manager of the Spring and Axle Company. (1870s)

Scotchman," judged the credit investigators), to Richard Colton with his three-man cloth cording mill that put out $8,500 worth of cloth a year.[25] One can find certain shared characteristics of this small factory and merchant group but no convincing indications of social cohesion among them. They shared, for example, a highly competitive environment, and one sees them circling like so many piranha in a cramped aquarium. Even the most upstanding of them

25 Examples from 1871 manuscript census, "Schedule No. 6 – Return of Industrial Establishments," passim. Quotation from R.G. Dun and Co, "Leeds Co., Canada West" 18: 86.

Industrialist's reward: the home of Charles L. Parmenter who in 1869 formed with William Bullock a rivet company still in existence. (1870s)

were hard-edged ("Scotch and close-fisted" was the description of James Anderson, clothier merchant), and the credit investigators found others to be "untruthful and not upright, although a good workman" (C.W. Ingram, maker of Harness mountings), of "small business, limited means, irregular habits" (Daniel S. Allen, Blacksmith), "very slippery and not to be trusted without security, old man called very dishonest" (Skinner and son, Hardware makers), "too sharp to be upright" (J. Thorp Henry, general store keeper).[26]

It was not at all uncommon for a man to fail, occasionally several

26 R.G. Dun and Co, "Leeds Co., Canada West" 18, quotations respectively from 91, 86, 91, 86, 71.

*Stylized view of the mouth of the Gananoque
River. Note the sawn-timber raft. (1870s)*

times, but failure in business was only a passing misfortune, not a
disgrace. The Skinners previously were in business in Brockville
where they made scythes and agriculture tools of a quality to win an
Exhibition Medal at the Crystal Palace in 1851. They got into
financial difficulties, however, became insolvent, allegedly through
the fault of other parties, moved to Gananoque, and started over.
That is not unusual; what is notable is that when the *Gananoque
Reporter* did a series of articles in 1860 on local industries, the earlier
failure was reported as just a normal part of business history, neither
worthy of special comment nor demanding to be ignored.[27] Again,
the Dun reports are full of examples of failure. One merchant and

27 *Gananoque Reporter*, 20 June 1860.

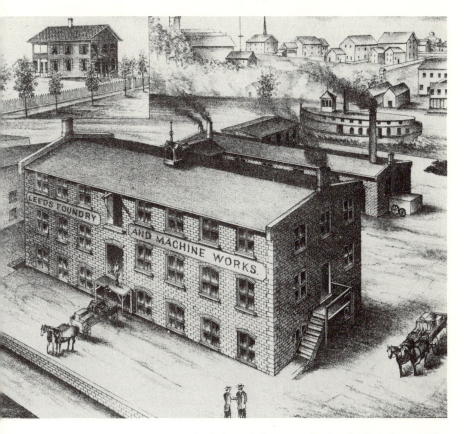

American influence: the Leeds Foundry, estab-
lished in 1858 by E.E. Abbott, a Connecticut
Yankee. His house is shown in the inset. (1870s)

tavern keeper, J.K. Laughton, became "smashed up and not worth
anything. Makes enough to live and that is all. Is trying to get into
business again." Later, it was reported that he "has given up his
store long since, is now keeping tavern – pretty good customer at his
own bar." Then, three months later, he "failed and made an
assignment to creditors of goods." One feels a certain sympathy
for a young blacksmith (Thomas Cruse) who, "though a good
mechanic," failed, and one can also understand the disgust of the
creditors of Haig Middleton, a wheelwright, when they discovered
he had "ran away six week ago." According to the credit investigator, he returned and then "burst up." William Wooland, formerly
a steward on a steamboat, who became briefly a small businessman

in Gananoque and then was described as "Gon away ... farming near Kingston," probably showed sound judgment, for by laying down the ledger and taking up the plow he was replacing the eristic with the eirenic.[28]

Those middling merchants and small-time manufacturers did not act as a group. They were willing (as in the election for the first village council) to be deferential to the local power élite, but beyond that each seems to have sought his own ends. They were a potential class, but not an actual one.

If one takes the manuscript census of 1871 as accurate (and, in contrast to that of 1861, it has no obvious gross discrepancies)[29] one can sort the village according to occupation. This is not exactly the same as a social class categorization, but in a local study, where one knows the nature of virtually every firm and shop, the occupational categories can be arranged so as to approximate social-class

28 R.G Dun and Co, "Leeds Co., Canada West" 18, quotations respectively from 89, 41, 18, 87.

29 Anyone using the 1861 census on occupational matters should be very careful, because the instructions to enumerators told them to classify all children who worked for the benefit of the fathers as being of the same occupation as the father, but in an inconsistent manner. If a father was a tradesman, the son was to be entered as the same, but if the father was a farmer, the son was to be listed as a labourer. (The full directions to enumerators are found in the *Annual Report, Year II* of the Peel County History Project 1974, 104–8.) Besides introducing two incompatible enumerating principles, these instructions left great scope for misplaced literalness on the part of the enumerator. In the census district which included Gananoque, the census-taker seems to have assumed that most male children did at least some work for the benefit of their fathers and therefore classed them as instructed by the central authorities. The result was that, for example, the seven-year-old son of one Irish-born labourer was classified as a labourer, the seven-year-old son of an Irish immigrant carpenter as a carpenter, and the four-year-old son of the Anglican rector as already a minister! and so on, through the whole batch of data.

These enumeration procedures mean (1) that one cannot use the 1861 data to determine the age at which children actually entered the labour force, and (2) that in practical terms one must limit use of the occupational data for the 1861 census to persons who are heads of household and of at least the age of majority. It is possible, however, that one may have the good fortune to come across a census district or several contiguous districts in which the census takers made appropriate descriptions of age of entry into the labour force, but even then the labelling of occupations probably will be inaccurate. (Was an adolescent carrying stones for his mason father really a mason, as the census instructions dictate? If anyone else were doing this unskilled manual task, he would be a "labourer" in the census categories.) Even though there may be a few census districts in which both labelling and age of entry into the labour force were handled accurately, the province-wide tallies will have to be abandoned entirely, since the data of so many districts will have been badly tainted.

groupings. (There are, of course, several standardized occupational scales, but none is appropriate to the local historical situation.) In Gananoque in 1871 one finds an occupational social structure as follows.[30]

	Occupation of all employed persons	
	number	% of total
Gentlemen	4	0.7
Farmers	18	3.4
Professionals, government officials, factory owners	37	7.1
Merchants and inn-keepers	49	9.4
Skilled tradesmen, clerks, factory hands	305	58.2
Unskilled labourers	95	18.1
Servants	16	3.1
Total	524	100.0

Three comments on methods. First and most important, the placing of factory hands in the same category with the skilled tradesmen and clerks is dictated in small part by the desirability of averaging two small data cells but chiefly by the skilled tenor of the firms in which they worked. In these firms the factory hands were clearly differentiated from the unskilled manual labourers and in fact most often were artisans who practised trades for which there was not as yet a special name (such as the new processes in the carriage spring factory) or which were specific to a relatively small industry (as in the shovel factory). Second, it is best to forget farmers altogether when surveying the village's occupational-social structure. They either lived on the outskirts or were retired farmers who had moved into town for their last years and were not a functional part of the industrializing economy. Third, the reason that the number of professional government officials and factory owners taken from the nominal census (thirty-seven persons) is smaller than the number of factory owners on the industrial census of the same year (forty-nine factories) is that the nominal census was more rigorous in defining a factory owner. If a man had only himself and one or two employees, he was classed as an artisan in the nominal census rather than as a factory owner. For our purposes that is all to the good, for it means that the

30 Compiled from the manuscript census of 1871, "Schedule No. 1 – Nominal Return of the Living," 67 (PAC).

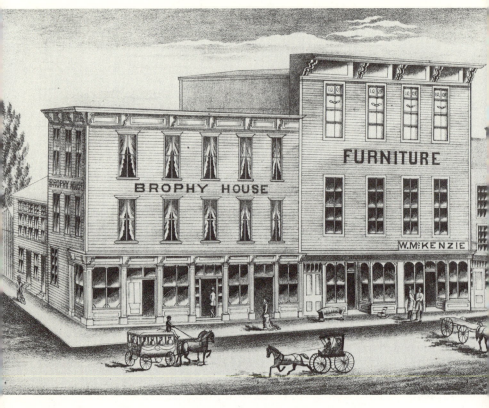

*The best hotel in town: notice the Odd
Fellows' temple in upper story of McKenzie's
furniture store. (1870s)*

*Brown's drug store: notice that the shrewd
store owner rented out his top storey to three of
Gananoque's ubiquitous lodges. (1870s)*

category composed of professionals, government officials, and factory owners actually does constitute an élite.

Had a consciousness of class emerged among the workers, it most likely would have been among the skilled rather than the unskilled. As grouped here, the skilled tradesmen, white collar workers, and factory hands shared both a high level of technical expertise and, for the most part, a dependency upon wages (or, more accurately, upon vouchers, for this rather than cash was the usual method of

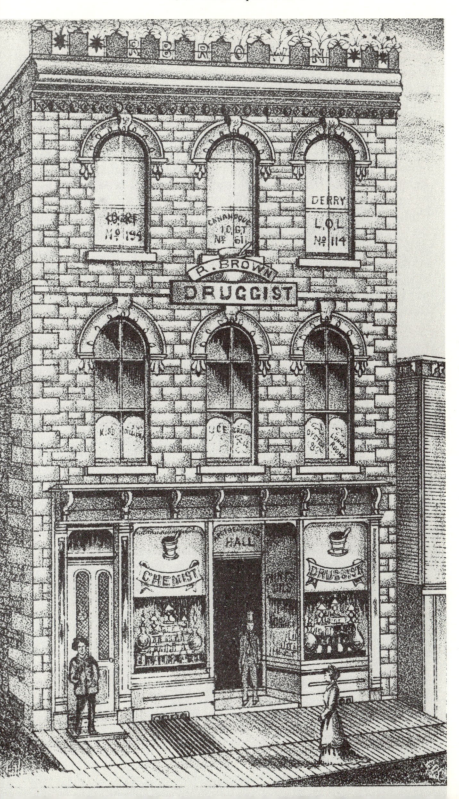

payment).[31] Unlike the *petit bourgeoisie*, the skilled workers and factory hands, once taken on by a firm, were not in direct daily competition with their fellows in the same line of work. Potentially, workers in a given shop had a common economic interest, workers in the same industry had a shared concern, and all members of the skilled sector had shared class interests.

There seems, however, no specific evidence of working-class consciousness in this period. (I am more than willing to be corrected on this; judgments made from absence of evidence are inevitably tentative.) It is not until the organization of the local branch of the Knights of Labour in Gananoque in 1881 and its blossoming into three lodges in the late 1880s and 1890s that unmistakable signs of working-class consciousness appear.[32] This occurred, however, after the village's economic base had changed from one based on high skill levels and many small firms to a true industrial structure of markedly larger firms and increasing mechanization, implying skill dilution, increasing standardization of tasks, and the alienation of the work force. In 1871, however, the village of Gananoque was close to, but not yet at the point of becoming a class-segmented society.

5

This proto-class structure was crisscrossed by three important variables, religious affiliation, place of birth, and ethnicity, and in charting these we come to the question, where did the Irish fit in? To approach this issue, one must first cross-tabulate the relationship between religious persuasion and place of birth. This is done in table 11. Then, one must do the same for the relationship between ethnicity and religion; this relationship is presented in table 12. The place of birth data tell us that most of the population was native-born but that there were three significantly sized cells of new immigrants: Irish-born Catholics, Scottish-born Presbyterians, and English-born Anglicans. This information, when combined with data on place of birth and occupational-social grouping (see table 13), seems to suggest that at the lower end of the social spectrum

---

31 McKenzie (179) reports that the Jones company was the first to do away with the voucher system and pay cash instead, but does not give a date.
32 I am grateful to Bryan Palmer for giving me copies of his file on the organization of labour in Gananoque in the 1880s, including the reminiscences of two early organizers.

each of these groups constituted something halfway between an ethnic group and a class, that is, an *ethclass*.[33]

Comparison of the data in table 11 with those in table 12 gives some indication of the degree to which ethnic associations in this village diminished over time (and thus, *mutatis mutandis*, an indication of the temporal limits on the concept of ethnic class). For many ethnic groups, a specific religion is an important part of their cultural system and slippage away from that religion is therefore an indirect evidence of the decline of the group's sense of ethnic identity. As far as Scots-born Presbyterians and English-born Anglicans are concerned, table 11 can be taken as providing a set of locally applicable norms concerning the association of the foreign-born with the dominant church in their homeland. (The Protestant-Catholic divide in Ireland obviously makes a similar association impossible.) To this one can add data on the association of Quebec-born French persons with Roman Catholicism. These, then, give us norms that we can compare with the pattern of religious persuasion of the generations born in Canada (or, in the case of the French Canadians, born in Ontario):[34]

percentage of Scottish-born who were Presbyterian	75.7%
percentage of persons of Scottish ethnicity, born in Canada, who were Presbyterian	49.8%
percentage of English-born who were Anglican	73.9%
percentage of persons of English ethnicity, born in Canada, who were Anglican	31.4%
percentage of Quebec-born French Canadians who were Roman Catholic	100.0%
percentage of persons of French-Canadian ancestry, born in Canada West (Ontario), who were Roman Catholic	81.0%

These data (which, it must be emphasized, apply only to this specific local context) suggest that in this industrializing village the ethnic cultural matrix weakened quite radically among the children of the immigrants.

33 On the concept of ethclass, which, suitably modified to fit Canadian historical circumstances, is a very useful way to show the way that ethnicity and class interact, see H. Edward Ransford, *Race and Class in American Society: Black, Chicano, Anglo* (Cambridge, Mass.: Schenkman Publishing Co. 1977), 55ff.
34 The Scots and English figures are derived arithmetically from tables 11 and 12. The French-Canadian data required reprocessing of the 1871 manuscript census material.
   Incidentally, although the census specified ethnicity in terms of "French," not "French Canadian," one is perfectly safe in this context in interpreting the former to mean the latter.

TABLE 11

1871 Census of Gananoque
Cross-tabulation of Religion and Place of Birth, Entire Population

	Anglican	Various Methodists	Various Presbyterians	Roman Catholic	Other	No info.	Total
Ireland	36	13	34	102	0	0	185
Scotland	4	11	56	2	0	1	74
England	102	29	5	2	0	0	138
All other foreign-born (97% from U.S.)	12	61	47	28	7	0	155
Native-born Canadians	299	491	264	406	5	3	1,468
TOTAL	453	605	406	540	12	4	2,020

	Anglican	Various Methodists	Various Presbyterians	Roman Catholic	Other	No info.	Entire population
Ireland	7.9%	2.1%	8.4%	18.9%	0.0%	0.0%	9.2%
Scotland	0.9	1.8	13.8	0.4	0.0	25.0	3.6
England	22.5	4.8	1.2	0.4	0.0	0.0	6.8
All other foreign-born	2.7	10.1	11.6	5.2	58.3	0.0	7.7
Native-born Canadians	66.0	81.2	65.0	75.1	41.7	75.0	72.7
TOTAL	100.0	100.0	100.0	100.0	100.0	100.0	100.0

	Ireland	Scotland	England	All other foreign-born	Native-born Canadians	Entire population
Anglican	19.5%	5.4%	73.9%	9.7%	20.4%	22.4%
Various Methodists	7.0	14.9	21.0	39.4	33.4	30.0
Various Presbyterians	18.4	75.7	3.6	30.3	18.0	20.1
Roman Catholic	55.1	2.7	1.5	18.1	27.7	26.7
Other	0.0	0.0	0.0	4.5	0.3	0.6
No information	0.0	1.3	0.0	0.0	0.2	0.2
TOTAL	100.0	100.0	100.0	100.0	100.0	100.0

Source: Manuscript census of 1871, "Schedule No. 1 – Nominal Return of the Living," PAC

TABLE 12
1871 Census of Gananoque
Cross-tabulation of Religion and Ethnicity, Entire Population

	Anglican	Various Methodists	Various Presbyterians	Roman Catholic	Other	No info.	Total
Irish	140	169	140	293	4	0	746
Scottish	45	73	180	23	0	2	323
English	243	261	66	15	1	1	587
French	7	24	6	200	0	0	237
All others	14	58	12	8	6	1	99
Unknown	4	20	2	1	1	0	28
TOTAL	453	605	406	540	12	4	2,020

	Anglican	Various Methodists	Various Presbyterians	Roman Catholic	Other	No info.	Entire population
Irish	30.9%	27.9%	34.5%	54.3%	33.4%	0.0%	36.9%
Scottish	9.9	12.1	44.3	4.2	0.0	50.0	16.0
English	53.6	43.1	16.2	2.8	8.3	25.0	29.1
French	1.6	4.0	1.5	37.0	0.0	0.0	11.7
All others	3.1	9.6	3.0	1.5	50.0	25.0	4.9
Unknown	0.9	3.3	0.5	0.2	8.3	0.0	1.4
TOTAL	100.0	100.0	100.0	100.0	100.0	100.0	100.0

	Irish	Scottish	English	French	All others	Unknown	Entire population
Anglican	18.8%	13.9%	41.3%	3.0%	14.1%	14.3%	22.4%
Various Methodists	22.6	22.6	44.5	10.1	58.6	71.4	30.0
Various Presbyterians	18.8	55.7	11.2	2.5	12.1	7.1	20.1
Roman Catholic	39.3	7.1	2.6	84.4	8.1	3.6	26.7
Other	0.5	0.0	0.2	0.0	6.1	3.6	0.6
No information	0.0	0.7	0.2	0.0	1.0	0.0	0.2
TOTAL	100.0	100.0	100.0	100.0	100.0	100.0	100.0

Source: Manuscript census of 1871, "Schedule No. 1 – Nominal Return of the Living," PAC

Tables 13 and 14 provide data on the relationship of occupation to place of birth and ethnicity. The tally includes all whom the census showed as employed. Slightly under one in four of the villagers either had a job or was self-employed. Most, but not all of these individuals were heads of households, although it was not unusual for a family to have both the father and a son, or even two, at work. Women rarely were found in the employment marketplace unless they were heads of household, that is widows, abandoned wives, or spinsters.

When one examines the place of birth data (table 13) it appears that the ethclasses did indeed exist. For instance, if the minimum threshold which must be obtained before a village group was sizeable enough to be a distinct cohort were set at fifteen wage earners (an arbitrary but reasonable number, for in the village the census data indicate that fifteen wage earners can be expected to be supporting a total of roughly fifty-eight people, a sufficient number to form a distinct social group), then table 13 indicates the existence of the following ethnic classes:

1 Scottish-born skilled workers
2 English-born skilled workers
3 Irish-born Protestant skilled workers
4 (a) Irish-born Catholic skilled workers
  (b) Irish-born Catholic unskilled workers

Through a reprocessing of the census data to distinguish the French Canadians born in Quebec from the rest of the native-born Canadians, one can add

5 Unskilled French-Canadian Catholic workers[35]

Ethclass, in the context of the village of Gananoque, can be thought of as a halfway station on the way to class consciousness among the workers. One would expect that as the ties of the Old Country weakened, the class element in ethclass gradually would predominate while the cultural aspects of ethnicity diminished. Based upon the strong ethclass cohorts of skilled workers for the British Isles as shown in 1871, one would expect that class consciousness would first arise among the skilled workers. The union activities of 1881 can be taken as the fulfilment of such an expectation.

35 Of the twenty-four Quebec-born French-Canadian Catholic workers, sixteen were unskilled, seven skilled, and one was a servant.

6

In a reversal of procedure, instead of examining the part played by ethnicity in the evolving class structure, let us see what the information on occupational-class levels tells us about the position of various immigrant and ethnic groups in this particular industrializing village. Here one must avoid falling into the fallacy of false precision. In other words, it would be relatively easy to set up a ranking scale of occupations and to relate this either to place of birth or to ethnicity by running sets of correlations. This would give a set of nice clean numbers that would relate social status to birthplace and ethnicity but would be chimerical: there is no historical ranking scale that handles adequately the occupations which we have in this village.[36] Instead, one must have the courage to be imprecise in interpreting tables 13 and 14; one must try to apperceive the *gestalt*, the entire profile, of each ethnic group, particularly as it compares to the other groups in the fundamental aggregates of élite occupations, skilled trades, and unskilled employment. Several patterns are clear, but, as with a pointillist painting, one has to look not at individual dots but at the overall pattern.

Were the immigrants lower on the social scale than those born in Canada? Even to ask seems at first idiotic, but for the fact that the economic-social structure of the surrounding countryside had favoured immigrants and disadvantaged the Canadian-born. An examination of table 13 shows that there was little difference in the distribution of the occupational-class profile between native-born

36 For a succinct comment on status or prestige rankings of nineteenth-century occupations, see A. Gordon Darroch and Michael D. Ornstein, "Ethnicity and Occupational Structure in Canada in 1871: The Vertical Mosaic in Historical Perspective," *Canadian Historical Review* 61 (September 1980): 309–10.
  If there is no satisfactory scale developed elsewhere, why not create one specifically for Gananoque? Even at a very gross level it is impossible, given the available data, to create a scale that would not be a reflection more of twentieth-century conceptions than of nineteenth-century reality. For instance, should a merchant be ranked lower on the scale than a factory owner? It depends largely on the size of the operation of each and, more important, on the profitability of each man's operation, and these data are missing for many entrepreneurs. Was a journeyman carpenter more skilled than a factor worker who hand-forged components for an agricultural implement? The factory hand well may have been more skilled, better paid, and held higher in local regard. The census data make discriminations among the labouring class possible only on the most general level: skilled (including factory hands), labourers, and servants.

TABLE 13

1871 Census of Gananoque

Occupation of All Those Employed, by Place of Birth

	Gentlemen	Farmers	Professionals, government officials, factory owners	Merchants, inn-keepers	Skilled tradesmen, clerks, factory hands	Unskilled labourers	Servants	Total
Ireland: Protestant	1	2	4	5	27	4	2	45
Catholic	0	1	1	2	24	15	2	45
Subtotal, Ireland	(1)	(3)	(5)	(7)	(51)	(19)	(4)	(90)
Scotland	1	4	5	2	22	4	0	38
England	1	0	5	5	41	6	2	60
All other countries (94.1% from U.S.)	0	4	5	9	25	8	0	51
Subtotal, all foreign-born (3)	(3)	(11)	(20)	(23)	(139)	(37)	(6)	(239)
Native-born Canadians	1	7	17	26	166	58	10	285
TOTAL	4	18	37	49	305	95	16	524

	Gentlemen	Farmers	Professionals, government officials, factory owners	Merchants, inn-keepers	Skilled tradesmen, clerks, factory hands	Unskilled labourers	Servants	Entire population
Ireland: Protestant	25.0%	11.1%	10.8%	10.2%	8.9%	4.2%	12.5%	8.6%
Catholic	0.0	5.6	2.7	4.1	7.9	15.8	12.5	8.6
Subtotal, Ireland	(25.0)	(16.7)	(13.5)	(14.3)	(16.7)	(20.0)	(25.0)	(17.2)
Scotland	25.0	22.2	13.5	4.1	7.2	4.2	0.0	7.3
England	25.0	0.0	13.5	10.2	13.5	6.3	12.5	11.4
All other countries	0.0	22.2	13.5	18.4	8.2	8.4	0.0	9.7
Subtotal, all foreign-born	(75.0)	(61.1)	(54.0)	(47.0)	(45.6)	(38.9)	(37.5)	(45.6)
Native-born Canadians	25.0	38.9	46.0	53.0	54.4	61.1	62.5	54.4
TOTAL	100.0	100.0	100.0	100.0	100.0	100.0	100.0	100.0

	Ireland: Protestant	Ireland: Catholic	Subtotal, Ireland	Scotland	England	All other countries	Subtotal, all foreign-born	Native-born Canadians	Entire population
Gentlemen	2.3%	0.0%	1.1%	2.6%	1.7%	0.0%	1.2%	0.3%	0.7%
Farmers	4.4	2.3	3.3	10.5	0.0	7.8	4.6	2.5	3.4
Professionals, government officials, factory owners	8.9	2.3	5.6	13.2	8.3	9.8	8.4	6.0	7.1
Merchants, inn-keepers	11.1	4.4	7.8	5.3	8.3	17.7	9.6	9.1	9.4
Skilled tradesmen, clerks, factory hands	60.0	53.3	56.7	57.9	68.3	49.0	58.2	58.2	58.2
Unskilled labourers	8.9	33.3	21.1	10.5	10.0	15.7	15.5	20.4	18.1
Servants	4.4	4.4	4.4	0.0	3.4	0.0	2.5	3.5	3.1
TOTAL	100.0	100.0	100.0	100.0	100.0	100.0	100.0	100.0	100.0

Source: Manuscript census of 1871, "Schedule No. 1 – Nominal Return of the Living," PAC

The squire's residence: "Bellevue," home of the Hon. John McDonald, built 1831–2. (Photo credit: G. Innes)

Another McDonald house: "Blinkbonnie," built 1843–4, the residence of William Stone McDonald. (Late 1880s. Photo credit: Archives of Ontario)

The Provincial Hotel, built 1856, shown in the late 1880s. The business still operates and the building is fundamentally unchanged. (Photo credit: Archives of Ontario)

A section of the Canadian Birmingham in the late 1880s. Note the efficient use of the waterfront. The Spring and Axle Factory is in the foreground. (Photo credit: Archives of Ontario)

A small waterfront shop: the Cowan and Britton Wringer Factory in the late 1880s. In 1871, under earlier management, it had five fulltime employees. Notice the outlet for the water which passed through the building and powered all the equipment. (Photo credit: Archives of Ontario)

A harness works, a furniture factory, and a grist mill on the upper dam. Note the conduits for apportioning and delivering water power as developed in the 1860s. (Late 1880s. Photo credit: Archives of Ontario)

*A typical waterfront plant: Skinner's Factory.
In 1871 it had twenty-nine fulltime employees,
turning out hardware, saddlery, grain cradles,
and other items. (Late 1880s. Photo credit:
Archives of Ontario)*

*The Jones Shovel Factory. In 1871, the firm
employed forty-eight men and seven boys. (Late
1880s. Photo credit: Archives of Ontario)*

Canadians and the foreign-born, although the native-born were somewhat overrepresented among the unskilled labourers. Actually, the aggregate profiles of the foreign-born and the native-born Canadians hide two widely disparate groups. The first of these was the American-born. Gananoque, situated right on the border, always had close trade links with the United States and throughout its history American capitalists as well as skilled workers and a few labourers saw opportunity in the village and migrated to it. In this period several of the industries and mercantile firms were either owned or managed by Americans. Thus, the American-born (who are found in table 13 as comprising 94.1 percent of all immigrants from outside the British Isles) actually were the most advantaged group that one can identify in the village. Their categories had by far the highest proportion in the managerial and mercantile classes and the lowest proportion of persons in the combination of the skilled, unskilled, and servant categories.[37]

On the other side of the ledger, the native-born profile was brought down by the camouflaged presence of the least-advantaged group in the society, those individuals of French-Canadian ethnicity who had been born in Quebec. This group had no persons whatever above the level of labourer.[38]

skilled tradesmen, clerks, and factory hands	7 (29.2%)
unskilled labourers	16 (66.6%)
servants	1 (4.1%)

Within the context of Gananoque village, these people were foreigners, even though they had been born in British North America. They had emigrated to the village from a culture that was highly dissimilar in many aspects, especially in dominant language, to that which prevailed in this insular municipality. The cultural

37 One of the great follies of the organizers of the 1871 and succeeding Canadian censuses was the decision not to permit "American" as an ethnic designation. Children of American-born persons had to be designated "English," "Irish," and so on, as appropriate. For this study, this means that it is virtually impossible to determine if the Americans' position as the leading cohort in village society was passed on to succeeding generations or was merely a single-generation phenomenon. This refusal to permit "American" not only loses track of a major immigration group but taints all ethnicity data because, for example, individuals born in the United States but of distant English ancestry were placed in the same "English" ethnicity cohort as persons who had been born in England. The same distortion holds across the spectrum as a result of the Canadian government's magisterial decision that only Europe could constitute a true ethnic homeland.
38 The figures come from my processing of the manuscript census data.

adjustment for someone from the United States, England, Scotland, or Ireland was much much less than that required by the Quebec-born French Canadians. These Quebec immigrants moved into a new and strange world and, like the Chinese on the west coast of North America in the migrant generation, formed an isolated, almost hermetic, disadvantaged minority.

Therefore, in terms of social reality one would be justified in treating statistically the Quebec-born French Canadians as foreign-born. If one does this (which is to say, removes them from the native-born Canadian aggregate and transfers them to the foreign-born), then the following two occupational profiles result.

	A			B		
	Foreign-born and Quebec-born French Canadians			Native-born Canadians, less Quebec-born French Canadians		
Gentlemen	3	(1.1%)		1	(0.4%)	
Farmers	11	(4.2%)		7	(2.7%)	
Professionals, government officials, factory owners	20	(7.6%)	⎫ 16.5%	17	(6.5%)	⎫ 16.5%
Merchants and inn-keepers	23	(8.7%)	⎭	26	(10.0%)	⎭
Skilled tradesmen, clerks, factory hands	146	(55.5%)	⎫	159	(60.9%)	⎫
Unskilled labourers	53	(20.2%)	⎬ 78.4%	42	(16.1%)	⎬ 80.4%
Servants	7	(2.7%)	⎭	9	(3.4%)	⎭
	263	(100.0%)		261	(100.0%)	

The profiles are so similar that it is clear that in general *in this community* there was no great disadvantage in being an immigrant and no great advantage in being a native-born Canadian. When one seeks a general explanation for this situation, one can only go in a circle: the foreign-born brought with them to the village skills and, in some cases, capital, and this accounts for their being in skilled trades and in ownership positions as frequently as the native-born. That, of course, is tautological. It may be that Gananoque, which was quite far from the debouchment points for European immigrants and was known to have an economy based on skilled production, only attracted the "best" immigrants in terms of skills or capital in hand. That, however, is speculation. What is clear is

that the classic simplicity of the American model of occupational mobility, in which immigrants are found on the bottom rungs of the occupational ladder and the native-born on the higher one (*pace* Handlin, Thernstrom, and Katz), cannot by any stretch of the imagination be applied to this little Birmingham.

Among the foreign immigrants, those from England and Scotland as groups each had higher profiles than did the native-born Canadians (as defined in B above). The Scottish-born were disproportionately high in the professional-managerial class, and the English-born bulked large among skilled labourers. Both groups were proportionately very low among unskilled labourers.

Where were the Irish immigrants? For the first time in this study, one encounters a situation that approximates the stereotypic: the Irish-born Protestants were notably better off than the Irish-born Catholics. The Protestants, like the Scottish and the English-born, actually had a slightly higher social-occupational profile than did the native-born Canadians (as defined in B above). The Irish-born Catholics, however, were considerably overrepresented among the unskilled labourers and underrepresented sharply among the managerial and merchant groups. This situation dovetails with a change which characterized Irish emigration generally. After the Famine (one cannot be precise on dating, as the censuses of Ireland took place, as in Canada, only at decennial intervals), the pattern of whole families of former commercial farmers emigrating together was replaced by two sub-patterns: increasingly, persons from around Belfast and the industrializing Lagan region left, and simultaneously a strong stream of emigrants from among the landless labourers of Munster and Connaught began to run in full spate.[39] Although it would be wrong simplemindedly to label the

---

39 At this point, it is well to remind the reader that accurate direct data on the place in Ireland from which emigrants came are not available until 1876. Material from 1851 onwards shows the home counties of emigrants, but it is far from accurate. Thus, for the period before 1876 (and especially for that of 1841–51) scholars must inevitably use either indirect data or surrogates to indicate migration levels from specific parts of Ireland as well as to obtain indications of the type of person who left.

For the period 1841–51, the most thorough and satisfactory work is that of S.H. Cousens. He developed a data-base on regional emigration patterns, 1841–51, by relating the loss of population in each locale to the death-rate in that same locality: the excess of population loss over deaths was ascribable to emigration. To reinforce these data on the geographic source of emigration, he used a set of surrogates based on poor-law data, to indicate the sort of person most likely to have emigrated in this period. See especially his article, "The Regional Pattern of Emigration during the Great Irish Famine, 1846–51," *Institute of*

first "Protestant" and the second "Catholic," the former stream undoubtedly did verge towards the Protestant vector and the second towards the Catholic. Of course one cannot argue in lockstep that just because in general post-Famine Irish emigration seems to have had the same pattern – relatively skilled Protestants, relatively unskilled Catholics – that appeared in the urban areas of Canada West generally, and Gananoque in particular, the latter was a direct cause of the former, for intermediate filters certainly operated. In fact, although the Irish-born Catholics were proportionately over-represented locally among the unskilled, the important point is that most of them nevertheless were in skilled jobs.

British Geographers Publications 29 (1968): 119–34, as well as his other items cited in chapter 1, n40.

David Fitzpatrick's "The Disappearance of the Irish Agricultural Labourer, 1841–1912," *Irish Economic and Social History* 7 (1980): 66–92, uses agricultural labourers as a surrogate for emigration statistics and is at once very illuminating and slightly misleading. Two qualifications to this otherwise fine study need to be made. First, his surrogate does not work very well for northeast Ulster (Belfast and region), for obvious reasons related to the diversified nature of the economy of that region. Second, he misreads his own data and misleadingly stretches his conclusions back to 1841 rather than limiting them to 1851 and thereafter: his data show that only two counties in Connaught had a sharp decrease "in the ratio of male farm workers to 100 farm workers" (an emigration-rate surrogate) and that in fact the ratio actually *increased* in most of Munster (see his map, 85). In other words, until the Famine migration was well and truly done, the far south and west of Ireland were not major sources of migration. After 1851, his dat convincingly indicate that they were important sources (although not necessarily the source of the majority of emigrants).

This point requires emphasis because elsewhere (in "Irish Emigration in the Later Nineteenth Century," *Irish Historical Studies* 22 [September 1980]: 128–9) Fitzpatrick states that from 1841 (not 1851) onwards Connaught had the highest emigration rate. In confirmation he refers vaguely "to my findings" (128 n3) and to an article of Cormac O'Grada's, "Some Aspects of Nineteenth Century Irish Emigration," in *Comparative Aspects of Scottish and Irish Economic and Social History, 1600–1900*, ed. L.M. Cullen and T.C. Stout (Edinburgh: John Donald Publishers [n.d., c. 1977]), 65–73. Actually, this is a think-piece and not a confirmation in any sense of Fitzpatrick's view. In his conclusion (71) O'Grada carefully limits even his speculative suggestions to the post-Famine period. This is wise, because his pre-Famine data consist of only 320 cases from a single parish in county Cavan. One should add that Fitzpatrick's IHS article (126–43) as it covers the years from 1876 onwards (for which he has excellent data) has several very important insights.

Finally, to keep matters in perspective, let me underscore the danger in this matter of falling into the fallacy of the false converse: the mere fact that emigration took proportionately more people from the west and south of Ireland from 1851 onwards does not mean that emigrants from these areas necessarily made up the great bulk, or even necessarily the majority, of migrants from Ireland.

TABLE 14
1871 Census of Gananoque
Occupation of All Those Employed, by Ethnicity

	Gentlemen	Farmers	Professionals, government officials, factory owners	Merchants, inn-keepers	Skilled tradesmen, clerks, factory hands	Unskilled labourers	Servants	Total
Irish: Protestant	1	7	5	16	75	13	5	122
Catholic	0	1	2	7	47	19	3	79
Subtotal, Irish	(1)	(8)	(7)	(23)	(122)	(32)	(8)	(201)
Scottish	1	5	10	6	56	13	4	95
English	1	3	16	17	87	26	2	152
French	0	0	2	0	22	21	2	47
All others	1	2	2	3	18	3	0	29
TOTAL	4	18	37	49	305	95	16	524

	Gentlemen	Farmers	Professionals, government officials, factory owners	Merchants, inn-keepers	Skilled tradesmen, clerks, factory hands	Unskilled labourers	Servants	Entire population
Irish: Protestant	25.0%	38.9%	13.5%	32.7%	24.6%	13.7%	31.3%	23.3%
Catholic	0.0	5.5	5.4	14.3	15.4	20.0	18.7	15.1
Subtotal, Irish	(25.0)	(44.4)	(18.9)	(47.0)	(40.0)	(33.7)	(50.0)	(38.4)
Scottish	25.0	27.8	27.0	12.2	18.4	13.7	25.0	18.1
English	25.0	16.7	43.3	34.7	28.5	27.4	12.5	29.0
French	0.0	0.0	5.4	0.0	7.2	22.1	12.5	9.0
All others	25.0	11.1	5.4	6.1	5.9	3.1	0.0	5.5
TOTAL	100.0	100.0	100.0	100.0	100.0	100.0	100.0	100.0

	Irish: Protestant	Irish: Catholic	Subtotal: Irish	Scottish	English	French	All others	Entire population
Gentlemen	0.8%	0.0%	0.5%	1.1%	0.7%	0.0%	3.5%	0.7%
Farmers	5.7	1.3	4.0	5.3	2.0	0.0	6.9	3.4
Professionals, government officials, factory owners	4.1	2.5	3.5	10.5	10.5	4.3	6.9	7.1
Merchants, inn-keepers	13.1	8.9	11.4	6.3	11.2	0.0	10.3	9.4
Skilled tradesmen, clerks, factory hands	61.5	59.5	60.7	58.9	57.2	46.8	62.1	58.2
Unskilled labourers	10.7	24.0	15.9	13.7	17.1	44.6	10.3	18.1
Servants	4.1	3.8	4.0	4.2	1.3	4.3	0.0	3.1
TOTAL	100.0	100.0	100.0	100.0	100.0	100.0	100.0	100.0

Source: Manuscript census of 1871, "Schedule No. 1 – Nominal Return of the Living," PAC

Thus, if one considers only information on place of birth, one can draw up an order of local groups according to their occupational-social profile:

American-born
Scottish-born, English-born, Irish-born Protestants (roughly equal)
Native-born Canadians (excluding French Canadians born in Quebec)
Irish-born Roman Catholics
French Canadians born in Quebec

Ideally, one would like to be able to draw some direct conclusions about the mobility of ethnic groups over time, but that requires longitudinal data and the 1871 census was the first of its sort to deal with ethnicity. Nevertheless, the ethnic data presented in table 14 have some use. When compared with the information in table 13 these data seem to suggest that a regression towards the mean occurred in all groups, that is, for those born in Canada the effects of their family's Old Country cultural background was greatly diminished. The French Canadians' and the Irish Catholics' disadvantages diminished and the advantaged position of other groups lessened.[40] This corresponds with our earlier suggestion (based on religious data) that the effect of ethnicity upon class (or proto-class) would diminish rapidly once the immigrant generation was past. Thereafter, the local occupational structure was largely independent of ethnic factors.

7

Relationships within ethnic groups are as complex as those between groups and much more difficult to document. Both the Catholics and the Protestants of Irish ethnicity spread over a wide occupational range. Even if one considers only the immigrant generation in the village, the range within each group still was great. Clearly, one had not ethnic stratification but what has been called an ethnic division of labour woven throughout occupational structures.[41]

40 It is well to remember that Table 14, containing as it does all working persons in the village, understates the change in position between the first and second generations born in Canada. This occurs because the ethnicity table necessarily includes all the foreign-born.
41 Darroch and Ornstein, 329.

The interesting relationship, however, comes when one remembers that the industrializing village of Gananoque was set in a hinterland dominated by commercial agriculture. In the country, the Irish-born Protestant farmers were considerably better off than the average local farmers, but this caused no rural-village dissonance, as the Irish-Protestant immigrants in the village were above the average in occupational profile. For the Irish-born Catholics, however, the situation was different: they comprised an élite sector in commercial farming in the countryside but were a somewhat disadvantaged group in the village. Thus, in Gananoque and its hinterlands as a whole, an economic and social cleavage existed among the Irish-Catholic immigrants. This coincided with the functional divide between commercial farming and village occupations and with the general dissonance between village and countryside that is virtually inevitable in any largely rural area. Unhappily, unless public politics are involved, such intra-ethnic cleavages usually leave little or no historical evidence. In this township there exists today, preserved as a fossil from that earlier era, a pattern of Catholic worship that is as revealing in its configuration as it is vestigial in its continuation: today, in the front of Leeds township and in the adjoining parts of Pittsburgh township, the farming élite, still Irish-Catholic as was the case a century and a quarter ago, maintains its own tiny house of worship rather than mix with the workies in the parish church in Gananoque.

CHAPTER SEVEN

And What Is the Significance?

I

This study is intended to have some significance for Canadian social history, for the study of the Irish diaspora, and for the history of the Irish homeland. "Significance," however, is a word employed by historians only at their own peril. Like the original shibboleth, it is a litmus test, by which historians of antagonistic methodologies sort out friends from enemies. To quantitative historians of the narrower stripe, the term is usually employed in the sense of statistical significance: when they talk about someone's miscalculation of the significance of an item, they are referring in a very precise way to his having calculated wrongly the degree of accuracy of a given number or set of numbers. Others, especially those social historians who are more interested in chronological changes in the quality of life than in pure statistics, use the term to determine whether something is generally illuminating or is representative of a wider phenomenon. Still other historians, most notably those who concentrate on political history, describe an event or personage as significant or insignificant according to its or his effect upon the shaping of policy or governmental action, particularly at the highest levels. And intellectual historians, when they judge some historical figure to have been insignificant, usually mean that he was stupid, although the delicacy of their craft precludes their using such a commonplace.

Significance, as it concerns this book, and particularly the local study which is its centrepiece, has little to do with the first sense of the word (one has been dealing not with a sample but with an entire, if small, universe), nothing to do with significant figures in intellectual history, and only incidentally points to the significance of the Irish in the political development of the province of Ontario. This study is centrally concerned with showing that an examination of the social and economic chemistry of a specific community

can be of significance by illuminating the history of the Irish in the province of Ontario in particular and in North America in general. David Gagan, in one of the few thuddingly wrong sentences in his fine study of Peel county, declared that his was "not, except incidentally, a piece of local history."[1] In fact, his work was almost entirely a piece of local history, and triumphantly so, and that is why the book is so significant. Given the quality of most local historical writing, it is understandable that Professor Gagan wished to dissociate himself from the local antiquarians and to underscore the fact that his work had a wider purpose than the mere satisfaction of local piety. His work was both a local history and of general significance.

In interpreting the significance of this local study of Leeds and Lansdowne townships, one must first realize that the place was not typical. No community is. Even if one took "typical" to mean "average" and studied only local societies in Ontario that were close to the average on various major indices (population, age, ethnic source, and economic structure), one still would not have analysed a typical community, for most communities were far from being average on all the major indices. The key to interpreting a local study is to discern where on the entire spectrum of the provincial experience the particular locale fit. A set of local studies are like the colours of light that issue from a prism: each is part of the overall provincial picture, but no one colour is typical or average in any meaningful sense. One wants to know where, in the entire visible spectrum, each colour, that is, each community, fit. When the question of significance is posed in that way, it frees the local historian from having to argue that his case-study is more typical (and thus more important) than that of someone else. Collectively, scholars who do local studies are trying to understand the nature of the entire social and economic spectrum of the province, and for this reason the deviant case, the one which swings far to one end or the other of the societal spectrum, is as important as one in the middle, for we must know what the possible range of behaviour is if we are to know where the centre is.

Unhappily, Canadian economic historians have not as yet provided us with a breakdown for the nineteenth century of the various townships in the province on the basis of the leading social and economic indicators. Thus, one has to be satisfied with impressionistically fitting Leeds and Lansdowne into several crude

1 David Gagan, *Hopeful Travellers: Families, Land, and Social Change in Mid-Victorian Peel County, Canada West* (Toronto: University of Toronto Press 1981), xix.

typologies. Taking the date of earliest settlement as an important variable, for instance, one finds that the township did not fall into either the category of original loyalist township or that of late-filled inland area, but instead into a third category, an area on or near the St Lawrence system in which the pioneering work for the main part was done after the beginning of the nineteenth century and which "filled up" sometime in the middle third of the century. (Peel county, the area of Gagan's study, largely falls into this category.) To note another variable, if one looks at urban-rural breakdown in the township, it is clear that there was nothing even resembling a city, but neither was Leeds and Lansdowne the back of beyond. Provincially, in 1871, 78.0 percent of the total population was rural and in the same year 75.2 percent of the inhabitants of Leeds and Lansdowne lived outside Gananoque (the only "urban" centre in the townships).[2] The township, like most in Ontario, lay between two ends of a spectrum, at one extreme the city of Hamilton, representing the most American-style industrialized locality in Ontario, and at the other the lumbering townships of the Shield, in which the population was completely rural and largely seasonal.

This is primarily a study in ethnic history, and therefore discussion has necessarily been excluded of many items of social description that, while fascinating in themselves, are tertiary to this particular exercise.[3] That said, the sequence of local development

2 Compiled and computed from *Census of Canada, 1870–71* 1: 86–145, 252–81, and 358–9. These figures are statistically comparable: the census collected "urban" data by incorporated villages. Gananoque was incorporated, the other small villages in Leeds and Lansdowne were not.

3 Specifically, in the context of Leeds and Lansdowne township, it was found that ethnic history was not illuminated by considering man-land ratios, age profiles, birth and death rates, or age-specific fertility and mortality rates, to name a few. Some of these (such as age-specific death and fertility rates) would be untrustworthy in a population the size of the one here discussed. However, in another context, I hope to take up some of these matters as an aspect of Irish cultural transfer, as pioneered by John J. Mannion in *Irish Settlements in Eastern Canada: A Study of Cultural Transfer and Adaptation* (Toronto: University of Toronto Press 1974).

There is one piece of seemingly relevant inquiry that I have rejected for methodological reasons, the collection of data on transience. This may at first seem surprising: transience is presently a very fashionable topic in Upper Canadian social history and one finds it forced into interstices of otherwise cogent studies of local societies. The degree to which Canadian historians were surprised to discover that there was a good deal of transience in nineteenth-century Ontario is in itself surprising. Can they really have thought that individuals who lived on a continent of frontiers and who often had travelled thousands of miles before even arriving in Upper Canada would simply plop down in one place and remain? Transiency as a phenomenon in itself

charted here for Leeds and Lansdowne township relates to larger issues that transcend the ethnic focus of this volume. Although virtually completed by the time Douglass C. North's brilliant *Structure and Change in Economic History* appeared,[4] the present microstudy can be taken as an almost tailor-made empirical example of many of the theoretical principles which he adumbrates.

North has argued that an absolute requisite for development in western economies has been the obtainment of a secure set of property rights: western economic behaviour proceeds from this basis, not from any abstract ideology. This fundamental process was seen in this microstudy in chapter 2, where it was shown that acquisition of firm title to property was the primary piece of social behaviour upon which all other economic and social arrangements were predicated. Second, North suggests that the first duty demanded of the state by citizens in western societies is to guarantee property rights; thereafter, its job is to protect against anarchy, either economic or social. In chapter 2 of the present study, it was

---

requires attention, but the problem with most studies (and here one must include even Michael Katz's monumental work on Hamilton) is that they tell us little either about transiency or about the communities in which it occurs. Most studies simply note the proportion of a base population which arrives or leaves between two dates, usually dicennial censuses, although a few sophisticated studies use age-cohort data to provide a refined picture.

If, however, we want to know about transiency as a phenomenon, then, instead of counting the number of persons who arrive in and disappear from a given area, we should look at the transients themselves, tracing them through their successive occupations and habitations as they moved about the country. This is incredibly hard work, but the usual attempts to discuss transiency without studying transients are profitless.

Nor does the enumeration of those who disappeared from a given community tell us much about the nature of the community in question. The excessive emphasis upon defining levels of transiency obscures the fact that continuity and stability in the patterns of social evolution characterized most communities despite the continual rotation of population. Below a certain threshold (represented by wholesale out- or in-migration) transience was virtually irrelevant to the way in which an integrated local society operated. The rules stayed the same, even if the players changed. I am reminded of the story told me by an old and delightfully mendacious Irish senachie. He pointed to a hatchet in the corner of his tool shed and said, "That came over with the Norman conquerors." He continued, "It's the very same hatchet, so it is. Yes. Of course it has had a few different heads and handles since then." Communities, especially predominantly rural ones, are like that.

For a methodological analysis of the technical shortcomings of most Upper Canadian transiency studies, see Herbert J. Mays, "'A Place to Stand': Families, Land and Permanence in Toronto Gore Township, 1820–1890," in *Canadian Historical Association: Historical Papers*, 1980: especially 185–7.

4 (New York: W.W. Norton 1981).

shown that the inhabitants' participation in local government was highly conditional and was conducted in a series of individual bargains. Not accidentally, the most important actions of local government agencies (such as the quarter sessions) involved the protection of property rights from trespass, theft, and abuse, and of individuals against disorder and violence.

Of course, ideology has implications for both the preservation and the destruction of any system of property rights, and these implications are many and complex. One relationship, North argues, is for ideology to justify a system of property rights once that system has developed. That is precisely what happened in Leeds and Lansdowne township. As shown in chapter 3, the so-called "loyalist ideology" had its real impact on the distribution of power and property only after the war of 1812. Loyalist ideology was in fact not a primary determinant of economic and social behaviour but was a *post hoc* justification of a system of property and power that had developed independently of political beliefs. Actual behaviour as concerned landed property was shown to be the same for loyalists and nonloyalists alike.

Finally, North suggests that any system of individualistic economics is particularly vulnerable to attack by any group of persons who have a sense of collective identity. This sense of identity can emerge from a conscious ideology (such as revolutionary socialism) or from familial (clan), racial, or ethnic ties which produce a common set of understandings on how a social and economic system should be organized. As discussed in detail in chapter 4 of this book, the Irish in the township, by virtue of their collective identity, produced a virtual revolution in the distribution of power in the local society.

Although the emergence of social class structure is not a major part of North's argument, chapter 6 in the present volume indicates how one form of collective identity can begin to merge into another. In this case, ethnicity was gradually being replaced by ethclass, on the road to the eventual formation of a class-segmented local society. (The completion of this process is beyond the time-boundary of this study.)

Certainly one does not want to overstate the ecumenical significance of a single microstudy, but as encouragement to future scholars who may be contemplating engaging in such a study one may suggest: the great advantage of studying a Canadian community that was erecting anew an economic and social order in the wilderness is that the process brought to the fore, in a clear and

observable fashion, the inherent and central aspects of the western economic and social system of its time.

2

Returning to the narrower issues of Irish ethnicity in Ontario, it is logical to ask, where did Leeds and Lansdowne township fit on the spectrum of Irish settlement in the entire province? The township was not a community created to attract the Irish (like the Peterborough or the Talbot settlements), nor was it one of those in which settlement by the Irish was inhibited by virtue of the community's being established primarily to serve some other national group (as was the Glengarry Scottish settlement). Leeds and Lansdowne was open to the Irish on the same basis as to everyone else. The timing of the filling up of Leeds and Lansdowne meant that not only the industrializing village of Gananoque but the rural areas as well were open both to the pre-Famine Irish migrants and to those who left Ireland because of the Famine.

The proportion of Irish-born in the local population was slightly, but only slightly, higher than that of the province as a whole: in 1842, 18.7 percent of the combined population of the combined townships had been born in Ireland while 16.1 percent of the entire province was Irish-born. In 1871 the corresponding figures were identical: 13.7 percent for the combined townships and for the entire province.[5]

Within the combined townships of Leeds and Lansdowne, the 1871 census showed that 82.2 percent of those of Irish descent lived outside the incorporated village of Gananoque (this is the census definition of "rural"). Throughout the province of Ontario in the same year, 77.5 percent of all those of Irish descent lived in localities that were rural by the same criterion, that is, they lived in the countryside or in small incorporated villages.[6]

This local study has been largely, but not entirely, a piece of rural history and has focused upon the Irish, both Catholic and Protestant, as farmers. This fits well with what has recently become clear about the Irish as a group in the nineteenth century: farming was their most common occupation, at least as of 1871, and almost certainly since loyalist times. Darroch and Ornstein's massive

5 Sources: MS census of 1842, for Leeds and Lansdowne township (AO), 1842 census as found in *Census of Canada, 1871* 4: 136; *Census of the Canadas, 1860–61* 1: 62–3, 178–9.
6 Compiled and computed from *Census of Canada, 1870–71* 1: 86–145, 252–81.

restudy of the 1871 census of Canada revealed that in the province of Ontario 48.1 percent of the Catholics of Irish descent and 59.4 percent of the Protestants of Irish descent were farmers.[7] This was by far the most common occupation; the next most common drew only one-fifth of either cohort. Darroch and Ornstein found that the same conclusion held nationally, with some regional variation. Their work, like the present study, argues against the usual view of the Irish Catholics as having undergone urban proletarianization, and their quietly acid-dipped explanation is worth quotation: "The difference between more conventional interpretations of the class position of Irish Catholics and [their study's] national view would appear to result from exclusion from prior studies of the rural farm and nonfarm population."[8]

Leeds and Lansdowne township was very close to the provincial average in its distribution between urban and rural segments of the population, in its proportion of Irish-born, in the rural residence pattern of those of Irish descent, and in farming as the chief occupation of all those of Irish descent, Protestant and Catholic alike. It is not suggested, however, that the locale was "typical" of the provincial situation. What is being suggested is that, in the fundamental social variables discussed above, Leeds and Lansdowne was roughly somewhere near the middle of the spectrum of possibilities, the extremes of which are defined by the city of Hamilton at one end and the transient lumber camps at the other.

Not surprisingly, given that position on the spectrum, most of the conclusions drawn in this study confirm and illustrate the specific mechanism of certain common patterns. For instance, both in the countryside and in Gananoque, it was shown that place of birth was much more closely related to occupational success than was ethnicity (although it was related by quite different mechanisms in the village and on farmsteads), and this is shown by province-wide studies as well.[9] Given the facts that the local agrarian social-economic system favoured immigrants (they were better off than the native-born), that the system of the industrializing village did not penalize them (immigrants in Gananoque were distributed in nearly the same occupational profile as the native-born), and given that all ethnic groups moved towards the mean as the generations

7 A. Gordon Darroch and Michael D. Ornstein, "Ethnicity and Occupational Structure in Canada in 1871: The Vertical Mosaic in Historical Perspective," *Canadian Historical Review* 61 (September 1980): table 7, 326.

8 Ibid., 314.

9 Ibid., 319.

passed,[10] then it is natural that there should have been very little inter-ethnic conflict in the locality: "if there is an iron law of ethnicity, it is that when ethnic groups are found in a hierarchy of power, wealth, and status, then conflict is inescapable. However, where there is social, economic, and political parity among the constituent groups, ethnic conflict, when it occurs, tends to be at a low level and rarely spills over into violence."[11] As was discussed in chapter 6, ethnic bonds for the most part were quite weak and there was a sharp decline in ethnic affinities among the first generation born in Canada. This makes sense, given the openness of the local economic system: "since the manifestation of ethnic solidarity appears to be a response to the perception of patterns of structural discrimination in the society at large, it is not useful to conceive of it as a traditional or primordial sentiment."[12] The sense of ethnicity faded fast and seems to have remained strong only in small pools of the élite, Scottish Presbyterian businessmen who centred on St Andrew's church in Gananoque and the band of successful Irish Catholic farmers in the countryside.

3

Not everything in the local area was central to the province's social spectrum. In particular, the élite position of the Irish-Catholic farmers is unusual. Fortunately, on this matter it is possible to locate accurately the centre of the province-wide spectrum. This is done through the use of the Canada West Farm Survey, 1861, which

10 Although it relates to a later period (the 1880s), T.W. Acheson's work on the Canadian business élite of the 1880s is both relevant and fascinating: he shows that among Canadian business leaders the native-born were proportionately underrepresented and the immigrants strongly overrepresented. This was the situation which prevailed in Gananoque from the coming of the McDonalds in the 1810s until the 1860s, when the McDonalds began to slip sharply. See T.W. Acheson, "The Social Origins of the Canadian Industrial Elite, 1880–1885," in *Canadian Business History: Selected Studies, 1497–1971* (Toronto: McClelland and Stewart 1972), 147.

11 Stephen Steinberg, *The Ethnic Myth: Race, Ethnicity and Class in America* (New York: Atheneum 1981), 170.

12 Michael Hechter, *Internal Colonialism: The Celtic Fringe in British National Development, 1536–1966* (London: Routledge and Kegan Paul 1975), 340. The opposite case, appertaining to the Irish Americans, in which a high degree of ethnic solidarity is shown to be a function of the discriminatory social-economic structure of the United States, is detailed in Thomas N. Brown's brilliant volume *Irish-American Nationalism, 1870–1890* (Philadelphia: J.B. Lippincott Co. 1966).

TABLE 15

Canada West Farm Survey, 1861

Total Physical Value of Farm

(Land and Buildings, but not including Livestock)

	Irish immigrants			General population			
	Roman Catholic	Non-Roman Catholic	All Irish	All Roman Catholic	All non-Roman Catholic	Entire sample
Less than $1,000	57.1%	42.3%	46.9%	48.1%	29.4%	32.6%
1,000–1,999	18.7	27.9	25.0	26.5	26.6	26.6
2,000–2,999	14.3	14.9	14.7	13.3	15.9	15.4
3,000–3,999	2.2	5.0	4.1	4.4	9.4	8.5
4,000–4,999	4.4	5.5	5.2	5.0	6.6	6.4
Over 5,000	3.3	4.4	4.1	2.7	12.1	10.5
TOTAL	100.0%	100.0%	100.0%	100.0%	100.0%	100.0%
	(N = 91)	(N = 201)	(N = 292)	(N = 181)	(N = 875)	(N = 1,056)

TABLE 16

Canada West Farm Survey, 1861

Farm Progress: Cultivated Acreage as a Percentage of Acreage Occupied

	Irish immigrants			General population			
	Roman Catholic	Non-Roman Catholic	All Irish	All Roman Catholic	All non-Roman Catholic	Entire sample
0–19.9%	27.5%	25.9%	26.4%	26.0%	16.0%	17.7%
20.0–39.9%	22.0	18.4	19.5	18.2	18.4	18.4
40.0–59.9%	24.2	26.9	26.0	27.1	23.7	24.2
60.0–79.9%	9.9	15.9	14.0	14.9	23.5	22.1
Over 80.0%	9.9	7.0	7.9	9.9	12.3	11.9
No information	6.5	5.9	6.2	3.9	6.1	5.7
TOTAL	100.0% (N = 91)	100.0% (N = 201)	100.0% (N = 292)	100.0% (N = 181)	100.0% (N = 875)	100.0% (N = 1,056)

Professor R. Marvin McInnis has assembled and has generously made available for the present study in its relevant portions. McInnis's survey is extremely valuable because of its comparability to the data generated in the present local study. The year 1861 is the only year in which the agricultural census data are in dollar amounts and it was this year that was used as the basis of the analysis of the local farm economy in chapter 5. Further, the Canada West Farm Survey is organized according to farm units rather than by total population (as was the analysis in chapter 5), and on matters such as place of birth and religion the background of the head of household was determinative (again as was done in chapter 5).

Given then that the Canada West Farm Survey is directly comparable to the material in this local study, it has one further virtue: instead of doing a simple random survey, Professor McInnis has developed a "two-stage random sample." This allowed maximizing of the usefulness of a sample of about twelve hundred farm enterprises, and, equally important, guaranteed admission to the examples of the entire spectrum of Ontario townships. All of the approximately 300 Ontario townships were first classified into six strata according to the dates of their initial settlement, and a random selection within each of these strata was made, so that 150 townships in all were selected. Thus, recently or sparsely settled townships were represented as well as the older, more populous ones. Then, within each of the 150 townships, 8 farm households were randomly selected and information on more than 140 variables (some of them derivative but most of them primary) was collected.[13]

Many of these 140 items are fascinating, but for the purpose of this study the ones that count are the various indices of success for the several farm enterprises. These can be distilled down to three: the value of each farm enterprise in terms of land and buildings, the proportion of the land of each enterprise that was cultivated, and the number of non-family members within each farm household (usually an indication of whether a farm operation was large enough to require hired hands).

These data indicate that on the province-wide spectrum (unlike the case of the commercial farms in Leeds and Lansdowne township) Irish immigrants in 1861 were not better off than was the

13 For a detailed description of the procedure see R. Marvin McInnis, "Child-bearing and Land Availability: Some Evidence from Individual Household Data," *Population Patterns in the Past* (Center for Advanced Study in the Behavioral Sciences 1977), 208–13.

TABLE 17
Canada West Farm Survey, 1861
Non-Family Members in Household

	Irish immigrants			General population		
	Roman Catholic	Non-Roman Catholic	All Irish	All Roman Catholic	All non-Roman Catholic	Entire sample
0	80.2%	79.6%	79.8%	76.8%	75.7%	75.8%
1	13.2	14.4	14.1	13.8	14.4	14.3
2	3.3	3.5	3.5	5.5	6.2	6.0
3	1.1	1.0	1.0	2.2	2.5	2.5
4	0.0	0.5	0.3	0.0	0.7	0.6
5	0.0	0.5	0.3	0.0	0.2	0.2
6	1.1	0.0	0.3	0.6	0.1	0.2
7	1.1	0.5	0.7	1.1	0.2	0.4
TOTAL	100.0%	100.0%	100.0%	100.0%	100.0%	100.0%
	(N = 91)	(N = 201)	(N = 292)	(N = 181)	(N = 875)	(N = 1,056)

general population; and Irish-Catholic immigrants were not more successful, as measured by these indices, than were Irish-Protestant immigrants.

This does not mean that the Leeds and Lansdowne situation was ephemeral, by virtue of its being atypical, any more than the proximity of the township to the average of the several social indicators mentioned earlier made it typical and therefore important. Clearly, with regard to the Irish-born commercial farmers, Leeds and Lansdowne township represents one important type of social chemistry, no less real for its difference from the average. Doubtless there were other townships which, because of their social and economic patterns and the timing of their development, also attracted immigrants with capital and high abilities. Townships of this sort will determine one end of a spectrum of receptivity *vis-à-vis* immigrants, and the other end those localities where social and economic filters severally discriminated against new immigrants. One awaits further local studies and reminds oneself of the message implicit in tables 15, 16, and 17, that within the province an extraordinary range of success was possible, which is to say that a wide range of economic and social configurations was extant.[14]

5

Can a discussion of the Irish as a rural people in Ontario contribute anything of significance to the literature on the Irish diaspora, particularly on the Irish in North America? According to one of the most accomplished historians at present teaching in American universities, "Americans cannot understand their own history without understanding Canadian history."[15] Well over a century earlier, Thomas D'Arcy McGee, one of the few Canadian Irishmen with whom American historians are acquainted, noted, "the ignorance as to the United States in Ireland is only equalled by the

14 For local studies which help to place the Leeds and Lansdowne Irish on the province-wide spectrum, see three valuable studies: Julian Gwyn, "The Irish in Eastern Ontario: The Social Structure of Huntley Township in Carleton County, 1851–71," in *Exploring Our Heritage: The Ottawa Valley Experience*, ed. Vrenia Ivonoffski and Sandra Campbell (Arnprior: Arnprior and District Historical Society 1980), 20–31; Glen J. Lockwood, *Montague: A Social History of an Irish Ontario Township 1783–1980* (Smiths Falls: Corporation of the Township of Montague 1980); and Enoch Padolsky and Ian Pringle, *A Historical Source Book for the Ottawa Valley* (Ottawa: The Linguistic Survey of the Ottawa Valley 1981).
15 Robin Winks, *The Relevance of Canadian History: U.S. and Imperial Perspectives* (Toronto: Macmillan 1979), 60.

ignorance as to Canada in the United States."[16] Thus, one may be emboldened to ask, is it not possible that the experience of the Irish in Ontario casts some doubts on the adequacy of the most generally accepted analyses of the Irish migrants south of the border?

In particular, a central strand in the historiography of the Irish Catholics in America explains that they settled largely in cities because they were incapable of doing otherwise. (The presence of some Irish Catholics in the countryside sometimes is admitted in passing, but they are noted as deviants from the urban norm.) In an essay in a major volume on the Irish-American identity commissioned for the American Bicentennial of 1976, Lawrence McCaffrey, one of the most active historians in the field, states; "Unequipped to cope with the challenges of large-scale American farming and unwilling to confront the isolation of existence in the vastness of rural America, most Irish immigrants preferred to congregate in cities as the pioneers of the American urban ghetto."[17] Elsewhere, McCaffrey has elaborated: "Lack of work skills was far more important than a shortage of funds in determining the Irish-Americans' decision to become city dwellers. Because manorialism and serfdom had not encouraged agrarian skills or knowledge, Irish peasants were among the most inefficient farmers in Europe and were not equipped for life in rural America. Irish agriculture traditionally was more a cultural life-style than an economic system, and Irish peasants still used only simple tools – the spade, the scythe, and the hoe."[18] Although various historians argue which factor was more important, these quotations illustrate what in bare

16 Thomas D'Arcy McGee, *The Irish Position in British and Republic North America: A Letter to the Editors of the Irish Press, Irrespective of Party* (Montreal: M. Longwood and Cox 1866), 14.

17 Lawrence J. McCaffrey, "A Profile of Irish America," in *America and Ireland, 1776–1976: The American Identity and the Irish Connection*, ed. David N. Doyle and Owen Dudley Edwards (Proceedings of the United States Bicentennial Conference of Cumann Merriman, Ennis August 1976), 81.

18 Lawrence J. McCaffrey, *The Irish Diaspora in America* (Bloomington: Indiana University Press 1976), 63.
   Citation of McCaffrey's view as representative of the opinion of most historians of the Irish Catholics in nineteenth-century America is not endorsement of his judgments. In particular, the description of Irish farmers as the most inefficient in Europe is acceptable only if one adopts highly anachronistic criteria of agricultural efficiency (such as total output in relation to labour input). In fact, given the Irish problem (which was simply to feed a burgeoning population) the Irish farmers were amazingly efficient. They undoubtedly produced more calories per acre than did the English "high farmers." Indeed, if the primary criterion of efficiency is the calories of consumable foodstuffs produced per acre, then the highly labour-intensive Irish potato culture was

bones would be the generally accepted explanation of why the Catholic Irish in the United States did not settle in rural areas and did not farm: they were too technologically backward to farm in the New World; and they had a cultural drive to live in close physical proximity to others of their sort, rather than upon isolated farmsteads.[19]

All this has been put forward literally scores, perhaps hundreds, of times by serious scholars. Yet the case of Canada is unsettling, for it shows that in the same period in which the Irish Catholics in America were allegedly ghettoized most of those in Canada – not just Ontario – were settling in rural areas and that much their most frequent occupation was farming.[20] The Catholics of Irish birth or of Irish descent in Canada (especially those in Ontario) were *not* too technically backward to farm in the New World and did *not* have an overwhelming cultural drive to live in close proximity to one another. They *were* capable of facing life on lonely farmsteads and *were* able to accumulate enough capital to become commercial farmers. On the surface at least, this poses a problem: is it possible that those explanations of Irish-Catholic behaviour in America which posit certain inherent technological, cultural, and therefore economic limits on the behaviour of the Irish Catholics in the nineteenth century are wrong?

It is possible to argue that the cases of Canada and the United States are not perfectly comparable, and there is some justification in such a contention: the Irish Catholics in Canada may have had proportionally more of their members arrive before the Famine than did their counterparts in the United States. This, however, is hardly

---

probably the most – not the least – efficient in Europe. Whether the Irish farmer could change from intensive farming in the Old World to extensive farming in the New World is an entirely different question and has nothing to do with the relative efficiency of Irish agriculture.

19 Two decades ago, a third, generally agreed, point of explanation would have been mentioned, that the Irish either did not or could not accumulate enough capital to enter the American agicultural economy. This belief in the capital-bereft position of the Irish Catholic stemmed chiefly from the work of Oscar Handlin. It has been so widely questioned by recent studies as to have been virtually disproved. For an acute summary, see Cormac O'Grada, "Irish Emigration to the United States in the Nineteenth Century," in Doyle and Edwards, 97–8. The classic indication of the high propensity of Irish-born persons to acquire real property is found in Stephan Thernstrom's *Poverty and Progress: Social Mobility in a Nineteenth Century City* (Cambridge: Harvard University Press 1964), especially 156–7.

20 Analysis of the 1871 census shows that only in Nova Scotia was farming not the most common occupation of Irish Catholics. There they most often were semi-skilled workers (Darroch and Ornstein, table 7, 376).

a sufficient explanation of the Irish-Canadian Catholics and the Irish-American Catholics seemingly acting as if they were members of different species. Any suggestion that the Canadian experience is an inapposite comparison to the American must come down to an assertion (necessarily disguised to make it palatable to Americans) that among the Irish-Catholic migrants to North America, Canada received the winners and the United States the losers. Canada received those who were able to adapt to forms of agricultural technology unknown in the home country, had the character to overcome the insecurity of living in physical isolation in the countryside, and in addition had the tenacity to amass enough resources to enter commercial farming. This is hard to accept, but, unless one is willing to argue that the difference between Canada and the United States with regard to Irish Catholics was simply the difference between winners and losers, and unless one can also specify the set of mechanisms that resulted in such an efficient social sorting between the two countries in the New World, then one must agree that the two groups are indeed legitimately comparable and, perforce, that the Canadian experience is a valid laboratory case which permits testing – and, in the actual event, disproving – of the generally accepted explanations of Irish-Catholic behaviour in the United States in the nineteenth century. If it is indeed true that only a tiny fraction of the Irish-Catholic immigrants and their descendants in the United States settled in rural areas and even fewer actually farmed,[21] then the explanation

21 This, of course, is a major supposition and one for which the empirical data are surprisingly weak. The standard technique in documenting the residential and occupational structure of the Irish immigrants and their descendants in the United States is to use official federal census data. The problem with this approach is that the United States censuses are a very weak source of data on matters of ethnicity and religion. Consider, specifically,
  1 that no question regarding an individual's definition of his own ethnicity was asked until 1970 and even then it was misprocessed and therefore useless;
  2 that no information on the religious affiliation of specific individuals *ever* has been collected and published.
  Further note
  1 that from 1790–1840 inclusive no question concerning the place of birth of the inhabitants of the United States and territories was asked;
  2 that, therefore, only from 1850 onwards does one have data on the Irish born in the United States. This date, crucially, is post-Famine, so that one lacks knowledge of the base-line set by the normal migration which preceded the Famine years;
  3 that only in 1880 was a quasi-ethnic item introduced and then it had to do with where one's mother and father were born. Thus (a) all individuals of the second generation born in the United States were officially without

must lie in circumstances specific to the United States, not factors of cultural background vaguely ascribable to the Old Country.

One hesitates to go farther, especially in view of Professor McCaffrey's stricture that "only Irish-Americans can fully appreciate the nuances of the American-Irish experience."[22] (An intellectual revenge, one suspects, of the old placard "no Irish need apply"), but the Canadian experience may suggest to historians of the Irish in America another point, that Irish Protestants existed and that many of them migrated to the New World. "Irish-American" is a code-phrase for Irish Catholic and discussions of the Irish in the United States usually devote a small section, or a footnote, to mention of the "Scotch-Irish," a group of Presbyterians from Ulster, most of whom settled in rural areas in the late eighteenth and early nineteenth centuries and whom the author of the study in question then proceeds to ignore. This is quadruply damaging to an understanding of the phenomenon of the Irish in the New World. In the first instance, refusal to integrate the Scotch-Irish into the general story of Irish ethnicity in the United States is harmful not only because it obliterates an important part of the story but because it robs the history of the Irish in North America of a valuable set of natural comparisons between sub-sets of Irishmen who settled in the United States. Third, and perhaps more misleading, the ritual reference to the Scotch-Irish has permitted the erection of an invisible but seemingly impermeable time barrier: it

---

ethnicity and (b) an individual, of whatever generation, had no opportunity to express what he felt his own ethnicity to be. Moreover, even given the information which the United States officials did collect,

1 they did not cross-tabulate the quasi-ethnic item (that is, mother's and father's birthplaces) with any other variable whatsoever;

2 only from 1860 onwards does one find a cross-tabulation of place of birth with residency in certain large urban areas (this does not, however, constitute a thorough rural/urban breakdown of the foreign-born);

3 and only for 1870 and thereafter were the data on occupations and place of birth cross-tabulated.

This means that in the nineteenth century we know very little about the whole range of the Irish-born population as to religion, occupation, and place of residence, even less for the first generation born in the United States, and virtually nothing at all for the second and subsequent generations born in America. One can find easily several studies of urban-concentrated Irish communities in the nineteenth century, many of them excellent; but studies of concentrated populations of the Irish in America tell nothing about the range of their dispersal. For a discussion of the primary sources available, see Donald H. Akenson, "An Agnostic View of the Historiography of the Irish-Americans," *labour/le travailleur* (forthcoming, fall 1984).

22 McCaffrey, *The Irish Diaspora*, 181.

is assumed that, once the Famine starts, the only significant emigration from Ireland to America is by Catholics. Naturally, if one assumes that Protestant migration is nonexistent from the mid-nineteenth century onwards, one is unlikely to find evidence of its having occurred. Yet the Canadian data make it abundantly clear that Irish Protestants continued to emigrate in sizable numbers and the Ontario data show that they comprised roughly two-thirds of the migrants to that part of the world both before and after the Famine. Certainly, the proportion of Irish Protestants migrating to the United States was much, much lower, but, concerning the numbers of people, is it reasonable to suggest that the Famine actually reduced the number of Protestants migrating to the United States? Many of the Protestants in the Old Country were severely hurt by the Famine, and that great catastrophe can only have increased their migrant flow, just as it did that of the Catholics. Only if one is willing to make the tendentious argument that almost all the Irish Protestants went to Canada can one have even an attenuated excuse for ignoring Irish-Protestant immigrants into the United States, from the Famine onwards. Fourth, the usual throw-away reference to the Scotch-Irish in America encourages the false equation of Irish Protestant with Ulster-Scottish Presbyterian. The data from the Old Country, however, make abundantly clear that most Irish Protestants were Anglicans, who tended to be chiefly, but not entirely, of English ancestry. From the Canadian data we know that Irishmen of Anglican background were more frequent migrants, at least to that part of the New World, than were the Presbyterians.[23] Unless one wishes to posit that almost all the Irish Protestants of Anglican background went to Canada and virtually none to the United States, one must consider that perhaps a very significant segment of the ethnic history of the Irish in America has been allowed virtually to disappear.[24]

23 See Darroch and Ornstein, table 1, 312.
24 Chronicling the post-Famine Protestant migrants to the United States, especially the Anglicans, is a very difficult task. It is made more difficult because Protestant migration formed a thinner and a more scattered stream than did the Catholic. The only reliable way to find out the probable ranges and character of Protestant participation in the Irish diaspora is by a study which begins neither with civic boundaries as its limits (that is, with cities), nor with the census tabulations of place of birth, but with the actual immigrants. One needs a longitudinal study of a large body of Irish immigrants to the United States (4,000–5,000 would be the minimum acceptable) which identifies immigrants by their religion and traces the individual immigrants throughout their lives. This is an immense amount of work but no more so than computer-aided studies that are being done elsewhere.

Thus, one of the values of the Canadian case to historians of the American Irish may simply be to remind them that, just as the Irish polity in the homeland included both Catholics and Protestants, so the chronicle of those persons of Irish ethnicity in the New World must include all Irishmen, Catholic and Protestant alike.

6

It is on the vexed matter of the alleged differences between Protestants and Catholics that the Canadian case, particularly that of Ontario, may indirectly shed light on the history of Ireland itself. Perspective on the difference between the Catholics and Protestants in nineteenth-century Ireland is extremely difficult to achieve. It is easy to caricature the situation and thus suggest that the two main groups had nothing in common. Certainly, if one takes at face value the statements and actions of many nineteenth-century Irish Catholics and Protestants, one could easily conclude that they were as different from each other as good and evil. Yet at our distance in time the intriguing point is not that they were fighting with each other but that they were fighting by the same rules. Just as the precondition of a boxing match is that both fighters accept the same assumptions about the nature of their temporary squared universe and what one properly can and cannot do in it, so Protestants and Catholics in nineteenth-century Ireland shared a fundamental agreement on the nature of their world and on what counted in it.

I first became aware of this several years ago when I was completing the last volume of a trilogy on the history of Irish education in the nineteenth and twentieth centuries. The nurturing of children is an issue central to any society, and Catholics and Protestants fought viciously about education in the nineteenth century and again, after Partition, in the twentieth. Gradually, what long should have been obvious dawned on me: that the two sides were fighting not because of their differences but because of what they held in common. Both major groups agreed that the education of children was at the heart of the maintenance of their own cultural system, that schooling was related to universally accepted assumptions that the child, as a sufferer from Original Sin, was imperfect and had to be led to salvation, that religion had to be inculcated, and that, therefore, religious authorities had a prerogative to primary influence upon the educational system. This agreement marked the Irish as radically different from most Europeans (who increasingly viewed education in economic, not theological, terms), and from the American practice in most states.

Flail at each other though they did, Irish Catholics and Irish Protestants resembled each other more than anybody else.

To see the nineteenth-century Irish in this light is to run against the grain of some very adept and thoughtful recent historical writing. For example, in an issue of *Irish Historical Studies*, Kerby A. Miller recently has presented an intricate and erudite argument concerning the way in which linguistic, religious, and other cultural determinants of individual behaviour account for the difference in success of the Irish Catholics and Irish Protestants in North America. His argument has many facets, but the operational kernel of his thesis is this: "Our sources suggest that during the age of migration, 1790–1922, many Catholic Irish were more communal, dependent, fatalistic and prone to accept conditions passively than were the Protestants they encountered in either Ireland or America; and less individualistic, independent, optimistic and given to initiative than were these Protestants. In short, they were more sensitive to the weight of tradition than to innovative possibilities for the future. Indeed their perspectives were so pre-modern that to observers from modern business cultures, they often seemed 'irresponsible,' even 'feckless' or adolescent."[25] If this is true, then one has both a primary definition of the difference between Protestant and Catholic cultures in Ireland and an explanation of their quite different behaviour in the United States.

No matter how elegant an hypothesis may be, however, it has to face the same cruel cry as any other speculation: test it! Ideally, one should find a laboratory that is clean, that is, one which is neutral and in which empirical tests can be made fairly so that the results are expressed in terms of legitimate comparisons. Here, nineteenth-century Ontario in particular, but all of Canada if one wishes a wider arena, is useful.[26] Here one can test empirically the behaviour of Irishmen of both major cultures in a setting outside the homeland (that is, in a laboratory). Here one can observe a fair competition between Protestant and Catholic Irish in the sense that (unlike the homeland) there were no direct legacies of penal laws against either group, and here one may observe roughly comparable social groups: emigrants, Protestants, and Catholics alike tended to be neither

25 Kerby A. Miller, "Emigrants and Exiles: Irish Cultures and Irish Emigration to North America, 1790–1922," *Irish Historical Studies* 22 (September 1980): 105.
26 For a discussion of the usefulness of Canadian census data to historians of Ireland, see C.J. Houston and W.J. Smyth, "The Irish Abroad: Better Questions through a Better Source, the Canadian Census," *Irish Geography* 13 (1980): 1–19.

predominantly paupers nor well-off. For the purpose of this empirical test they can be thought of simply as belonging to a single "emigrant class." The number of Irish subjects who were tested in this laboratory numbered several hundred thousand.

In this test, the hypothesis that there were cultural differences between the two major religious groups in the homeland, differences so crucial as to relate to their fundamental economic orientation, is disproved. As discussed earlier, the evidence of Darroch and Ornstein, of the Canada West Farm Survey, and of this present study shows that Catholics and Protestants shared the same most common fundamental occupation (farming), the same ambience (rural), and the same familiar environment (most often the isolated Canadian farmstead), and that, although Protestant Irish farmers did slightly better overall than did the Catholic Irish, the difference was not overwhelming and there was a great deal of local variation. Further, there was a large Catholic, as well as Protestant, rural bourgeoisie. The only situation in which Irish Catholics and Irish Protestants behaved differently was in the major cities (where only a small proportion of each cohort lived) and there, as in the United States, the Catholics were markedly less successful than the Protestants. That, however, is merely a qualification to the overall conclusion that, basically, Irish Protestants and Catholics shared the same approach to the New World and exhibited roughly equal abilities in confronting its difficulties.

How can it be that competent, serious historians of Ireland have generally overestimated the difference between the Catholic and Protestant components of nineteenth-century Irish culture? One suspects that this has occurred because reification of culture is endemic to Irish historical writing; that is, culture (and its Irish subcomponents, Irish-Catholic culture and the two Protestant variants, Anglo-Irish culture and Ulster-Scots culture) is treated as something that has a life of its own, which is a direct cause of events, and which is itself mysteriously independent of the other aspects of life. It is very easy to fall into this trap, especially concerning a country in which a theological sensibility has been important, in which dogma has been omnipresent, and in which most inhabitants (now as then) view the visible world as a mere crystallization of a greater invisible reality. It is natural to analyse the differences between Protestants and Catholics in the visible world as in some way derivative from their views concerning the invisible one, and it is natural to tack on to religion the associated matters of language, superstititions, folk culture, and so on. How else, indeed, shall one proceed?

Instead the possibility may be considered that what appear to have been primarily culturally determined differences between Catholics and Protestants in nineteenth-century Ireland possibly were direct reflections of economic "class" (or whatever one wishes to term economic position and status in a pre-industrial society). This is not to say that there are not meaningful and fascinating differences among the cultures of Gaelic speakers, of the descendants of the Lowland Scots, and of the derivatives of English planters, and certainly these matters are intrinsically worthy of attention; nor is it being forgotten that religion in the form of the Protestant imposition of the eighteenth-century penal laws was the direct cause of the low economic position of many Irish Catholics in the nineteenth century. Nevertheless, it may be predicted that if one were to study comparable groups of Protestants and Catholics (agricultural labourers, small farmers, provincial businessmen, and so on) one would find that their behaviour and achievement in fundamental matters of economics and social adaptation were very similar. Indeed, they would be found to have acted more like each other than like their coreligionists who had markedly different class origins. Historians of Ireland have interpreted as being cultural differences between Protestant and Catholic which really are a function of the quite different economic-class profiles of the two groups.

Religious differences were undeniably real and important in nineteenth-century Ireland; equally undeniably, the differences in dogma, liturgy, and devotional enthusiasm among the various Irish faiths were significant. But these matters have to be kept in perspective. If historians really wish to chart accurately the differences between Protestants and Catholics, they would do well to start by isolating comparable economic groups and then running empirical tests not on how they talked but on how they behaved and on what they achieved. That, certainly, is one lesson which the data on the Irish migrants to Canada teach.

If there is any single lesson of this study that ought to be underlined, it is that the Irish-Catholic migrant to the New World was much quicker, more technologically adaptive, more economically alert, and much less circumscribed by putative cultural limits inherited from the Old Country than is usually believed. That knowledge is one direct benefit of studying the Irish in Ontario.

Appendix A
Aggregate Census Data

There is an oral tradition which holds that the census data for Ontario prior to 1851 are very shaky. This may be true, or it may not, as these comments stem from people who have done local studies and there has been no general study of the material on a province-wide basis which would allow us to correct local returns for systematic distortions in the procedure. Thus, a judgment of the usefulness of the data for any given township must be made for that township on the basis of internal evidence and whatever corroborating material one can find.

The pre-1851 censuses were compiled by a local civic official, usually the same person who tallied the assessment information or at least someone who was in close contact with the chief assessor. Hence, the first questions one must ask in a local context are, does it appear that the census data were based directly on the assessment data, or was the enumeration compiled separately? Ideally, there should be a fundamental similarity between assessment and census rolls, but the census should include a larger number of heads of households, because there was a time-lag before new residents found their way on to the tax rolls. This was the case in both the front and rear of Leeds and Lansdowne township.

A second question needs to be asked in evaluating the local enumerations: how do they mesh with the agricultural censuses of 1842 and 1848? Those two enumerations were conducted on a much wider information base and with much greater care than the annual enumerations. It is especially important for a rural study that the 1842 and 1848 censuses clearly included tenants as well as owner-occupiers, a fact which provides a valuable check on whether tenant farmers had been excluded or under-reported in the ordinary annual census of the locale. In the case of Leeds and Lansdowne township, the census for the rear of the township for 1848 is missing, but there is a very close relationship between the extant agricultural censuses and the ordinary ones and it is reasonable to conclude that, at least from the mid-1830s, the annual enumerations quite faithfully report the entire permanent population, whether owner or tenant. Transients, on the other hand, seem to have slipped through the statistical net. This is not fatal to the usefulness of the census material, as

long as one continually reminds oneself of both what the data include and what they exclude.

Of course there are finite problems with the annual enumerations and these will vary from township to township. Successive enumerators presented the data in varying ways (for instance, in some years the deaf and dumb and insane were enumerated separately) but these problems are not insuperable. Nor is the fact that the annual census date often varied from year to year and in fact often is not specified. Such distortion would be significant in province-wide studies but in a microstudy is virtually irrelevant.

Too much mention of the limitations of the data is apt to obscure their virtues. Although the data of a given township in Upper Canada often are not compatible with those compiled for a neighbouring one, the data *within* a township are at least compatible with themselves over long stretches of time. In Leeds and Lansdowne, for instance, local officials stayed on the job year after year and kept doing things in the same way year by year. Fortuitously, a useful "control" was introduced for Leeds and Lansdowne in that in 1840–2 the long-serving clerk of the Johnstown district, James Jessup, compiled a set of abstracts for the district going back to the earliest enumerations. This abstract can be checked against the originals and one finds that for a few years Jessup judged the censuses to have been compiled in a manner incompatible with that of the general run of data. In most instances, the deviations came in the definition of sub-categories of the population.

The reader will notice that I have not included a series for population of the entire Johnstown district. This is not because of the boundary changes in the district (see the notes on these changes in the introductory comments to Appendix B), for these can be understood easily enough, but because the Johnstown totals very often were incomplete. It was not at all uncommon for an entire township to be left out in a certain year or for one or two townships to report their data in a form incompatible with the practice accepted in the district as a whole. There are years for which the Johnstown figures are complete and compatible but not enough to permit the compilation of a time series.

The aggregate census data for several, but not all, of the censuses of the Johnstown district in the period 1824–49 inclusive are found in the *Journals of the Legislative Assembly*, as follows: 1828, Appendix; 1829, Appendix 5; 1830, Appendix; 1831, Appendix; 1831–2, Appendix; 1832–3, Appendix; 1835, Appendix, vol. 2, no. 41; 1836, Appendix, vol. 1, no. 46; 1836–7, Appendix no. 8; 1837–8, Appendix; 1839, Appendix, vol. 2, pt. 1; 1839–40, Appendix, vol. 1, pt. 1; 1841, Appendix T; 1842, Appendix GG.

One should, however, refer to the manuscript copies of the returns, not only to fill in all the years before 1824 and those missing after 1824 but to resolve the arithmetical errors in published totals which sometimes occur. A number of census abstracts for 1802–42 inclusive made by James Jessup, clerk of the Johnstown district, are found in the Archives of Ontario in the F.P. Smith papers. Also, several census abstracts are found in the Archives of Ontario, RG 22, ser 7, vol. 59-D, "General Quarter Sessions. Johnstown District, Sundry Municipal Papers." A complete tabulation of all the

townships of the Johnstown district for the 1842 agricultural census is found in the F.P. Smith papers in the Archives of Ontario.

The manuscript versions of the population returns, giving data on specific individuals as well as (in most instances) township aggregates are found in the Archives of Ontario, RG 21, Municipal Records, Section A, "Census Roll of the Municipalities in the United Counties of Leeds and Grenville," under the following titles: "Leeds and Lansdowne front division, 1805, inhabitants numbered," "[Illeg.] of the Population of the front of the township of Lansdowne and of Leeds for the year 1806," "A Return of the population of the front of Leeds and Lansdowne in the district of Johnstown for the year 1813," "Lansdowne front, April 10th, 1819," "Population, 1820," "A return of the population of the front of Leeds and Lansdowne for the year 1821," "1823, Population of Leeds and Lansdowne front," "Front for Leeds, 1824, March 13," "Returns of the population in front of the townships of Lansdowne and Leeds for the year 1825," "Return of the population in front of Leeds and Lansdowne for the year 1826," "Return of Census for front of Lansdowne and Leeds for 1827," "Census for the front of Leeds and Lansdowne for the year 1828," "Return of the population [illeg.] Return of the township of Leeds and Lansdowne in front for 1831," "Return of the population for the front of Lansdowne for the year of our Lord one thousand eight hundred and thirty-three," "Return of the population for the front of Leeds for the year of our Lord one thousand and thirty-three [sic]," "List of the census of the township of Leeds and Lansdowne in front for 1839," "List of the census of the township of Leeds and Lansdowne [front] for 1840," "List of the census of the township of Leeds and Lansdowne in front for 1841," "Return of the enumeration of the inhabitants of the front of Leeds and Lansdowne for the year 1842," "List of the census of the township of Leeds and Lansdowne in front for 1844," "List of the census of the township of Leeds and Lansdowne in front for 1845," "Return of the inhabitants of front of Leeds [and Lansdowne] (1848)."

For the rear of Leeds and Lansdowne, see the same Archives of Ontario series, under the following titles: "A List of the population of the rear end of Lansdowne for the year 1806," "A List of the population of the rear end of Leeds for the year 1806," "A List of the population of the rear end of Lansdowne for the year 1807," "A List of the population of the rear end of Leeds for the year 1807," "List of the number of inhabitants 1818" (copy partially illegible), "The no. of inhabitants for the rear of Lansdowne and Leeds for the year 1809" (copy partially illegible), "A List of the number of inhabitants in the rear of Lansdowne and Leeds for the year 1810" (copy partially illegible), "A List of the number of inhabitants contained in the rear of Lansdowne and Leeds for the year 1811," "Population of the inhabitants in the rear of Lansdowne and Leeds for the year 1812, the 15 of May" (copy partially illegible), "Return of the population of the rear of Lansdowne and Leeds in the district of Johnstown for the year 1813," "A report of the population of the rear end of Lansdowne and Leeds for the year 1814," "Return of the population of the rear, Leeds and Lansdowne in the district of Johnstown for the year 1815," "Return of the population of the rear of Leeds and Lansdowne in the district of Johnstown for the

year 1816," "[illeg. title and largely illegible copy] 1819," "A return of the Souls in the rear of Leeds and Lansdowne taken on the [illeg.] of March 1820," "[illegible title, 1821]," "Return of the population in the rear of the township of Leeds and Lansdowne in the year 1823," "Return of the population of the rear of Leeds and Lansdowne for the year 1824," "[return is incomplete] Return of the population of the township of Leeds and Lansdowne [rear] for the year 1825," "[untitled return 1826]," "A list of the inhabitants in the rear of the township of Leeds and Lansdowne, 1827," "[untitled return, 1828]," "Rear of Lansdowne and Leeds, 1829." "Names of heads of families in rear of Lansdowne [and Leeds] for the year 1830," "Names of heads of families [in rear of Leeds and Lansdowne, 1831]," "Census for the year of township of Lansdowne and Leeds commenced on the first Monday in January 1832," "The number of inhabitants in the rear of the township of Leeds [and Lansdowne, 1833]," "Names of heads of families [in rear of Leeds and Lansdowne, 1838]" (partially illegible), "List of the census of the township of rear of Lansdowne and Leeds for 1839," "List of the census of the township of rear Leeds and Lansdowne for 1840," (partially illegible) "List of the census of the township of rear of Leeds and Lansdowne for 1841," "List of the census of the township of Leeds and Lansdowne (in rear) for 1844," "List of the census of the township of Leeds and Lansdowne (in rear) for 1845."

TABLE A1
Aggregate Census Data:
Front and Rear of Leeds and Lansdowne Township, 1803–49

1803	Front	Rear	Combined
Total population		176	

1805			
Male children	29		
Adult males	34		
Female children	36		
Adult females	26		
Subtotal: males	63		
Subtotal: females	62		
Subtotal: children	65		
Subtotal: adults	60		
Total population	125	236	361

1806			
Male children	31		
Adult males	36		
Female children	36		
Adult females	27		
Subtotal: males	67		
Subtotal: females	63		
Subtotal: children	67		
Subtotal: adults	63		
Total population	130	229	359

1807			
Total population		304	

1808			
Total population	168		

1811			
Subtotal: children		114	
Subtotal: adults		80	
Total population		194	

1813			
Male children		79	
Adult males		52	
Female children		60	
Adult females		51	
Subtotal: males		131	
Subtotal: females		111	
Subtotal: children		139	
Subtotal: adults		103	
Total population		242	

1814	Front	Rear	Combined
Total population		249	
1815			
Male children		89	
Adult males		57	
Female children		76	
Adult females		64	
Subtotal: males	115	146	261
Subtotal: females	104	140	244
Subtotal: children		165	
Subtotal: adults		121	
Total population	219	286	505
1816			
Male children		98	
Adult males		73	
Female children		75	
Adult females		69	
Subtotal: males		171	
Subtotal: females		144	
Subtotal: children		173	
Subtotal: adults		142	
Total population		315	
1819			
Subtotal: males		166(?)	
Subtotal: females		148(?)	
Total population	167	314(?)	481(?)
1820			
Male children	141	134	275
Adult males	90	73	163
Female children	121	111	232
Adult females	78	66	144
Subtotal: males	231	207	438
Subtotal: females	199	177	376
Subtotal: children	262	245	507
Subtotal: adults	168	139	307
Total population	430	384	814
1821			
Male children	164	145	309
Adult males	137	76	213
Female children	131	115	246
Adult females	102	78	180
Subtotal: males	301	221	522
Subtotal: females	233	193	426
Subtotal: children	295	260	555
Subtotal: adults	239	154	393
Total population	534	414	948

1823	Front	Rear	Combined
Male children	177	172	349
Adult males	110	91	201
Female children	142	134	276
Adult females	88	89	177
Subtotal: males	287	263	550
Subtotal: females	230	223	453
Subtotal: children	319	306	625
Subtotal: adults	198	180	378
Total population	517	486	1,003
1824			
Males under 16	161	114	275
Males 16 & over	201	151	352
Females under 16	120	118	238
Females 16 & over	128	115	243
Subtotal: males	362	265	627
Subtotal: females	248	233	481
Subtotal: under 16	281	232	513
Subtotal: 16 & over	329	266	595
Total population	610	498	1,108
1825			
Males under 16	167	137	304
Males 16 & over	179	178	357
Females under 16	126	138	264
Females 16 & over	140	113	253
Subtotal: males	346	315	661
Subtotal: females	266	251	517
Subtotal: under 16	293	275	568
Subtotal: 16 & over	319	291	610
Total population	612	566	1,178
1826			
Males under 16	134	143	277
Males 16 & over	139	165	304
Females under 16	202	138	340
Females 16 & over	156	127	283
Subtotal: males	273	308	581
Subtotal: females	358	265	623
Subtotal: under 16	336	281	617
Subtotal: 16 & over	295	292	587
Total population	631	573	1,204
1827			
Males under 16	156	135	291
Males 16 & over	189	157	346
Females under 16	126	130	256
Females 16 & over	126	125	251
Subtotal: males	345	292	637
Subtotal: females	252	255	507
Subtotal: under 16	282	265	547
Subtotal: 16 & over	315	282	597
Total population	597	547	1,144

1828	Front	Rear	Combined
Males under 16	175	159	334
Males 16 & over	236	215 (?)	451 (?)
Females under 16	152	157	309
Females 16 & over	149	138	287
Subtotal: males	411	374 (?)	785 (?)
Subtotal: females	301	295	596
Subtotal: under 16	327	316	643
Subtotal: 16 & over	385	353 (?)	738 (?)
Total population	712	669 (?)	1,381 (?)
1829			
Males under 16	189	139	328
Males 16 & over	208	183	391
Females under 16	156	161	317
Females 16 & over	156	140	296
Subtotal: males	397	322	719
Subtotal: females	312	301	613
Subtotal: under 16	345	300	645
Subtotal: 16 & over	364	323	687
Total population	709	623	1,332
1830			
Males under 16	184	158	342
Males 16 & over	195	199	394
Females under 16	152	156	308
Females 16 & over	161	148	309
Subtotal: males	379	357	736
Subtotal: females	313	304	617
Subtotal: under 16	336	314	650
Subtotal: 16 & over	356	347	703
Total population	692	661	1,353
1831			
Males under 16	196	180	376
Males 16 & over	301	238	539
Females under 16	177	193	370
Females 16 & over	192	194	386
Subtotal: males	497	418	915
Subtotal: females	369	387	756
Subtotal: under 16	373	373	746
Subtotal: 16 & over	493	432	925
Total population	866	805	1,671
1832			
Males under 16	237	212	449
Males 16 & over	339	223	562
Females under 16	226	203	429
Females 16 & over	223	204	427
Subtotal: males	576	435	1,011
Subtotal: females	449	407	856
Subtotal: under 16	463	415	878
Subtotal: 16 & over	562	427	989
Total population	1,025	842	1,867

1833	Front	Rear	Combined
Males under 16	291	221	512
Males 16 & over	367	227	594
Females under 16	261	208	469
Females 16 & over	251	196	447
Subtotal: males	658	448	1,106
Subtotal: females	512	404	916
Subtotal: under 16	552	429	981
Subtotal: 16 & over	618	423	1,041
Total population	1,170	852	2,022
1834			
Males under 16	329	238	567
Males 16 & over	386	227	613
Females under 16	294	209	503
Females 16 & over	279	177	456
Subtotal: males	715	465	1,180
Subtotal: females	573	386	959
Subtotal: under 16	623	447	1,070
Subtotal: 16 & over	665	404	1,069
Total population	1,288	851	2,139
1835			
Males under 16	345	247	592
Males 16 & over	380	250	630
Females under 16	336	239	575
Females 16 & over	298	217	515
Subtotal: males	725	497	1,222
Subtotal: females	634	456	1,090
Subtotal: under 16	681	486	1,167
Subtotal: 16 & over	678	467	1,145
Total population	1,359	953	2,312
1836			
Males under 16	371	250	621
Males 16 & over	366	250	616
Females under 16	326	233	559
Females 16 & over	285	226	511
Subtotal: males	737	500	1,237
Subtotal: females	611	459	1,070
Subtotal: under 16	697	483	1,180
Subtotal: 16 & over	651	476	1,127
Total population	1,348	959	2,307
1837			
Males under 16	399	265	664
Males 16 & over	358	241	599
Females under 16	367	234	601
Females 16 & over	304	210	514
Subtotal: males	757	506	1,263
Subtotal: females	671	444	1,115
Subtotal: under 16	766	499	1,265
Subtotal: 16 & over	662	451	1,113
Total population	1,428	950	2,378

1838	Front	Rear	Combined
Males under 16	391	275	666
Males 16 & over	428	256	684
Females under 16	345	265	610
Females 16 & over	316	230	546
Subtotal: males	619	531	1,150
Subtotal: females	661	495	1,156
Subtotal: under 16	736	540	1,276
Subtotal: 16 & over	744	486	1,230
Total population	1,480	1,026	2,506
1839			
Males under 16	428	276	704
Males 16 & over	409	235	644
Females under 16	364	247	611
Females 16 & over	338	233	571
Subtotal: males	837	511	1,348
Subtotal: females	702	480	1,182
Subtotal: under 16	792	523	1,315
Subtotal: 16 & over	747	468	1,215
Total population	1,539	991	2,530
1840			
Males under 16	465	275	740
Males 16 & over	447	277	724
Females under 16	393	271	664
Females 16 & over	366	254	620
Subtotal: males	912	552	1,464
Subtotal: females	759	525	1,284
Subtotal: under 16	858	546	1,404
Subtotal: 16 & over	813	531	1,344
Total population	1,691	1,077	2,748
1841			
Males under 16	498	273	771
Males 16 & over	479	293	772
Females under 16	451	273	724
Females 16 & over	398	258	656
Subtotal: males	977	566	1,543
Subtotal: females	849	531	1,380
Subtotal: under 16	949	546	1,495
Subtotal: 16 & over	877	551	1,428
Total population	1,826	1,097	2,923
1842			
Total population	2,173	942	3,115

1844	Front	Rear	Combined
Males under 16	615	234	849
Males 16 & over	589	248	837
Females under 16	552	238	790
Females 16 & over	504	232	736
Subtotal: males	1,204	482	1,686
Subtotal: females	1,056	470	1,526
Subtotal: under 16	1,167	472	1,639
Subtotal: 16 & over	1,093	480	1,573
Total population	2,260	952	3,212
1845			
Males under 16	601	332	933
Males 16 & over	590	303	893
Females under 16	553	331	884
Females 16 & over	494	294	788
Subtotal: males	1,191	635	1,826
Subtotal: females	1,047	625	1,672
Subtotal: under 16	1,154	663	1,817
Subtotal: 16 & over	1,084	597	1,681
Total population	2,238	1,260	3,498
1846			
Males under 16	642	329	971
Males 16 & over	602	308	910
Females under 16	582	300	882
Females 16 & over	536	287	823
Subtotal: males	1,244	637	1,881
Subtotal: females	1,118	587	1,705
Subtotal: under 16	1,224	629	1,853
Subtotal: 16 & over	1,138	595	1,733
Total population	2,362	1,224	3,586
1847			
Males under 16	636		
Males 16 & over	566		
Females under 16	640		
Females 16 & over	518		
Subtotal: males	1,202		
Subtotal: females	1,158		
Subtotal: under 16	1,276		
Subtotal: 16 & over	1,084		
Total population	2,360		
1848			
Males under 16	707		
Males 16 & over	690		
Females under 16	659		
Females 16 & over	583		
Subtotal: males	1,397		
Subtotal: females	1,242		
Subtotal: under 16	1,366		
Subtotal: 16 & over	1,273		
Total population	2,639		

1849	Front	Rear	Combined
Males under 16	732		
Males 16 & over	655		
Females under 16	695		
Females 16 & over	597		
Subtotal: males	1,387		
Subtotal: females	1,292		
Subtotal: under 16	1,427		
Subtotal: 16 & over	1,252		
Total population	2,679		

Appendix B
Aggregate Assessment Data

It is very easy to point out the shortcomings in the assessment data collected before the rearrangement of the municipal system in 1849 and the introduction of improved assessment methods by an act of 1850. Undeniably, the assessment data were not collected in a manner that a present-day historian would like: categories changed over time, several categories were defined with maddening numerical illogic, the earliest reports are very uneven, there were time-lags between land patenting and assessment, many things we would like to know about were left out while other, virtually useless, data were included, and individual assessors obviously were idiosyncratic in their methods.

Emphasis on the deficiencies of the data, however, may give the scholar an air of profundity but it obscures the point that the assessment data are very useful if used with intelligent caution. To anyone familiar with the data available for comparable rural areas in the British Isles, the riches of information given to the historian of central Canada are a veritable cornucopia. Nothing comparable to the data available for Upper Canada from the early years of the nineteenth century is found for the British Isles until mid-century. Instead of complaining we should delight in the richness of the information and subject its use only to a single imperative: the data should be understood for what they are – not modern census material but information gathered as part of financing local government services, which related the ability of local individuals to pay for those services. One reads the data "sideways," that is, with a consciously different purpose in mind than the compilers had, and of course compares them to nominal and agricultural census data whenever possible.

One must compare the assessment data to other material (especially the 1842 and 1848 agricultural censuses) because they were based on information the ratepayer himself provided. The assessor had to swear to the authenticity of the report and was liable to fine if the report was proved false, but the ratepayer was not under similar penalty, so that there was an incentive to understate one's wealth. The assessor, however, had an interest in keeping the reports at least reasonably accurate, and the

public posting of the assessment list meant complaints from neighbours at a gross understatement of assets.

In compiling a series-over-time of assessment data, the chief difficulty to overcome is the changes of categories that occurred. The most important of these is that from 1803–7 houses were assessed only grossly, as being in town or in the country. An act of 1807 introduced a useful typology of houses, ranging from round logs to more refined two-storey dwellings. In 1811 round logs ceased to be tallied (or taxed) and only dwellings of squared timber, frame, brick, or stone were counted. Obviously, this seriously affects any conclusions one wishes to draw about dwellings of the entire population, because the round-log house was favoured by the newer, or poorer, settlers. Similarly, the livestock reporting was affected when, after 1811, swine ceased to be assessed, pigs being an especially important starter crop for newcomers. Only in 1820 did lands unpatented but held under lease or promise of fee simple become taxable.

Despite all these caveats the data are revealing, so long as one knows that they do not report the entire story. One can rearrange the scrambled assessment categories into a logical order that will give useful time-series, and, if one is doing a local study, one readily can become aware of local shifts that may produce untrustworthy discontinuities in the data, in particular the appointment of new assessment officers.

An extremely valuable discussion of the historical changes in the early assessment laws is found in H.E. Manning, *Assessment and Rating, being the Law of Municipal Taxation in Canada*, 2nd ed. (Toronto: Canadian Law List Publishing Co 1937), 1–16. See also Verschoyle B. Blake and Ralph Greenhill, *Rural Ontario* (Toronto: University of Toronto Press 1969), for a discussion of the relation of house-types and assessment categories. Within the limits described above, the time-series for the front and the rear of Leeds and Lansdowne township is straightforward. However, the reader should treat the series of assessment material on the Johnstown district (compiled for selected years only) as being only crudely indicative of the context in which the much more reliable Leeds and Lansdowne township data were generated. This is necessary because the boundaries of the Johnstown district changed significantly during the first half of the nineteenth century. An act of 1821 (2 Geo IV, c. 3), effective in 1823, took the county of Carlton out of the Johnstown district and formed that county in the Bathurst district. Further, an act of 1838 (1 Vict. c. 25), which became effective 19 March 1842, allotted the townships of North Gower and Marlborough to the Dalhousie district and the north part of the townships of Burgess and Elmsley to the Bathurst district.

In the following tables, the years from 1825 onward for the Johnstown district are found in the *Journals of the Legislative Assembly*: 1828, Appendix; 1829, Appendix; 1830, Appendix; 1831–2, Appendix; 1832–3, Appendix; 1833–4, Appendix; 1835, Appendix, vol. 2, no 40; 1836, Appendix, vol. 1, no. 45; 1836–7, Appendix no. 9; 1837–8, Appendix; 1839, Appendix, vol. 2, pt. 1; 1839–40, Appendix, vol. 1, pt. 1; 1841, Appendix U; 1842, Appendix N; 1843, Appendix, vol. 2, DD; 1844–5, Appendix R;

1846, Appendix H; 1847, Appendix O; 1848, Appendix V; 1849, Appendix L; 1850, Appendix P.

For earlier years shown on the table, see Archives of Ontario, RG22, ser. 7, Court of General Session, Johnstown district, Sundry Municipal Papers, Box D, entitled: "A General Account of all rateable property in Distict of Johnstown [7 March 1803–8 March 1804]," "A General Account of all rateable property in District of Johnstown [5 March 1804–6 March 1805]," "A General Account of all rateable property in District of Johnstown [3 March 1806–1 March 1807]," "A General Account of all rateable property in District of Johnstown [2 March 1807–3 March 1808]," "Aggregate account of all rateable property in District of Johnstown [7 March 1808–8 March 1809]," "Aggregate account of all rateable property in District of Johnstown [March 1816–March 1817]," "An Aggregate account of all rateable property in District of Johnstown, commencing in January 1820," "An Aggregate account commencing in January 1821."

For the front of Leeds and Lansdowne these should be supplemented with the manuscript assessment returns, found in the Archives of Ontario, RG 21, Municipal Records, Section A, under the following titles: "Assessment for Lansdowne and Leeds for the year 1812," "Assessment for the year 1814, Lansdowne Front devishion [sic] and Leeds," "[Untitled for 1815]," "Assessment roll for the Township of Leeds and Lansdowne in Front, District of Johnstown, for the year 1816," "Assessment Roll for the Township of Leeds and Lansdowne in Front, District of Johnstown for the year 1817," "Assessment Roll for the township of Leeds and Lansdowne Front, commencing on the first Monday in the month of January 1821," "Assessment List of the Front of the townships of Lansdowne and Leeds for the Year commencing February 7th, 1825," "Assessment List of the front of the townships of Lansdowne and Leeds for the year commencing February 14th, 1826," "Assessment for Leeds and Lansdowne in front for the year 1827," "Assessment List for the Front of the townships of Leeds and Lansdowne for the year 1828," "Assessment for the front of Leeds and Lansdowne for the year 1829," "Assessment for Leeds and Lansdowne in Front for the year 1830," "Return of property assessed in the Front of the township of Leeds and Lansdowne in the year 1833."

For some of the years not mentioned above, there are incomplete returns available in the RG 21 series which are useful for dealing with specific individuals.

For the rear of Leeds and Lansdowne one should supplement the material printed in the *Journals of the Legislative Assembly* with the manuscript assessment returns in the Archives of Ontario, RG 21, Section A, found under the following titles: "List of the Rateable Property of the rear end of Lansdowne and of Leeds [1804]," "A Bill of the Rateable Property of rear end of Lansdowne and Leeds for the year 1805," "Assessment for the rear of the township of Lansdowne and Leeds for the year 1807," "Assessment for the rear of Lansdowne and Leeds for 1808," "Assessment for the rear of Lansdowne and Leeds for 1809," "An Assesssment roll for the rear end of Lansdowne and the rear end of Leeds for the year 1813," "An Assessment for the rear of the township

of Lansdowne and Leeds for the year 1814," "Assessment for the rear of the township of Lansdowne and Leeds for the year 1815," "Assessment for the rear of the township of Lansdowne and Leeds for the year 1816," "An Assessment for the rear of the township of Lansdowne and Leeds for the year 1817," "The Assessment for the rear of the township of Lansdowne and Leeds for the year 1818," "An Assessment for the rear of the township of Lansdowne and Leeds for the year 1819," "An Assessment for the rear of Lansdowne and Leeds for the year 1820," "Assessment of the rear of the township of Leeds and Lansdowne for the year commencing the first Monday in the month of January, 1821," "Assessment of the rear of the township of Lansdowne and Leeds for the year commencing the first Monday in the month of January 1822," "Assessment of the rear of the township of Leeds and Lansdowne for the year commencing the first Monday in the month of January 1825," "Assessment of the rear of the township of Leeds and Lansdowne for the year commencing 1st Monday, January 1826," "Assessment of the rear of the township of Lansdowne and Leeds for the year commencing the first Monday in January, 1827," "Assessment of the rear of the township of Lansdowne and Leeds for the year commencing the first Monday in January 1828," "Assessment of the rear of the township of Lansdowne and Leeds for the year commencing the first Monday in January 1829," "A true list of the rateable property in the rear of the town[ship] of Leeds [and Lansdowne] for the year commencing the first Monday in January 1830," "Copy of the assessment of the rear of the township of [Leeds and] Lansdowne for the year commencing the 1st Monday in January 1831," "List of the rateable property for the rear of the township of Lansdowne and Leeds commencing the first Monday in January 1832," "List of the rateable property in the rear of Leeds [and Lansdowne] for the year commencing the 1st Monday in January 1833."

Again, it is worth noting that there exist incomplete or untabulated returns for some of the years that are missing in the list above and that for information on specific individuals these incomplete returns are of value.

TABLE B1

Assessment Data: Johnstown District, Selected Years, 1803–49

	1803–4	1804–5	1806–7	1807–8	1808–9	1816–17	1821	1826	1831	1836	1841	1846	1849
Land													
Cultivated (acres)	18,215		22,692	24,441	25,596	31,745	46,368	50,249	65,784	90,892	118,922	131,731	147,453
Uncultivated (acres)	159,206		236,944	246,916	245,554	224,729	324,384	228,917	277,690	346,139	399,750	367,432	397,796
Livestock													
Horses (3 years & up)	921	868	999	1,070	1,112	1,582	1,876	2,092	2,890	4,256	6,084	6,465	7,271
Oxen (4 years & up)	672	689	877	1,017	931	922	1,333	2,383	3,301	3,566	3,363	3,073	2,548
Milch cows	2,072	2,141	2,375	2,537	2,474	3,175	4,675	5,307	7,599	9,964	12,919	14,133	15,022
Horned cattle (2 years & up)	1,036	984	1,389	1,175	1,117	1,117	1,961	2,414	2,999	3,946	4,175	3,781	4,977
Swine	805	415	292	354	286								
Mills													
Grist (1 pair of stones)	17	18	17	17	21	22	27	29	29	28	32	29	32
Grist (additional stones)	3	3	2	2	2	2	1	4	10	15	28	29	39
Saw mills	12	12	15	16	20	28	43	44	47	55	55	60	66
Business Premises													
Store houses			4	5	6	2	5	8	8	24	16	15	2
Merchant shops			7	12	8	35	36	37	72	78	90	111	78
Private Dwellings													
Round-log houses				662	673								
Square timber, under two stories				56	59	95	185	186	212	256	209	212	248
Square timber, two stories				1	1	7	1	23	23	6	2	3	4
Frame, under two stories				176	183	261	392	462	455	960	1,154	1,355	1,300
Brick or stone, under two stories				1	3	8	18	40	236	195	270	400	430
Frame, brick, or stone, two stories				15	19	47	88	129	172	243	301	319	154

TABLE B2
Assessment Data: Front of Leeds and Lansdowne, 1812–49

	1812	1814	1815	1816	1817	1821
Land						
Cultivated (acres)	796	830	806	910	867	1,112
Uncultivated (acres)	10,620	9,551	13,705	11,353	11,119	12,355
Livestock						
Horses (3 years & up)	51	47	48	65	64	56
Oxen (4 years & up)	75	35	28	46(?)		48
Milch cows	116	102	89	109(?)		152
Horned cattle (2 years & up)	14	26	29	42		
Mills						
Grist (1 pair of stones)	1	1		1	1	3½
Grist (additional stones)						2
Saw mills		3		3	3	
Business Premises						
Store houses						
Merchant shops				2		
Private Dwellings						
Square timber, under two stories	3		5	9	7	3
Square timber, two stories						
Frame, under two stories	4			10	12	17
Frame, two stories						
Brick or stone, under two stories						
Brick or stone, two stories						
Frame, brick, or stone, two stories				1	1	2

TABLE B2—(Continued)
Assessment Data: Front of Leeds and Lansdowne, 1812–49

1825	1826	1827	1828	1829	1830	1833	1834
1,441	1,583	1,692	1,854	2,241	2,220	2,856	3,188
13,293	15,662	14,383	15,748	16,449	16,224	18,831	19,864
59	59	60	57	59	71	110	133
92	119	115	123	148	141	175	171
175	187	210	233	275	292	346	379
206 (?)	131	111	129	130	167	156	212
1	1	2	2	2	2	1	1
1	1	4	4	4	4	4	4
3	3	3	2¾	2¼	2¼	2¼	1¼
1	1	1	1	1	2	2	2
2	3	2	2	2	4	18	21
19	21	21	28	29	26	58	68
	2			2	2	4	
					1	1	2
						2	6
2		2	2				

TABLE B2—(Continued)
Assessment Data: Front of Leeds and Lansdowne, 1812–49

	1835	1836	1837	1838	1839	1840	1841
Land							
Cultivated (acres)	3,421	3,589	3,781	4,354	4,591	4,987	4,921
Uncultivated (acres)	19,978	20,649	19,205	22,655	22,214	23,473	22,438
Livestock							
Horses (3 years & up)	137	148	156	192	212	234	255
Oxen (4 years & up)	182	191	141	144	158	150	133
Milch cows	457	436	464	514	507	558	607
Horned cattle (2 years & up)	177	224	180	195	192	227	226
Mills							
Grist (1 pair of stones)	1	1	1	1	1	1	2
Grist (additional stones)	3	3	3	4	4	4	5
Saw mills	1¾	1½	1¾	1¾	1	1	1
Business Premises							
Store houses				1	1	1	1
Merchant shops	2	2	2	3	3	4	6
Private Dwellings							
Square timber, under two stories	24	20	18	20	19	20	18
Square timber, two stories							
Frame, under two stories	71	59	67		77	81	79
Frame, two stories			4				
Brick or stone, under two stories	3		2		2	2	3
Brick or stone, two stories	6		8	8	7		
Frame, brick, or stone, two stories		5			7	8	8

TABLE B2—(Continued)
Assessment Data: Front of Leeds and Lansdowne, 1812–49

1842	1843	1844	1845	1846	1847	1848	1849
5,238	5,527	5,821	5,916	6,494	6,776	6,913	7,418
25,053	27,110	27,496	25,658	27,139	27,364	27,191	31,301
288	297	305	319	334	360	413	429
185	188	199	203	185	176	160	142
682	810	806	843	851	858	930	902
253	286	294	335	206	293	315	300
2	2	2	2	3	1	2	2
6	6	6	6	6	1	6	6
2	4	4	4	3	2	4	3
1	1						
5	5	6	7	4	4	5	8
47	58	64	63	64	71	62	62
		1		1			
92	93	106	112	116	121	118	127
4	3	4	7	5	7	12	13
8	9	9	7	10	12	13	10

TABLE B3

Assessment Data: Rear of Leeds and Lansdowne, 1804–49

	1804	1805	1807	1808	1809	1813
Land						
Cultivated (acres)	525	606	819	947	937	906
Uncultivated (acres)	3,390	2,492	6,729	8,956	8,371	4,673
Livestock						
Horses (3 years & up)	17	23	24	30	32	32
Oxen (4 years & up)	28	25	65(?)	42(?)	49	32
Milch cows	60	75	104	92	87(?)	84
Horned cattle (2 years & up)	41	43	56(?)	54(?)	65	24
Swine	22		13		16	
Mills						
Grist (1 pair of stones)						1
Grist (additional stones)						
Saw mills	1	½	1	1	1	2
Business Premises						
Store houses						
Merchant shops						
Private Dwellings						
Round-log houses			28		26	
Square timber, under two stories						1
Square timber, two stories						
Frame, under two stories			6	6	6	5
Brick or stone, under two stories						
Brick or stone, two stories						
Frame, brick, or stone, two stories						

TABLE B3— (Continued)
Assessment Data: Rear of Leeds and Lansdowne, 1804–49

1814	1815	1816	1817	1818	1819	1820	1821
841	1,012	879	997	1,135	1,225	1,272	1,384
5,814	5,952	6,072	5,991	5,815	8,026	9,513	10,592
43	49	46	37	49	58(?)		60
28	32	43	46	38	38(?)		41
94	97	107	89	84			115
64	57	38	38	36			83
1	1	1	1	1	1	1	1
1	1	1	1	1	1	1	1
2	2	1	2	2	2	4	3
						2	
4	5	5	6	7	5	10	10
2		2	2	2	2		2

TABLE B3—(Continued)
Assessment Data: Rear of Leeds and Lansdowne, 1804–49

	1822	1825	1826	1827
Land				
Cultivated (acres)	1,372	1,591	1,627	1,690
Uncultivated (acres)	9,044	10,793	11,868	11,890
Livestock				
Horses (3 years & up)	57	67	68	67
Oxen (4 years & up)	56	118(?)	117	128
Milch cows	121	158	183	210
Horned cattle (2 years & up)	67	129	169	149(?)
Swine				
Mills				
Grist (1 pair of stones)	1		1	
Grist (additional stones)				
Saw mills	1			
Business Premises				
Store houses				
Merchant shops				
Private Dwellings				
Round-log houses				
Square timber, under two stories	4	3	11	9
Square timber, two stories				
Frame, under two stories	12	11	11	13
Brick or stone, under two stories				
Brick or stone, two stories				
Frame, brick, or stone, two stories	2	3	2	3

TABLE B3—(Continued)
Assessment Data: Rear of Leeds and Lansdowne, 1804–49

1828	1829	1830	1831	1832	1833	1834	1835	1836
1,832	1,576	2,039	2,150	2,260	2,399	2,482	2,640	3,075
12,737	11,078	13,620	13,322	11,725	12,780	12,410	12,948	14,361
79	83	85	101	101	112	111	139	147
133	128	129	161	172	152	129	159	169
230	261	275	297	330	314	302	347	358
167	174	158	151	154	127	176	175	192
1	1							1
	1							1
1	2	1		1				1
							1	1
11	7	5	18	17	12	13	17	14
						1		
15	13	14	19	17	12	20	25	35
						1	2	
						3	6	
4	5	5	5	3	4			5

TABLE B3—(Continued)
Assessment Data: Rear of Leeds and Lansdowne, 1804–49

	1837	1838	1839	1840	1841	1842
Land						
Cultivated (acres)	3,316	3,651	3,866	4,089	4,492	4,391
Uncultivated (acres)	14,266	16,189	17,859	17,118	16,946	15,294
Livestock						
Horses (3 years & up)	169	167	174	196	201	199
Oxen (4 years & up)	138			136	129	126
Milch cows	377	383	380	429	439	406
Horned cattle (2 years & up)	188	159	169	193	224	279
Swine						
Mills						
Grist (1 pair of stones)	1	1		1	1	1
Grist (additional stones)	1	1		1	1	1
Saw mills		2	1	2	2	2
Business Premises						
Store houses		1				
Merchant shops	1			2	2	1
Private Dwellings						
Round-log houses						
Square timber, under two stories	8	11	12	14	13	10
Square timber, two stories					2	
Frame, under two stories	27	31	33	37	40	39
Brick or stone, under two stories	2	2	2	2	2	1
Brick or stone, two stories	6	6				
Frame, brick, or stone, two stories			5	5	6	3

TABLE B3— (Continued)
Assessment Data: Rear of Leeds and Lansdowne, 1804–49

1843	1844	1845	1846	1847	1848	1849
4,646	4,978	4,661	4,699	5,013	5,186	5,747
17,499	18,212	17,933	16,544	16,369	16,504	17,477
211	241	232	241	266	285	298
122	118	156	137	132	106	100
446	462	509	512	546	541	540
346	285	285	163	192	298	333
1	1	1	1	1	1	1
1	1	1	1	1	1	1
2	1	2	1	2	2	2
2	1	1	2	2	4	1
12	9	9	9	6	6	10
40	48	50	52	52	54	70
3	3	3	3	3	3	6
6	6	4	5	5	5	5

TABLE B4

Assessment Data: Front and Rear of Leeds and Lansdowne, Combined, 1814–49

	1814	1815	1816	1817	1821	1825	1826
Land							
Cultivated (acres)	1,671	1,818	1,789	1,864	2,496	3,032	3,210
Uncultivated (acres)	15,365	19,657	17,425	17,110	22,947	24,086	27,530
Livestock							
Horses (3 years & up)	90	97	111	101	116	126	127
Oxen (4 years & up)	63	60	89(?)		189	210(?)	236
Milch cows	196	186	216(?)		267	333	370
Horned cattle (two years & up)	90	86	80			335(?)	300

	1827	1828	1829	1830	1833	1834	1835
Land							
Cultivated (acres)	3,382	3,686	3,817	4,259	5,255	5,670	6,061
Uncultivated (acres)	26,273	28,485	27,527	29,844	31,611	32,274	32,926
Livestock							
Horses (3 years & up)	127	136	142	156	222	244	276
Oxen (4 years & up)	243	256	276	270	327	300	341
Milch cows	420	463	536	567	660	681	804
Horned cattle (two years & up)	260(?)	296	304	325	283	388	352

	1836	1837	1838	1839	1840	1841	1842
Land							
Cultivated (acres)	6,664	7,097	8,005	8,457	9,076	9,413	9,629
Uncultivated (acres)	35,010	33,471	38,844	40,073	40,591	39,384	40,347
Livestock							
Horses (3 years & up)	295	325	361	386	430	456	487
Oxen (4 years & up)	360	279	282	280	286	262	311
Milch cows	794	841	897	887	987	1,046	1,088
Horned cattle (two years & up)	416	368	354	361	420	450	532

	1843	1844	1845	1846	1847	1848	1849
Land							
Cultivated (acres)	10,173	10,799	10,577	11,193	11,789	12,099	13,165
Uncultivated (acres)	44,609	45,708	43,591	43,683	43,733	43,695	48,778
Livestock							
Horses (3 years & up)	508	546	551	575	626	698	727
Oxen (4 years & up)	310	317	359	322	308	266	242
Milch cows	1,256	1,268	1,352	1,363	1,404	1,471	1,442
Horned cattle (two years & up)	632	579	620	369	485	613	633

Appendix C
Agricultural Census of 1842

The problems with the 1842 agricultural census may seem daunting, and one should therefore emphasize the value of the material before dwelling on its defects. The 1842 census was the most ambitious conducted before 1848 and it collected not only the usual enumeration data but information on each individual's religion, place of origin, and possession of land, house, livestock, and other objects. As a means of compiling a social profile of an area it is invaluable. It is especially useful for studying immigrant assimilation as it asked each individual not born in the country how long he had been in Canada (this question was dropped from the next agricultural census, that of 1848). The 1842 data are the first which allow us to identify clearly the ethnic background of the local population.

Just like all the other censuses before mid-century, the 1842 census probably under-counted by not including all transients. However, if one starts with the clear understanding that the individuals who were enumerated in such full detail in 1842 did indeed exist (and no one seriously has suggested fraud by "creation" of individuals on the part of the enumerators), one can recompile the census data to provide the information one wants. For instance, although the aggregate results did not separate Irish Catholics from Irish Protestants or cross-tabulate other items by ethnic or religious background, one can do so, if one starts with the individual cases and works up (always provided, of course, that the items one needs were filled in on the forms and that they are legible; there is a serious legibility problem with some of the sheets for Leeds and Lansdowne township).

The Johnstown district aggregrates are not elsewhere available, and I am including them in the hope that they will be of use to other historians of the district as well as useful context for the Leeds and Lansdowne data. The source of the aggregate district material is the holograph aggregate summation found in the F.P. Smith papers in the Archives of Ontario.

There are certain problems in the Johnstown aggregates of which the user should be aware. I have rearranged (but not substantively redefined) the categories under which the original aggregates were presented. Where arithmetical errors were made

by the original compiler, I have corrected them. Nevertheless, the user will still find incompatible categories: in particular, the categories for aggregating men and women were not the same. Also, on some items the enumerator of a given township simply did not collect the desired information.

In several cases aggregates, although arithmetically correct, seem untrustworthy. The following should be scrutinized carefully before being employed: (1) the total of women between fourteen and forty-five in Elizabethtown which shows only two of 842 to be married; (2) the total of females in Elizabethtown over forty-five, as none are shown; (3) the total of female lunatics for the entire district and especially for Kitley, as sixty-five of a total of sixty-eight female lunatics in the district are shown to reside in that township; (4) the huge arithmetical errors in the clerk's totalling of the population of the townships of Elizabethtown and Kitley; (5) the very large number of persons omitted in computing national origin in the townships of Bastard, Elizabethtown, and Kitley; (6) on the question of religious affiliation, the massive omissions in Kitley and Yonge and an overcount of considerable size in Elizabethtown.

Those are just the major problems and anyone working on a specific township will find many more of lesser import. For the township of Leeds and Lansdowne, the material on the front is excellent, the best in the district as far as the aggregate data are concerned. The rear of the township, however, is only of uneven quality. Particularly irritating is the fact that the data for sex and age of population are totally unreliable. Specifically, for the rear of Leeds and Lansdowne township, the aggregate numbers in the age and sex categories indicate a total population of 1,406, while those of birthplace indicate a population of 942. This cannot be sloughed off as an instance of under-reporting of places of birth (although that degree of under-reporting would be ominous in itself). It is a possible indicator of serious problems with the run of censuses for the rear of Leeds and Lansdowne for the era: the 942 figure, not 1,406, fits with the trend reported in other censuses, and if the larger number were correct it would indicate that the entire run, except for 1842, was invalid. Fortunately, it is the 1,406, not the 942, which is invalid. The evidence is that, most important, a rerunning of the age-group numbers shows gross errors in calculation, as much as 100 percent on some items. The errors are not correctable, however, because the whole set of age data was very sloppily collected. It must be thrown out entirely, as unreliable. Second, it is relevant that James Jessup, the Johnstown district official who was responsible for doing an aggregate table of the returns, added a final column to those specified by the official district forms in aggregating "total number of persons," and he specifically set down 942, even though this fit with the place of birth numbers, not with the age of population numbers that the census takers had given him.

In the case of the township of Leeds and Lansdowne, the census data for 1842 mesh well with those for the other years in the 1840s (once one has completely disregarded as unreliable the age and sex data for the rear of the township). Comparison with the assessment data is rather harder, however, as the assessors used certain taxation

categories for their work, while the 1842 agricultural enumerators used others suited to their purpose. One suspects that the 1842 enumerators were rather closer to reality. For example, although quite close in total acreage in both the front and rear of Leeds and Lansdowne township, it is clear that the census takers were more strict in defining "improved" land than were the assessors in defining "cultivated" land for tax purposes. In the matter of livestock, the census takers and the assessors counted horses differently; I cannot discover the reason for this and thus suggest that these equine data be treated very tentatively. By and large, however, the categories do not overlap; the agricultural censuses include sheep, hogs, and neat cattle (meaning all milch and young cattle, except calves, not merely horned cattle two years of age and above as in the assessment), as well as a very wide range of information on crop outputs and domestic manufacture.

TABLE C1

1842 Census: Johnstown District, Census of population

	Front of Leeds and Lans-downe	Rear of Leeds and Lans-downe	Sub-total, Leeds and Lans-downe (front & rear com-bined)	Augusta	Bast
SEX AND AGE GROUPINGS (excluding servants, indigents and the incapacitated, and persons engaged in trade or commerce)					
Children					
5 years and under					
Boys	220			477	
Girls	233			517	
Above 5 and under 14 years					
Boys	307			645	
Girls	241			520	
Males, adolescent and adult					
Above 14 and under 18 years					
Married	3			7	
Single	87			185	
Above 18 and under 21 years					
Married	7			4	
Single	76			94	
Above 21 and under 30 years		NOT RELIABLE	NOT RELIABLE		
Married	40			128	
Single	55			139	
Above 30 and under 60 years					
Married	282			578	
Single	30			58	
60 years and upwards					
Married	13			63	
Single	10			38	
Females, adolescent and adult					
Above 14 and under 45 years					
Married	286			649	
Single	128			410	
45 years and above					
Married	47			136	
Single	11			34	
Subtotal	2,076			4,682	2,

th gess	South Crosby	North Crosby	Edwards-burgh	Eliza-bethtown	South Elmsley	South Gower	Kitley	Oxford	Wolford	Yonge
5	87	88	243	622	94	78	314	341	218	388
8	93	67	250	637	80	57	325	298	236	369
11	75	72	320	765	97	96	380	360	255	533
8	88	60	340	682	83	75	386	317	140	541
	9	9	36	84	5	5	10			
6	21	16	127	281	30	38	191	117	86	193
		9	14	54		1	26	1	20	3
1	32	18	87	147	22	19	93	74	46	100
	22	21	77	35	17	19	243	108	44	97
	36	12	79	158	35	23	155	93	82	123
10	106	62	294	17	107	68	468	313	176	429
	5	13	32	38	10	5	30	25	19	29
1	15	5	54	3	4	9	69	42	16	64
	5	5	17		3	1	69	6	9	18
10	120	77	283	2	113	75	730	383	252	459
3	86	25	148	480	46	47	382	184	50	357
1	24	9	111		13	21	93	80	52	134
	5	3	32		7	6	22	26	9	46
64	829	571	2,544	4,005	766	643	3,986	2,768	1,710	3,883

TABLE C1—(Continued)
1842 Census: Johnstown District, Census of population

	Front of Leeds and Lansdowne	Rear of Leeds and Lansdowne	Subtotal, Leeds and Lansdowne (front & rear combined)	Augusta	Ba
PERSONS ENGAGED IN TRADE OR COMMERCE	15			12	
INDIGENTS AND INCAPACITATED					
Deaf and Dumb					
Male	3			1	
Female					
Blind					
Male	1				
Female					
Idiots					
Male	1				
Female				1	
Lunatics					
Male					
Female					
Subsisting on alms, or paupers	2				
Subtotal	7			2	
SERVANTS					
Coloured					
Male	13			8	
Female	18			7	
Other male servants					
Farm servants	10			12	
In private families	12			23	
Other female servants					
In private families	22			36	
SUBTOTAL	75			86	
TOTAL POPULATION					
Uncorrected total per clerk's MS	2,185			4,671	
Corrected total	2,173	942	3,115	4,782	

ss	South Crosby	North Crosby	Edwards-burgh	Eliza-bethtown	South Elmsley	South Gower	Kitley	Oxford	Wolford	Yonge	
0	3	3	0	45	0	7	3	23	0	7	
			1	6			2	3			
		1					2	2			
	1					1	2			1	
	1			2		1	1		1	1	
				2			1	1		4	
			1	4			1	1		2	
				2			1				
							65			2	
	1									1	
0	3	1	2	16	0	2	75	7	1	11	
			2	4			5				
		2	1	4							
	10			54	16	5	11	16	11	21	
	5	10	3	113	1	1	1	1	12	13	
	14	5	10	115	5	7	6	12		21	
0	29	17	21	290	22	13	23	29	23	55	
63	883	600	2,446	6,835	767	675	2,850	2,825	1,732	3,870	
64	864	592	2,567	4,356	788	665	4,087	2,827	1,734	3,956	33,019*

of corrected township figures.

TABLE C2

1842 Census: Johnstown District, National Origins (Place of Birth)

	Front of Leeds and Lansdowne	Rear of Leeds and Lansdowne	Sub-total, Leeds and Lansdowne (front and rear combined)	Augusta	Bastard	South Burgess	South Crosby	N(C
NATIVE OF CANADA								
Of French origin	44	23	67	65	21		54	
Of British origin	1,205	690	1,895	3,007	49	47	534	
NATURALIZED CANADIANS BORN OUTSIDE OF CANADA								
England	83	15	98	354	78	1	32	
Ireland	459	125	584	968	644	15	183	
Scotland	136	2	138	137	12		9	
Continental Europe	1	4	5	13	7		4	
United States of America	166	83	249	80	131		61	
ALIENS (BORN ABROAD AND NOT YET NATURALIZED)	82		82	14	18		5	
TOTAL AS DERIVED FROM ABOVE FIGURES	2,176	942	3,118	4,638	960	63	882	
TOTAL POPULATION AS GIVEN IN TABLE	2,173	942	3,115	4,782	2,622	64	864	
NUMBER OF PERSONS NOT ACCOUNTED FOR (overcounts are designated "−")	−3	0	−3	144	1,662	1	−18	

rds-	Eliza-bethtown	South Elmsley	South Gower	Kitley	Oxford	Wolford	Yonge	Uncor-rected total, Johnstown district (as reported in clerk's MS)	Corrected total, Johnstown district
102	140	16	12	44	79	33	95	753	753
,516	3,440	376	412	1,415	1,551	1,125	2,760	18,465	18,465
74	275	30	31	78	76	58	103	1,331	1,332
474	2,290	223	153	908	923	474	587	8,531	8,532
142	254	105	30	64	75	38	84	1,122	1,122
7		2		1	2		1	56	56
127	338	13	30	305	71		144	1,581	1,581
4	63	2	4	16	25	4	42	286	286
,446	6,800	767	672	2,831	2,802	1,732	3,816		32,127
,567	4,356	788	665	4,087	2,827	1,734	3,956		33,019
121	−2,444	21	−7	1,256	25	2	140		892

TABLE C3

1842 Census: Johnstown District, Religious Affiliations

	Front of Leeds & Lansdowne	Rear of Leeds & Lansdowne	Sub-total, Leeds & Lansdowne (front & rear combined)	Augusta	Bastard	South Burgess	South Crosby	No[rth] Cr[osby]
RELIGIOUS DENOMINATIONS								
Church of England (Anglican)	506	220	726	1,279	924	26	217	
Church of Scotland (Presbyterian)	424	9	433	762	79		32	
Roman Catholic	300	45	345	790	268	1	65	
British Wesleyan Methodists	11	85	96	54	11	17		
Canadian Wesleyan Methodists	237	81	318	884	10		105	
Episcopal Methodists	80	67	147	493	195	1	91	
Other Methodists	95	3	98		269		79	
Presbyterians (not associated with Church of Scotland)	9	36	45	51	36			
Congregationalists or Independents	2	1	3	19	1			
Baptists and Anabaptists	32	54	86	124	224		30	
Lutherans		5	5					
Quakers	1	18	19	1	42	8	2	
Moravians and Tunkers								
Dutch Reformed							1	
Jews	5		5					
"All other denominations"	13	23	36	5	589	9	160	
Total as derived from above figures	1,715	647	2,362	4,462	2,648	62	782	
Total population as given in table C2	2,173	942	3,115	4,782	2,622	64	864	
Persons not accounted for (overcounts are designated "−")	458	295	753	320	−26	2	82	

wards-rgh	Eliza-bethtown	South Elmsley	South Gower	Kitley	Oxford	Wolford	Yonge	Uncorrected total, Johnstown district (as reported in clerk's MS)	Corrected total, Johnstown district
442	2,066	195	119	894	748	549	881	9,111	9,111
866	238	214	275	420	632	114	373	4,468	4,468
364	573	219	56	466	471	163	277	4,130	4,130
203	387	24	13	217	174	148	322	1,743	1,743
236	242	9	149	139	319	28	76	2,524	2,524
168	422	15		193	59	99	438	2,325	2,325
	64			48		32	8	618	598
	584	5		19	8		13	761	761
	24	4						51	51
8	57		40	63	28	9	33	711	711
	6		1	17	10			39	39
	26				7	6	100	213	213
								7	7
	5				4			10	10
								5	5
	771			5	427	10	16	15	2,060
2,287	5,465	685	658	2,903	2,470	1,164	2,536		28,756
2,567	4,356	788	665	4,087	2,827	1,734	3,956		33,019
280	−1,109	103	7	1,184	357	570	1,420		4,263

TABLE C4

1842 Census: Johnstown District, Material Culture and Educational Institutions

	Front of Leeds & Lansdowne	Rear of Leeds & Lansdowne	Sub-total, Leeds & Lansdowne Front & Rear	Augusta	Bastard	
HOUSES						
Inhabited	354	57	411	747	431	
Vacant	1		1	2	3	
Being Built	11	5	16	4	4	
LAND						
Occupied land (acres)	19,671	14,064	33,735	50,357	34,982	
Improved land (acres)	5,028	3,827	8,855	14,539	9,386½	
AGRICULTURAL PRODUCE (WB-Winchester bushels)						
Wheat (WB)	5,613	5,514½	11,127½	15,546	14,237	
Barley (WB)	795½	2,118	2,913½	4,536	2,451	
Rye (WB)	116	712	828	624	289	
Oats (WB)	13,664	30,351½	44,015½	60,894	30,109	
Indian corn (WB)	396	1,773	2,169	4,942	5,166	
Buckwheat (WB)	174	110	284	2,671	485	
Potatoes (WB)	34,486	20,827	55,313	96,564	19,668	
Pease (WB)	3,594	1,002½	4,596½	1,583	2,794	
Maple sugar (lb)	6,763	9,702	16,465	22,480	25,313	
LIVESTOCK						
Neat cattle	1,978	1,336	3,314	3,454	3,186	
Horses	368	116	484	945	835	
Sheep	2,166	2,184	4,350	5,008	4,585	
Hogs	1,117	837	1,954	2,466	2,480	
Bee hives	7	10	17	24	7	
DOMESTIC TEXTILE MANUFACTURE						
Full cloth (yd)	2,238	1,865	4,103	5,914	1,746	
Linen, cotton, & other thin cloth (yd)	46	302	348	503	3,991	
Flannel and other n-f wool (yd)	2,986	4,799	7,785	8,893	4,083	
Wool produced (lb)	5,511	3,674	9,185	12,705	10,824	

th ...sby	North Crosby	Edwards-burg	Eliza-bethtown	South Elmsley	South Gower	Kitley	Oxford	Wolford	Yonge	Corrected total, Johnstown district (provided only for items on which all townships reported)
33	100	410	996	137	109	502	498	n/a	450	
						6	12		2	
2			22			5	1		2	
043	6,509½	27,149	n/a	13,849	13,462	38,013	38,606	n/a	53,267	
556	1,511½	7,420	n/a	3,297	4,006	9,141	9,992	5,752	14,960	
070	1,787	4,229	28,535	4,595	4,983	17,580	14,975	7,344	23,203	155,406½
146	41	1,478½	4,687	325	621	2,075	1,400	750	2,864	24,288
55	31	880	248		50	35	187	282	251	3,760
636	1,801	33,622	60,944	10,232	15,647	30,218	36,483	20,436	33,049	387,235½
359	1,614	5,848	4,711	825½	1,614	2,098	6,910½	2,863	5,831	47,023
556	50	1,303	1,875	6	192	131	489	557	962	9,591
286	8,162	62,322	82,498	25,895	27,345	58,518	71,147	42,309	70,503	640,218
770	209	3,096	5,332	971	833	4,446	1,363	1,060	6,191	33,249½
095	4,759	16,116	23,319	5,626	1,824	21,959	21,810	15,209	33,139	213,928
162	500	2,366	4,398	930	790	3,206	2,305	1,725	4,210	31,584
223	121	675	1,396	171	195	621	404	433	848	7,358
790	739	3,136	7,479	1,021	1,070	4,412	2,867	2,409	6,977	45,863
754	346	1,619	3,232	537	486	2,688	1,543	1,142	2,699	21,975
41		43	94		5	4	8	10	72	325
758	540	3,614	7,190	893	1,383	4,190	3,256	1,906	7,636	44,139
374	42	3,960	4,013	20	151	4,177	515	313	460	18,867
092	808	1,784	6,685	1,954	1,923	3,486	5,735	3,453	9,081	58,762
293	1,509	7,439	19,794	2,910	2,620	10,006	7,120	5,716	16,107	110,258

TABLE C4

1842 Census: Johnstown District, Material Culture and Educational institution

	Front of Leeds & Lansdowne	Rear of Leeds & Lansdowne	Subtotal, Leeds & Lansdowne Front & Rear	Augusta	Bastard
AGRICULTURAL PRICES (average)					
Wheat since last harvest/bu.	6/0	5/0		5/6	6/0
Day labour (shillings/pence)	3/6	3/9		2/6	3/0
RETAIL OUTLETS FOR SPIRITS					
Taverns and public houses	4	3	7	15	7
Stores selling spirits	3	3	6	8	2
MILLS					
Grist Mills	2		2	3	3
Mill stones (pr)	8		8	12	
Oatmeal mills				1	
Barley mills				1	
Saw mills	1	3	4	3	2
Oil Mills					
Fulling mills	1	1	2	1	1
Carding mills		1	1	3	2
Threshing mills	2	3	5	1	7
Paper mills					
MANUFACTORIES					
Iron works					1
Nail factories	1				
Distilleries				2	
Breweries				2	
Tanneries	1		1	2	3
Pot and pearl ash manufactories	1		1	2	16
Wind, steam, or wind-powered manufactories	1		1		
EDUCATIONAL INSTITUTIONS					
Colleges, academies, and universities					
Elementary schools	2	4	6		
Pupils in elementary schools					
Male	59	56	115		
Female	37	45	82		

uth osby	North Crosby	Edwards-burg	Eliza-bethtown	South Elmsley	South Gower	Kitley	Oxford	Wolford	Yonge	Corrected total, Johnstown district (provided only for items on which all townships reported)
5/6	5/0	5/0	5/6	5/6	5/6	6/0	5/6	5/0	5/9	
1/11	2/0	2/6	1/3	2/6	2'6	3/0	2/6	1/8	2/8	
	1	4	20			1	4	4	8	71
	7		8			1	5	3	2	42
	1	2	4			1	2		5	23
	2	3	7				4		1	37
1		1	1			1				5
										1
2		2	7			1	5		11	37
	2									2
		1	2				2		4	13
	1	1	2				1		4	15
3		3	11			3	5		4	42
										0
										1
										1
										2
			1				1	2		6
	1	2	3				3		3	18
2	7	1	5	48		49	3	3	7	145
			2				5	1		9
										0
4						3		4	4	21
48						41		126	54	384
44						35		28	49	238

Index

Material in the Introduction to the Second Edition is not included in the index.